The Liverpool & Manchester Railway

The Liverpool & Manchester Railway

R. H. G. THOMAS
Foreword by Jack Simmons

B. T. BATSFORD LTD
LONDON

FIRST PUBLISHED 1980
© R. H. G. THOMAS 1980
ALL RIGHTS RESERVED. NO PART OF THIS PUBLICATION
MAY BE REPRODUCED IN ANY FORM OR BY ANY MEANS
WITHOUT PERMISSION FROM THE PUBLISHERS
PRINTED IN GREAT BRITAIN BY
THE ANCHOR PRESS LTD.
TIPTREE, ESSEX
FOR THE PUBLISHERS, B. T. BATSFORD LTD,
4 FITZHARDINGE STREET, LONDON W1H 0AH
ISBN 0 7134 0537 6

1 *George Stephenson (1781–1848), portrait by T. L. Atkinson, after John Lucas, with railway across Chat Moss in the background*

Contents

	Acknowledgments	6
	Foreword *by Jack Simmons*	7
CHAPTER 1	The Formation of the Company	11
2	The Construction of the Railway	33
3	The Rainhill Locomotive Trials	63
4	The Opening of the Railway	76
5	Travelling on the Railway	91
6	Relations with Other Railways	95
7	Stations	108
8	The First Railwaymen	135
9	Locomotives and Rolling Stock	151
10	Operating the Railway	186
11	Accidents	208
12	Rules and Regulations	216
13	Conclusion	223
	Main Events and Developments *affecting the Liverpool and Manchester Line after 1845*	235
APPENDIX A	The Opening Ceremony, 15 September 1830	
	1 List of prominent guests	241
	2 Order of trains	243
APPENDIX B	List of locomotives	244
	References and Notes	247
	Index	257

Acknowledgments

The author wishes to express his gratitude for the assistance he has received from numerous individuals, libraries and record offices in the preparation of this book. In particular, he would record his indebtedness to the following: Messrs E. Craven, H. Paar, Peter Gulland and S. H. Pearce Higgins; Mr Harold Hart for translating technical matter from Old German script; Miss Janet Smith, Archivist, Liverpool Record Office, Mr B. Ironmonger, The Science Museum, London, Mr John Edgington, National Railway Museum, York, Mr J. Gordon Read, Merseyside County Museums; the Librarian, Institution of Civil Engineers for permission to quote from the Telford Papers, The Earl of Dundonald and the Trustees of the Broadland Archives for permission to quote from letters to the 10th Earl and to Lord Palmerston respectively, and to Susan Greatrex for preparing the plan of the L&MR on page 36; the staff of the Public Relations Department, British Rail, Liverpool; Roger Hansford for his services in typing the text, and to Mr W. F. Waller of B. T. Batsford.

This work was undertaken at the suggestion of Professor Jack Simmons of Leicester University, for whose valued help and continued interest the author wishes to thank him sincerely.

The author owes a particular debt of gratitude to his old friend of the Railway & Canal Historical Society, Peter Roos, who undertook a great deal of research on his behalf and discovered hitherto untapped material at the Public Record Office. His scholarship in the field of governmental control of railways through the Board of Trade in the nineteenth century has also been placed at the author's disposal. Not least has been his invaluable help in draft and proof reading. The writer, however, accepts full responsibility for matters of fact or opinion expressed in the following pages. Finally, he would pay tribute to his wife Marjorie, for her infinite patience and for her practical help in checking and indexing.

ILLUSTRATIONS

The author and publishers wish to thank those who have kindly granted them permission to use the following illustrations:
British Rail, London Midland Region: 16, 43, 44, 105, 107. The Institution of Civil Engineers: 37, 39, 40, 55, 63. Liverpool City Libraries: 3, 4, 5, 6, 18, 20, 64, 118. National Railway Museum, York; Crown Copyright: 19, 22, 49, 58, 67, 69, 70, 110, 115, 116, 119, 120, 121, 122. National Railway Museum, York: 38, 51, 74. The Director, Science Museum, London: 1, 7, 8, 10, 11, 13, 15, 24, 26, 30, 31, 32, 36, 42, 48, 52, 54, 60, 61, 71, 79, 104, 106, 108, 109, 112. Science Museum, London, Crown Copyright: 2, 23, 25, 27, 41a, 53, 59, 72, 75. *The Builder*: from the issues of 17 February 1849, 62a, 62b; 13 January 1844, 68. *The Engineer*: 77, 78. R. Lamb, Esq., of Liverpool Polytechnic for the photograph of the bust of Jesse Hartley, 12, owned by the Mersey Docks and Harbour Co, and in the care of Merseyside County Museums.

Foreword

by Jack Simmons

The formal opening of the Liverpool & Manchester Railway on 15 September 1830 was an event in world history; a thunderclap that was heard throughout Europe and across the Atlantic. 'It burst rather than stole or crept upon the world', wrote an American 40 years later. 'Its advent was in the highest degree dramatic. It was even more so than the discovery of America.' Of what other railway could that be said, at its opening, at any time anywhere?

The Liverpool & Manchester combined in itself, as never before, all the essential elements of what we know as a railway today. It conveyed both passengers and freight, entirely by mechanical traction; it provided a public service, open to all; and it did so under the authority of Government, by Act of Parliament. The locomotive was the most spectacular element in the whole organism; but it was, as we can now see looking back, only one element, side by side with others less dramatic but scarcely less remarkable. The promotion and construction of the railway had been followed attentively far beyond Lancashire; the trials of the locomotives, staged by the company at Rainhill in 1829, were watched from across the Atlantic. When the formal opening came, and then as trains began to move in regular service between Liverpool and Manchester, it was clear at once that a new instrument of social and economic life had been forged. Some people disliked and feared it. Others gave it their immediate admiration, and set themselves to apply the example it offered elsewhere, in their own parts of Britain or in countries overseas. Nobody, whether a critic of the railway or an enthusiastic supporter, could deny that it was a portent for the future. And anyone now, looking back over the history of the past 150 years, can see that its significance has endured.

More than one valuable account of the railway was written at the time of its opening: J. S. Walker's *Accurate Description of the Liverpool & Manchester Railway*, for example; the record of Henry Booth, the company's Secretary and Treasurer, which was reissued almost immediately in Philadelphia and in a French translation in Paris. The hundredth anniversary of its opening in 1930 called forth Dendy Marshall's *Centenary History*, the fullest account written up to that time, valuable for its plates and for its discussion of the iconography of the subject. Since then two American scholars, Robert E. Carlson and Thomas J. Donaghy, have surveyed the evidence much more extensively, making considerable use of the company's surviving archives, which are now in the custody of the Public Record Office at Kew. We have still, however, had to wait for a comprehensive history of this outstandingly important undertaking. Now, just in time for the 150th anniversary of the railway's opening, we have got what we have wanted so long, from Mr Thomas.

Seven years ago he published a careful history of the London & Greenwich company, *London's First Railway*: another pioneer enterprise, in suburban transport, which pointed the way to profound and striking social change in the future. Here his field is a wider one. The company he is studying was much bigger, and so was the range of its operations. The literature is correspondingly larger too. The Liverpool & Manchester Railway engendered much controversy throughout its promotion and building; and as a successful operator it was not only described with admiration and assailed by critics, it was also the target for much abuse from jealous rivals—other railways, canal companies and turnpike trusts. All this found expression in pamphlets, articles in the press, debates in Parliament, as well as in private letters and diaries. Mr Thomas sets out this complicated evidence for us and takes us through it surely.

Too much attention has perhaps been given in the past to the technology of the undertaking; certainly that has been investigated more thoroughly than any other part of the story. Here it is recounted as fully as it should be, but kept in proportion within the framework of a true company history. The locomotives earn the closest attention, for they did most to give the railway its peculiar, unprecedented character, and their performance in service had a powerful influence upon the practice of other railways, again not in Britain alone but in Russia, in Germany, and in the United States. So here they all are, the historic band of 105, their characteristics discussed in Chapter 9 and their individual histories summarised in Appendix B. But Mr Thomas does not stop there. He has also much to tell us about the men who were responsible for working these machines—not an easy task, sometimes a dangerous one. He records, with a hint of just sympathy, the first major railway strike in Britain, in 1836. He also shows us in detail the duties and conditions of service of the rest of the staff—some 700 men by 1832, 1100 by 1843. He has a good deal to say about conditions of travelling on the line and the services it provided. There has been much discussion in recent years of the origins of excursion trains. It will startle some readers, brought up on the notion that they were invented by Thomas Cook in 1841, to find an excursion train running on the railway within three weeks of its opening, and another, privately organised (a charter train, one might well call it, for a Manchester Sunday School), in May 1831. Mr Thomas considers these to be the earliest recorded railway excursions; and that is a reasonable claim.

Not all the judgements here on matters of opinion will command everyone's agreement. To take a single instance, I think Mr Thomas is ungenerous towards George Stephenson—though he might fairly point out that George himself was very rarely generous to others. To say this is not to make any fundamental criticism of the book. Rather, it affords an example of one of its best qualities. It does not provide a mere narrative of events or a dry analysis. It displays the railway to us as a great achievement in planning, execution, and management; an achievement worked out by limited and faulty human beings, to be appraised by us as best we can. Too often, in the brief summaries of the past, the history of the railway has appeared as a simple success story, a record of the conquest of difficulties by experience and ingenuity. It was that, but the conquest was far more arduous than might be supposed; and it was not always complete, even at the end of the company's independent life in 1845. Mr Thomas's clear presentation of the development of techniques, in construction and working, enables us to feel much more clearly than ever before that we are watching the enterprise ourselves as it unfolds in irregular stages, sometimes almost from day to day. Though the railway used machines, it was not itself a mechanical organism. It was a human instrument, developed, adapted, and controlled by men to serve the needs of their fellow men. That is the way in which it is shown to us here, in this admirable book. And that is how it ought to be seen in history.

Liverpool & Manchester Railway Acts of Parliament

7 G4 c xlix 5 May 1826 Incorporation
7 & 8 G4 c xxi 12 April 1827 Further powers
9 G4 c vii 26 March 1828 Further powers
10 G4 c xxxv 14 May 1829 Further powers
1 W4 c li 22 April 1831 Further powers
2 & 3 W4 c xlvi 23 May 1832 Further powers

7 W4 & 1 Vict c xxvii 5 May 1837 Further powers
2 & 3 Vict c xli 14 June 1839 Further powers
5 & 6 Vict c cviii 30 July 1842 Further powers
8 & 9 Vict c cxxiii 21 July 1845 Further powers
8 & 9 Vict c cxcviii 8 August 1845 Amalgamation

List of Abbreviations

B&LR	Bolton & Leigh Railway
B&ORR	Baltimore & Ohio Railroad
C&WR	Canterbury & Whitstable Railway
D&KR	Dublin & Kingstown Railway
ECR	Eastern Counties Railway
GJR	Grand Junction Railway
GPO	General Post Office
GWR	Great Western Railway
L&BR	London & Birmingham Railway
L&MR	Liverpool & Manchester Railway
L&NWR	London & North Western Railway
L&YR	Lancashire & Yorkshire Railway
LMSR	London, Midland & Scottish Railway
M&LR	Manchester & Leeds Railway
M&SR	Manchester & Sheffield Railway
MB&BR	Manchester, Bolton & Bury Canal Navigation & Railway
NER	North Eastern Railway
NMR	North Midland Railway
NUR	North Union Railway
RS&Co	Robert Stephenson & Co
S&DR	Stockton & Darlington Railway
W&NR	Warrington & Newton Railway
Y&NMR	York & North Midland Railway

CHAPTER ONE

The Formation of the Company

Casually, under the heading 'Iron Railway between Liverpool and Manchester', the *Liverpool Mercury* on 2 August 1822 referred to a meeting of several leading men in the fields of commerce and industry, which had recently been held to consider means of improving communications between their two towns. Eight years later the world's first railway in the modern sense was to be opened, heralding the 'Railway Age' with all the incalculable benefits to civilisation and mankind which it would bring.

Few men living then could remember the day, 60-odd years before, when the Duke of Bridgewater's Canal was opened in their district, inaugurating an earlier phase of the Industrial Revolution, the great period of the artificial Inland Waterways. Authorised in 1759 – the 'Year of Victories', the days of Wolfe and Clive – the first section had been opened in 1761, enabling the Duke's coal from Worsley to be sold in Manchester for less than 7s. per ton. By this time many rivers in various parts of the country had been made navigable by the installation of locks, by dredging and by other means; in the next 60 years hundreds of miles of canals were cut to form a reasonably adequate network.

Manchester's proud claim to the title 'The Cradle of the Industrial Revolution' is justifiably based on its early application of the factory system to the textile trade, long established in that part of Lancashire, following the invention of spinning and weaving machinery; the development of the steam engine to provide the power coincided to some extent with the improvements to the original crude machines. Within a few years other villages in the district grew into towns, each with its specialised products, and the drift of workers from the countryside gradually increased; Manchester and Salford had a population of about 57,000 in 1790, 95,000 by the turn of the century, and 133,788 by 1821, maintaining a considerable lead over Birmingham and Glasgow.

Liverpool in the latter part of the eighteenth century overtook Bristol as the second port of the kingdom, although its growth can be traced to the beginning of the century. Established as the port for commerce with Ireland, its geographical position gave it a natural advantage when England's pattern of trade gradually shifted from being predominantly with Europe and the Near East to the world-wide markets opened to her through the extension of the Empire. During the early years of the eighteenth century the number of ships using the port amounted to a hundred or so a year; by 1820 over 7,000 vessels were handled annually, and a great variety of raw materials were discharged in ever-increasing quantities at her congested docks. To these same quays flowed an endless stream of manufactured goods, not only from the mills in and around Manchester, but from the Yorkshire textile mills and cutlers, the potteries and factories of the Black Country and much of the output of salt from Cheshire.

The wars of the eighteenth and early nineteenth centuries tended only to increase the volume of trade since they generally resulted in massive additions to the Colonial Empire; still further markets were opened up by the discovery and colonisation of undeveloped territories, notably Australia, although this was necessarily a gradual process.

American cotton played little part in the industrial growth of Lancashire until after the War of Independence; then in 1784 the first small shipment reached Liverpool – a mere eight bags, and even that was seized by customs officers under the conviction that it could not have been the produce of the USA as stated on the manifest. Until this time the chief sources of raw cotton were the West Indies and the Near East, the imports being made through London and thence by road to Lancashire. Thirty-five years later some 290,000 bags a year were discharged at

Liverpool from the USA alone to feed the hungry mills.

A tragic consequence of the developments in the Western World was the rapid growth of the slave trade. General Tarleton MP, speaking in 1805 against Wilberforce's attempts at abolition, ventured the rather unsavoury argument that 10,000 persons in Liverpool alone were completely engaged in it '... besides countless numbers affected and benefited by it.'[1] The port continued to flourish and expand after abolition however, legitimate trade apparently absorbing all those who feared unemployment; and many leading citizens of Liverpool campaigned afterwards for the total elimination of slavery in the British Empire.

Until 1831 all the merchandise carried between Liverpool and the wide area it served went either entirely by road or by road and canal. In general the Lancashire roads, in common with those in the rest of the country, were in a poor condition for most of the eighteenth century. Even the turnpike between Liverpool and Manchester was described as 'circuitous, crooked and ... rough' and its surface 'infamous', since the Trustees spent little in maintenance. Much of the traffic was carried by pack horses as it had been from time immemorial, and the rest by the many waggoners along the rough paved highways.[2] Collieries remote from the canals relied on the irregular service provided by country carts to send their coal to Liverpool; 'When the farmers have little to do they bring large quantities; when busy, a few or none come'.[3]

Water-borne traffic between Liverpool and Manchester became economically practicable after the passage of the Mersey and Irwell Navigation Act in 1720, which gave powers to a Board of 'Undertakers' (39 in number), to dredge, straighten, enlarge and shorten by cuts, the rivers connecting the two towns. This concern enjoyed a monopoly of the barge traffic until 1776, when the Bridgewater Canal was opened through to Runcorn from Manchester, but despite the concern's misgivings leading to its strenuous opposition to the Duke's project, there soon proved to be more than sufficient traffic for both, and price-fixing agreements quickly followed.

These canals were open to all who owned suitable barges or 'flats' as they were termed, and paid the appropriate dues, but the proprietors exercised almost total control over the use of the waterways through their ownership of virtually all the warehouses accessible from the canal or river banks. The Mersey and Irwell Navigation Company, as the original body became in 1794, operated as a carrier through its subsidiary, the Old Quay Company.[4] The Duke of Bridgewater had been a carrier on his own canal from its inception.

The third waterway that connected Liverpool with Lancashire and Yorkshire was the Leeds and Liverpool Canal. Authorised in 1769, it was operated in two sections for over 40 years, business on the Yorkshire side commencing in 1773 and on the Lancashire side a year later. In taking the canal across the Pennines, heavy engineering works were involved, including 97 locks and two tunnels, one nearly a mile long, and it was not until 1816 that the waterway could be opened throughout. After protracted negotiations the canal was linked with the Bridgewater Canal by a cut from Wigan on the former to Leigh on the Duke's canal, thus providing the third waterway between Liverpool and Manchester; this branch was opened in January 1821.

William James,[5] a solicitor and land agent, who became interested in railways at least as early as 1799, probably first conceived a plan for a railway between Liverpool and Manchester, or at least a rail connection between some of the canals in the district, during a visit in the autumn of 1802. By the end of the Napoleonic Wars he was a wealthy man, deriving £10,000 a year from his land agency alone; he was by this time a coal-owner, the Superintendent of the Stratford-on-Avon Canal and a shareholder in the Croydon, Merstham and Godstone Railway, although the latter did little to enhance his fortune. He was a much-travelled man, and his wealth enabled him to pursue his interest in formulating railway schemes in many parts of the country.

However, still in the throes of a desperate war, Britain was not ready to embark on these costly projects and even the enthusiasm and persuasive powers of the far-sighted James failed to kindle much interest in his plans. It was not that they were nebulous schemes, devised by an eccentric visionary; he was not only one of the most successful men in his chosen profession and generally an astute business man, but in his efforts to establish a railway system he took the trouble to acquaint himself with every new development or improvement in track and machinery. He was familiar with the principles of civil engineering and equally so with those of the steam locomotive, from that of Trevithick to those of Stephenson; for he had followed the improvements of Blenkinsop, Hedley and others, and his commitment to the locomotive as the source of power for railways was confirmed on 1 September 1821, when he entered into a business agreement with Stephenson and his

2 *William James (1771–1837)*

partner Losh to help promote the sale of their products. In April 1822 he refers to '. . . the invention of the Land Agent Steam Engine and the Malleable Iron Plate Rails secured to the present Company by Letters Patent.'[6]

James had been increasingly active during the previous 18 months in planning lines on a grand scale, and while on a routine business visit to Lancashire in the summer of 1821 he became aware of the difficulties being experienced by the merchants of Liverpool and the manufacturers of Manchester with their inadequate roads and canals. He appears to have canvassed the idea of a railway among several businessmen in Manchester, and one of these, Joseph Cowlishaw, a corn merchant, was sufficiently interested to introduce him to Joseph Sandars, corn merchant and underwriter of Liverpool. The moment was propitious, for Sandars and his fellow traders were becoming increasingly vocal on the question of the cost and inadequacy of the services offered by the canals at a time when trade was booming following a long period of depression. Sandars, who seems to have known everyone of influence in Liverpool, was their leader in the attack on the canal interests, and James had little difficulty in convincing him that a steam-operated railway would go far towards solving their problems.

The idea was not particularly novel; railways between the two towns are said to have been proposed before the end of the eighteenth century, by William Jessop in 1797 on behalf of a group of Liverpool merchants and by his business partner Benjamin Outram a year later for railway promoters in Manchester.[7] Jessop's line through country to the south of the two towns was to have been laid with his newly-invented edge rails, while Outram's took a northern route and was envisaged as an iron plateway; both would naturally have been horse-operated. Two separate railways would have been uneconomic, and the rival promoters could come to no agreement, so in the end neither was built.[8]

About this time James produced his first rough surveys of railways in the area, the original plan being to link the various canals by short lines. In the years that followed a number of small lines appeared in various parts of the country and in 1821, after three years effort on the part of its promoters, the Stockton and Darlington Railway Act was passed. A year before, Thomas Gray had published his *Observations on a General Iron Rail-way* in which he urged the construction of a line between Liverpool and Manchester as the first link in a network connecting the principal towns and cities of England. The stage was thus set for the meeting between James and Sandars, the outcome of which was the acceptance of James's offer to prepare a preliminary 'ocular' survey for the line, to be used by Sandars in enlisting support for the project.

Joseph Sandars, then a member of the Society of Friends, was prominent in the commercial community of Liverpool; prosperous in business, he was also active in politics supporting the Whig Cause and Parliamentary Reform. He has been described as 'active and perhaps impulsive, moderate yet persistent' and it was probably these qualities, as much as business acumen, that accounted for his success. Possessed of the gift of persuasion, he could fire others with his enthusiasm for an enterprise, and this he proceeded to do for the railway undertaking.

His first step was to form a provisional committee in Liverpool and a similar, though smaller, one in Manchester: the former eventually totalled 21 members, and the latter 10. Here were gathered the leading spirits of the two most important towns in the north-west, between them representing practically every shade of opinion in religion and politics, many spheres of commercial and philanthropic activity, the

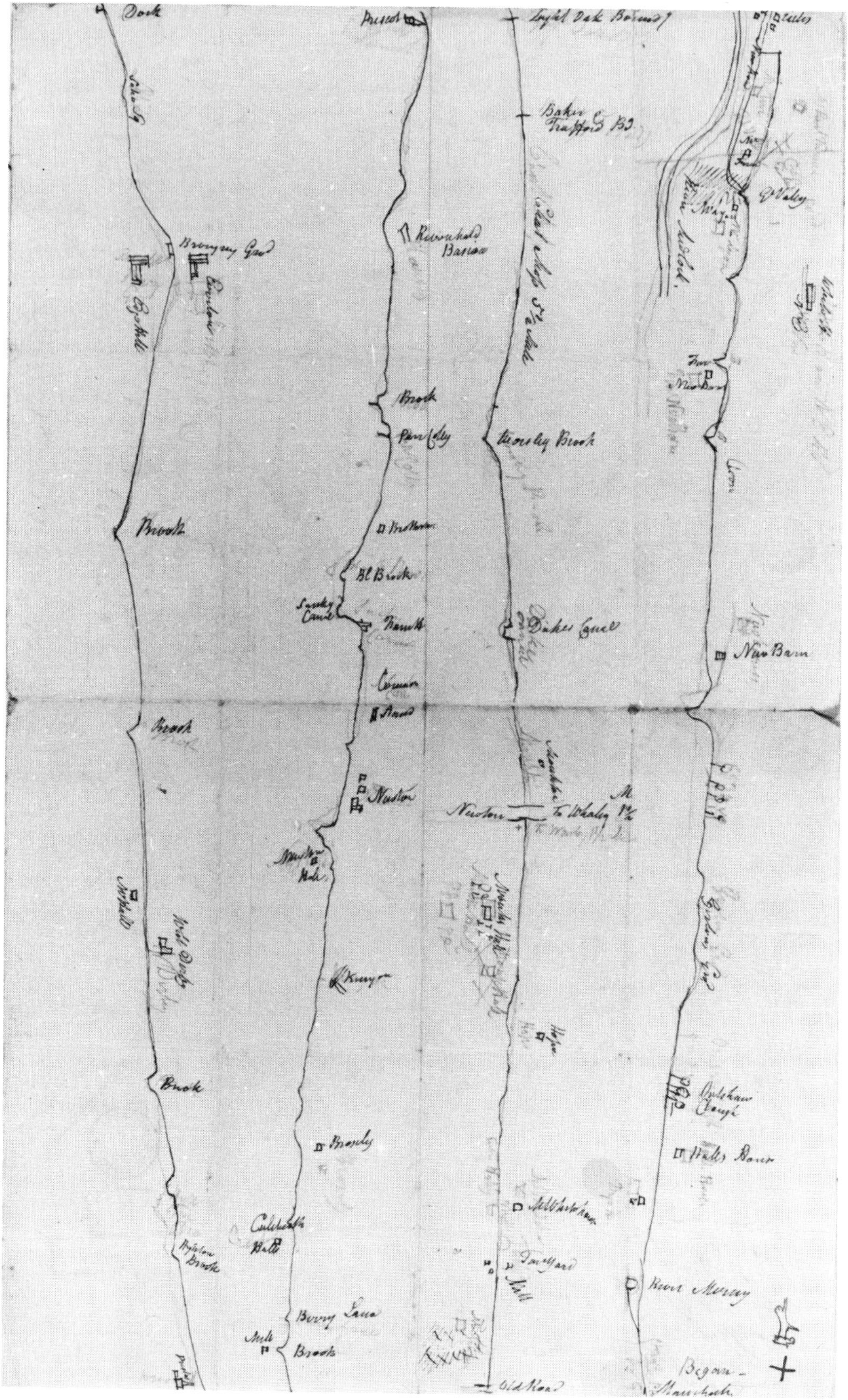

sciences and engineering: Sandars knew them all and they knew and trusted him.

Liverpool's leading banker, John Moss, was among his earliest supporters, as was James Cropper, the wealthy Quaker merchant and philanthropist, John Gladstone MP, father of Britain's future prime minister, importer, owner of a fleet of merchant ships and of large sugar and coffee plantations, and his friend and fellow-merchant William Ewart joined the committee; a former Mayor of Liverpool Sir John Tobin, friend of Canning and Huskisson, and a future Mayor, William Rathbone, of the family of cotton importers,[9] were there. The Chairman of the Corn Exchange, Sandars' partner Samuel Blain, lent his support; Dr Thomas Stewart Traill, a founder of the Royal Institution, the Mechanics' Institute and the Liverpool Infirmary, and Charles Tayleur, later to establish with Robert Stephenson the famous locomotive building firm, The Vulcan Foundry, were willing recruits.

Meanwhile in Manchester men of similar calibre were responding to Sandars' invitation to support the railway, and these for the most part were successful and prosperous members of the cotton industry. Peter Ewart, Thomas Harbottle and William Garnett were directors of the Manchester Chamber of Commerce, as also was Hugh Birley who, as a Major in the Manchester Yeomanry, had been present at the Manchester riots of August 1819 – the so-called 'Peterloo Massacre'; Major Joseph Birley of the same military family was also on the committee. Sandars was fortunate in recruiting to his Manchester committee John Kennedy, the engineer and inventor friend of James Watt; among other things he had improved Crompton's 'Mule', was a partner in the firm which built them, and was a wealthy cottonspinner on his own account. A staunch advocate of the steam locomotive, his expert knowledge of mechanical engineering was invaluable to the committee.

Such was the prestige of the Provisional Committee, its members embracing as they did so diverse a range of interests, that the railway project received widespread acceptance in the business circles of industrial Lancashire.

While the Provisional Committee was being organised, James set to work to prepare his preliminary survey, in which he was assisted by two of his sons, his brother-in-law Paul Padley[10] as Chief Surveyor, George Hamilton, Hugh Greenshields and the young Robert Stephenson. By the summer of 1822, under pressure from the Committee, he produced his 'Preliminary Report' in which he estimated that the whole line could be built in 18 months for £100,000, and he stated that the sums required by the contractors for undertaking the work would be detailed in the Parliamentary surveys and estimates.

The Provisional Committee had in the meantime agreed to Sandars' proposal to petition the Bridgewater Canal for a reduction in their rates; this appears to have been a shrewd move on their part, for they cannot have been so naive as to suppose that any concession would be forthcoming, and a written refusal to meet their request would provide valuable evidence of the need for a railway. Predictably the Superintendent of the Bridgewater Trust, Robert Haldane Bradshaw, rejected the memorial, on 9 April 1822, and in his pursuit of 'Profit-extraction to the utmost limit . . .'[11] he contributed to the eventual success of the Liverpool & Manchester Railway, at the same time hastening the decline of those profits the waterways had so long enjoyed.

Until this time the Provisional Committee had been a loose, rather informal association, meeting at infrequent intervals owing largely to the difficulties of travelling the 30-odd miles between Liverpool and Manchester. Now, however, the time had arrived for a permanent Committee to be organised, and this was accomplished at a meeting of the members from both towns held in the summer of 1822 at the offices of Pritt and Clay, Solicitors of Liverpool; John Moss was elected Chairman of the Committee and George A. Pritt its legal adviser. The Committee then decided to await James's completed survey in the hope of approaching Parliament for leave to introduce a Bill the following year.

Within a short time the first hint of the project reached the Press; on 27 July 1822 the *Manchester Guardian*, under the heading 'Iron Railway between Manchester and Liverpool', suggested the possibility of public meetings to consider the scheme and an early application to Parliament; the use of 'steam carriages' was foreshadowed. The article was reprinted in *The Times* two days later, and, with the order of the towns reversed, in the *Liverpool Mercury* on 2 August. On 20 September the *Liverpool Mercury* reported that the Committee had taken the first steps to establish the railway and that notice of their intention to apply to Parliament had been given.

The first setback to the railway came in the autumn of 1822 when it gradually became apparent that James had encountered difficulties in surveying the

3 *William James' 'Ocular survey'; rough notes in pencil, inked in later. 1821*

4 *John Moss (1782–1858), the first Chairman of the Liverpool & Manchester Railway*

line and that the plans and estimates were not likely to be ready in time to meet the requirements of Parliamentary Standing Orders, for an application in 1823. Unfortunately for himself and the Committee, James pretended that all was going well and in response to repeated requests to produce the plans he assured the Committee that they were on the point of completion, promising delivery in a matter of days. About November there is a change in the tone of his letters on the subject; although claiming that the plans were now completed he refers to illness and distress overtaking him.

The surveyors meanwhile were under some pressure to complete their work, for on 3 September Robert Stephenson wrote to James informing him that it would be impossible to finish the plan before the 16th and asking for another surveyor to assist him; he also asked James where the line was to finish. On 23 September Hamilton sent in part of his survey, pointing out that the needle of his surveying instrument differed from Padley's. At about the same time Robert Stephenson reported that his level (theodolite) had been kicked over and asked for a replacement; he also wanted the 'draft of the fields' for the tenants' names.[12] It appears that the draft plans were completed in October, although James told Sandars that a plan had been lodged with the clerk of the peace in September, and that the reduced Parliamentary plans were completed in November.

Padley, described as a first-rate surveyor, clever artist and draughtsman, is said to have lithographed all the plans for James, who confided everything to him.[13] From letters of Robert Stephenson, it seems that James himself was occupied during October 1822 with surveys for the Bolton & Leigh Railway and with the invention of a new tubular rail.[14]

Plans and sections of the line obviously existed in October 1822 for on the 15th a complete section of the line showing levels and gradients over the whole 32 miles was sent by James to George Stephenson for his comments and advice as to the practicability of his supplying stationary steam engines and locomotives to work the line. Stephenson furnished a certificate dated 28 October showing the estimated performance of a locomotive with various loads ranging from 40 tons over 32 miles in 8 hours to 10 tons over the same distance in $2\frac{1}{2}$ hours.

James's original route was roughly on the course of that eventually adopted for the L&MR. Starting at the Everton boundary in Soho Street, the line rose on a gradient of 1 in 37 for 1166 yards, ran level for 1030 yards and then fell at 1 in 43 for 1188 yards. This section was to be worked by a stationary engine at first, but when the railway was established a tunnel was to be driven through Everton Hill, then barren of houses. A novel feature of the scheme was that of retaining the steam engine so that when buildings covered the site it could be used as a pumping engine to raise water. The proposed line ran through West Derby, Huyton, Prescot, Newton, Kenyon and Bury Lane, to cross Chat Moss and reach Manchester via Eccles.[15]

It would appear that up to this time the Committee were unaware of the route their railway would take, for when the plans were revealed they demanded an alteration in the entrance to Manchester. Gladstone and Ewart insisted on an extension to the Liverpool docks, regardless of the cost, and an alternative route was required that would avoid the lands of Lord Derby and other noblemen. These fresh surveys were made in early November despite very severe weather, and the plans were produced for Lord Derby's approval. In a letter of 13 November, however, he indicated that he was '... so decidedly averse to any plan of the sort that it would be useless to lay this, or any other plan before him ... ', adding that if brought to Parliament, he would oppose the scheme.[16]

THE FORMATION OF THE COMPANY

For some time, a suit in Chancery had been hanging over William James, and he was in fact on bail of £15 in the late autumn of 1822. His surety, Edward Hinton, rescinded the bail however, and James was committed to the Kings Bench Prison on 18 November, where he served a three-month sentence, being released on 19 February 1823 under the Insolvency Act.[17] During this, his first period of imprisonment, he wrote a long letter to Sandars in which he asserted that the plans were complete and that there would still be time to get the measure through Parliament that session although he thought it prudent to postpone the application and in the interim have the plans engraved and published along with the reports. He went on to say that the cost of the survey had been seven months labour and about £500 (of which he had received £290), adding 'No one knows my labours and privations in the progress of this work; but if my friends are firm in their intention they will find that, against another session, many of our present difficulties will be removed'.

George Hamilton, one of James's assistant surveyors, wrote to him on 19 March 1823 suggesting that the plans for the Bolton Railway be removed from Everton ' ... as I dare say you will agree that they will be safer in our custody than Miss M'George's ... '. At this time James was also planning a line between Portsmouth and Chatham among others, and it was becoming apparent to the Committee that they could not rely upon him to produce the final plans of the L&MR in a reasonable time. His imprisonment must have caused serious misgivings among the Committee Members, and when on 30 May he was again committed to the Kings Bench Prison as a result of a claim by his brother-in-law, Peter Mudie, and others, a meeting of the subscribers was called in Liverpool under the chairmanship of Charles Tayleur to consider the position. One of the resolutions was that Jesse Hartley, Engineer to the Liverpool Docks Board, should 'go over the proposed line and give his opinion in respect to it.' At an adjourned meeting held about the middle of August, and thinly attended, it was proposed that a general meeting be held ' ... at some convenient place between Liverpool and Manchester, for the purpose of going more decidedly into the business and at the same time confirming the appointment of Mr Hartley.' David Holt, who conveyed this information to James on 16 August 1823, urged him to comply with Sandars' request to send Padley with the plans and estimates:

' ... if thou cannot be here thyself ... so that he may

5 *James Cropper (1773–1840)*

not only attend Mr Hartley, and give him information which thou appearest to think indispensable, but be able also to attend the general meeting as thy representative, there to sustain thy interests and satisfy the minds of the subscribers that in thee they have every security for the due performance of what thou hast undertaken.'

James, who was not released from prison until 22 October, could not attend the meeting; although there is no record that Padley was there it is likely that he did attend to represent James. Hartley's appointment was confirmed and he proceeded to resurvey the line, submitting a long report by the spring of 1824.

The year 1823 was well advanced when these meetings took place, and about 18 months had elapsed since the project was first launched. The Committee only now started taking matters into their own hands, and began the long process of acquiring the technical knowledge that would enable them to undertake the very complicated task that lay before them.

It would seem that until this time the Committee members, heavily engaged in their various business activities, were not prepared to devote sufficient time to the railway, believing that James could be trusted to plan and build it.

Early in May 1824, four members of the Provisional Committee, Booth, Ellis, Kennedy and Sandars, went to inspect railways in the North-east and to report on the engineering aspects. They examined the Stockton & Darlington Railway, still under construction, the Killingworth Colliery Railway, where they first saw locomotives, two of Stephenson's, although they were not actually working. At Hetton Colliery, however, they not only saw locomotives at work, but rode on one of them.

At this moment the unfortunate James found himself back in prison for the third time, having been arrested for debt and committed to the Kings Bench on 14 May.

A full meeting of the Provisional Committee was held in the Liverpool Underwriters' Rooms on 20 May, when the Report of the delegation was received. All its members were very impressed by what they had seen, and were unanimously in favour of employing locomotives on the proposed railway. The Committee resolved to form a Joint Stock Company to construct the line as soon as Parliament authorised it, to raise £300,000[18] capital in 3,000 shares of £100 each (no person to hold more than ten), to open subscription lists in Liverpool and Manchester, and to make a first call of £3 by 1 August. At this meeting the Provisional Committee was formally dissolved and a new one formed to direct the affairs of the undertaking; it consisted of 24 members, and included the stalwarts from the old Committee, under the same Chairmanship – that of John Moss.[19]

However, the most momentous decision taken that day was to invite George Stephenson to become the Company's Engineer; its consequences went far beyond the Liverpool & Manchester Railway itself and were to influence the development of railways as yet unthought of, in Great Britain and throughout the world.

George Stephenson had had about 20 years experience of steam engines, having been concerned with their installation at a number of mines on the north-eastern coalfield, and he had had a great deal to do with the various types of tramway and railway associated with these collieries; furthermore, he was engineer to the Stockton & Darlington Railway, then nearing completion. He had been building locomotives since 1814 and was a partner in Robert Stephenson & Co., the principal (and almost the only) locomotive-building firm then in existence.

James had recommended him to the railway committee, although probably as a supplier of equipment rather than as a civil engineer, and Sandars had met him at Killingworth within a short time of the delegation's visit. By reason of their business interest in the locomotive, Stephenson undoubtedly knew of James's plight, and Sandars must have mentioned the committee's impatience at the failure of their former engineer to produce the plans so long awaited. It is reasonable to suppose that arrangements for Stephenson to replace James were made at that meeting, and that the invitation of 20 May was a formality. Stephenson accepted it immediately, for on 25 May Sandars, in the course of a reply to a letter James had sent on 7 May, notified him of his dismissal and of Stephenson's appointment, adding, rather naively, that he was certain that the arrangement would be agreeable to James, and inviting him to hand over his plans in return for which his name should receive prominence and his reputation be enhanced by association '... in such a mighty affair.'

After having made arrangements for his assistants[20] to take over his work on the Stockton & Darlington Railway, Stephenson arrived in Liverpool on 12 June, where he was met by his son and Sandars. That evening he dined at Sandars' house and entered another world. Overwhelmed by the gracious living of Liverpool's commercial elite, he wrote to Longridge giving details of the lavish hospitality he had enjoyed both there and at Ellis's home the next evening. He was not only impressed by the number of servants and the variety of costly wines, but by his hostesses, of whom he wrote 'Mrs Sandars is a fine woman, and Mrs Ellis very elegant.'

Less than a week later Robert sailed from Liverpool for Colombia via Venezuela, to be absent for three vital years. When working on the L&MR survey he became very attached to William James, whom he respected and admired. The friendship was to endure, and after James's death, Robert paid him the highest tributes, assigning to him the coveted title 'The Father of Railways', much to George Stephenson's annoyance. It has been suggested by biographer L. T. C. Rolt that Robert was not only anxious to escape from intolerable parental domination, but was disgusted by the way in which his father supplanted his own former friend and business associate and then sought to take advantage of what work he had done, according him neither thanks nor credit.

Robert's plans had been made for some months but the fact remains that he made no attempt to secure his release from the Colombian venture to assist in the L&MR project, but was ready to withdraw from active partnership with his father and the locomotive-building business. It is reasonable to suppose that they discussed the railway project in the weeks before his departure, and it may well have been that Robert did not wish to be associated in an undertaking that might prove to be beyond his father's ability to complete.

One of George Stephenson's first steps was to engage Paul Padley in June 1824 as a surveyor; James, writing to his son shortly afterwards, said 'He knows my plans of which he and Stephenson will now avail themselves. I confess I did not calculate upon such duplicity in either.' Padley was apparently working on the final copy of the plan in October 1822. Others engaged at the time were Hugh Steel, Thomas Blackett, James Clough and Elijah Galloway Jnr. Although engaged by Stephenson they were paid by the Committee, as shown by Elijah Galloway's account for £148 19s.[21]

It is fairly certain that the course of the line was not planned by Stephenson as Galloway, who arrived from Newcastle by coach on 18 June, started '... assisting in the levels between Liverpool and Manchester' the following day, and worked continuously until 19 July, a total of 31 days, including Sundays, for which his fee was 31 guineas. After their experience with James, the Railway Committee was taking an active part in the planning of the undertaking. With at least a rough idea of what James's plan had been since they had amended it, if not actual plans of some description, together with the report following Hartley's survey, it is unlikely that they would have been willing to consider an entirely new route. The probability is that Stephenson was presented with the results of the previous work and asked to check the levels, make what deviations were necessary and produce detailed plans, sections and estimates.

The interval between Stephenson's arrival in Liverpool and the start of the survey was less than a week, and quite insufficient to permit of his working out a new route across country with which he was unfamiliar. James, released from prison on 18 August, wrote shortly afterwards that his plans, approved by the Board, and then at Liverpool, had been used by both Hartley and Stephenson.

It was at this time that James's connection with the L&MR was finally severed, occasioning him '... a more severe pang of anguish' than all his other misfortunes. Evidently he had been offered some appointment in the Company, but he said that he could not humble himself to be employed, having been accustomed to circumstances so very different.

Here lies the clue to his failure; not content with having his suggestions adopted and being encouraged to survey a railway that others were willing to finance, he seems to have been determined to see the whole project through Parliament to a successful conclusion, expecting the proprietors to wait patiently while he attempted to do single-handed work requiring a team of experts. To James the L&MR was one of a number of schemes in which he was involved, and a section of the national railway network he envisaged, whilst to the Committee it was a vital means of communication, urgently required if the commerce of the two towns was not to grind to a halt. In these circumstances the Committee had already shown commendable forbearance.

Meanwhile on 1 June the Committee made its first approach to the Common Council of Liverpool for the support it considered essential to the success of the Bill; the Council met immediately to discuss the Committee's memorial but decided to consider it fully when the railway's plans were more mature. At about the same time John Moss decided to relinquish the Chairmanship of the Committee on the grounds that he felt temperamentally unfitted to undergo the stresses of guiding the Committee's fortunes in the months and years ahead. He proposed Charles Lawrence, then Mayor of Liverpool, as his successor, and he was duly elected. It was a fortunate choice, for Lawrence, a West India merchant, was a man of high standing in Liverpool and was described as gracious and possessed of a charm of manner and presence that impressed all with whom he had dealings. It is probable that Henry Booth, Secretary to the Committee since 1822, became full-time salaried Treasurer at this time, abandoning the corn trade, in which he had not been spectacularly successful. Sir John Tobin withdrew from the Committee and John Gladstone MP resigned in favour of his son Robert, but continued to serve the Company well in Parliament.

From Galloway's account, the main part of the survey was completed before the end of July and in a letter of 11 July George Stephenson wrote:

'The Liverpool line will soon be finished. I have Hugh [Steel] and Mr Galloway carrying on the levels who will manage the whole line without any other assistance. They have now got nearly half way and through the worst of the ground.'

Preoccupied with the survey of the Liverpool & Birmingham Railway, Stephenson himself was absent from the L&MR for long periods during the survey; he was in Birmingham at the end of June, and seems to have spent July and August visiting West Auckland, Newcastle, Stourbridge, Newport,

Newcastle-under-Lyme and, after becoming involved with the Newcastle & Carlisle Railway, Brampton. On 11 July he had four sets of surveyors on the Birmingham Line and expected to have another eight or ten pairs at work on his return from the North – at least 24 men compared with the two on the L&MR. Padley is not heard of again in connection with the L&MR although he was still with Stephenson; presumably he and the other experienced surveyors were on Stephenson's other projects. Some time in August Stephenson did manage to spend two days on the L&MR when Galloway was occupied in 'Looking over the line and shewing Mr Stephenson the direction of the levels.'

Possibly the Committee were becoming rather concerned at Stephenson's apparent neglect of the railway for during August the shadowy figure of Mr Awty appears on the scene; Galloway records 'Waiting on Awty by directions of Mr Sandars 2 days', but what his brief was is not clear. The only other reference to him is in a letter to Sandars dated 27 September in which Stephenson wrote:

'I am quite shocked with Auty's [sic] conduct; we must throw him aside as soon as possible. Indeed, I have begun to fear that he has been fee'd by some of the canal proprietors to make a botch of the job.'

This was the first of several instances where Stephenson sought the dismissal of men in authority who had not been appointed by him. In December he refers to a Mr Straker of the Newcastle area, who had been called to Liverpool to give his opinion on Railroads (he assumed by Ewart), adding 'I will not state my opinion of Mr Straker's principle ... ' leaving the Company to form their own conclusions.[22]

September 1824 saw the setting up of a Finance Committee which included the banker Lister Ellis, and the opening of a campaign to secure local support for the undertaking. Press announcements detailed the advantages the railway would bring, petitions in its favour were organised, and a pamphlet was prepared attacking the canals.[23] This was published on 6 October, to be followed on 29 October by the Committee's first Prospectus, prepared by Henry Booth and signed by Lawrence, in which the capital required had increased to £400,000. The Prospectus was given wide publicity in local and London newspapers, and copies, accompanied by Sandars' pamphlet, were sent to MPs and others who were thought to have some influence.

6 *Henry Booth (1789–1869), Secretary, Treasurer and later General Manager of the Railway*

Public interest was now thoroughly aroused, and letters poured into the editorial offices of the newspapers, the sympathetic, the hostile, the sarcastic, the frivolous – contributions from all shades of opinion. This in turn led to editorial comment, and the reprinting of material that had appeared elsewhere; little information on railroads was available to the journalists of the day, and practically none of an impartial nature.

About mid-October 1824 a 24-page printed '*Synopsis of the Proceedings necessary in soliciting the Bill, with observations*'[24] was prepared to enable the Committee and officers of the Company to deal systematically with the intricate requirements of Parliament's Standing Orders for Private Bills. By this time Thomas Moulden Sherwood had been engaged as Parliamentary Agent, and Francis Mewburn, the Darlington Solicitor who had seen the S&DR Bill through Parliament, was advising the Committee and its Solicitors on various matters from his own experience.[25] In addition, Messrs Dyson and Jones were also advising the Committee and William George Adam, KC, the leading counsel for the Committee, had been briefed. The views of all these were set out in the synopsis and taken into account by the Committee and its Solicitors; where there was a divergence of opinion, that of Sherwood was invariably accepted.

The Committee had to ensure that a notice giving the names of all parishes and townships through which the railway was to pass or would be affected by it appeared in a county newspaper three times, and that a similar notice be 'affixed to the principal outer door of the Session House' at Lancaster, Preston, Salford and Kirkdale. The person posting these notices was required to remain near the door until the Magistrates had entered and the court commenced business.

The map and section of the line and the Book of Reference containing a list of the owners and occupiers of all the land required to be compulsorily purchased, had to be deposited for public inspection with the Clerk of the Peace for the County and the Town Clerks of Liverpool and Manchester by 30 November. Their preparation, and responsibility for their accuracy, rested with the Engineer, their deposit with the Solicitor. Every owner and occupier of land over which the railway was to run had to be interviewed and a record made as to whether they 'assented to, or dissented from, such Railway, or are neuter in respect thereto.' The writer of the synopsis observes, 'The operation here required will be one of great nicety and labour', and Mewburn stressed that

'The clerk who takes the assents must be *well versed in the business* of the Railway, know all its bearings, and be able to talk about it; he must be candid and of good address ... he must be careful to *note down the precise* words of the owner, &c., and read them over to him, when they do not amount to a clear avowal of his being assenting, dissenting or neutral.'

Moreover,

'... he should be a man of self possession and acquainted with the rules of evidence. For on his evidence as to matters of form, and on the engineer's as to merits, the Bill will mainly hinge.'

W. C. Clay was selected for this onerous duty and it undoubtedly comforted and encouraged him to reflect that the Committee were satisfied that he embraced these admirable qualities during the cold winter days when he was confronting hostile tenants with documents and large scale maps. He was assisted by

'... Mr James Woods, whose local knowledge is accurate as far as Newton, and to Mr Johnson, of Manchester, whose local knowledge seems very good as far as Worsley, the intermediate ground being Chat Moss, and the contiguous country seems to be intimately known to Mr Borron the magistrate, who lives in that neighbourhood, and has offered his assistance in giving information.'

The real purpose in sending two men was to provide a witness to the written comments and signatures of the tenants and owners, for, as Mewburn observed, 'I know by sad experience that some men will deny their hand-writing.' So far as Parliament was concerned, everyone owning or occupying property along the line had to be visited; whether they supported the project or not was immaterial.

Meanwhile Sherwood was advising on the preparation of the Petition to Parliament for leave to introduce the Bill, and while stating that it was unimportant whether this document was signed by 20 or by 5000 subscribers and proprietors of land, he suggested that

'... so far as regards the success and respectability of the application, it may be as well to obtain as many signatures as can be conveniently procured amongst the *proprietors of land*, with a view to repudiate any imputation which may be cast upon us, that the undertaking is one which has for its object, the emolument of the subscribers and not the benefit of the public ... '

The Committee was to be careful not to allow anyone whose evidence might be required at the enquiry to sign the Petition, since this would invalidate their testimony and the document had to be ready for presentation within two weeks of the opening of the Parliamentary Session in January 1825. By this time all the other papers required had to be ready, including the Subscription List showing the name of each subscriber and the amount of his subscription. The Committee was advised to have every signature to the Petition or Subscription List witnessed, and that the Committee's solicitor should attest all those of persons outside London; although this would mean many journeys, it would be cheaper than to have to call numerous witnesses to London from various parts of the country.

Amid all this activity the Bill itself had to be drafted; the Committee was warned that 'The Bill must be drawn with great care. Mr Mewburn recommends Mr Crawford to settle it.' Also, 'Mr Mewburn recommends that we should *not* introduce a specific clause respecting turnpike-roads, but slip in some words in the first clause, conferring great powers on the company.'

Copies of the Bill and a printed map of the railway of 1 inch to the mile were to be held in readiness for distribution to every Parish Clerk along the line after the Bill had been brought in; notices that these papers had been deposited with the Clerks were to appear in newspapers and to be nailed to the church doors of every parish affected.

The synopsis of proceedings outlines the principal duties of the Engineer: to survey the country, fix on the best line, take levels, make a map or plan and section and to make a Book of Reference. Much of this work was finished or well in hand. A paragraph headed 'Observations' was intended to prepare him for appearing before the Committee of the House:

'The points to which the engineer will be examined, will be many and important: he will have to verify his Surveys, Levels, Maps, Section, and Book of Reference; to prove the depositing; to prove the estimate; to speak to the line selected; to substantiate the advantages of the proposed undertaking, including the superiority of locomotive engines over other propelling powers; and he must particularly be prepared to meet, and answer at the moment, any objections that may be raised, either against the proposed line, or against the nature of the road, or of the machinery intended to be used.'

Finally, the duties of the Parliamentary Agent and the Committee were specified; the former was to give advice and information, and after the Bill was brought in, to undertake all the practical work of conducting it through both Houses.

'Beyond this, it would be difficult to define his duties; but from his high character for zeal, industry, and talents, there is no doubt that his department will be most effectively filled.'

The Committee undertook to attend to the general correspondence, the appropriation of shares, collection and distribution of the Company's funds, the superintendence of the other departments, the literary department and the canvassing of members.

Someone, most probably Sherwood, ' ... recommended that the Liverpool and Manchester Rail-road Bill should sail in the wake of the Birmingham and Liverpool Bill' on the grounds that this project stood a good chance of success since the landowners were generally favourable and it did not ' ... interfere with the interests of a powerful Canal Proprietary.'[26]

Meanwhile in the field Galloway is found accompanying George Stephenson and James Walker on a three-day inspection in August, and during the same month, spending two weeks making estimates and calculations. During the second week of October he spent two days showing the line to Thomas Oliver, another of Stephenson's assistants who evidently joined the Liverpool and Manchester team at that time, and on 26 October he started a nine-day period 'levelling a proposed line on the South of Liverpool.' During November he spent one day assisting in the survey of the property of Lords Sefton and Derby, returning to Newcastle on 2 December, his work finished for the time being.

The surveyors met a considerable amount of opposition when attempting to carry the survey across the lands of Lords Sefton and Derby, and a flat refusal from Robert Bradshaw to allow them on the Bridgewater Trustees' property. It was claimed that an earlier survey had been made in the middle of the night, without permission, and that the tenants' crops had been damaged. In October Stephenson wrote to Joseph Pease complaining of his difficulties with these particular landowners whose ground was 'blockaded on every side' to prevent the survey. There were instances of damaged instruments,[27] but it seems likely that a certain amount of guesswork was substituted for accurate observation when the small surveying party encountered any determined opposition.

It does not appear that Stephenson himself did much of the surveying, and the final plans dated 20 November 1824 were prepared by his draughtsman Thomas O. Blackett, and countersigned by him. Apart from new projects in which he was involved, Stephenson's Stockton & Darlington Railway, then under construction, and the Locomotive Works at Newcastle, occupied much of his attention.

The Committee, in attempting to arouse public interest in the project, inevitably stirred up opposition, primarily from landowners and their tenants, turnpike trustees, carriers and carters, and all who had a vested interest in defeating the plan for a railway; Clay attributed much of this opposition to the efforts of Lords Derby and Sefton and to the Canal managements. G. F. Bury, the Committee's solicitor in Manchester, encountered bitter resentment to the railway project when attempting to rally support, and Hugh Birley, Committee Member, also of Manchester, reported a rumour that some tenants had given notice to quit in fear of the railway.[28]

Foreseeing a bitter contest looming up when the Bill reached Parliament, the Committee, somewhat belatedly, sought to accumulate as much additional information as was available on engineering and technical matters in order to combat any arguments sprung upon them by their opponents. To this end, Charles Sylvester, Engineer, was commissioned to inspect and report on locomotives and railways in the North-east; his Report delivered on 15 December 1824, recommended the employment of the locomotive engine, which he averred was capable of much improvement. In January 1825 at the request of the Committee, further detailed experiments were made at the Killingworth, Hetton and Ford Collieries in the presence of eight prominent engineers: George Stephenson, William Cubitt, John Rastrick, William Brunton, Philip Taylor, Charles Sylvester, James Walker and Nicholas Wood. Some of the Railway Committee were also in attendance together with representatives of railway interests from London, Birmingham and other places.

Using various locomotives, trial runs were made at Killingworth up and down a gentle gradient on 18 and 22 January, attaining speeds between 3.1 and 7.1 mph, with trains varying in weight between 32 and 59 tons. At another colliery speeds of $5\frac{1}{2}$ mph were recorded with a locomotive and 10 mph with stationary engines. Coal and water consumption were also recorded.

About the time of the railway trials the Mersey and Irwell Navigation Company conducted some experiments to determine how quickly a barge could be horse-towed from Manchester, loaded in Liverpool and returned to Manchester. Leaving Manchester in the early hours of the morning, the loaded barge was back before midnight, but although the ideal conditions in which the tests were made did not normally obtain, the results were nevertheless given in evidence against the Railway Bill.

The approval of the Liverpool City Council had not been given by the end of 1824 and on 5 January the Railway Committee petitioned that body to allow the railway to enter Liverpool and to lend their support in Parliament. The Council was very much divided on the whole question of the railway and eventually agreed to its entering the town only if locomotives were prohibited from travelling along or using the streets. Accordingly in March the Committee had a clause inserted in the Bill excluding steam engines from the streets of both Liverpool and Manchester.

The L&MR Bill came to Parliament at a time when that body was seriously perturbed at the number of joint stock companies being brought before the public. A list of 276, involving a total capital of £174m, was published in February 1825 by *The Monthly Repository of Theology and General Literature*, and reprinted as a pamphlet for the benefit of those who did not subscribe to that journal by a firm in the City of London. The L&MR was only one of 49 Rail Roads in the list, which included canals, docks and a variety of other public utilities, both in the British Isles and abroad. Some were respectable, some dubious; some were over-ambitious, others fraudulent.

The Subscription Contract, required under Standing Orders before Parliament would proceed with the Bill, appears to have been complete by 12 January 1825, a notice to this effect appearing that day in *The Times*. This document listed by name the shareholders and their separate holdings, and had to represent at least four-fifths of the capital required to complete the undertaking, in order to demonstrate that the project was a serious one.

The past few months had seen the Committee, once it had been galvanized into action, pressing forward rigorously with its preparations, and the short period ahead, before the opening of the 1825 Parliamentary Session, was one of even more intense activity as, pursuing its timetable, the final steps were taken.

During December and January Sandars, Moss and Lawrence spent some time in London canvassing Members of Parliament for support and Booth prepared a short summary of the Committee's objects based on the prospectus and recent published statements. In Parliament William Holmes, MP for Bishops Castle,[29] promoted the Committee's interests and mobilised support for the Bill, whilst Thomas Creevy, member for Appleby and close friend of Lords Sefton and Derby, organised the opposition.

By the end of January 1825 all the documents were ready and those required in advance by the Private Bill Office had been lodged; the plans had been deposited in November with the Clerks of the Peace. Lister Ellis and other Members of the Committee had taken rooms in the Royal Hotel, St James's Street, in readiness to watch the Bill's progress through Parliament. On 8 February the Petition for leave to bring in the Bill was read in the House of Commons; after its examination by the Committee on Standing Orders, Lord Stanley and General Gascoyne were instructed to bring in the Bill, and it had its first reading on 18 February, its second on 28th. A long debate followed, and it was adjourned until 2 March by which time a petition claiming that Standing Orders had been infringed was presented by John Shaw Leigh of Liverpool. He also declared that the plans submitted to the Private Bill Office differed from those deposited with the Clerk of the Peace, and that both sets were grossly inaccurate, particularly as to the levels.

Leigh's petition was referred to a separate committee, and the debate proceeded. Following several other members, William Huskisson, Member for Liverpool and President of the Board of Trade, rose to speak in favour of the Bill, making an exception in the case of the railway to his self-imposed rule never to interfere with Private Bills. Claiming to be unconnected with any railway or canal, and not to have any particular preference for either, he urged that any improvement in transport facilities could only reinforce Britain's commercial supremacy over the rest of the world, and that the promoters must be moved by similar considerations, since they had agreed to accept an annual return of 10% on their limited investment. Several other Members took part in the debate before the Second Reading was carried without a division, and the Bill was sent to a Committee under the Chairmanship of General Gascoyne.

Sandars had evidently learned in advance of Leigh's petition and made hurried arrangements for Stephenson's plans to be checked by William Cubitt. The engineer was just completing his report on the Killingworth experiments and was already engaged in projects in Lincolnshire and elsewhere, but by rearranging his programme, and incidentally spending most of the week coaching between Cambridge, London, Lincoln and Folkingham, he contrived to attend the railway committee to receive instructions.

Cubitt had discovered a pamphlet entitled 'Public Reasons against Railways and Loco-motive Engines',

7 *The Right Hon. William Huskisson MP (1770-1830)*

based on some aspects of the Killingworth trials, and circulating among MPs '. . . who were quick enough to believe all the contents.' Sandars, profoundly disturbed by this and other information reaching him, wrote anxiously to Ellis in London that he had seen '. . . a gentleman . . . who has had an opportunity of conversing with all the engineers who are to be arrayed against us', and from whom he had received advance details of the lines of argument the opposition would pursue. They would attempt to prove that Stephenson's 'Darlington Road' was badly executed and a complete failure, and would dwell on the high cost of railway maintenance. They intended calling as a witness the Manager of Hetton Colliery; 'I am inclined to think there is a feud between Stephenson and the Agent' added Sandars. While still writing his letter he received confirmation from Cubitt that the levels and estimates for the section of line across Knowsley Moss were inaccurate, and he also heard that the opposition would claim that the errors in all would amount to a falsification of the Estimates by £100,000. 'The time is drawing nigh and we are very far indeed from being prepared', he wrote, urging Ellis to have Steel, Galloway and Blackett questioned on the survey in the presence of himself, Stephenson and Cubitt.

Cubitt meanwhile asked if he should examine any other parts of the line '. . . and endeavour to reconcile the same so as to be consistent in evidence with Mr Geo. Stephenson on that subject. I think there is no time to be lost'.[30]

Cubitt's reports were anything but reassuring. He, with two of his own assistants and Hugh Steel, from Stephenson's original party, took new levels from the stone of a door which he marked, 260 yards north of Canning Street, and he found Stephenson's levels throughout the line to be from 10 feet to 50 feet out.

On 21 March 1825 the Committee on the Bill[31] started the examination. Principal counsel for the railway were W. G. Adam and Robert Spankie, and for the opposition George Harrison and Edward Alderson; there were in addition three others for the Bill and five against. After Adam's opening speech, which occupied the whole of the first day, a procession of witnesses followed, each saying more or less the same thing whether they were timber or cotton importers, brokers or cotton spinners; all were dissatisfied with the canals. This part of the evidence drew tediously to its close on the twelfth day, and the next six meetings taking the enquiry to 29 April were of a more positive nature, involving engineers supporting the project. The first to be called was John Rastrick, an established civil engineer and locomotive builder, who was questioned at great length and cross-examined by opposing counsel. He had an excellent grasp of the subject of railways and his replies rattled Alderson who, in his confusion, became insolent to the engineer. George Stephenson's turn came on 25 April, and his testimony in the opening stages was firm and unshakable so far as general principles of steam-operated railways were concerned, since he was on familiar ground and could draw upon his experiences in the North-east.

The next two days, however, were to see a complete reversal of the situation, for Stephenson was now cross-examined on his survey and estimates and it soon became apparent that he knew little about either. It was quickly revealed that the opposition were fully aware of the serious errors in the survey and Stephenson was soon reeling under the ruthless interrogation of their counsel on matters of detail. From his evasive answers, his constant pleas that he could not remember, his frequent admission of mistakes and his monumental ignorance of measurements relating to the line he was supposed to have surveyed, Alderson built up a formidable case against the railway and in doing so not only humiliated the wretched engineer, but also embarrassed his employers.

William Cubitt gave evidence on 29 April, but when questioned about the levels he had checked, he had to admit that he had found none of Stephenson's figures correct. Nicholas Wood testified in favour of the locomotive later that day, and on 2 May the Railway's case was wound up by Robert Spankie who, in his summary, made a gallant but forlorn attempt to retrieve some part of Stephenson's reputation.

The following day the case for the opponents of the railway was opened by Harrison, who launched a fierce attack on the railway project and on its engineer; the rest of the week was mainly devoted to evidence by engineers on behalf of the Bill's opponents. The first was Francis Giles, an experienced Civil Engineer and associate of Sir John Rennie who had recently surveyed a route for a canal between Liverpool and Manchester and had also surveyed the proposed line of the L&MR with his assistant Alexander Comrie, on the instructions of the petitioners against the Bill. It was during his examination on 5 May that he made the oft-quoted observation that 'no engineer in his senses would go through Chat Moss, if he wanted to make a Railroad from Liverpool to Manchester.' In his opinion, the cost of doing so would be nearer £200,000 than the £40,000 estimated by Stephenson. Henry Robinson Palmer, engineer to the London Docks, who had received his engineering training under Telford, asserted that any calculations made from Stephenson's plans and sections would be useless, while George Leather[32] agreed, but went further; no engineer could construct the railway from such drawings.

Alderson then returned to the attack, castigating the bewildered Stephenson for his ignorance and complete lack of common sense, and claiming that he had no plan, was incapable of making one, and had no idea as to how he would set about constructing the railway if the powers to do so were granted; but he urged Parliament to withhold these powers from a company that would place its fortunes in such incompetent hands.

In a frantic effort to save the Bill at this late stage, the Committee ordered Cubitt to re-survey the whole line, and he started on 14 May with the branch from Princes Dock to the main line and on to Bootle.

Four days later, assisted by his younger brother, he had completed an uninterrupted line of levels to a spot near St Helens, having met no opposition more serious than a warning about trespass from Lord Sefton's steward and a couple of tenants, who then walked quietly away; he hoped to get to the far side of Chat Moss in the next two days. It does not appear that the Railway were able to make use of the new survey but it did have the effect of vindicating Cubitt, whose earlier figures had been questioned by Giles; each had taken a different base line, but their levels were found to agree.

The Committee sat for over another fortnight hearing the witnesses, some 20 of them, called by the canal interests and turnpike trustees, and the proceedings drew to a close at the end of May with the final speeches by Harrison and Adam. The Committee met on 1 June to vote on the separate clauses of the Bill, but the vital Clauses 2 and 3, powers to make a railway and power to take lands, were lost by fairly substantial majorities, and after a brief consultation with Sherwood, Adam withdrew the Bill.

Its opponents were jubilant; Creevy wrote[33] '... this devil of a railway is strangled at last', and reported that his friend Lord Sefton was in ecstasies at the result. Creevy had good cause to congratulate himself since he had ensured the attendance of all the Bill's opponents on the vital day when voting on the Clauses took place, whereas Holmes had failed to rally its supporters.[34]

There were, of course, a number of reasons for the failure of the Railway to obtain its Act, not the least being its inexperience. Much time was consumed in attempting to demonstrate the shortcomings of the canals, but when the positive advantages of the railway were argued, notably its far greater speed, the widespread prejudice against the locomotive was misjudged, and even the modest claims made on its behalf enabled the opposing counsel to play upon the fears of the ignorant. Its case was not helped by the publication of an article in the influential *Quarterly Review* of March 1825 questioning the possibility of persuading passengers to entrust themselves to trains travelling at 18 or 20 mph, nor by Nicholas Wood's *Practical Treatise on Rail-roads* in which he asserted that 12 mph was too fast. It was, however, Stephenson's performance that undoubtedly sealed the fate of the Bill and there can be no excuse for his almost total unpreparedness before the Committee. He had been warned well in advance of what he might expect, but either arrogance born of over-confidence, following his partial success in the North-east or a failure to appreciate that this concern was no mere coal-carrying line of the type with which he was familiar, brought about all that loss of money and effort, and set the project back another year.

He blamed his own apprentices, Galloway and Steel, for the errors in the survey, a charge stoutly resisted by the former. Galloway does not appear to have had any further association with Stephenson or the L&MR, but Steel, who had been assigned to prepare the survey for the Bolton & Leigh Railway, became Surveyor to that company.[35]

The Committee did not allow itself to remain a prey to despondency for long. A meeting by invitation was held on 4 June at the Royal Hotel, St James's Street, at which 21 influential supporters of the project were present. Under the chairmanship of General Gascoyne, William Huskisson and Thomas Spring Rice moved resolutions in favour of attempting to get the Bill through next year. The Committee was urged not to be discouraged, and the general opinion was that the prospects were favourable. Back in Liverpool they called a meeting of subscribers on 17 June and presented their report. It was agreed that, since ample funds for the purpose were in hand, a second attempt should be made, but not with George Stephenson as Engineer. Although some members of the Committee were ready to defend him, it was recognized that the whole project would be put at risk if he remained even remotely connected with it, and he was accordingly dismissed.

A successor to Stephenson had already been approached; Lord Lowther, a staunch supporter of the railway, discussed the project with John Rennie, one of the country's leading engineers, and presumably acting on behalf of the Committee, offered him the position of Engineer to the Company. He and his brother George accepted the appointment on 1 July, on the understanding that they would not be bound by any plans or arrangements made by Stephenson, and as their Chief Surveyor they appointed Charles Blacker Vignoles.

Then in his early thirties, Vignoles had had several years experience as a surveyor in England and America, and he arrived in Liverpool in early July fresh from having surveyed a railway line between London and Brighton for the Rennies. After a few

8 *Sir John Rennie (1794–1874)*

9 *Charles Blacker Vignoles (1793–1875), when President of the Institution of Civil Engineers*

days spent in a preliminary inspection of the line planned by Stephenson, he proceeded to plan a new route intended to be less objectionable to landowners and other vested interests. The new line was to the south of Stephenson's, and ran almost directly east through Huyton, Parr Moss, Newton, Chat Moss and Eccles. No streets were to be crossed either in Liverpool or Manchester; they were avoided in Liverpool by taking the railway in a tunnel under the town, and in Manchester by terminating the line at Salford on the west side of the River Irwell, although it is unlikely that this was intended to be a permanent arrangement. The proposed line was about two miles shorter than Stephenson's, but it included some bold engineering features, notably the $1\frac{1}{4}$-mile tunnel from Edge Hill to the Docks and the rock cutting at Olive Mount. On 18 July the plan was presented to the Directors and the next day John Rennie and Vignoles went over the proposed line and agreed on its adoption. The next three weeks saw Vignoles, Rennie and a band of assistants making the preliminary survey, submitted to the Board and accepted on 12 August, on which date Vignoles was officially appointed Surveyor to the Company.

Then began the detailed survey from which drawings and estimates were prepared, involving much outdoor work and the usual clandestine visits to hostile territory, the observations taken by moonlight and the ever-present threat of violence.

Robert Bradshaw, however, was now more amenable to the railway, possibly because of the professional approach adopted by the new Engineer and Surveyor. Vignoles, speaking 45 years after the event, said he was brought before Mr Bradshaw at Worsley Hall on a pretended charge of trespassing, and the encounter developed into a discussion on the railway question.

Bradshaw wrote to J. Loch on 27 September 1825 referring either to this meeting or a subsequent one:

'The Manchester and Liverpool railroaders are certainly going to Parliament again next session. Their existing surveyor has just been here to show me their new plans, etc., and ask permission to go over our lands; to which (you will scarcely believe it) I have consented; but the man behaved so fairly and openly that I really could not refuse; am I not a Liberal?'[36]

The reason for the change in attitude may have been the expense of opposing a second Bill, the contest over the first having cost the Bridgewater Trust £10,000. But there was no capitulation at this stage and Bradshaw declined to accept an allocation of shares on behalf of the Trust, demanding sole proprietorship as the only alternative to uncompromising opposition.

However, Vignoles conveyed the details of his conversation with Bradshaw to the Railway Committee, and he was of the opinion that this led to the opening of negotiations with the Marquis of Stafford, the virtual owner of the Bridgewater Canal. Details of these discussions do not appear to have been recorded, probably for the reason that all those involved were well-known to each other and in some cases lifelong friends.

W. Adam, counsel for the railway, arranged with his relative, James Loch MP, business adviser to Stafford and auditor to the Bridgewater Trustees, to approach the Marquis with a view to opening negotiations. Several meetings followed between Loch and the railway representatives, Lawrence, Moss and Robert Gladstone, culminating in an agreement by Lord Stafford in December 1825 to take 1,000 Shares in the Railway. This was no hasty decision, for Loch had suggested the possibility of a compromise with the railway a year earlier; it was the intervention of William Huskisson, however, that settled the matter. He had been Secretary to Lord Stafford (then Lord Gower) at the Paris Embassy during the French Revolution, and had remained the close friend of the Stafford family ever since; his staunch support of the railway project cleared any lingering doubts from the mind of the Marquis.

The new estimates prepared by Vignoles totalled about £100,000 more than Stephenson's, and Stafford's investment saved the Committee from having to raise this additional capital in the depressed financial situation of that time. It also removed from the scene the most formidable of potential opponents to the new Bill, since the Bridgewater Trust could not now oppose a project in which the life tenant of the Trust Estates was so deeply involved.[37]

To what extent Bradshaw was a party to the arrangement is not clear, but it is unlikely that he was enthusiastic. Nevertheless, even had he wished to oppose the Bill, which is by no means certain, he could not have done so without the signatures of the other two trustees on the petition. These, Sir Archibald Macdonald and the Archbishop of York, were both brothers-in-law of the Marquis, and were kept fully informed of the progress of the negotiations by Loch; it is reasonable to suppose, therefore, that the successful outcome of the discussions depended largely on their agreement, and they would not then be disposed to challenge the Bill.

It is perhaps significant that the negotiations between the Railway Committee and Lord Stafford took place during the early months of the S&DR – Bradshaw's letter, by an odd coincidence, was written on the Opening Day – and it is very probable that the success of this Company coupled with the fact that the new route was both less objectionable and was being properly surveyed, persuaded the Bridgewater interests that the renewed application for the L&MR Bill would be difficult, if not impossible, to defeat.

Encouragement came from another unlikely quarter; Albinus Martin, Resident Engineer to the Leeds and Liverpool Canal, had become friendly with Sandars and the Stephensons, and now strongly supported the project.

During the autumn of 1825 the Committee were occupied in ensuring that all the requirements of Standing Orders were met; again the announcements appeared in the Press, plans were deposited, notices were nailed to church and sessions house doors, new scrip was issued to replace the original share certificates and owners and occupiers of land affected were canvassed.

To avoid the possibility of the premature disclosure of confidential plans and arrangements, a special committee of six had been formed in Manchester; these were Lawrence, Sandars, Moss, Booth, Gladstone and Harrison, and upon them fell the main burden of preparing for the introduction of the new Bill, then being drafted.

In December a new Prospectus was issued outlining the causes of the earlier failure, and setting forth the measures taken to ensure success at the next attempt. At the same time the railway's case was presented to the Liverpool Corporation and, after some acrimonious discussion, the plan was accepted by a majority of two.

By early 1826 the Subscription Contract had been sufficiently filled to satisfy Parliament; about 80% of the capital of £510,000 now required had been taken up. Nearly £200,000 was subscribed in Liverpool, £100,000 by Lord Stafford, and a mere £12,000 by Manchester interests; this was about one seventh of the amount represented by the 844 shares held in London. One of the London shareholders was Thomas Richardson of Overend, Gurney & Co., who held 75 shares in the L&MR and was a director of the S&DR and Canterbury & Whitstable Railway.[38]

At the beginning of February those members of the Railway Committee responsible for watching the Bill's progress gathered in London and Sherwood, with W. Adam, William Brougham, Henry Joy and Serjeant Spankie, prepared for the presentation of the Bill to Parliament. Read for the first time on 10 February, it had its second reading on the 20th and then went to a Commons Committee from which it emerged on 22 March, its Preamble proved and all its clauses having been accepted by substantial majorities. No details of its passage through the Committee have survived, since no order for the minutes of Evidence to be printed was made, and the original manuscript notes appear to have been lost in the fire which destroyed the Houses of Parliament in 1834. A final effort to defeat the Bill in the Commons was made on 6 April, when it came up for its third reading, but it was saved largely by Huskisson who, in a brief but masterly speech, weighed the inconveniences feared by a few against the benefits the railway would bring to the country as a whole.

The next day the Bill had its first reading in the Lords, and on its second reading, three days later, Lord Derby launched a fierce attack on it; the Bill was committed, however, without a division, but His Lordship petitioned against it, thoroughly frightening the members of the Railway Committee in London. But William Holmes, who was again looking after their interests, was quite confident of being able to muster between 18 and 25 peers to support the Bill, and wrote 'I do not know what the devil it is that alarms them.'

The Committee started its proceedings on 13 April, and its Report with the Minutes of Evidence was subsequently printed.[39] Counsel for the petitioners against the Bill were the same as on previous occasions, Messrs Harrison, Alderson and Earle, but now they were dealing with experienced Civil Engineers in Vignoles and G. Rennie, and these, the principal witnesses for the Railway, could not be shaken or bullied. After assuring Alderson that the plans and sections were 'perfectly correct', Vignoles was questioned on the possibility of the Wapping end of the tunnel being flooded. He thought it might be flooded to a depth of six inches in the unlikely event of a hurricane sweeping over the docks, but if the volume of water overflowing from the docks stood two feet deep in the tunnel, as Alderson suggested, then 'All Liverpool would be in the same situation.'

On the north side of Smithdown Lane, near the Edge Hill tunnel mouth, stood a large stone house in extensive grounds owned by Mrs Earle and valued at £12,000. Having established that the trains would be in a deep cutting all through her land, Vignoles was asked 'How deep?', to which he replied, 'Averaging about 40 feet.' To the next question, 'So that some part only of the loading will be visible?' he replied, 'We shall hardly load 40 feet high'; this line of questioning then ceased. Later, when George Rennie

10 *George Rennie (1791–1866)*

was giving evidence, Harrison took up the question of the height to which trucks would be loaded with cotton and was told 12 feet from the ground. Asking what effect a gale would produce, Rennie pointed out that the prevailing westerly winds would be favourable to the cotton trains travelling towards Manchester, and does not appear to have been perturbed by Harrison's retort: 'So that you have substituted Sails of Cotton Bags instead of locomotive engines; is that a part of your power?'

The vexed question of the locomotive did not arise directly in connection with the L&MR as the Rennies had planned the line for horse operation; if the Company subsequently decided to employ locomotives, their level railway would be ideally suitable, but that was no concern of Parliament for the present. The Engineers' plan was to operate the railway by dividing it into three 10-mile stages, changing the horses at the end of each stage.

Rennie stated that he had never seen the S&D Railway, and from the references to it by other witnesses, he would probably not have been very impressed if he had. Hardman Earle referred to the sound of its engines as a '... loud, hoarse barking ... every time the piston goes up and down ...', while Thomas Lingard, a witness for the canal interests, must have been one of the first railway passengers to record train timings. He made at least two return journeys, the fastest by the horse-drawn 'Experiment' coach which covered the 11½ miles from Darlington to Stockton in 1 hour 33 minutes and the slowest on a train of empty waggons drawn by a locomotive driven by '... Mr Stevenson's [sic] brother'. This train was in motion for 3 hours 22 minutes and at a standstill for various reasons for 1 hour 13 minutes, achieving an average speed of 2½ mph. The reasons given for the stoppages were the derailment of waggons on the train, obstructions caused by other waggons off the single track road, taking in water and the necessity of stopping the engine before horses could be induced to pass it at the 100-yard passing places. Horse-drawn carriers' waggons were also operating on the S&DR at this time.

When examining Josias Jessop on the weight-bearing capacity of the railway over Chat Moss, Alderson referred to the Kilmarnock and Troon Railway, which was laid over a similar morass where the locomotive had been tried but laid aside; replied Jessop, 'That was because the locomotive was good for nothing. I understand that it was not an Engine made for the purpose; it was an Engine made for a saw mill, which they put upon wheels.'

The examination of witnesses ended on 27 April and on 1 May the Lords Committee voted in favour of the Bill by 30–2, the dissentients being the Earls of Derby and Wilton; on 5 May the Act received the Royal Assent.[40] The Company promised to start construction in three weeks, and expected the work to be completed in three years.

The Company spent an estimated £27,000 in finally obtaining its Act;[41] Bills from the witnesses were coming in during August 1826 – J. U. Rastrick £182, Josias Jessop £59 10s.

Although since 1802 some 34 separate railways had between them obtained 50 Acts, that incorporating the L&MR was the most comprehensive document of its kind up to that time, and it formed the pattern for railway Acts of Incorporation for some years to come. Nearly 60 of the original proprietors were named, and the Company was established in perpetuity. From a terminus on the east side of Wapping Street, Liverpool, the parishes through which the line was to pass were listed, to its eastern terminus at Hampson Street, near the New Bailey Prison, Salford. Rights of compulsory purchase of land were bestowed upon the company, and it was given virtually unlimited powers to construct the earthworks, bridges, tunnels, warehouses, stationary steam engines and all other works and buildings it required on its own land; these powers had to be exercised with as little disturbance to the property of its neighbours as possible, and

11 *Share Certificate dated 28 December 1826*

compensation was payable to landowners and others whose property was damaged. Where the demolition of property resulted in a reduction of rates to a parish or other local authority, the loss was to be made good by the Company. The railway was not permitted to encroach upon the land of anyone not named in the Book of Reference, nor to deviate more than 100 yards from the line specified in the plans; neither could it compel an owner to dispose of an excessive amount of land. The maximum normal width to be taken was 22 yards, but this was extended to 150 yards for stretches of cutting or embankment, and for the sites of junctions.

Several sections of the Act contained restrictions on the Company's activities to safeguard the interests of property owners along the route, and several more laid obligations upon the Company to provide facilities such as the provision of bridges over cuttings, or tunnels through embankments, for the same purpose. The Liverpool Common Council, the Docks Trustees and the Bridgewater Estates were among other public and corporate bodies who secured special provisions.

A large part of the Act, about 60 of the 200 sections of which it comprised, concerned the capital, financial arrangements and internal organisation of the Company. The duties and responsibilities of the Directors were detailed here, along with the powers of the shareholders and the frequency of General Meetings. The provisions for the payment of dividends from the profits of the undertaking, but not from its capital, were set forth, and the Board was given the discretionary power to withhold 10% of the profits to build up a Reserve Fund to a total of £100,000. The undertaking that dividends should not exceed 10%, made at the express wish of Huskisson before the 1825 Bill was launched, was fulfilled in a curious and unique way. So long as the dividend remained at 10% or less, the Company was empowered to charge the maximum rates for Tolls or Carriage as specified later in the Act, but if this rate were exceeded, then all charges would have to be reduced in the following year. The restriction applied only to dividends, and not to profits, and provision was made for the Reserve Fund to be used to supplement the dividend when the profits fell below the amount sufficient to distribute the maximum of 10%.

Schedules of tolls on several classes of merchandise, animals and passengers were incorporated in the Act, and other sections gave the Company the right to act as carriers, again setting out the maximum charges it could demand. Although the Company was regarded as the proprietor of a public highway, albeit a specialised one, it was authorised, in the interests of safety and efficiency, to frame rules and regulations to be observed by those who sought to run their own vehicles upon it.

It was soon discovered that the Act of Incorporation, comprehensive though it was, did not give the Board all the powers it required and a second Act, principally to enable the Company to borrow

£100,000 from the Exchequer Loan Commissioners, was passed on 12 April 1827.[42] The loan, for a term of 20 years from 23 June 1827 at $3\frac{1}{2}\%$, was secured by a first mortgage on the railway and all its property, and by a lien on the last 30% of the Share Capital. This would be released only when the Commissioners were satisfied that the works were sufficiently advanced to afford full security.

CHAPTER TWO

The Construction of the Railway

WITH THE PASSING of the Act of Incorporation the Company was at last able to make its plans for constructing the railway after five years of optimism, anxiety, frustration and expense. A General Meeting of the Shareholders was held on 29 May 1826 in the Exchange Building, Liverpool, under the Chairmanship of Charles Lawrence. After receiving a report on the recent activities in Parliament to secure the Act, the proprietors elected Henry Booth Treasurer at a yearly salary of £500 and then proceeded to elect 12 of the 15 directors, the remaining three being nominated by the Marquis of Stafford under arrangements made in December 1825. These were awarded one guinea for each Board Meeting attended, up to a maximum of 52 meetings a year.

The Meeting closed with a vote of thanks to William Huskisson and General Gascoyne for their assistance in steering the Bill through the Commons, coupled with an expression of mild disgust at the attitude adopted by the two members for the County who had strenuously opposed the Bill, Lord Stanley and John Blackburne. A lengthy and detailed Report was issued to the Shareholders outlining the Company's prospects and estimated income; this document reassured the proprietors that annual dividends were not limited to 10%, as many had feared, and the possibility of the future use of steam locomotives was mentioned.

At this time the Company had not appointed an Engineer, and in recognition of the services rendered by the Rennie Brothers and Vignoles before the Parliamentary Committee, they were the first to be asked their terms for building the line. Whilst awaiting the brothers' reply, the Board invited Vignoles to stake out the line at a fee of four guineas per day, which he commenced to do a few days later; he was thus the Company's first engineer, and he let the first construction contracts – those for the preliminary drainage of Chat Moss.

In the meantime G. and J. Rennie's terms had reached the Board, and gave rise to prolonged discussion, the details of which are not recorded but would have made interesting reading had they been. The Board was evidently sharply divided between those whose confidence rested on the professional ability of the Rennies, and the supporters of George Stephenson, and to a lesser degree of J. U. Rastrick. It was eventually decided to ask the Rennies whether they would share the responsibility with either Rastrick or Stephenson, or possibly both, and their reaction to this proposal could not have come as a surprise. George Rennie attended the Board Meeting of 17 June 1826 and explained in some detail the conditions he and his brother were offering; when it is remembered that these two were among the leading civil engineers in the Kingdom, their proposals do not seem unreasonable.

They claimed the right to appoint a resident engineer, for whose activities they would accept complete responsibility, and they undertook to visit the works six times a year, spending up to ten days on each occasion. They guaranteed to build the railway within the estimates they had submitted, but in turn demanded a completely free hand in executing the work for which they had prepared the plans. George Rennie assured the Board that neither he nor his brother would have any objection to the appointment of Josias Jessop, Thomas Telford (both men of advanced age) or any member of the Society of Engineers as Consulting Engineer, but they would have nothing whatever to do with Rastrick or Stephenson, as they could foresee only trouble as the outcome of such an association. They did concede, however, that George Stephenson might supervise the locomotive department so long as they were not accountable for it. For these services they claimed a joint salary of £500–£600, which, considering their prestige, seems far from exorbitant.

G. and J. Rennie, in offering these terms, indicated their absolute confidence in the project they had planned, involving as it did 31 miles of railway including tunnels, bridges, viaducts, miles of earthworks and the crossing of Chat Moss, and it is difficult to understand why the Board did not appoint them after the long years of uncertainty and disappointment that had gone before. But there were strong elements in the Board Room who opposed their engagement, and they succeeded in first delaying the acceptance of the Rennie brothers' terms, and finally in persuading the Board to reject them. Years later John Rennie said that they 'naturally expected to be appointed the executive engineers, after having with so much labour and anxiety carried the Bill through Parliament. The Executive Committee of the Railway behaved extremely ill to us!'

Whether or not the Board was wise in depriving the Rennies of the opportunity of building the Liverpool and Manchester Railway is a matter for conjecture. In the event a number of modifications were made to their original plan, at least one of which led to difficulties in the early days of the Company's operation; this was the substitution of inclined planes of 1 in 96, intended to be worked by stationary engines, for the gentle gradients of 1 in 256 and 1 in 226 planned for horse or locomotive working at Sutton and Whiston respectively.

Having rejected George and John Rennie the company next considered George Stephenson and John Urpeth Rastrick for the position of Chief Engineer. The inclusion of Rastrick in the short list appears to have been something of a formality, for although Sandars visited his Stratford & Moreton Rail Road and heard very favourable reports on the abilities of its engineer, his name was eliminated before he had been given the opportunity of stating his terms on the grounds that they might be unaccepable to the Company. This left Stephenson as the only candidate, and at the Board meeting of 3 July letters from Michael Longridge and Joseph Pease were read, both strongly recommending him as engineer to the railway. These two men were undoubtedly the best qualified from personal experience to testify as to Stephenson's capabilities as a practical engineer at that period, and the Board could not have been unaware that they were also his partners in both the locomotive and engineering firm of R. Stephenson & Co. and the civil engineering and contracting company of George Stephenson & Son. Invited to state his terms he requested a yearly salary of £800, in return for which he undertook to spend a minimum of nine months per year on the works, personally directing operations. This appears to have satisfied the Directors, who without further ado, appointed him as Chief Engineer to the Liverpool & Manchester Railway.[1]

As one of its Consulting Engineers the Company appointed Josias Jessop, who had already served the Committee during its Parliamentary contest, but he had little to do with the enterprise for he died in October 1826. In their other Consulting Engineer, Jesse Hartley, the Company had a skilled professional of outstanding ability, upon whose judgement they placed the utmost reliance. Appointed Engineer to the Liverpool Docks in 1824, he built or reconstructed every dock in that extensive system during the next 36 years. A year older than Stephenson, he was described[2] as a man '... of large build and powerful frame, rough in manner and occasionally rude, using expletives which the angel of mercy would not like to record; sometimes capricious and tyrannical, but occasionally, where he was attached, a firm and unswerving friend.' Although, like Stephenson, he dreaded examination before Parliamentary Committees, he was, nevertheless, an engineer of original genius whose services to the Company, like those of others, received little or no mention either at the time or since.

12 *Jesse Hartley (1780–1860)*

He was associated with the Company at least as early as 1824, and he lent George Stephenson surveying instruments, some of which were returned in a damaged condition without a word of thanks or explanation, bringing forth a fairly strong letter of protest from Hartley. However, he appears to have been on reasonably friendly terms with Stephenson in the years they worked together; the latter probably realised that Hartley was not a man it would be prudent to offend.

Stephenson's first task was to recruit a band of resident engineers, and deliberately ignoring all the established professionals he chose four young men who had been apprenticed to him and were on the books of his own contracting company. Joseph Locke, apprenticed in 1823 at the age of 18, was first employed on the construction of locomotives and in 1825 he built his first small railway, the Black Fell Colliery line. After assisting Stephenson with the surveys of the Newcastle and Carlisle and Canterbury and Whitstable Railways, he was made responsible for the western end of the L&MR in 1826.

William Allcard came from a well-known Quaker family and started as one of Stephenson's pupils in the drawing office of the steam engine factory. In 1826, at the age of 17, he was entrusted with the preliminary drainage work on Chat Moss, later moving to the central section of the line. The eldest of the four was John Dixon, whose engineering career dated from 1819 when he assisted in the survey of the S&DR, and later became its Resident Engineer; he was 30 years old when appointed to the L&MR in 1826. John Gooch, formerly cashier to the Bedlington Iron Works, apprenticed his son Thomas to Stephenson for six years from October 1823, two years to be spent building steam engines and four as a draughtsman and civil engineer. He was summoned to Liverpool some months before his 18th birthday to join his chief, in whose house he lived for two and a half years during which time he was the Company's principal draughtsman. He made nearly all the plans and working drawings at the Railway Office in Clayton Street, and spent his evenings acting as secretary to Stephenson. Many of the drawings had to be made from Stephenson's verbal instructions or from little rough sketches on scrap paper. Lithography had not yet been applied to the production of duplicate plans, and copies were laboriously traced on drawing boards into which glass plates had been inserted, with lamps giving a strong light underneath.[3]

As time went on superintendents were employed to assist the resident engineers, supervising some particular piece of specialised work. These, too, were

13 *Joseph Locke (1805–60)*

friends of George Stephenson. James Scott was placed in charge of the excavations at Olive Mount, while Anthony Harding assisted Locke at the Wapping Tunnel works, where his brother Thomas was one of the contractors. Both brothers had previously worked with Stephenson on the S&DR, along with John Harding, another brother who found his way to the L&MR.

The Company had decided to allow Stephenson to build the line under a confusing system of direct labour and small contracts, Stephenson himself being one of the contractors, against the advice of William Jessop, who early in August had suggested letting a contract for the whole line and that it be built by 'one responsible party by a single contract.' Since the system had been employed by the leading civil engineers of that time in the construction of canals, docks and other public works, its application to railway building was the obvious solution, since the techniques to be employed would be very similar to those with which a contractor would be conversant.

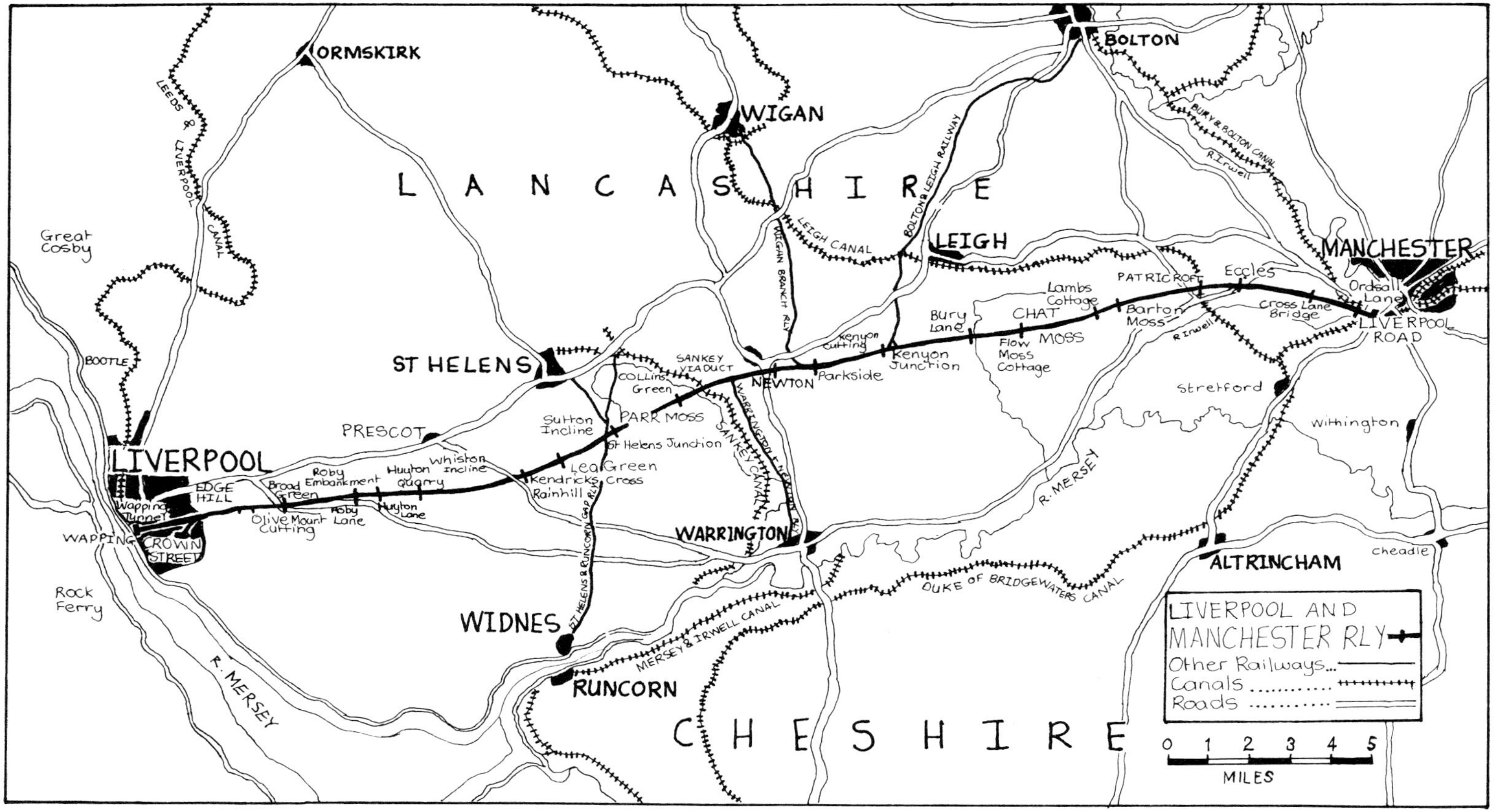
LIVERPOOL AND MANCHESTER RLY
Other Railways
Canals
Roads
0 1 2 3 4 5
MILES
LANCASHIRE
CHESHIRE
ORMSKIRK
WIGAN
BOLTON
LEIGH
MANCHESTER
ST HELENS
PRESCOT
LIVERPOOL
WARRINGTON
WIDNES
RUNCORN
ALTRINCHAM
Great Cosby
BOOTLE
Rock Ferry
WAPPING
Wapping Tunnel
CROWN STREET
EDGE HILL
Olive Mount Cutting
Broad Green
Roby Embankment
Roby Lane
Huyton Quarry
Huyton Lane
Whiston Incline
Kendricks Cross
Rainhill
Lea Green
Sutton Incline
St Helens Junction
PARK MOSS
Collins Green
SANKEY VIADUCT
NEWTON
Parkside
Kenyon Cutting
Kenyon Junction
Bury Lane
Flow Moss Cottage
CHAT MOSS
Lambs Cottage
Barton Moss
PATRICROFT
Eccles
Cross Lane Bridge
Ordsall Lane
LIVERPOOL ROAD
Stretford
Withington
cheadle
LEEDS & LIVERPOOL CANAL
LEIGH CANAL
BOLTON & LEIGH RAILWAY
WIGAN BRANCH RLY
SANKEY CANAL
BURY & BOLTON CANAL
R. Irwell
R. MERSEY
DUKE OF BRIDGEWATERS CANAL
MERSEY & IRWELL CANAL
ST HELENS & RUNCORN GAP RLY

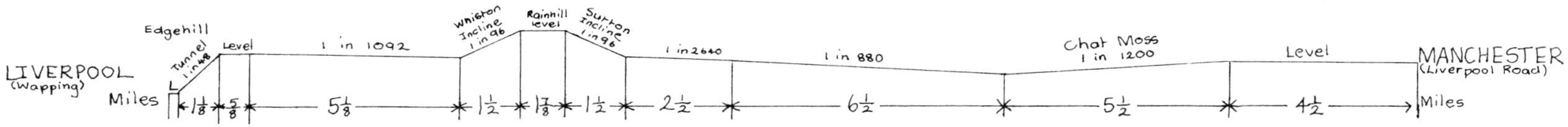
LIVERPOOL (Wapping)
Miles
Edgehill Tunnel 1 in 48
Level
1 in 1092
Whiston Incline 1 in 96
Rainhill level
Sutton Incline 1 in 96
1 in 2640
1 in 880
Chat Moss 1 in 1200
Level
MANCHESTER (Liverpool Road)
Miles
1 1/8
5/8
5 1/8
1 1/2
1 7/8
1 1/2
2 1/2
6 1/2
5 1/2
4 1/2

The L&MR Board did not, however, invite tenders for the whole, or even substantial portions of the construction, but only for specialised work on tunnels and bridges. Although there are many references to contractors in the Company's Minutes, in contemporary records and in the following pages, most of these were men who were originally foremen of labouring gangs. Showing initiative and a certain shrewdness, they were willing to accept the responsibility for completing specified tasks, usually limited at first, but extended when they proved to be reliable. All the arrangements were made verbally between these small contractors and the resident engineers or superintendents along the line, no written contracts involving the Company ever being entered into.

Stephenson appears to have had only a sketchy idea of costing, and the Board had no experience of such matters. In February 1828 after work had been in progress for over a year, Horatio Allen[4] wrote:

'There appears to be a want of accurate information as to the cost of doing several kinds of work. And when a contract was let, it is their practice to keep an accurate account of the work done, time, &c, in order to determine whether they are giving too much or too little, and they seem to have the power of doing pretty much as they please with their contractors, who are with them only a promoted labourer.'

A year later Telford was to make a similar observation, only more forcefully.

The detailed accounts, now regrettably lost, must have been exceptionally complicated, as often men were engaged by the day – one account refers to Stephenson indicating to a group of men how many he needed by holding up that number of fingers.[5] Payment was made fortnightly by the Resident Engineers who drew the cash from Liverpool, and at the same time, marked up on a wall-map or scale diagram in the Board Room, the progress of the work in their area.

The first purchases of land were being completed by 4 August 1826 and by October, ballast waggons had been purchased from Joseph Pease and the Butterley Iron Works; larch wood for the temporary tracks was arriving from Scotland and the first iron rails were delivered by Jevons & Sons. In the months that followed the Company made increasingly large purchases of the stores and equipment needed from a variety of firms – castings and ironwork from Mather

14 *Plan and section of the Liverpool & Manchester Railway*

Dixon and the Bedlington Iron Works, rails from John Bradley of Stourbridge, iron chairs from Foster Rastrick, wheels and axles from Robert Stephenson & Co., and bricks, made under contract by Henry Haydock at Newton Common.

In January 1827 Robert Stephenson, George's brother, wrote from Stratford on Avon offering patent waggons, but whether they were accepted is not recorded. The Company's first workshops were established at Tabley Street, Liverpool, but in January 1827 they were removed to Whites Field, Crabtree Lane.

Work was started on Chat Moss and the Wapping Tunnel in the summer of 1826 and the whole line was marked out in the autumn, but it was January 1827 before sufficient equipment had been assembled for work on the rest of the line to begin.

In the interval between the Company's decision not to employ the Rennie brothers and the appointment of George Stephenson as Chief Engineer, the Board on 27 June appointed the engineer and architect, John Foster,[6] to be the Principal Engineer in charge of the Tunnel at £400 a year. It seems highly probable that differences of opinion soon arose between these two engineers, for on 8 August the Board was informed that Foster had declined to act as Tunnel Engineer. It was about this time that Locke was made responsible for the western end of the line, including the tunnel, and it may well have been that Foster was unwilling to serve under one so recently out of his apprenticeship. The Board, however, was equally unwilling to entrust the construction of this major work entirely to Stephenson or his assistants and on 4 September Jesse Hartley was formally appointed Civil Engineer to the Company, and Inspecting Engineer and Arbitrator for the Tunnel.

During the following week contracts were let to James Copeland of Newcastle-on-Tyne, Matthew Burnett, Thomas Harding and J. Stevenson for excavating the shafts at 3s. per cubic yard and driving the tunnels at 2s. 5½d. By mid-October a model of the tunnel had been made by R. Edmondson & Sons, and work on the first shaft was well ahead. Vignoles had already marked out its path, unfortunately for him a few feet out of true alignment. This was discovered by Stephenson who made observations from the tops of buildings that commanded a view of the shafts after work on them was well forward, and led to the final breach between Vignoles and Stephenson, a situation that had been developing in the eight months they had worked uneasily together; Vignoles resigned as resident engineer, though with much regret, on

2 February 1827. In a letter of 14 January 1827[7] Vignoles said:

'It is true there was an error in the survey of the tunnel made by me, but it was one which might have been rectified without trouble or expense; and it was one which would not have originated if I had been here alone.'

George Stephenson, in a curiously incoherent letter to his son dated 23 February 1827, does not disguise his satisfaction at having rid himself of the last direct link with the Rennies:

'... it was said that Renney had some of the best surveyors in England with him here and one of the best was left with me which I supposed was expected by menny of our directors to be a guid to me & set him to surveye the tunnal and mark out the different shafts after which I found a meathat of cheking his work and found eny shaft out of the line this was after we had spent about 1000£ in that part ... a finishing blay to Renny and his ... my asstance is now all of my own chosen ... I hope you will make a fair holing in your shaft it is a very difficult job to work from Compass in such a situation Renny man got one of our shafts 13 feet from the line and none of them in the line my methet of prouf was by pendulums in the arc supported by 3 triangles legs so that I had a plume line from the top to the Bodom and got the sights over the tops of the houses.'

By February 1827 several rectangular shafts 6ft by 10ft had been sunk, varying in depth from 28 to 70 ft, and each brick-lined; to correct the error in the survey short connecting drifts were made at right-angles to the main tunnel alignment. From these passages the

15 *Wapping Tunnel, 1833. Some earlier views incorrectly show locomotives in the tunnel*

tunnel was driven in both directions, about 20 men being employed in each of the ten gangs. The men could work for only a limited period in the darkness and cramped conditions, and one party relieved another at definite intervals; two shifts were employed and the work went on night and day.

The shafts or 'eyes' were numbered from the Wapping end;[8] No 1 was at the corner of Gt George Square and was 30ft deep and No 2, of 40ft, was behind the Gt George Chapel. Shafts 3 and 4 were called White Delf and Yellow Delf respectively and were near Duke Street and Hope Street. Yellow Delf was at the bottom of a small quarry and being only eight feet deep, could be entered on foot by a small inlet, a method recommended to reporters and other visitors who tended to become nervous at the prospect of descending in a bucket. The deepest shaft was No 5, 70ft from the surface, on vacant ground east of Bedford Street. At Mosslake Fields, east of Vine Street, No 6 descended 46ft, and from Millfield, near Crown Street No 7 went down 30ft. The last shaft, No 8, was at the top of the tunnel at Edge Hill, and was 36ft deep. Horse gins were employed for raising and lowering men and materials, and some constables were engaged early in January 1827 to guard the tunnel shafts and machinery; the works at Yellow Delf were particularly vulnerable.

Starting at the top of the arch, the outline of the tunnel was scooped out of the rock face to a depth of two to five feet, depending upon the texture of the rock. Where this was solid, the great mass of material left in the centre was used as a working platform and, as the work proceeded, was removed by pick or blasting, and taken by horses working on light railways to the shafts, where it was raised and dumped about 50 yds from the top. Here it was sorted, the large stone to be dressed and used for sleepers or other purposes on the railway, and the small stone and rubble taken to various places in the town to be used for elevating the sites of intended new streets or filling in hollows preparatory to building. The clay went to the Company's brickworks, established at Edge Hill in March 1827, to be returned in the form of bricks for lining the tunnel.

When unstable rock, clay or sand was encountered, requiring a brick lining, only about 18in. of the tunnel outline was driven at a time, and the brick lining, starting from a ledge at the top of the five foot perpendicular side wall, was built almost to the crown of the arch from the inside of the centering. When the arch was complete broken bricks and pieces of stone were rammed into the space between the brick arch and the rock or clay above, and the whole bonded with Pozzolani cement; at no time was the tunnel more than two feet ahead of the brickwork. In some places small patches of brickwork were used to fill in holes left when insecure rock was removed from the sides of the arch; at only a few places did the brickwork go down below the level of the tunnel floor. The brick lining varied from 18in. to two feet in thickness, and 6000 cu. yds went into lining the tunnel. The original intention had been to use stone for the lining, but this was found to be impracticable. Part of the tunnel under Crown Street, only a short distance in from Edge Hill, fell in May 1827, owing to an insufficient number of props being used to support the roof. Its depth here was about 30ft, and the mass of moss-earth and sand left a subsidence in the ground above.

In one or two places water was encountered, and under Mosslake Fields the works were for a time flooded to a depth of seven feet. At the Wapping end the tunnel was very near the surface, and the bottoms of several wells were cut away by the workmen; here the rock could be split only by hammer and wedge, and despite all precautions the foundations of one or two houses sank. In the vicinity of Hope Street and Crabtree Lane, however, the tunnel roof was 70ft below the surface.

The Wapping end of the tunnel curved gently to the south-east on the level for 270 yds; the remaining stretch of 1980 yards was perfectly straight but on an incline of 1 in 48 ascending to Edge Hill. The correct alignment was achieved in the blind and disconnected sections by means of plumb-lines suspended from points known to be correct, and by the trembling needle of the mariner's compass, by some miracle not deflected seriously enough by stray ironwork to throw any of the sections more than an inch or so out of true when they met. The inclination was determined by adjustable spirit-levels. The working line was the underside of the crown of the arch.

The miners laboured in appalling conditions, and on more than one occasion they refused to work until persuaded, cajoled or bribed by Locke or Stephenson. Writing of these incidents in 1830, Henry Booth said:

'Nor is this suprising, considering the nature of the operation: boring their way almost in the dark, with the water streaming around them, and uncertain whether the props and stays would bear the pressure from above till the arch-work should be completed. Those who visit the Tunnel in its present state, illuminated with gas-lights, and traversed by horses, carriages, and crowds of passengers, will not easily picture to themselves the original dark and dangerous cavern, with the roof and sides supported by shores, while the miners pursued their arduous task by the light of a few candles, whose feeble glimmer glancing on the water which ran down the sides, or which spread out in a sheet below, was barely sufficient to show the dreariness of the place.'[9]

A frequent visitor to the works in progress was James S. Walker, who wrote:

'Seen and heard from a distance through the intermediate darkness, the labour of the miners was truly interesting. Their numerous candles twinkled in the thick obscurity like stars on a gloomy night, and their figures here and there marked out in dark profile, while they flung about their brawny arms, – together with the frequent explosion and the fumes of gunpowder, conveyed no contemptible idea of some infernal operation in the regions of Pluto.'[10]

The Company's policy of providing the heavy materials and contracting only for the more specialised labour led to some very complicated arrangements with the contractors. The Company provided the temporary rails and timbers, the machinery at the shafts, the waggons, bricks, cement and other materials for making the mortar. They also found the wood for making the ventilation ducts, wooden conduits of eight inches square section extended along the tunnel as the workings progressed. The contractor employed the men and furnished the tools, lights, horses and gunpowder at a rate that had risen to 4s. per cu. yd by February 1828. The rate for brickwork was 3s. per sq. yd of inside surface of the arch, regardless of the thickness required. All materials were delivered to the contractors at the top of the shafts, and it was their responsibility to move them to the required position. Once the horses had been lowered down the shafts they remained in the tunnel for the duration of the work; stables were provided for a number of horses in each section.

On 26 November 1827 Copeland's section of the tunnel met the workings from Mill Field Shaft 'within a very few inches' and by May 1828 the great work was nearing completion; two sections met on 12 May, and a week later other gangs broke through to each other under Nelson Street. On 9 June the Board recorded that the final sections were joined and the tunnel open throughout. At the Wapping end

'... a few paces from the entrance there is a huge round-topped gate, formed of framework and upright iron rods. This ponderous portal is fixed on a centre pivot in the roof and another in the middle of the Railway, so that it is easily turned either way, and effectually closes up the vault from intruders, yet admits a free passage of air.'[11]

16 *Edge Hill excavation and tunnel under construction*

Arrangements were made with the Liverpool Gas Company for lighting the tunnel, and the gas pipes, supplied by M. & W. Grazebrook, were laid with gas-jets every 50 yds during the early part of 1829. On the completion of this work in July the Board ordered the tunnel to be whitewashed throughout in readiness for its opening to the public view, and for the next few weeks a small number of workmen were employed finishing the tunnel, the first to run completely under a city.

From Edge Hill to the passenger terminus at Crown Street ran a short tunnel of 290 yds, parallel to and to the right of the Wapping tunnel but inclining upwards. This tunnel was only 15ft wide and 12ft high, and the trains were to be worked through it by rope haulage up to Crown Street and by gravity in the other direction. Like the Wapping Tunnel, it was whitewashed and gas-lit, and inscribed on the keystone at the Crown Street end may still be seen the date '1829'.

By the spring of 1827 work had started on most of the line; although the country between Liverpool and Manchester is reasonably flat, it nevertheless required about nine miles of embankment and 13 miles of cutting.

Where the tunnels emerged at Edge Hill a large area had to be excavated to provide room for the stationary steam engines, locomotive sheds and several lines of rails for accommodating the trains. This cutting, to a depth of 40ft through rock, was made by Harding, one of the tunnel contractors. Between Edge Hill and Wavertree Lane an excavation known as the Marle Cutting was driven by Thornton & Co. Although of no great difficulty it was still unfinished in 1829 because of the impossibility of removing the spoil to the Broad Green Embankment until the intervening Olive Mount Cutting was completed. Eventually most of the spoil was disposed of in spoil banks by the lineside.

A major undertaking was the excavation of the Olive Mount Cutting, lying between the Marle Cutting to the west and the Roby Embankment to the

17 *Edge Hill; entrances to the tunnels, 1831*

east, and about half a mile north of the former Wavertree village.

Like the Wapping Tunnel, this was inherited by Stephenson from the Rennie-Vignoles plan of 1826, and by March 1827 he had informed the Board of his proposals for commencing the work. The task was formidable, although straightforward, involving the cutting of a deep and narrow ravine nearly a mile long and on a very slight curve through solid rock at places to a depth of 70ft, and originally just over 20ft wide. John and George Stevenson and Jos. Thornton & Co. were the contractors, and the Company's Superintendent was Scott, until he left to supervise the works at Whiston, when he was replaced by John Gillespie.[12]

On 14 May 1827 Hartley suggested that some of the vast quantity of stone to be excavated, nearly half a million cubic yards, might be used in the reconstruction of the Liverpool Docks, upon which task he was then engaged, and shortly afterwards a contract was arranged under which the company would supply up to 5000 cu. ft per week at 6d. per cu. ft, delivered on the Dock Quays. Much of the material was used by the Railway for sleepers, and in May 1830, 7000 stone blocks were supplied to the contractor for the Kenyon & Leigh Junction Railway from Olive Mount. It was said at this time that the cutting was being widened 'as the stone at each side was valuable', but a more likely reason was the obvious danger of the original small clearance between the walls of the cleft and the passing trains.

As the stone was loosened, it was hoisted out of the cutting by horse-gins. Two bridges spanned the ravine; that carrying the Wavertree to Old Swan Road was of brick, while the other was of wood, resting on brackets formed of stone left projecting beyond the surface of the cutting walls.

One of the difficulties encountered was the liability to flooding at those points where the excavation was deepest, since the water could not escape or drain through the rock, and pumps worked by steam engines were installed. In May 1828 the workmen reached the bottom of the cutting at one place, and the first few yards of permanent way were laid there.

The cutting was not completed until 1830, by which time there had been a number of casualties among the labourers; the dependants of one who was

18 *Olive Mount Cutting from the Broad Green end; works nearing completion, 1830*

killed by a falling gin in July 1827 were awarded £10 compensation. All cases of injury, wherever they occurred along the railway, were considered individually by the Board, and usually an award was made.

From Olive Mount Cutting the line continued on the Broad Green (or Roby) Embankment, one mile long and reaching a height of 45ft, with a base varying between 60ft and 135ft. This was constructed in three separate stretches in order to employ a greater number of labourers, the sections eventually joining to form the complete embankment, or 'battery' as it was often called in those days. The western section used the spoil from Olive Mount Cutting while the Huyton cutting supplied the material for the eastern part. The central section was made with soil from a field at Twig Lane, bought for that purpose.

The Huyton Cutting yielded 47,000 cu. yds of spoil and rock, the latter providing material for bridges and walls. The section was finished in 1829. The principal contractor along the section of line from Broad Green through Huyton to the Whiston Inclined Plane was McLeod.

Had the railway been constructed exactly as planned by Vignoles and the Rennies, the next five miles would have been in cutting through Rainhill, rising gently to the summit at 1 in 226 and then falling eastward at 1 in 256. George Stephenson, however, proposed a number of amendments to the Parliamentary plans including the substitution of inclined planes, each of one and a half miles at 1 in 96 at Whiston and Sutton, with an elevated level stretch of nearly two miles separating them, later known as the Rainhill Level. At the top of each gradient two stationary steam engines were to be erected for the purpose of hauling the trains up to the level section. Stephenson claimed that this plan would save £37,000 in construction costs and could be completed more quickly. It seems an extraordinarily short-sighted policy to sacrifice what could have been a practically level line with all the operating advantages that would follow, for one on which delays and stoppages would be inevitable, for a saving of a mere 5% of the railway's total cost. Uncharitable observers at the time suggested that the steep gradients were introduced to prevent the adoption of

19 *Olive Mount Cutting: widening works in progress.* c. 1848

horse traction on the line, but, whatever the reason, and against the advice of Josias Jessop, the Board agreed to Stephenson's plan.

Even the modified line involved heavy earthworks, principally in levelling the 1⅞ miles through Rainhill and excavating the cutting through which the Sutton Inclined Plane ran. Four contractors working here, McLeod, Allcock, Copeland and Pickering, removed 220,000 cu. yds from the Rainhill section and 144,000 cu. yds from the Sutton cutting. In May 1828 a petrified tree trunk was dug up at Whiston and presented by the Board to the Liverpool Royal Institution.

Compared with the works at Chat Moss, those at Parr Moss were uncomplicated and gave the engineers little trouble. Situated half a mile from the eastern end of the Sutton Incline, Parr Moss is about ¾-mile across and 15 to 18ft deep. With an area of 400 acres, it was less than one-twelfth the size of Chat Moss, and not nearly as saturated. Into Parr Moss was tipped all the spoil from the adjacent Sutton Cutting. The work here was done by Thomas Eaton's men, and as at many other sections of the line, a temporary tram-road was laid along which the spoil-waggons were drawn. At length a concealed embankment about 25ft high formed of clay, stone and shale built up across the Moss, eventually to carry the railway about four feet above its surface.

The line now ran through Collins Green to enter the valley of the Sankey Brook where, alongside the stream, ran the Sankey Navigation (St Helens Canal).

Just over 14 miles from Liverpool stands the most spectacular engineering work on the L&MR, the Sankey Viaduct. The Rennies' original plan entailed a viaduct of 712ft overall length, including the approaches, the main section comprising seven arches of 50ft span and one, that over the canal, of 60ft; the height above the water was 60ft and the width 25ft.

In a letter to his son dated 23 February 1827, Stephenson included a rough sketch of the viaduct he planned to build, a curious design of interlaced 'Gothick' arches as he put it, 20 in number and each of 40ft span. Taking the width of the piers into account, this would have produced a structure over 800ft long, or nearly twice the width of the valley to be crossed. It was evidently to be of brickwork, for he had already recommended the Board in January to establish a brickworks on Newton Common to supply the bricks for both this and the Newton Viaduct. The Directors, on being presented with the plan on 19 March, were apparently not very impressed and they asked Hartley to confer with Stephenson on the matter. Some five months later he recommended a viaduct of elliptical arches of 65ft span, but Stephenson favoured the alternative 9-arch semi-circular design of 50ft span. It seems to have mattered little to Hartley, who was among other things a professional bridge builder, and he thereupon designed the Sankey Viaduct, carrying out the survey and preparing the plans and estimates for a fee of £27 7s. 6d. The contract for the western embankment approaches to the viaduct went to Greenshields and work started in June 1827. This long embankment reached a height of 60ft at its eastern end, and as there was no accessible cutting to supply the 200,000 cu. yds of spoil required, fields alongside the line were purchased and the earth moved from there.

20 *George Stephenson's original sketch for the Sankey Viaduct*

In September the Board considered whether to have the viaduct built by a single contract, '. . . or separate contracts or divisions under the more immediate control of our own surveyors.' The second course was adopted and the viaduct was eventually completed under the supervision of Allcard and his assistant Fyfe. A protracted series of negotiations between the Company and the Sankey Navigation now followed over the approval by the latter of the plans. This and other matters of contention were finally settled by the Company undertaking in March 1828 to pay the canal company £500 compensation for encroaching upon their property and £30 per day when building operations held up their traffic.

Meanwhile timber for the foundations of the piers was purchased and the pile-drivers prepared, and in the spring the work of driving the 200 piles upon which the ten piers were to be raised was begun; each pile had to be driven 20 to 30ft through the sandy, alluvial valley bed. Booth refers to '. . . the heavy ram . . . hoisted up with double purchase and snail's pace to the summit of the Piling Engine, and then falling down like a thunderbolt . . .', to drive the timber perhaps half an inch. Some of the piles were driven upright, others at an angle to form struts, and upon them platforms 40ft × 20ft were built to form the foundations of the piers.

By the early summer of 1829 the piers had been built; either for reasons of economy or for ease of construction, they were of brick faced with stone. It

21 The Sankey Viaduct, 1831

was Hartley's intention that the arches should have been of solid masonry, but he assented to these being turned in brickwork providing the materials and workmanship were good.[13] When Huskisson visited the railway on 21 August, he crossed the nearly-completed viaduct, a temporary path having been laid across the one unfinished arch. By February 1830 the parapet walls were in position and the majestic viaduct towering 60ft above the stream was virtually finished.

On the far side of the Sankey Brook the 40ft Sandy Mains or Newton Embankment carried the line out of the valley and through Newton, where a four-arch viaduct spanned the turnpike road and the old Mill Dam at a height of 27ft. Built of stone-faced brickwork, it was a smaller version of the Sankey Viaduct, and, completed in 1828, it provided the builders with valuable experience.

The railway now entered the Kenyon Cutting, the greatest single earthwork on the line. Begun in May 1827, the work was divided among several contractors including Baird, Hutchinson, Parkinson and Simmons. The immense amount of earth shifted, nearly three-quarters of a million cubic yards, provided ample material for the Newton Embankment and for the Brosley Embankment to the east, leaving a large surplus which could have been put to good use in the western approach embankment had it been possible to transport it across the valley. Since this was not feasible a field at Kenyon Lane '... of about one Cheshire Acre[14] and full of hollows and pits' was purchased in February 1825 as a dumping ground; several more fields were required for the same purpose before this section was finished in 1830.

The Brosley Embankment, 1½ miles long and 18 to 20ft high, was entrusted to John Blacklock, and took the line to the edge of Chat Moss.

The passage of the line across Chat Moss was to cause the Board and George Stephenson much anxiety and foreboding, for once having launched the railway on this route, to have abandoned it in favour

22 Newton Viaduct and Station, c. 1847

of another would have involved expense and delay they were loath to contemplate.

There was, in fact, nothing particularly novel in building a railway across the Moss, for railways had existed there from 1793 when William Roscoe and a Mr Wakefield of Liverpool had started to drain the Moss under an Enclosure Act. This first railway was described as a

'... road of iron, cast in bars of six feet long, and joined together by dove-tailed steps, resting upon wood sleepers. Upon this road one horse will with ease take seven waggons of marl or sand, of six hundredweight each. The extremity of the road where it diverges on each side from the principal road, is daily changed; and a single person will, with ease, take up, remove, and lay down two hundred yards of it in a day.'[15]

About 1816 Robert Stannard,[16] then Roscoe's steward, introduced an improved railway system on Chat Moss, using wrought iron rails of an inverted V section in conjunction with specially designed trucks.

When James made his first survey in 1822 he planned the line across Chat Moss (falling into it in the process), and was evidently quite familiar with the railways already at work there.

George Stephenson, resurveying the line, followed James's plan almost exactly; he, too, saw the many deep drains that had been cut in the Moss and the tramways and wagons at work. He also talked to those who worked there, including one Jim Hirst, later to become an engine driver on the Liverpool & Manchester Railway, and his father. Visiting the Moss one day in 1825 Stephenson hired these two to accompany him, Hirst taking a long staff to sink into the Moss while the boy carried '... flint and steel to light a candle, in order that when a sounding was made George might be able to test whether the air coming from below was coal-pit air or not.' When water was detected, but no coal, Stephenson remarked, 'You lads know better than I do.' In a letter of 12 December 1824 Stephenson had expressed his belief in the existence of a coalfield beneath Chat Moss:

'It is my opinion that coal will be found under Chat Moss. I think there will be none under Kirkby Moss;

but immediately on the southeast point of Mossbro Road from when the Railroad crosses I think it will be found: and I believe the coalfield will pass up even under Knowsley Hall and continue through the whole of that high country by Prescott. But I should not advise any purchase to be made of coal fields until a closer investigation is made, even though you were certain of the Act passing.'

At that time Chat Moss covered about 5000 acres, measured about four miles from east to west, and was unstable to a depth of 10 to 35ft, below which was a solid bed of clay. The surface was covered with coarse rough grass, and in places it was dangerous to venture, but with the years of work that had gone into its drainage, and the accumulated experience of those engaged on this task, it was not the formidable obstacle to the railway that Francis Giles had suggested it to be, when his evidence had contributed to the defeat of the first Bill. George Rennie wrote that when he and his brother surveyed the line in 1826 '... we found a good road over the middle of it capable of bearing a horse and cart...' He went on to mention the work of Roscoe and Mr Borron of Wolden Hall '... from whom we derived much valuable information; so that, guided by former experience in draining extensive marshes, we felt no apprehensions about Chat Moss.'[17]

Other engineers who endorsed the plan were Vignoles, who, under the Rennies, had actually made the survey, Josias Jessop, at that time engaged in building the Cromford & High Peak Railway, and Alexander Nimmo, whose civil engineering activities in Ireland had involved crossing bogs and mosses. The horse-operated Kilmarnock & Troon Railway, opened in 1810, had been successfully carried over such terrain. This is not to suggest that the construction of four miles of a main line railway over such land should have been an easy task; the contractors and their men worked continuously for months on end with very little apparent progress, but they were fully aware that it would take years to accomplish their object.

Within seven weeks of the passing of the Act, Vignoles had staked out the line across Chat Moss and had let contracts for four open ditches the whole length of this section. G. Rennie had recommended a width of 44 yds to allow for slopes and drainage, but it was decided in July to buy sufficient land from the occupier, Mr Borron, for 100 yds width at £2 per acre; the cost of the four-mile strip was less than £300.

The largest contracts were undertaken by Robert Stannard, who also excavated the cutting between Salford and the Moss; among the other contractors were a Mr Blacklock and a Mr Willy.

When Vignoles staked out the line he directed that a temporary path of wooden planks be laid across the Moss, and this was in position when John Dixon the Assistant Engineer in charge of the eastern end of the railway took up his duties. The railway labourers followed the practice of those who had worked on the Moss for generations, and strapped wooden boards to their boots, thus distributing their weight over a wider area; specially designed pattens were made for the horses employed on the works. In October the Board refer to a working railway already in operation on Chat Moss, one presumably constructed by Robert Stannard who had been awarded the contract for the three miles west from Eccles. This light railway eventually extended right across the Moss and over it all the materials required for building the line were carried, in loads of about a ton, on waggons propelled by boys; these lads quickly acquired the skill necessary to enable them to run with the waggons and, by stepping on the sleepers, to avoid falling into the Moss. Labourers in parties of eight or ten were also conveyed in the waggons to their place of work.

About this time one of the directors, James Loch, visited the works and voiced the opinion, shared by others, that progress here was too rapid for safety. Accordingly, the chairman with Booth and two other directors inspected the works in November and expressed themselves very satisfied with the operations there; they did, however, suggest that a small committee of directors should superintend the works on Chat Moss, and Sandars, Brandreth and Ellis undertook the task. They also invited a Mr Wilson of Troon,[18] an engineer familiar with the Kilmarnock & Troon Railway, to report on the line, which he did in April 1827, commenting favourably on most aspects of the work being carried out. A few weeks earlier James Roscoe had offered his services as superintendent of the Chat Moss works but there is no record that he was engaged.

It is apparent that during the winter of 1826-7 the first difficulties on Chat Moss arose at a place called Blackpool Hole; here they could not find the bottom of the morass and the contractor tipped spoil for more than three months without making the slightest progress. Quantities of old sugar casks were chained together with brushwood and moss, but these came to the surface again at some distance from the side of the line. Altogether about 70,000 cu. yds of spoil were tipped and disappeared here, and when at length the directors began to complain, Stannard urged them to purchase a plantation of young larch trees about half

23 *Chat Moss, near Lamb's Cottage, 1831*

grown, nearly a mile distant from the line at Botany Bay Woods, near Worsley Hall. Part of the wood was bought, the trees grubbed up by the roots and dragged to the Moss. These trees were laid together 'herring-bone' fashion, and when pieces of rock, spoil, earth and loose material were tipped upon this timber, the road gradually formed.

It was thus that the principle of allowing the railway to float on the Moss was established, although it was evidently not Stephenson's original plan:

During the controversy between Stannard and Stephenson, it seems there was great difficulty in convincing Stephenson that the raft system was the best, as Stephenson always insisted that if they put spoil enough on the Moss it would find a bottom; but although it did no doubt sometimes reach the bottom it did not stay there as the bog had a specific gravity like a quicksand and assisted a flow from each side; but after many anxious discussions Stephenson said to Stannard, 'Have your own way'. The contractor replied, 'Yes, I will, but I want some money'. Stephenson then said, 'The Directors have none, but I have £400 in one of the Liverpool Banks of my own, and I will lend it to you'. He got the money and, with a fresh supply of wagons obtained from Manchester and the weft and warp of the trees of Botany Bay Wood, he became successful in obtaining a foundation.[19]

The main drainage ditches ran parallel with the railway and 16 yds apart; they were three to four feet deep, and as they grew longer the volume of water carried off was such that the soft peat sides slipped away and choked the channel. The problem was overcome by the purchase of a large number of empty tar-barrels from Liverpool which, when laid end-to-end along the ditch and partially sealed with clay, formed a wooden sewer or conduit. When the flow of water from the space between the ditches subsided the partially drained ground was prepared for the permanent way. On it were laid tree-trunks and branches; in places rough wooden frames similar in size to farm gates were made up to form the foundations. These were then covered with heather, moss or any other light materials to hand, interspersed with more brushwood hurdles, to form the base of the floating road-bed. A covering of earth, sand, shingle and cinders completed the work, which after settlement and consolidation, was levelled in readiness for the laying of the permanent way.

This method of construction was adopted for most of the line over Chat Moss, but at each end an embankment was required to cover the transition from floating road-bed to railway laid on firm ground. These were constructed by tipping spoil into the bog until at length, by its very volume it formed a solid, but mostly invisible embankment. At the Manchester end 670,000 cu. yds of material were used in these operations, and although the work had been proceeding steadily for some two years, there was little evidence that it was anywhere near completion when Telford inspected the works in 1829. Almost another year was to elapse before this causeway groped its way into the Moss to join the floating section to the Barton Embankment. On the western side much less difficulty was encountered, the ground there being comparatively firm and dry, and the embankment had been finished before Telford's visit.

About 200 men were normally employed upon the line over Chat Moss; some of them worked for the principal contractors or for sub-contractors, of whom there were several; others were employed directly by the company. Claiming to have been the first man to have put a spade into Barton Moss, Hirst worked on the line from the beginning of operations; later he became a small contractor, employing nine or ten men. Another, named Higginson, died during the work and the Company paid his widow £10. The piecework rate of wages paid for the main drains was from 1¼d. to 1⅓d. per cu. yd, at which rate men earned from 3s. to 3s. 6d. per day.

Progress throughout the line had been hampered by the unusually wet summer and autumn of 1828, and on the approach of spring 1829 the Board ordered that double shifts of labourers be employed where possible to hasten the work, now falling seriously behind schedule; at Chat Moss work went on continuously, the night gangs working in the fitful light of flares and bonfires by the lineside.

At last, towards the end of 1829, the railway over Chat Moss was finished and one line of rails had been laid. From December trial runs were made over the section with increasingly heavy loads;[20] and by April a train of about 45 tons crossed the Moss at over 15 mph without damage to itself or the track, no doubt to the great relief of John Dixon, the Assistant Engineer, whose unremitting work over three and a half years had produced four miles of railway at the remarkably low cost of £27,720.

Beyond Chat Moss the line continued for about one mile over low-lying country on the Barton Embankment, made from the spoil from the Eccles cutting to the east. The contractor here was Robert Stannard, and his men moved 300,000 cu. yds in the construction of these two works. The Eccles cutting was the last major earthwork before the railway entered Manchester.

In 1828 the Board considered the possibility of seeking powers to extend the line from Salford to Manchester; this involved little more than a bridge over the Irwell and a terminus in nearby Water Street. Approval for an application to Parliament was given at a Special General Meeting on 3 November, and Dixon was sent to discuss the matter with the Manchester Surveyors of Highways, but since he was furnished with no plan, section or elevation of the proposed Water Street bridge and works, little headway could be made.

The surveyors then sent two of their members to Liverpool to secure details of the height of the bridge, only to find that Stephenson had not made a drawing, but promised to do so. In March a meeting of Leypayers[21] was held in the Town Hall, but little enthusiasm for the project was evident. One speaker was suspicious of the plan since it emanated from Liverpool – 'They brought the nuisance to us, not we to them' – while another warned that locomotives '. . . sent forth noise, smoke, steam and fire. There was no engine of so infernal appearance.' A Mr Candelet was opposed to incurring any expense in objecting to the Bill on the grounds that 'The nuisance created by the smoke was nothing, enveloped as we were in perpetual smoke' from mills, whose owners failed to abate it. Those who actively supported the scheme argued that the town would benefit from cheap Irish provisions, appearing oblivious to the wider commercial advantages that the plan offered.

Both the Bridgewater Canal and the Old Quay Company made arrangements with the railway company under which the land required for the extension would be sold in return for wharfage and other facilities, and the Company agreed to a demand from the Manchester authorities that iron fences be erected along either side of the line where it crossed the streets. The Bill was presented early in 1829, and meeting no opposition, it received the Royal Assent on 14 May.[22]

This was the Company's fourth Act, and it authorised the abandonment of its original plans for a terminus among the canal locks and basins at Hampson-street, Salford, and for the line to be taken instead by Kent-street and Ordsall Lane to cross the Irwell; here in Manchester it was empowered to erect a station on the unbuilt land occupied as timber yards and bleaching grounds near Water-street. The previous year another Act[23] had allowed for some trifling deviations from the original line to be made

24 *Manchester, Irwell Bridge, with Old Quay warehouses visible through right-hand arch, 1833*

near the Sutton Workhouse, Burtonwood, Newton and Culcheth; it also stipulated the gauge as 4ft 8in. and 5ft 1in. between the inside and outside edges of the rails respectively, and set a penalty of 40s. for trespassing on or walking along the railway.

Jesse Hartley had already designed both the Irwell and Water Street bridges. The river bridge was of two arches, each of 63ft span, and 30ft above the waters of the Irwell, which it crossed askew; it was of brick, encased in solid ashlar. In June the building contract was awarded to J. Brockbank and Alexander Fyfe, who were to supply all the materials and equipment required; by October the foundations for the side piers were laid and the coffer dam with a steam engine working the pumps was in position for the base of the central pier. Advances of a few hundred pounds were made periodically to the contractors, who lacked sufficient capital to finance the work themselves.

Towards the end of April 1830 a tragic accident occurred when a boat carrying twelve workmen was upset in the river and they were all drowned. On 3 May the Board received a list of the families of the dead men and resolved to afford relief to such of them who '... were in distressed circumstances, to a limited extent, as in previous cases.'

The Directors were showing some anxiety in July 1830 at the still unfinished state of the works on the Irwell, and received a forecast that the masonry would be completed by mid-August.

Under a separate contract Brockbank and George Findlay built the 22 brick arches and the bridge over Water Street that carried the line to its Manchester terminus. In April 1830 it was decided to widen Water Street, and to support the lengthened bridge by eleven cast iron Doric columns 17½ft high, erected along the edge of each footpath, upon which rested massive cast iron beams, arched between with brickwork. These castings were supplied by Nasmyth, who also cast the 45-ton columns. The Manchester Passenger Station had its frontage in Liverpool Road, at right-angles to Water Street, and behind it were erected large warehouses forming part of the goods station.

The building of the Liverpool & Manchester Railway brought George Stephenson into contact with most of the leading engineers of that time, and, it might be added, into conflict with quite a few of them. One of these, and a very redoubtable one, was Thomas Telford, engineer to the Exchequer Loan Bill Commissioners, to whom the company had applied for the lifting of their lien on the final 30% of the share capital. The Directors had already indicated that they were unable to pay the annual interest of £3500 due in June 1828. Without hesitation the Commissioners released 10%, and the Board called up that amount in December 1828. Before authorising any further call, the Commissioners instructed Telford to report on the state of the works and to estimate the cost of completing them. Accordingly, he spent a day on the line at the end of November and left his assistant, James Mills, to carry out the survey and make a preliminary report.

Whether by accident or design, on the morning that Mills started his survey both Stephenson and Locke left for Newcastle in order to observe the working of the railways in that area. They had not returned by 20 December when Mills reported to Telford:[24]

'Stephenson and Locke are trying experiments on the Darlington & Stockton Railway to see at what speed Locomotive Engines will carry coals and passengers *all together*; as they have but two Roads, and therefore mean to keep *one rate* of Travelling for Coals, Lime, Merchandize, Ladies and Gentlemen.'

Mills's first discovery was that no plan or section of the line existed apart from the one prepared by

Vignoles for the Rennies, and from copies of which every calculation was made; he at once employed a draughtsman to make a fair copy for his and Telford's use. His purpose being to ascertain the amount of work outstanding and to estimate the cost of completing it, he reported that there would be some difficulty

'... for in truth there does not appear to be a single Contract existing on the whole line. Stevenson [sic] seems to be the Contractor for the whole, and to employ all the different People at such prices as he thinks proper to give them, the Company *finding all materials*, not only Rails and Waggons, but even Wheelbarrows and Planks etc.'

The first man he asked about prices for work said there was no fixed price or specified distance; Stephenson would pay between 8d. and 1s. 1d., as he thought fit, and he might go on for 20 yards or half-a-mile. For masonry the Company provided the material and paid 1s. 6d. to 6s. per yd.

Mills does not seem to have received much co-operation from the directors, if he ever met any of them; they are not mentioned in his or Telford's reports as ever furnishing any information about the railway. Most of it was gathered from the two day men detailed to accompany him or from men working along the line, but he does mention '... a young man of the name of Gooch, an apprentice of Mr Stevenson [sic], who has given me some assistance as to computations &c, &c.' Of the Assistant Engineers, he wrote:

'... each of the Three have about 200 Day Men employed and pay them every fortnight as *Company Men* – for laying temporary Roads, moving Planks, making Wheelbarrows, Driving Piles, and in short doing *every thing*, but putting the stuff into the carts and barrows, which is done by a set of men who are also under their direction, and to whom they give from 3½d. per yard to 5 shillings as they think it deserves.'

25 *Manchester, approach to Liverpool Road Station showing Water Street Bridge, 1833. In the foreground are the water-tower and boiler-house where the locomotive water was heated*

During January 1829 Mills wrote his report for Telford, whom he met in Manchester early that month, and together they went over the line. Stephenson, now returned from Durham, accompanied them, but what passed between the two engineers during those winter days spent on the inspection is not recorded. That Telford was very disturbed by some of the practices employed in building the railway is evident from his final report, and that he was at a loss to understand how the Directors intended to operate it when it was finished is also apparent.

The Report contains 18 numbered paragraphs, dealing first with the Liverpool end, where work on 270 yds of excavation for warehouses had not been started. The Wapping Tunnel was nearing completion and appeared satisfactory, but much remained to be done between the tunnel and Wavertree Lane, where he suggested spoil banks would be required. From here to Broad Green, a distance of two miles, a great quantity of excavation still remained, but this would not produce the enormous quantity of spoil, nearly half-a-million cubic yards, required for the great Broad Green embankment. The section included not only the rocky Olive Mount Cutting but other stretches through marl and clay, and in his opinion the side-slope of 1 in 1 was too steep and should be flattened to 18 inches to 1 foot, giving not only stability but additional material for use in the embankment. His further remarks reveal some rather shoddy workmanship on these cuttings:

'... even with the proposed slopes, there would be required a wall along the bottom from four to five feet in height above the level of the roadway; it should be three feet in thickness, and built with well-bedded stones laid in good lime mortar for the whole thickness, not merely for a few inches in front, and the remainder laid loose and dry, worse than a common stone dyke, having only *one face* made for show – a part thus built, had tumbled when I was there, and if the other retaining walls now built, are constructed in the same manner, they are not likely to resist the pressure of slipping marl.'

He stressed the need for a drainage system constructed along the top of the bank to carry off the water before it could soak into the side of the cutting, a precaution which had been overlooked.

The seven-mile stretch from the eastern end of Broad Green Embankment to Leach Lane Road included the Whiston and Sutton gradients, and was substantially completed, there being no particularly heavy earthworks along the way. Coming now to Parr Moss, Telford was unwilling to commit himself as to how long it might take before the moss settled from draining and a stable road could be thrown across it. Through Collins Green the line was practically finished, but the great embankment leading on to the Sankey Viaduct still needed about 63,000 cu. yds to complete it, and Telford was critical of the method adopted by the contractor in forming it. He maintained that it should have been raised in stages so that each level had time to consolidate, whereas

'... having been formed by bringing the waggons forward on the top level and tumbling the earth down the whole height, which at the end of the bridge is 59 feet, I expect a considerable time will be required for its consolidation, and that it will be subject to slips.'

On the question of Chat Moss, Telford could only advance a 'conjectural estimate' of the amount of work still outstanding by forming a ratio from what had already been done, and he did not even guess how long it would take.

Of the bridges, about half were built or under construction, the Sankey 'Aqueduct', as Telford persisted in calling it, being two-thirds finished; he observed that the whole of the masonry work on the line had been '... performed in a very perfect manner.' He concluded that the earthworks and bridges could be finished in two years, i.e. by early 1831, but that it would not be possible to lay the rails by this time owing to the '... uncertainty that attends the Moss operations, and the slips which may take place in the extensive marl cuttings and embankments.'

It does not need much imagination to gauge Stephenson's reaction when a copy of the Report dated 4 February reached Liverpool, and the Board must have read it with some dismay since clearly its effect on the Exchequer Loan Commissioners would not be one of inspiring that confidence in the Company that would persaude them to release the remaining 20% of capital. The Report was examined closely and certain errors discovered, principally concerned with quantities of earth to be shifted. In the case of the number of bridges completed the figures were incorrect because faulty information had been given to the Board by its Engineer and passed on to Telford. The Report had in fact given the Commissioners the impression that a sum beyond the resources of the Company would be required to finish the railway, and that the completion date was distant and uncertain; at their next meeting they resolved not to release any further portion of the share capital without additional security. When their decision was conveyed to the Board a deputation of directors went to London and waited upon the Commissioners; their appeal resulted in their being given permission to make a further call of 10%.

Perhaps under pressure from Stephenson and those members of the Board who resented the intrusion into their affairs of an elderly engineer from London, but almost certainly to allay the fears of some shareholders, the Company published Telford's report in pamphlet form on 16 March 1829, printing opposite each section its own comments and contradictions. A copy of this document soon came to the notice of Telford and Mills, and the latter, presumably replying on behalf of his senior, gave the Commissioners, and through them, the Directors, the benefit of his advice, together with his observation on the Company's choice of engineer. The Board, in contesting several quantities listed in the Report, said that they '... rely upon the authority of their Engineer', to which Mills replied:

'... would it not have been better to have directed their Engineer to have compared his calculations with Mr Telford's – you well know, however, why the Board did not do this, you well know their Engineer is not capable of making the survey, and it would have been more candid to have said that one of the Engineer's Agents or Apprentices had made such statement to the Board.'

On the specific question of the cost of the Kenyon Cutting, where the Company claimed the estimates differed by £2380, he wrote:

'Now with respect to the price for this Cutting, it is exactly that passed by the Engineer's Agent to the Board in writing; it is certainly not the price at which Mr Telford would have rated it, but then it must be observed that Mr Telford was never called upon to value work conducted as the whole of this work has been. There never was any great public work before, I apprehend, where one Person was appointed to act as Engineer and to execute the work under the sole contraul [sic] of himself, his agents and own apprentices, hired as resident Engineers at a large salary.

'I am of opinion that if this work had been conducted as all other public works in which I have been engaged have been, by a competent and experienced Engineer and let under proper specifications in different parts to responsible Contractors totally disconnected with the Engineer, that at least one-third of the expense already incurred ... could have been saved to the proprietors ... every Engineer or Contractor at all acquainted with public works knows that the employment of Company's Men is at all times and in all situations to be avoided if possible, but in conducting the whole of this great and expensive Undertaking there has been scattered over thirty miles in length hundreds of day men not under the contraul [sic] of contractors who would for their own interest take care they were only paid according to the work performed, but who well knowing they were paid by the Company according to the Account returned by the Agents of the Engineer, would work as all Company's men do.'

The remaining portion of the letter reveals the uncertainty existing in the minds of many engineers at that time as to the precise manner in which railway transport was to be conducted; some of these matters had, of course, only recently received the Board's consideration and no decisions as to motive power, for example, had been reached. Telford had included £14,000 for 'fixed engines for tunnel and two inclined planes, with their machinery', in his estimates of the cost of completing the railway, but when the Board argued that this was not an expense of construction but a charge against the Carrying Department Account, Mills said:

'... by transferring it to the same Proprietors on another leaf, one cannot but smile. It is said that the Steam Engines form no part of the Road – True – but how is the Public to get up and down the Tunnel – is every Carrier to draw himself up and down by a contrivance of his own?'

He went on to say:

'... it is because I am most anxious this great experiment should ultimately succeed that I communicate to you thus fully my opinion for your consideration.

'I think that when the Directors discharged Mr Rennie, whose estimate, I believe, was £510,000, and who made the survey of the present line and assisted to carry the Bill through Parliament, they should have paused before they had allowed another Engineer whose estimate, I believe, was only £400,000 to have expended upwards of £600,000 upon Mr Rennie's line, and to have constructed two Inclined Planes in the middle of the line, which have totally changed the character of the whole Undertaking as designed by the Engineer who made the survey.

'By Mr Rennie's Plan horses would have travelled the whole way, as on the Stockton & Darlington Rail Road for conveyance of Passengers and light goods with safety and comfort to the Public at eight, nine or ten miles per hour and coals and other heavy materials might have gone with safety by Steam Engines at the rate of five miles per hour.'

He concluded by asking if it would not be better for the Company, even at this late hour, to consider reverting to the Rennies' original plan.

Perhaps on reflection the Directors realised that Telford's original report was a fairly restrained document; Mills's observations certainly appear to have had the effect of shaking them out of a certain complacency that had settled over them after the passing of the Act, and to that extent they profited from Telford's brief association with the Company, even though they did quibble before settling his account for £629. The final 10% was released by the Commissioners in the summer of 1830, following another deputation of directors.

Very shortly afterwards the decision to hold the Rainhill Locomotive Trials was taken and it is very likely that Mills's remarks on horse and locomotive traction strengthened Stephenson's already fierce determination to see that the locomotive should soon run unchallenged.

No fewer than 63 bridges were built ranging in size from the Sankey Viaduct to Hodgkinson's Cattle Bridge carrying the line over a nine-foot farm track.

26 *Rainhill Bridge, 1830. At this time Rainhill Station was a quarter-mile to the east at Kendrick's Cross*

About half the number were occupation bridges, and five spanned water. Stone, brickwork, timber or a combination of these materials was used in their construction, and although one subsequently collapsed, they were generally soundly built.

The Rainhill Bridge carrying the Liverpool-Warrington-Manchester turnpike road over the line was described as 'of very curious and beautiful construction' and as one of the 'most remarkable skew bridges in the Kingdom', a reference to its having been built at an angle of 34° to the line, the most acute of the 15 skew bridges on the L&MR. At a Board Meeting on 29 September 1828 the question of this bridge was discussed and Stephenson reported that he had '... measured the Stone Bridge at Coleshill ... and another at Lancaster', whereupon it was decided that the Rainhill Bridge should be 30ft in width between the parapets, similar to the one at Lancaster. Since Hartley had been familiar with this bridge since boyhood, it is probable that he actually designed the Rainhill Bridge, particularly as the mode of construction was similar to that used by him to build the Liverpool Docks; George Findlay secured the building contract.

Work started towards the end of 1828 when a full-sized model in wooden framework was set up in a field beside the line and the stone blocks, many of over two tons, were cut, dressed and numbered in advance, each being individually shaped to fit its exact position. The bridge was then constructed and the road raised on inclined embankments to pass over it.

The Railway crossed the Bridgewater Canal on a two-span masonry bridge at a height of 12ft above the water. The Glazebrook bridge of brick and stone carried the line 30ft above the stream by a single span also of 30ft; the original contractor for this '... bridge over the River Gless' was dismissed by Dixon as unsatisfactory in February 1827.

Little information has survived concerning the men who built the railway. Most of them were either Irish or local men, but the overlookers were mainly men from the north who had been engaged on the construction of the S&DR. From this group came '... the several intelligent contractors ... who urged on their respective parties of workmen with unremitting anxiety and perseverance.'[25] Describing the ordinary labourers, an engineering student wrote in August 1829:

'The men, who are the finest workmen in Europe, dig out 25 cubic yards of heavy clay each day – but their desire to run to the public houses and get drunk is so great that many of them perform their day's work in a few hours. These dissolute men exert themselves so violently in their work that I have seen many powerful, muscular men with their blood oozing out of their eyes and nostrils.'[26]

At this time it was found that an increasing number of workmen, navvies, masons and specialists of various kinds, were being enticed across the Atlantic by the offer of high wages made by agents of railways and canals constructing in the USA; several hundred were said to have gone from the railway, causing delays in the progress of the work.

The Assistant Engineers were given positive instructions in January 1830 that the wages of labourers were to be paid in the offices of the several districts and not in a public house, and that the contractors were, so far as practicable, to follow the same procedure. Thomas Nicholson, a contractor on Kenyon Cutting, failed about this time and on 8 February it became known that he was not only unable to pay his men's wages, but that he owed a Lowton shopkeeper, Cartwright, £177 19s. for

27 *View of the Railway crossing the Bridgewater Canal just to the west of Patricroft, 1831*

provisions supplied to them. The Company declined responsibility for the debt but undertook to submit Cartwright's case to a General Meeting after the completion of the works; in March 1831 he was given £100. The contractor had for some reason, been paid fortnightly in advance, and had nothing to collect at the end of the last fortnight.

A great deal of rock blasting was done, particularly in the Wapping Tunnel and Olive Mount Cutting. The charge of about three pounds of gunpowder was put into a tin canister 2in. in diameter and 30in. long, to which was attached a tin tube about five feet in length which held the priming; the canister was then placed in a hole drilled in the rock and exploded.[27] After several men had been injured by flying fragments of rock the Company adopted the suggestion of one of its labourers, Thomas Young, to use a screen of faggots when blasting, a practice he had seen in America; he was awarded £5 in August 1828.

By May 1830, with the main sections of the line completed, many of the labourers were laid off, but Stephenson was asked to prepare a list of reliable platelayers to be retained and to occupy the gate cottages.

Locomotives were employed on the construction of the line before any decision was made on whether they were to be used in working the railway. Stephenson and Henry Booth had been working on a plan for a smoke-consuming locomotive and on 7 January 1828 the Board authorised the construction of one engine of six tons to cost £550. This was the 'Liverpool Travelling Engine', later to be named *Lancashire Witch*,[28] but the Company decided in April that it should be transferred to the Bolton & Leigh Railway, who would be ready for it about June, since it could not be used on the temporary tracks of the L&MR. It was an 0-4-0 engine with 4ft wooden wheels and 9in. × 24in. cylinders inclined at 39° from the horizontal; it was fitted with springs, a hot water pump and bellows beneath the tender to produce a forced draught; in many respects it was a prototype for the *Rocket*.

Towards the end of July 1829 the Company borrowed *Lancashire Witch* for three months from the B&LR and put her to work at Eccles. The Engineers were anxious to use locomotives on ballast trains over the new permanent way as the horses played havoc with the carefully laid track, their hooves churning up the ballast as they slipped and strained at their task.

In March 1829 Stephenson was asked to provide a locomotive for work in the Marle Cutting and on the Broad Green Embankment; this, referred to as the 'Liverpool Coke Engine' by the makers and named *Twin Sisters* by the Company, reached Liverpool via Carlisle in July and was assembled in the Company's yard. It was a six-wheeled engine of curious design, having two separate boilers, fireboxes and chimneys; its 9in. × 24in. cylinders were set at an angle of 45°, and it developed about 12 hp. It was supplied with boiling water from reservoirs and boilers set up along the line, to avoid the need for it to carry a great weight of water.[29]

It gave some trouble at first both in starting and in generating steam and eventually Thornton the contractor asked for its removal when it became immobilized and all the roads were blocked with loaded waggons. The Company were on the point of reverting to the use of horses when an alteration in the position of the exhaust steam pipes provided the remedy. In a letter of 13 August 1829 Stephenson refers to the modifications, which appear to have been of the trial and error variety, and to the fact that the engine now looked neater, but he does not ascribe its improved performance to its more efficient blast.

From then it worked steadily from Sunday midnight until Saturday night every week and on Sundays it was handed over to the engineers. An observer described it as pushing a train of 12 loaded waggons, about 60 tons, at six or seven miles an hour.

Edward Bury's first locomotive, *Dreadnought*, came on to the line in March 1830 to undergo trials in the form of several week's ballasting. This was a six-wheeled engine with 10in. × 24in. horizontal cylinders working a crankshaft, the drive being transmitted to the wheels by chains; it was described by Hardman Earle as a 'clumsy machine'. His second engine, *Liverpool*, with 12in. × 18in. inside cylinders and 6ft coupled wheels arrived for its trials in July 1830, but had not been ballasting for long when her crankshaft broke. This happened about the time the railway was opened, and on 20 September Bury was ordered to remove both engines until they had been put into complete order. *Liverpool* was reported ready on 25 October and was allowed back on the line, but no trials were permitted until Gooch could go with the engine and keep an exact account of its performance. *Dreadnought* went to the B&LR where it worked well into 1831, being involved in an accident at Bolton on 13 June; *Liverpool* also was purchased by that company.

On 3 September 1827 the Board had recorded its opinion '... that the great work was advancing at too slow a rate' and decided that more superintendents were required. Some months before they had noted that Stephenson was also engaged on the C&W,

Bolton & Leigh and Nantlle Railways, in addition to his business interests at Newcastle, and while accepting that he was already committed to these projects, he was offered, and accepted, a further £200 per annum as an inducement to devote more time to the L&M and to undertake no further engagements.

The very wet weather of 1829 seriously hampered the progress of the work – it was the wettest summer for 14 years. After the Rainhill Trials in October Stephenson was ordered to complete one line of road through from Liverpool to Manchester by New Year's Day 1830 if possible, and an 'Expediting Committee' established at that time was authorised to spend an extra £1000 to speed the work. On 9 November Stephenson was told to offer premiums to several contractors to complete the work by Christmas Eve and each Assistant Engineer was promised £50 if the line was fit to carry a locomotive by New Year's Day. A fortnight later the Directors learned to their astonishment that the Surveyors of the Stockport Junction Railway had been using the upstairs part of the Company's office to prepare their plans and that Locke and Dixon had been absent from the L&MR, working on this project. Stephenson was made aware of the Board's views in most explicit terms, and reminded that the Assistant Engineers were their employees and not his servants, and were not to be engaged on any work not connected with the L&MR without their express permission. An apologetic Stephenson undertook to renounce his connection with the Stockport Junction Line and to prevent his assistants being called to give evidence before Parliament.[30]

However, on 28 December Locke reluctantly resigned in order to devote his attention to Stephenson's other interests and his place was filled by young Thomas Gooch at £250 per annum; the newly-apprenticed Frederick Swanwick, 19 years old, was then appointed Stephenson's private secretary. Another assistant was Edward Salvin who joined him from Croxdale Hall, Co. Durham in November 1829, but who died at the age of 19 the following year.[31]

In April 1830 Stephenson was given permission to survey the Liverpool & Birmingham Railway, of which John Moss was to become Chairman, but to leave notice in writing where he should be each night. In June the Sheffield & Manchester Railway sought

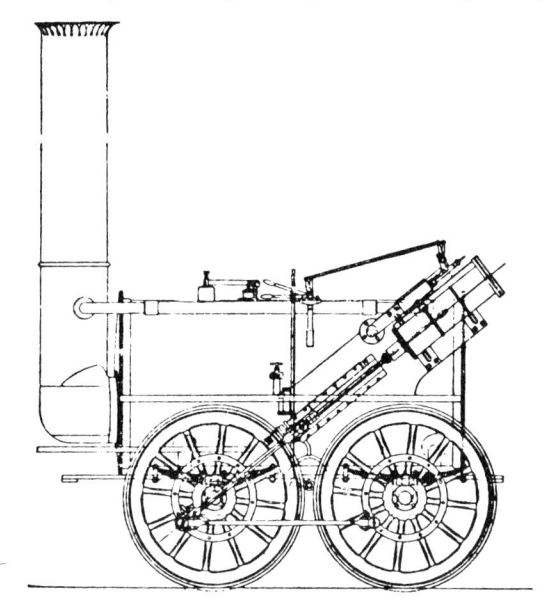

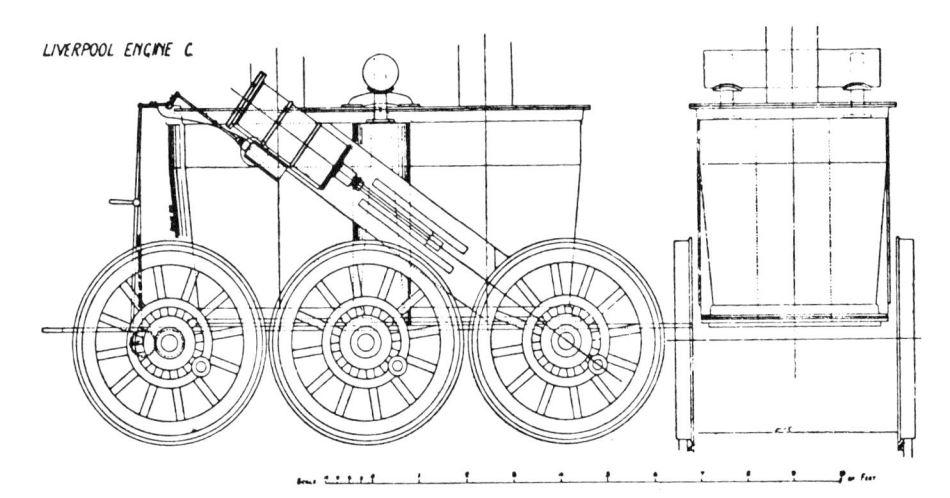

28 Lancashire Witch

29 Twin Sisters

the services of George Stephenson for its survey but the Board said he was too busy to be spared.

On 13 July 1829 the Board had engaged Captain James Chapman, RN, as 'Inspector of the progress of the Works', and a few days later at his suggestion mileposts were ordered to be erected. The Captain appears to have been zealous in the discharge of his duties, and to have enjoyed the support of several directors, for in December the engineman of *Lancashire Witch* was dismissed by the Board for insolence in answering Chapman's questions on the engine's performance and state of repair. At the same time Stephenson was told to 'make it known along the line' that the driver had been discharged for improper conduct. The driver in question had been brought over from the north by Stephenson, who in a letter to the Board, claimed that only such men were capable of operating the locomotives. He seized the opportunity of criticising both Chapman's activities and the Board's discretion in appointing a person 'entirely ignorant of Engineering', and after complaining of doubts and suspicions voiced by the Board on other matters upon which he had expressed opinions, he virtually presented the Directors with an ultimatum – he could not remain as Engineer if Chapman continued as Inspector of Progress. The Board thereupon withdrew Chapman and a week later, on 11 January 1830, awarded him £200.[32]

Stephenson had been instructed in January 1829 to complete the line without any unnecessary ornament on bridges or other works, and on 6 January 1831 the Finance Committee ordered him not to '... expend the smallest sum on the completion of the Road over and above what should be absolutely necessary for the stability of the Way.' Although the railway had been open for some months there remained a good deal to be done in minor works at a number of places and it was not realised at the time that for the next 15 years, except for a few short intervals, major works would be in hand either at Liverpool or Manchester. These included a new station at Lime Street, reached by a long tunnel from Edge Hill, and the Hunts Bank Extension across Manchester to the new Victoria Station.

As sections of the line were finished fences were erected; in some places these were stone walls, but usually wooden railings were put up and quickset hedges planted against them. As late as 1833, however, the railway across Parr and Chat Mosses was still unfenced. Distance posts painted white with black figures, were set up at ¼-mile intervals along the north side of the line, the distances being measured from Liverpool.

In December 1830 the Board considered having a guard rail erected along embankments similar to those on the B&LR but Stephenson said they were insufficient for their purpose of preventing trains from running over the edge. After further discussion it was decided to have continuous mounds of earth raised along each side of the embankments, and it was said in 1836 that such mounds were in general use. Although they remained on the L&MR, they do not in fact appear to have been widely adopted elsewhere. Only at Parkside were railings in use: these were erected in February 1832 to prevent carriages falling into a deep cutting beside the line. In December 1831 Stephenson recommended the adoption of check rails on the bridges. No details of these survive, but in view of his observations a year earlier, they were probably additional rails laid parallel with the running rails, but on the inside of the wheel flanges, to hold a train on the track.

The Company was under an obligation to build bridges for certain landowners, two at Eccles for a Mr Whitaker and one at Hea Field Moss for Thomas Legh; in each case the Company settled for a cash payment in lieu of the bridges. Years later some level crossings were replaced; that at Wavertree Lane by a bridge in 1838, and the Patricroft crossing by a side road and tunnel in 1841.

In December 1831 David Dockray[33] reported that the northwest wing wall and abutment of the Sankey Viaduct was settling, and a few months later he was apprehensive as to the stability of the structure. Hartley inspected it in May 1832, reporting favourably on its condition, but he instructed George Stephenson on the steps to be taken to ensure its safety. In fact, the viaduct had never been finished, and it was July 1833 before the coping was put on the parapet walls. In 1838 and again in 1842 piers were reported to be sinking; on the second occasion an arch at the eastern end was shored up and fairly heavy repair work followed.

Chat Moss caused little trouble, apart from the need for constant ballasting as the track sank with the drying and shrinkage of the moss. Back in September 1827 Cropper had exhibited a model wooden cottage costing £30 and the Company gave a trial order for six for the workmen on Chat Moss, directing that they be fitted with iron stoves. In July 1831 four permanent cottages were built on the Moss for the men who worked there, as they had to walk several miles from their lodgings, and a little later a small smithy was erected there from scrap materials. At this time the tar-barrel drainage system was extended, and to protect the railway from the digging of parallel drains or the dumping of waste materials by occupiers, a 50-yard wide strip of land was taken at points where this might occur.

The failure to install a drainage system caused several earth slips and in January 1834 Mr T. Studholme of Carlisle, a specialist drainage engineer, was consulted. He recommended a method of tile draining that he had used on the Newcastle & Carlisle Railway and when that Company confirmed that it was completely successful, work on Kenyon Cutting and 'Dr Parke's Cutting', near Wavertree, was put in hand. Studholme sent some men who were familiar with the work, and the cost was only about 67s. per chain lineal, including the sowing of grass. Parke's Cutting was a continual source of trouble; during a sudden thaw in 1841 the retaining wall bulged and had to be taken down.

The gauge of the L&MR was decided in July 1826, apparently without much thought or discussion, when on Stephenson's advice it was resolved that '... the width of the Waggon Way between the rails be the same as on the Darlington Road, namely 4ft 8in. clear, inside the rails'. This was at variance with G & J Rennie's plan, which was for a gauge of 5ft, but no provision for this was made in the first Act. Railways of various gauges existed at the time, but the Killingworth line and the S&DR were of 4ft 8in. and both used locomotives supplied by Stephenson. As the firm was equipped to construct locomotives of this size and expected to supply the L&MR, it was obviously convenient to build them to the same gauge, if only for the reason that they could be tested on existing railways around Newcastle before delivery. It would thus appear that the L&MR was made to fit the locomotives and what was to become the standard gauge in Great Britain and many parts of the world was established.

The odd half-inch seems to have been added to the gauge of the rails, but not the wheels, in order to prevent the flanges wearing against the inside edges of the rails – assisted by the conical shape of the wheel-tread and the inclination of the rails.

The main line of the L&MR consisted of two tracks, and was the first railway to be laid with independent rails for up and down traffic. It had been suggested by both Moss and Loch that four tracks should be laid, in order to separate the passenger and goods trains.

In October 1827 specifications were prepared by Stephenson for the permanent rails, which he had decided should be of wrought iron, although he himself had a financial interest with William Losh in a patent cast-iron rail. The rails required were of the fish-bellied type with provision for the supporting chairs to be 3ft apart and with a $1\frac{1}{2}$in. rolling surface; they were to be made in 15ft lengths and to weigh 35 lb. per yard.

Advertisements inviting tenders were placed in newspapers in Birmingham, South Wales and other centres of the iron trade, and the first contracts which stipulated the delivery of 100 tons per month at Liverpool – 1280 rails – went to John Bradley & Co. of Stourbridge and Michael Longridge of the Bedlington Iron Works at £12 15s. per ton or about £1 per rail. To support these rails some 220,000 cast-iron chairs were needed, 127,000 stone blocks and about 50,000 wooden sleepers. The 31 miles of double track alone required nearly 44,000 rails.

The rails were tested by subjecting them to a load of 18 tons on a 4-wheeled truck moving at $2\frac{1}{2}$ mph, or $4\frac{1}{2}$ tons per wheel; they were permanently bent by a weight of 7 tons applied between the chairs. Stephenson ventured the opinion that they would last for 60 or 70 years in a safe working condition, and then be valuable as scrap since malleable iron improved with age; he subsequently reduced his estimate to 30 years. He also propounded the theory that rails in daily use did not rust so quickly as those lying by the lineside because of electrical influences generated by passing trains.

Under Birkinshaw's system for producing fish-bellied rails, the red-hot metal went through the rolling mill six times; on its last passage through it passed between a pair of rollers one of which was of eccentric form to impart the bulges to the underside of the rail. No further rolling was possible afterwards.

Jesse Hartley disagreed with Stephenson's choice of rail and in February 1828 he designed a parallel rail for which he claimed several advantages. It would be cheaper to produce, requiring no complicated rolling technique and it could be rolled many times to achieve the final shape, greatly consolidating the iron in the process. The supports need not be confined to a particular distance apart, an advantage at points and crossings, or where a weakness in the track appeared.

About 13 miles of the line, those sections across the mosses or on embankments, were laid on wooden sleepers 9ft × 6in. × 5in., to facilitate ballasting as the track settled. Oak was chosen in preference to the larch used for the temporary tramroads, although it was found later that larch was preferable; the timber came down from the forests to the coast at Annan, Carlisle and Ravenglass for shipment to Liverpool.

Stone sleepers were used on the remaining 18 miles; most of them came from excavations along the line but some were bought from quarries at 1s. 6d. each.

They varied in size from 18in. to 2ft square, and 1ft deep. Two holes 6in. deep and 1½in. in diameter were drilled in the stone, into which oak plugs were driven and the cast iron chair was then fastened by iron spikes hammered into the plugs; squares of felt soaked in pitch were interposed between chair and stone to cushion any surface irregularities.

The road bed was of broken stone 6 to 12in. deep and firmly pounded down, and the stone sleepers were laid along it with a slight inclination inwards to correspond with the conical shape of the wheel-tread. The rails were then fixed, wooden keys being used for the intermediate chairs; where the rail ends met, a larger chair was used, with recesses into which lugs on the rails fitted, and a steel key which cut into the wrought iron held them firmly together. No expansion gap was left as Stephenson said the heat would be absorbed by the stone. Finally the whole space around the stones was filled with ballast sufficient to cover the sleeper and chair completely and leave about one inch of rail visible. The ballast together with the weight of the stones preserved the gauge, no tie-bars being used. At Olive Mount the rails were fastened directly to the stone floor of the cutting.

Where necessary the rails were bent with wooden mallets, and on curves the outside rail was raised. There were, however, very few curves on the line, the sharpest being that at the bottom of Wapping Tunnel; Olive Mount Cutting was on a very gentle curvature, as was the line over part of Chat Moss.

Roads and lanes, where they crossed the line, were built up to the level of the top rail, iron plates being used to keep a channel clear for the flanges of the wheels.

When finished and ballasted over, at some places with sand, at others with small coal, the line consisted of four equidistant rails laid with 'mathematical correctness', as one writer described it. The distance separating the up and down tracks was the same as the gauge, 4ft 8½in., the original purpose of which was to enable a train carrying a bulky load on approaching an overbridge, or going through the Wapping Tunnel, to be diverted to the centre pair of rails by means of suitably placed points. For that matter it could travel the whole distance on the centre track if traffic in the opposite direction were kept out of the way. There is, however, no record that the line was ever operated in this way, and this narrow clearance between trains was to cause problems for many years.

The number of broken rails discovered in various parts of the line caused the Board some concern in May 1832 and Stephenson was asked if stronger rails of a different shape should be ordered; his reply is not recorded but no immediate change was made. The heavier locomotives coming into service by 1833, partly as a result of the lighter engines being shaken to pieces on the flimsy track, only tended to aggravate the situation. The now frequent rail fractures occurred where a block or sleeper had sunk under the weight of a train, the points of support being the weakest parts of a fish-bellied rail. The sinking of blocks and sleepers was dealt with either by removing them and beating fresh ballast underneath or, if the settlement was slight, by raising the chair on thin slips of wood, replacing them by thicker pieces until a given limit was reached.[34]

Much thumping was caused by the unevenness of the rail-joints, the wheels depressing one rail end as much as half an inch, and then hammering the next one; where the joints did not coincide with those on the opposite rail, the consequent rocking and swinging of the carriages caused the passengers great discomfort and hastened the deterioration of vehicles and permanent way. Fragments of iron broken from the rails littered the track.

The decision was taken in November 1833 to employ 50 lb. fish-bellied rails and to experiment with the parallel type, of the same weight. Several hundred tons of each were ordered, the latter being of the same pattern as those used on the Wigan Railway, and in May 1834 the descending lines on the Inclined Planes were relaid, in each case half of each type being used.

By September relaying was proceeding at various parts of the line, both types of rail being used. The sound 35 lb. rails taken up were put aside for use in the new Lime Street Tunnel, where locomotives would not run. At the same time wooden sleepers were being replaced by stone blocks, and the original chairs by heavier ones. The stones were now set diagonally or 'diamond-wise', the corners almost touching to form a practically continuous line; the object was to make the four sides of each block more easily accessible for ballasting and maintenance.

The 50 lb. rail was still not strong enough, and in February 1835 Harford Davies & Co were asked for 300 tons of 60 lb. parallel rail at £8 per ton, the price paid by the North Union Railway. By December 75 lb. rail had been settled upon for the main line and the Company decided to use the surplus revenue from the half-year just ending, after paying a dividend of 4½%, to purchasing the heavy rail in order to put as much of the railway as possible into good condition before the Grand Junction and North Union Railways' traffic came upon it. An advantage of the 75 lb. rail was that sleepers could be placed at 5 ft. intervals, a welcome economy since the demand for British rails had increased to such an extent that the price had soared by 85% during the period June 1835 to February 1836.

All the new rails were of the parallel type, and about 2500 tons were laid in the summer of 1836; they now cost £14 5s. per ton from various makers. In November a mile of line was laid with the GJR pattern heavy rails and chairs, using compressed oak keys. The 60 lb. rails were still being bought, but not for the main line. In 1838 the line down Sutton Incline was again relaid, now with 75 lb. rail, and the Lime Street Tunnel with 60 lb. By 1839 all the original rails had been replaced; their sale at £9 per ton, and the old chairs at £8, partly offset the cost of relaying the line, although the work caused considerable inconvenience over nearly five years.

During the later stages of the relaying it was decided to discontinue the use of stone sleepers. In September 1832 the Board asked for a return of the number broken since September 1830; although there is no record of this number, in November 1836 it was reported that 200 were broken between the Edge Hill Locomotive Shed and the western end of Olive Mount Cutting – about 100 yards. There had been instances of deliberate damage being done to both stone and wooden sleepers by platelayers to ensure continued employment. Until 1834 there was no method of preserving wood, but in May of that year the Company looked into the cost of adopting Kyan's process for preventing dry rot and decay in timber, cordage and canvas, by the use of corrosive sublimate; they were not very impressed by experiments carried out on the tunnel rope. However, the process seems to have been improved by 1837, for the Company then purchased for £80 a licence to install a trough 20ft × 4ft × 4ft for 'steeping the larch sleepers'. The sleepers, 8ft × 8in. × 5in., were 'Kyanized' and the oak keys prepared by compression in one of Bramah's presses, in the Company's yard at Crown Street. From then onwards the stone sleepers were replaced and the opportunity was taken of increasing the width between the tracks to 5ft 2in.[35]

The points, called switches for many years, were of similar design to those of the S&DR, although there was some variety on different parts of the line. A pair of movable tongues, tapering at one end and loosely pivoted at the other, were mounted on iron plates and shifted independently by hand; they were then secured by wedges or crossing plates which were attached by light chains to the bed-plates to prevent their being stolen or mislaid. The wheel flanges supported the weight of the train as it passed over the bed-plate, lifting the wheel-treads slightly clear of the movable sections of rail which guided it. A crossing from one line to the other occupied 45ft of track. Another pattern used pieces of rail which were inserted or removed as necessary to divert a train. These, in use in 1833, were partly of wood, presumably for ease of handling on account of their large size, and were secured in position by hammer and iron pin. A reference in June 1832 to *Venus* being thrown off the line at Warrington Junction '. . . owing to the slide-over rails not having been removed after the crossing of a train' probably refers to this type. The wooden switches were in use at least as late as 1836; they were considered to be the safest, and engines which could not negotiate them at their trials were rejected.

These early switches had no automatic indication of the direction in which they were set and it was the driver's responsibility to check by observation while approaching slowly.

A new type of switch designed by John Cummings was tried at a siding on Chat Moss in June 1835 with a view to its adoption on the main line and in January 1838 the Treasurer was asked to see if some improvement could be made in the sidings, especially at the top of the inclined planes '. . . by eccentric switches, allowing a train of goods to proceed direct in and out of a siding without backing, as at present practised.'

By April 1839 sliding rails on the L&BR were being replaced by Fox's points 'with tell-tale or signal post attached.' It appears that these, or something similar, were adopted on the L&MR eventually, for when the Board of Trade wrote objecting to '. . . loose cross rails on lines open to the public', and recommending self-acting switches, the Company replied that the latter were already in use. The points in use in 1846 consisted of two 9ft cast-iron plates fixed on blocks or sleepers, with a single movable rail on each plate; the rails were connected by an iron rod which moved them laterally on the operation of a lever.

The question of permanent way maintenance by contract was considered in January 1832, when Dixon was asked to suggest the most suitable section to be let, but some directors were opposed to the idea, and it was shelved. The following year John Dent entered into a maintenance contract to commence on 1 October, but after the first week no men or materials had appeared, although Dent himself had been seen several times, on each occasion drunk. The contract was declared null and void, and James Scott and John Cummings took on the work in November initially at

£252 each per month; they had been until this time superintendents in the employ of the Railway. The Company supplied rails, sleepers and ballast and the cost was about £200 per mile; constant employment was provided for three platelayers to each mile of track. Their contract was renewed for the next two years, Scott being responsible for Edge Hill to Newton, and Cummings for the remainder, but in November 1836 it was reported that the line was very much out of order. Edward Woods, now Chief Engineer of the L&MR was instructed to employ fresh platelayers, charging the cost to the contractor, and when Scott protested in February 1837, by then the 'late contractor', the matter went to arbitration.

Continuous experiments and observations were carried out with a view to perfecting the track, and numerous plans and inventions were examined. In February 1833 the Dublin & Kingstown Railway asked the Company to test some rails, and a 100-yd stretch of their track was laid near Wavertree Lane. Another length of track under test for the GJR was laid nearby in October 1834; this was of Stephenson's new pattern with bearings 5ft apart. The Company considered that having permitted the experiments, the rails had become their property, but they agreed to return the D&KR rails, when replaced, as that Company appeared to be in a desperate state.

Joseph Locke conducted experiments in August 1833 on corrosion, discovering that a rail on the south main line lost about 1 oz per month over a period of 18 months, during which time 600,000 tons of traffic had passed over it; tests for wear and rusting in August 1840 yielded similar results, each accounting for the same loss of weight of 2 oz per yard each year. All broken rails were left by the lineside to be examined by the engineer before being collected each week and taken to Crown Street for sale.

In July 1833 William Jessop submitted drawings and a description of a cast-iron rail and Locke of an improved chair; both were referred to Stephenson who does not appear to have recommended them. The Board asked James Price of Gateshead for further details of his plan for reducing maintenance costs in November 1835, and read Thomas Parkin's description of his concrete sleepers in December 1836. Another invention of this period was Cassell's patent bituminous composition, a kind of plastic capable of being moulded, and claimed to be a substitute for wood or stone wherever these materials were used on the railway. One invention, James White's new chair, was given a trial in March 1837.

A successful experiment was carried out in May 1836, when wooden keys were inserted into the rail joints to reduce the noise; the expedient tried at first on half a mile of track, was later extended over most of the line.

Dixon strongly urged the use of T-section parallel rail rather than the type with a lower web, on grounds of safety. The former would fit tightly into the slot in the chair, and '. . . if they do work loose . . . the road continues safe although a rail or two may, until repaired, jingle or rattle a little as each train passes'.[36] With the other pattern, the chair required a slot the width of the web, and iron or wooden keys; the danger lay in the possibility of the key falling out at a rail joint and the rail ends moving laterally an inch or more out of alignment. This risk was overcome later with the introduction of fish-plates.

By the time the railway had been entirely relaid the maintenance had reverted to the Company. Staff records for 1842 show 132 men employed on 'maintenance of Way', including 18 engaged solely on repairing walls and fences. Of the 114 permanent way men, two were overlookers, 29 foremen and all but seven of the rest unskilled labourers. The overlookers, in charge of half the line each, earned £2 10s. per week, the foremen, responsible for about a mile each, 3s. 6d. a day, and the platelayers, 2s. 8d., a weekly total of £116.

CHAPTER THREE

The Rainhill Locomotive Trials

It was clearly the Company's intention to adopt steam power in some form for the railway from the beginning and although much of the evidence during the Committee Stage of the first Bill concerned the locomotive, the question was largely avoided during the passage of the second Bill. The Rennies were not convinced of the superiority of the steam locomotive and were not in favour of its use for passenger trains until such time as improvements in its reliability and performance made its use expedient.

By the autumn of 1828 it did not appear that any spectacular improvement had been made in the locomotive since it first went into regular service in 1812. Of 50 or so that had been built in England about half were in regular use, almost all on colliery lines; 17 had been built by Stephenson, but the most powerful engine at work then was Hackworth's *Royal George* on the S&DR.

The alternative method of propulsion was by rope and stationary engine, a system employed on several of the colliery lines, sometimes in conjunction with gravity-running down inclines. Thus the choice before the Board lay between the locomotive, or 'travelling engine' as it was still called, and the stationary engine, each method having its fervent advocates.

By this time the stationary steam engine was a comparatively efficient and reliable machine, having been steadily improved over a period of a century, and no dramatic developments in its performance or design were anticipated. The locomotive on the other hand was still very much in its infancy, but while the existing examples were slow, clumsy, at times dangerous and always subject to mechanical failure, radical improvements appeared only to await the day when leading inventors and engineers could be induced to give it their serious attention.

The first step taken by the Company to resolve the problem, after a discussion on 29 September 1828, was to despatch Messrs Cropper, Moss and Booth to Darlington to observe and report upon the S&DR where locomotives, horses and fixed engines were employed, and at the same time to view some of the many colliery railways concentrated in that district.

Cropper was strongly in favour of fixed engines, while Booth advocated locomotives; Moss was probably open-minded on the question. Their visit took place in October and their Report to the Board seems to have been inconclusive. It was referred to Stephenson who in turn reported upon it on 5 November in a long document[1] presenting all the points in favour of the locomotive and all the disadvantages attending the stationary engine. Not least of these was the estimate that 54 fixed engines, each of 19hp and costing £64,800 would be required, and that the five needed across Chat Moss would have to be supported on piles at considerable extra expense. He also pointed out that an engine working 12 hours a day could be expected to break down once a year, and if it took only three hours to repair, the 54 engines could account for a complete stoppage of traffic of about a fortnight a year, since the failure of one engine would immobilise the whole line.

Stephenson calculated that a maximum of 1200 tons per day could be moved by stationary engines, and that 12 minutes would be required for travelling the distance between each engine station, including the time taken in changing ropes and signalling to the next engine.

On 6 November the directors discussed Stephenson's Report at great length and instructed Booth to write to Mr Benjamin Thompson seeking permission for a deputation, including '. . . one or two professional or scientific men' to visit the Brunton and Shields Railway, where stationary engines worked the entire line. In the meantime Cropper and others had written to the Company urging the use of stationary engines, and on 17 November the Board decided to invite James Walker, Civil Engineer, of Limehouse, London, and J. U. Rastrick of Stourbridge, to report on the railways of Darlington and Newcastle. Both were busy men, however, and neither could undertake the commission until the new year. Meanwhile early in December Stephenson and Locke went to Darlington and spent about a fortnight conducting a series of experiments with the locomotives there while Mills was inspecting the L&MR for Telford.

Walker joined Rastrick at Stourbridge on 10 January 1829 (where he saw the latter's *Stourbridge Lion*, destined for the USA),[2] and both arrived at Liverpool on the 12th to receive specific instructions as to the points on which their professional opinion was required. Briefly this amounted to an unbiased assessment of the comparative merits of fixed and locomotive engines, their cost, performance and reliability; which was best adapted to moving up to 3000 tons of goods daily and conveying passengers at a minimum speed of 8 mph. After spending two days on the L&MR works, they inspected the Bolton and Leigh Railway on 15 January and the Blenkinsop locomotives of the Middleton Railway, Leeds the following day. From 17 January until the end of the month they saw practically all there was to see of railways in the north-east. At Darlington they came upon a party of American engineers from the Baltimore & Ohio Railroad also engaged in collecting data, and later Rastrick sought from Hackworth copies of the results of their experiments.[3]

The two engineers, having met in Oxford to compare notes, submitted separate reports which were read on 9 March. They had not, however, reached any definite conclusion as to the best method of operating the railway, other than to suggest that if the directors contemplated catering for heavy traffic immediately upon opening the line, then stationary reciprocating engines would be preferable on grounds of 'economy, despatch, safety and convenience'; locomotive engines were recommended only if the Company should decide 'to proceed by degrees and to proportion the power of conveyance to the demand ...', but with '... two fixed Engines upon Rainhill and Sutton planes, to draw up the loco-motive Engines, as well as the goods and carriages.' The Rainhill engines, it was suggested, would give the directors valuable experience of stationary engine working on that part of the line and enable them to judge whether to adopt the system throughout. On the whole both engineers tended to favour the stationary engine, having been very impressed with the operation of the Brunton and Shields Railway, but their preference was very marginal, probably because they hesitated to stake their reputations on opinions and advice stated too dogmatically; time had disproved other theories and Giles's derision of the plan to cross Chat Moss did not look so humorous now. Rastrick showed complete impartiality since, apart from the locomotives he was building for the USA, he was then constructing the *Agenoria* for the Shutt End Railway. Perhaps the most valuable suggestion, certainly the one with the most far-reaching consequences, came at the end of Walker's report. It was that the Company might offer a premium to the builder of the best locomotive submitted for trials on the railway as an incentive to those with inventive talent.

Very little reliable data on the locomotive was available at this time. Neither the optimism of its advocates nor the scepticism of its critics rested on much more than enthusiasm or prejudice unsupported by facts and figures. When most locomotives worked on the coalfields the fuel consumption and cost were matters of little importance, and speeds of 3 or 4 mph were acceptable. Even George Stephenson, who had built the S&DR and supplied most of its engines, had to spend that fortnight with Locke on the line before he could produce any figures of cost and performance approaching accuracy. In a period of six months, however, the L&MR Board had received six reports and a volume of correspondence, and had amassed more information on mechanical traction than had ever been gathered together before. The last of these reports, prepared by Robert Stephenson and Locke in March 1829, was mainly concerned with refuting Walker and Rastrick's arguments and presenting again the case for the locomotive; it was received by the Board on 20 April.[4]

At their meeting on that day the directors decided that no system would be adopted that might inhibit the Company from benefiting from any future developments in mechanical transport, and the locomotive was the machine where more improvements were likely to be made. The Directors, on the motion of Richard Harrison, resolved to adopt Walker's suggestion and offer a premium of £500 for a 'Locomotive Engine which shall be a decided improvement on those now in use ...' The advertisement, dated 25 April and addressed to Engineers and Iron Founders, appeared in the *Liverpool Mercury* on 1 May and in at least four other papers at about the same time.

Meanwhile the Board awaited the arrival of Stephenson's new locomotive, ordered on 16 March;

it appeared on 13 July having travelled from Newcastle to Carlisle, thence by steam packet to Liverpool, and was expected to be at work at Olive Mount Cutting in a week. This was the *Twin Sisters*.

For nearly three years the Board had been receiving proposals from inventors, engineers and others for operating the line, the earliest of which appears to be the offer made by Professor Leslie in October 1826 of a scheme for working inclined planes, while in June 1827 John Vallance of Brighton proposed the adoption of his tunnel and vacuum atmospheric system. The following December the Company was offered Samuel Brown's Gas Vacuum Engine and Gurney's loco-motive engine for coaches and passengers, but Stephenson advised against them all. The summer of 1828 brought an offer from D. Gordon, the patentee of a new Steam Carriage, of 200 shares in his invention, but this was declined on the grounds that the Railway was not authorised to invest in such a scheme; before the year was out Robert Wright, an accountant of Edinburgh, had had his plan and description of a new locomotive rejected by Stephenson. After the announcement of the £500 premium, Brown asked if his Gas Engine would be eligible and was told that it would, while Thomas Hill of Leeds, who offered the Company a locomotive in August 1829, was advised to enter it in the competition. During this month Timothy Burstall of Leith and O. W. Hahr[5] advised the Company that they were entering locomotives for trial, and in September enquiries about the conditions were received from William Crawshay of Merthyr Tydfil and W. Morgan of Broad Street, London, the proprietor of a patent steam engine. While the trials were actually taking place yet another offer of a locomotive was received from Messrs Anderson and James of London, the decision upon which was postponed.

In the event, however, there were only four serious entries, although other machines which did not qualify for the premium were exhibited. It was said that some engineers, who might have been capable of building an efficient locomotive, were unwilling to risk doing so on the off-chance of winning £500, but without any guarantee of reimbursement of their expenses or the purchase of their locomotive.

The conditions governing the contest were framed by Sandars, Cropper, Moss, Benson and Rotherham, but it is inconceivable that Stephenson, as the Company's chief engineer, and the principal locomotive builder of that time, should not have had a hand in the matter, together with Booth who had some knowledge of engines and machinery. When Stephenson announced his decision to enter for the premium, Booth suggested that the locomotive be constructed with a multitubular boiler, the tubes carrying the hot gases from the firebox and thus greatly increasing the heating surface to which the water was exposed with a consequent increase in the production of steam. He also proposed that the engine be entered jointly by himself and Stephenson, a suggestion readily accepted.

Booth was not the inventor of the fire-tube boiler, the patent for which had been granted to James Neville of Shad Thames, London, in 1826, and widely published in 1828, in which year M. Seguin applied the principle to one of Stephenson's old Killingworth locomotives. The fact that no mention was made of Neville's patent at the time of the trials suggests that it was invalid in that the fire-tube boiler was invented even earlier. It appears that the engine was planned in May 1829, and the drawings made by Robert Stephenson and Co.'s draughtsman, G. H. Phipps, assisted by William Hutchinson. It was planned specifically to win the prize and its capacity for useful work afterwards was an important but secondary consideration.

The actual construction started in June and from Robert Stephenson's letters to Booth on its progress, it is clear that work was well advanced by the beginning of August and complete by the end of the month, except that 'The Mercurial gauge and some other nick nacks are yet to be put on.'[6]

The engine was named *Rocket* by George Stephenson, from a reference to Congreave's military rockets in the *Quarterly Review* article on the Railway of 1825.[7] The main features of the *Rocket* were its boiler containing 25 three-inch copper tubes, its 8in × 17in. cylinders set at an angle of 35° from the horizontal, the chimney bolted directly to the front end of the boiler, but with its base spread out to cover the tube-ends and its driving wheels, the spokes and rims of which were of oak. The nave was of cast iron, and an iron band and flanged tyre were shrunk on to the wheel. The frames, of very light construction, were 4in. × 1in. wrought iron bars laid flat and bent where necessary; leaf springs were fitted above the driving axle and below the trailing axle. Two safety valves were fitted, one of a lock-up spring type in a small metal cover, secured by two padlocks, and the other a weighted lever type accessible from the footplate.

On 2 September the engine was given its first trials on the Killingworth Railway, when some minor defects became apparent; the reversing gear required adjustment and the technique of using coke had to be mastered. With a load of about 24 tons *Rocket* managed 8 mph up an incline and 12 mph on the level. Robert Stephenson thought the experiment was not as successful as it might have been, but that '... the Engine is capable of doing as much if not more than set forth in the stipulation.' Edward Fletcher, later locomotive superintendent of the NER, then in the last year of his apprenticeship, helped in the construction and attended the trials.

The modifications made, further tests were apparently carried out for the locomotive was delayed in Newcastle for some days, and was not finally despatched to Liverpool until 12 September. Dismantled, the parts reached Carlisle by horse-drawn waggon on 14 September and four days later arrived at Liverpool by the steamer *Cumberland* from Bowness-on-Solway. From the time of its arrival it took about a fortnight to assemble *Rocket*, subject it to further trials and paint it.

Robert Stephenson asked Booth to have the tender made at Liverpool as '... the coach makers that made the last tender will make one neater than our men.' It was built by Thomas Worsdell, and had a strong wooden frame on four cast iron wheels with outside bearings. The coke was stored on the floor beneath a 300-gallon water cask.

To create an impression of speed and lightness the *Rocket* was painted in the fashion of a mail coach; the wheels, boiler cladding and tender were yellow, lined in black, the chimney was white and the water butt green; the copper pipes and brass fittings were highly polished and the finished machine looked far removed from the ponderous black engines of the coalfields.

Some of Stephenson's men from the Forth Street Works, with Hutchinson in charge, were at Rainhill to ensure that all last-minute adjustments were carried out and the night before the trials started they appear to have touched up the paintwork, for Robert Stannard's young son, riding on the tender the following evening, became stuck to the tacky paintwork of the cask.[8] The chimney could not have retained its pristine condition without a coat of paint every night.

The *Novelty*, said to have taken its name from a theatre, was built in London by John Braithwaite to the designs of the Swedish engineer John Ericsson; in appearance and construction it was unlike any locomotive that had previously been built, although it bore some resemblance to a fire-engine Ericsson

30 Rocket *as she appeared at the Rainhill Trials, October 1829*

had recently patented. Its wheels were 4ft 2in. in diameter and placed 6ft apart, and its 6in. × 12in. vertical cylinders drove a cranked axle through bell cranks. The boiler was 10ft long but only 13in. in diameter, and contained a tapering flue which returned on itself twice; its water capacity was 45 gallons. Fuel was fed into the firebox from the top and a draught was provided by bellows worked by the engine. No tender was required as both fuel and water were carried on the engine frames, four bushels of coke in two small baskets and about 120 gallons of water in a tank of 20 cu. ft. Specialised parts of the locomotive were supplied by various firms, the springs by Thrupp and the wheels by Jones & Co. According to its makers, *Novelty* was of 8 hp and it weighed only 3 tons 17 cwt in working order.

The engine had been designed and built in the short space of seven weeks, Ericsson only having learned of the contest after more than three months had elapsed. He alone of the three principal contenders had never before built a locomotive, and he was the only one unable to test his engine, since no railway existed near London upon which trials could be conducted. *Novelty* was carried by Pickfords on the canal from London to Liverpool and they also took it on to Rainhill. Its dark blue paintwork and array of burnished copper fittings gave it a striking appearance and it quickly became the favourite among a large section of the spectators.

Timothy Hackworth, builder of the *Sans Pareil*, was Engineer and Manager of the S&DR; his salary was small and he was a comparatively poor man. With a few hundred pounds remaining from a legacy, he decided to build an experimental engine and his employers gave him permission to erect it in their Shildon Workshops at his own expense and in his own limited time. But their works were so small and ill-equipped that they had difficulty in maintaining their own locomotives. *Sans Pareil* was designed in odd moments and at night, and the work distributed among several engineering firms; Longridge's Bedlington Iron Works made the boiler, Robert Stephenson & Co. the cylinders, and other parts were made elsewhere and in some cases not delivered until well after the promised date.

The engine was assembled by working day and night but the time was so far spent that its construction was very hurried and after allowing some days for its transport to Liverpool by road, no thorough test was possible; a run of a few miles at midnight on the Aycliffe Level was all the trial it got, and it reached Liverpool only just in time to qualify for the competition.

Sans Pareil incorporated some of the features of the larger and very successful *Royal George*. Its boiler contained a large return flue from the fire-grate through the boiler and back to the chimney which was sited alongside the fireplace. The wheels were 4ft

31 Novelty

6in. in diameter, coupled, and fitted with hardwood spokes. Vertical cylinders of 7in. diameter and 18in. stroke drove the rear wheels through connecting rods working directly on to crank pins. The engine had an efficient blastpipe, Hackworth being more alive to the value of this method of urging the fire than most of his contemporaries. He achieved this by joining the two separate exhaust pipes, and running a single pipe into the chimney, although he did this to save weight, perhaps without being fully aware of its effect. Despite subsequent claims made on his behalf, however, he did not invent the blast pipe; the action of waste steam discharged into the chimney was known to Trevithick in 1804 and described in scientific journals in 1805 and 1806.

Robert Stephenson kept a pretty close watch on the progress of *Sans Pareil* during its construction, and his letters to Booth contain the latest information gleaned from Shildon, including on one occasion two rough sketches of Hackworth's boiler. Despite assurances that its design had a number of defects, a certain amount of anxiety can be detected as it was discovered that the locomotive's gear was similar to that employed on 'the large engine at Darlington', viz the *Royal George*.

The tender, which was pushed in front of the engine, appears to have been made in Liverpool; contemporary illustrations show it as identical with the one attached to the *Rocket*, and John Dixon, referring to Hackworth's dissatisfaction with the arrangements in general, said '... nothing our men did for him was right; we could not please him with the Tender nor anything.'[9] The fireman rode on the tender and the driver on a shelf-like footplate behind the boiler. *Sans Pareil* was painted green, yellow and black.

Timothy Burstall of Leith (Edinburgh) had built a steam road coach in 1824 and had patented an improved version in 1826. The locomotive *Perseverance* he entered for the Rainhill competition was, so far as may be judged from the scanty information that has come down, based upon the second model. It ran on four wheels, uncoupled, and two vertical cylinders drove a countershaft which turned the axle by gear

32 Sans Pareil

wheels. It weighed 2 tons 17 cwt and carried its own fuel and water. The boiler was upright and contained no flues or tubes, '... the heated air and flame escaping up the chimney immediately from the fireplace.' An old lithograph of a 'Locomotive Steam Engine of Mr Timothy Burstall's Construction' probably represents the engine as it appeared at Rainhill.[10] A scale beneath the illustration indicates that the engine's overall length was 12ft.

Perseverance had arrived at Millfield yard[11] by 28 September, but unfortunately it was damaged during transit from Liverpool to Rainhill, apparently falling to the ground when a chain broke during unloading operations; one of the cranks was injured, a pipe broken and the engine probably strained. Burstall spent the next fortnight making adjustments to the machine.

Two other machines were entered, but were not serious competitors. Thomas Shaw Brandreth, barrister and former director of the L&MR who opposed the employment of steam locomotives on grounds of their supposed danger, produced his *Cycloped*, a contraption powered by two horses. It consisted of a four-wheeled open truck the floor of which was an endless platform of wooden planks, 4in. wide and 1½in. thick, attached at their ends to ropes which were in turn supported by a series of rollers. At each end of the carriage the rope passed round a drum; that at the rear transmitted the drive to the axle through spur wheels. The machine was put in motion when the tethered horses, standing side by side and separated by a long barrier, attempted to walk or trot, whereupon the platform was driven round by their hooves causing the drums to revolve. A simple system of gears enabled the horses to start the carriage in low gear and to trot comfortably after it had gathered speed. A secondary purpose of the gearing was to ensure that the horses travelled in the direction in which they were facing. *Cycloped*, complete with two horses, weighed about three tons.[12]

Ross Winans,[13] who came over with the B&ORR party of engineers in 1828 and stayed to experiment with waggons on the L&MR, invented a 'Manumotive Carriage' propelled by two men. It was

33 Perseverance

simply one of his anti-friction waggons cranked by winch and lever, and at its trials in July doubts were expressed as to the propriety of passengers allowing men to toil for long hours that they might ride in comfort. Nevertheless, both the horse and manual system of traction still had their advocates years after the steam locomotive was fairly established.

Meanwhile the Company made its own preparations for the forthcoming contest. On 31 August the Board decided that the trials should be held at Rainhill, and Stephenson was ordered to prepare a double line there, with a single track down to the Roby Embankment. The Company arranged for the competing locomotives to be erected and prepared at its Millfield Yard by its own men, under the direction of the owners, or their superintendents, and on 7 September George Stephenson was instructed to have a temporary lock-up shed erected at Rainhill '. . . for the safe-keeping of the Specimen Engines at night and during wet weather.' A weighing machine of seven tons capacity was also set up at Rainhill.

On 28 September the directors noted that two

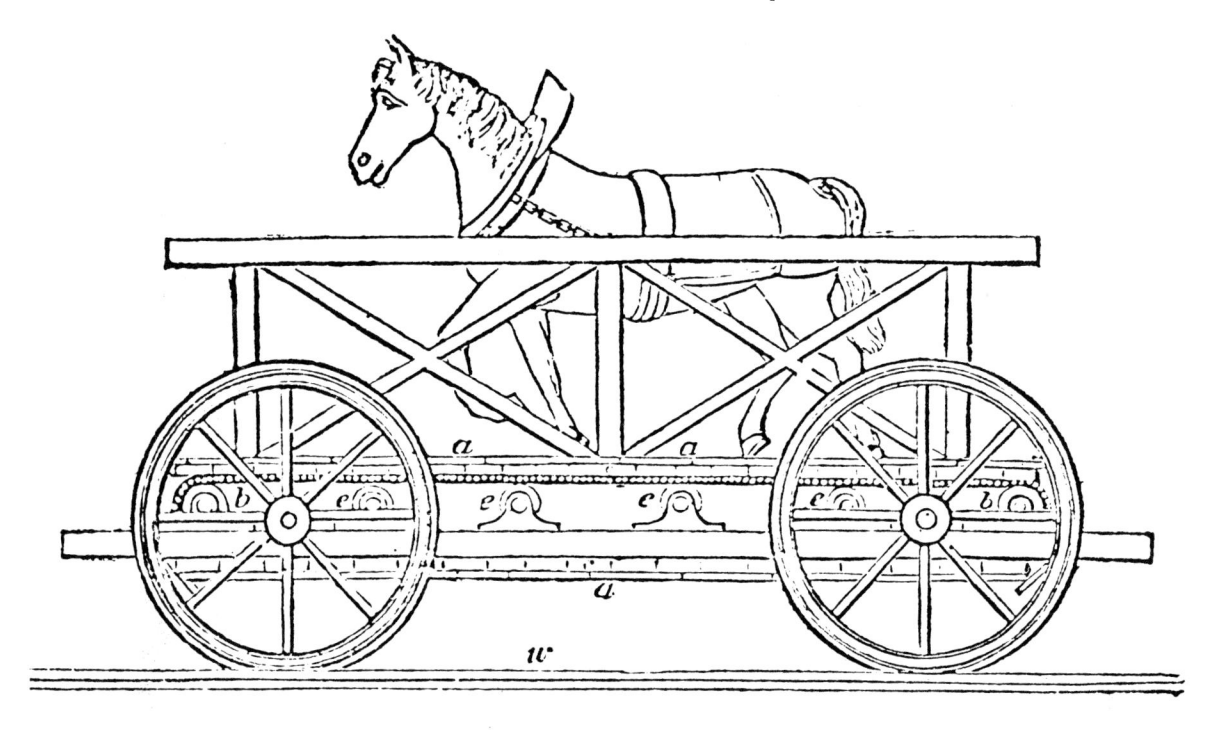

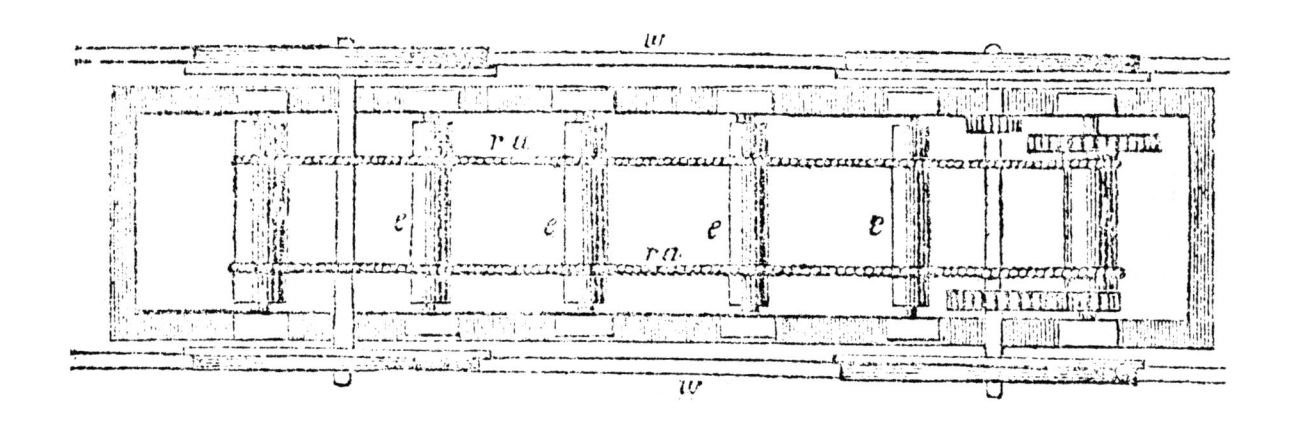

34 Cycloped

specimen locomotives had arrived at Millfield, Burstall's and that of Booth and Stephenson; *Cycloped* was on its way.

A great deal of public attention had been focussed upon the trials by the Press and it was known that engineers and railway promoters from all quarters would be taking a close professional interest in the proceedings. For the more distinguished guests a large stand was erected at Kendrick's Cross, ¼-mile east of the Rainhill Bridge and on 5 October the Board resolved to have 300 of its employees, the day men from the works, each armed with a staff, to act as special constables to control the less exalted spectators and keep them off the line.

Three judges were appointed, J. U. Rastrick, Nicholas Wood and John Kennedy. Rastrick and Wood were thoroughly familiar with the steam locomotive, although the latter had recently ridiculed the idea that locomotives could travel at over 12 mph. Kennedy, representing the directors, was the originator of several improvements in textile machinery, among other inventive activities. The judges were required to communicate the results of the trials to the directors, who reserved to themselves the awarding of the premium.

The general stipulations of the contest had been published on 25 April 1829, but these amounted to little more than the minimum requirements dictated by considerations of safety and the Company's Acts.

On 6 October, nearly a week after the closing date for delivery of the engines at Liverpool, and the day on which the proceedings at Rainhill started, more detailed conditions, under the title of 'The Ordeal', were published over the signatures of the three judges, to be followed on 8 October by new conditions, printed on a buff card about the size of a postcard, the judges having decided that the original ones were not sufficiently explicit. Essentially the conditions were that the engine should be capable of hauling three times its own weight in working order over a distance of 70 miles at a speed of at least 10 mph. Each engine was to make ten return trips, roughly equivalent to the distance from Liverpool to Manchester, and after a fresh supply of fuel and water was taken on, to repeat the performance.

The final preparations were made on Monday, 5 October; four posts were set up, the starting post, near the Weighing Shed, and, one furlong distant, Post No 1 at which Rastrick was to be stationed; after 1½-miles, Nicholas Wood's Post No 2 and 220 yards farther on the stopping post, the total distance of 1¾-miles including ⅛-mile at each end for gathering speed and stopping.

The organisation and general supervision of the

35 *The Rainhill Trials; from left to right,* Novelty, Sans Pareil, Rocket. *Probably conjectural, as the grandstand was ¼-mile east of the Rainhill Bridge*

contest was in the capable hands of Vignoles, who had no financial or other interest in any of the entries; he was later congratulated publicly by Rastrick on having discharged his duties to the satisfaction of all concerned.

The trials opened on Tuesday, 6 October, a fine autumn day, and from an early hour the spectators began to congregate along the line. Soon all the roads leading to Kendrick's Cross were choked with vehicles bringing visitors from Liverpool and Warrington, St Helens, Manchester and other parts of the country; the lowest estimate was 10,000. The gathering was likened to a great race meeting and the presence of several Quakers caused some flippant comment. The only two public houses within miles of the course did unparalleled business that day and the proprietoress of the Railway Tavern was congratulated for having prudently set aside a room for the better class of visitors.

Engineers and men of science had travelled hundreds of miles to witness the event, and there was undoubtedly a larger gathering of such men by the lineside that day than had ever assembled anywhere before. They held a meeting on the course, adjourning later to the Waterloo Hotel, and resolved that, before dispersing, they would give a dinner for the directors and officers of the railway on the following Saturday. A band played by the grandstand throughout the day, and shortly after 10 o'clock the directors, each wearing a white ribbon in his buttonhole, arrived from Huyton by a train drawn by one of Stephenson's engines, probably *Twin Sisters*.

The first day was devoted to demonstration runs by the competitors and the times and weights recorded were approximate and unofficial. The first runs were made by the *Rocket* which drew about 12½ tons at 12 mph and attained 18 mph running light. It was said to have emitted very little smoke, but to have dropped red-hot cinders all along the track. Hackworth then ran *Sans Pareil* light, but made no attempt to test it with any load. *Rocket* was driven throughout the trials by Mark Wakefield, one of the regular drivers of *Lancashire Witch* during the construction of the railway; William Gowland,[14] the driver of the *Royal George* on the S&DR, was Hackworth's engineman on *Sans Pareil*. Winans' machine was then demonstrated; carrying the two men who worked it and six passengers, it '... moved with no great velocity', probably handicapped by the fact that one of its wheels had been damaged during the afternoon by Hackworth's engine.

The crowds who thought the *Rocket*'s speed of

36 *William Gowland (d. 1875), driver of* Sans Pareil *at Rainhill*

18 mph incredible were now treated to the spectacle of the little *Novelty* flashing along at nearly 30 mph, with no load, and only Ericsson and Braithwaite riding on it; it quickly became the favourite among the general public.

Finally *Cycloped* was exercised, drawing some waggons round which clung about 50 persons and which brought the total weight, including the machine and horses, up to five tons. A speed of exactly 5 mph was achieved, the relative speed of the horses being only 1¼ mph. Neither *Cycloped* nor Winans' machine appear to have taken any further part in the Rainhill trials.

On Wednesday, 7 October, *Novelty* opened the proceedings but after doing one trip loaded, at 20¾ mph, the bellows burst and further trials were suspended. By this time it was raining heavily, and although most of the engineers were present, few other spectators remained. Stephenson, Hackworth and Brandreth made several exhibition runs, but the railway became so clogged with mud that further trials were abandoned.

The first serious trials under the inspection of the

judges and complying with their revised rules issued that day, took place on Thursday, 8 October, when *Rocket* was tested. Under the rules, it was weighed before 8 o'clock in the morning and then steam was raised, the load prepared and other preparations made. It started at 10.36 a.m. and finished its first series of runs at 1.48 p.m. Taking on fresh supplies of fuel and water, and with steam blowing off all the time, it started again just after 2 p.m. and finished at 5 p.m. Its 40 journeys had been made without any kind of hitch and after allowing time for oiling and greasing the engine and waggons, taking on water and reversing, an average speed of about 16 mph, with a maximum of just over 29 mph, was recorded. Speeds on the outward trips, travelling eastwards, were higher than on the return runs, when the engine running in reverse pushed the waggons back to the starting post. Towards the end of the proceedings, as the *Rocket* came up to the stopping post, some directors and their friends – Robert Gladstone, Henry Moss and Doctor Traill among them – took turns to ride along the course.

It was apparently intended to give *Novelty* its trials on Friday, but Braithwaite and Ericsson secured a postponement of one day on the grounds that they had not had time to comply with the amended conditions. Hackworth exercised his engine, but without attempting to submit it to an actual trial. There were again large crowds of onlookers that day and a number of men climbed aboard the train attached to *Sans Pareil*, refusing to get off when requested. At the moment of starting the engineers uncoupled the engine, leaving train and irate passengers stranded, to the delight of the spectators. There is no record of any other activity that day, although it is said that Stephenson, disconcerted by the more efficient blast produced in *Sans Pareil*, discovered that it resulted from the single exhaust pipe entering the chimney. He hastily had a union pipe made for the *Rocket* in Warrington and brought to Rainhill slung behind the stage coach; it was fitted immediately on arrival, apparently during the night.[15]

Large crowds assembled on the Saturday to see their favourite, and with a load of 6 tons 17 cwt she started off in fine style. Only a single trip in the easterly direction was made, however, when on the return journey the engineman closed the cock between the feed pump and the boiler, and the resulting pressure of water burst the feed pipe. The Company had not provided any facilities at Rainhill for repairs of this nature, and it was necessary to send to Prescot two miles away, to have it mended. This mishap effectively finished *Novelty*'s chances of completing her trials that day, and while it was being repaired Stephenson brought out the *Rocket* and made two runs, without tender or load, at 30 mph. The improved performance was attributed by some writers to the modified blast pipe.

During the afternoon *Novelty*, now once again in working order, made several exhibition runs, hauling the Directors' Carriage with 45 passengers at 30 mph. The times were taken by Charles Vignoles, who rode on the engine during these tests. On one of these trips, 'The gentleman[16] at the brake of the wheel, not being sufficiently experienced, the engine was not checked so soon as it ought to have been . . .', and the train went careering some way down the Sutton Inclined Plane.

The spectators were very impressed by all they saw that day, but Braithwaite and Ericsson unwisely decided to take the locomotive to pieces in an attempt to improve its performance and reliability, a task that occupied three days and nights.

All cares and anxieties were laid aside that evening, however, on the occasion of the engineers' dinner. Arranged to form a climax to the proceedings on what was expected to be the last day of the trials, it was a most convivial gathering, conducted in the style of the great public dinners held in London; Rastrick was chairman, with Hartley and Wood as vice-chairmen. Altogether 61 sat down to dinner, including about 20 guests.

'On the cloth being drawn, the health of "The King" was given from the chair, in a bumper toast which was drunk with three times three. Tune by the Harmonic Band, "God Save the King".
'The next toast was "The Liverpool and Manchester Railway, with our best wishes for its success". This toast was drunk with thrice three most enthusiastic cheers. Tune, "Off she goes".'

Thirty-one further toasts are detailed in the report, and there were several others. Hartley gave 'Mr Telford and the Institution of Civil Engineers', to which Vignoles replied in the absence of Telford, whom he described as the instigator of our most important public works. When the list of persons and institutions directly connected with the railway was exhausted, they moved on to the 'Engineers of Sweden', the 'Trigonometrical Survey of the United Kingdoms' and 'May every town in the kingdom be united by iron'. The company separated just before midnight, '. . . the steam of good fellowship and excellent feeling having been kept up during the whole of the meeting.'[17]

For the next two days, apart from any activities on the part of the competitors and their assistants, all was quiet at Rainhill; on Monday the weekly Board Meeting was held as usual at Liverpool. Tuesday, 13 October, saw the judges at their tents once more for the trials of Hackworth's *Sans Pareil*. The trial of this engine had been delayed through boiler leakage and much time had been spent in running copper into the defective joints and caulking them. Dixon wrote '... the Boiler runs out very much, he had to feed her with more meal and malt sprouts than would fatten a pig', a reference to the use of oatmeal in the boiler to staunch the leaks, as was then standard practice.

When Rastrick arrived he found that the engine had been at work all night and the water in the boiler quite hot, so that it did not take long to get up steam. The engine was over the stipulated weight of $4\frac{1}{2}$ tons but was allowed to compete, its load being assessed at 14 tons $6\frac{1}{2}$ cwt, comprising the tender and three waggons.

Sans Pareil started off and worked steadily for about two hours, at an average speed of just under 14 mph. At some point, however, the feed pumps failed, causing the water level in the boiler to fall to 8in., when the leaden plug melted, bringing the engine to a standstill half a mile short of completing its 16th trip. The plug was replaced, the pump cleared, steam raised and the engine was ready to resume its journeys, when the force pump failed again, and the trials were abandoned. It was noticed that the exhaust was excessively strong when the engine was running, the mighty blast sending coke and cinders high above the chimney; this had been caused by a crack in one of the cylinders, allowing the steam to escape directly into the blast pipe, although this was not discovered until the locomotive was examined after the Trials were over.

The judges had granted Braithwaite and Ericsson the time they had requested to put *Novelty* into working order, and arranged to test it on Wednesday, 14 October. Wood writes: 'On the arrival of the judges at Rainhill at the appointed time, they found that several parts of the engine having been taken to pieces, were not put together, and a considerable time elapsed before this was done.' Eventually steam was raised, a preliminary trip made, and the engine came up to the starting post. When returning westwards during the second trip, however, a boiler joint blew out, the cement applied only that morning not having

37 Iron Wonders, *1829; probably the first, and undoubtedly the worst, set of verses written about the railway*

Iron Wonders.
A NEW SONG.

J. Pannell, Printer, 68, Paradise St. Liverpool.

O have you been at Rainhill Bridge,
   And seen the racing there?
Or mark'd those Iron Wonders run,
   With power and speed so rare?
Or did you hear what odds were laid,
   The Novelty would beat the Rocket,
How Stephenson his power displayed,
   And well deserves the prize to pocket?
      CHORUS.—Whack row de dow.

His horse is of Newcastle breed,
   So famous on the Tyne,
And there his master rear'd his head,
   And there first made them shine:
His hard-won fame still hands him on,
   Among the bright he shines the brightest,
For all must own his work best done,
   His horse ne'er made a stop the slightest.

For both his wind and limbs are good,
   He's proved beyond a doubt,
Which like him stood the task assigned,
   Or gaily tript it out;
Such wond'rous feats he oft perform'd,
   The whole crowd cry'd out he's flying;
E'en scientific men were charm'd,
   Saying, were it thousands its worth buying.

Now Erickson and Braithwaite too,
   May fit things np for sale,
And paint and brush their horse's head,
   And make him cock his tail;
But faith, no more we'll hear their prate,
   'Bout what they can do in Lunnun,
For when their horse was tried with weight,
   He broke his wind and spoil'd his running.

Newcastle now may give her horn
   An animated bla',
And loudly tell to all around,
   How Robert beat them a';
His father too, mechanic's pride,
   May proudly boast a son so clever,
And while on Rail-roads we do ride,
   Their worth shall be forgotten never.
      Whack row de dow.

had time to set. This put an end to the experiment, and Ericsson withdrew from the contest.

Finally *Perseverance* came out and made some experimental runs, but could scarcely attain 6 mph, and recognising that it was unsuitable for the railway, Burstall spared the judges time and trouble by withdrawing.

At intervals during the trials the *Rocket* was brought out for experimental trips and early in the morning of the last day it drew a carriage with 25 passengers up on one of the Inclined Planes at a reported speed of 20 mph.

Thus ended the Rainhill Trials. The judges prepared their report and submitted it to the Board on 20 October. It was confined to a simple statement of the performances of the *Rocket*, *Novelty* and *Sans Pareil*, without any comment on the merits or defects of the engines. At its meeting that day the Board awarded '£500 to the proprietors of the *Rocket* engine, Henry Booth, Mr Stephenson and Mr Robert Stephenson.' The Company also purchased *Rocket* and offered to buy the two unsuccessful engines; Hackworth, who had invested all his capital in *Sans Pareil*, gladly accepted the offer of £550, but Braithwaite and Ericsson declined to sell *Novelty*, preferring to perfect her in the expectation of securing orders for a great number of such locomotives. Burstall was awarded £25 towards his expenses. The following February the Company paid Nicholas Wood £151 15s. 7d., his fee for judging the contest.[18] A pipe, brought home from Virginia by Raleigh and smoked by him just before his execution, was presented to George Stephenson after the *Rocket*'s success by a member of the Hetherington family of Northumberland.[19]

As might have been expected, the distribution of the prize among the Company's Treasurer, its Chief Engineer and his son inspired some caustic comment and a degree of resentment. It was argued that the other competitors had insufficient time to prepare their machines and hasty construction rather than any fault in the design had brought failure; no account was taken of any improvements or innovations for which their builders were responsible. Hackworth seems to have been disgruntled during the whole period; Dixon says '. . . he openly accused all George Stephenson's people of conspiring to hinder him of which I do believe them innocent'; be that as it may, he had some grounds for complaint when he was refused permission to see his engine weighed, and he could hardly be blamed for any feelings of bitterness towards Robert Stephenson & Co. after discovering the faulty cylinder they had sold him. There was no basis for supposing that the firm knew of the flaw in the cylinder, five or six having been cast and discarded before what was believed to be a perfect pair was produced.

Despite all the argument and recrimination, sustained as it was until near the end of the century, only *Rocket* had stayed the course and fulfilled all the conditions of the test. Had it failed as the others did, the locomotive would have been condemned, and its development retarded for years. The Stephensons were desperately anxious that the *Rocket* should win since it would have reflected little credit on them had it been outmatched by any of the others; all the advantages that experience could afford lay with them. The L&MR abandoned all notions of employing stationary engines for general traffic, and after *Rocket*'s performance on the inclined planes, even the plans to use them there were dropped; only for working the Edge Hill Tunnels were they to be employed.

At the next General Meeting the question of the impropriety of the railway's officers having any connection with suppliers of machinery to the Company was discussed, and despite denials by both Booth and George Stephenson that the former had any share in the *Rocket*, suspicions persisted.[20] A few directors, led by Cropper, disliked and mistrusted Stephenson, but he had powerful allies in Moss, Hardman Earle and Sandars.[21] The latter claimed that 'If he had not supported and encouraged him, under all the annoyance and vexation he had endured, Mr Stephenson would have relinquished his situation long since.'

CHAPTER FOUR

The Opening of the Railway

THE CONSTRUCTION of the Liverpool & Manchester Railway was a source of continual interest to thousands of people over the years, and those who could not watch the great earthworks and bridges taking shape were regaled with newspaper accounts of their progress. Sightseers walked freely over the completed sections, at their own risk and with the knowledge of the directors, who were not disposed to employ sufficient watchmen to keep them away.

So much interest was shown by the public in the Wapping Tunnel that the Company decided in July 1829 to admit visitors every Friday; a press announcement informed them that they could enter through the arch at Crown Street or the railway yard at Wapping. A charge of 1s. was made, but children under 12 were admitted free if accompanied by an adult. The entrance fee was charged '... to prevent the intrusion of too great a concourse of people', and the proceeds went to the local infirmaries. The tunnel was opened from 12 o'clock until 5 p.m. on 31 July, but at the next Board meeting it was decided that it should be whitewashed and extra lights provided, so that after the opening on Saturday 8 August, visitors had some months to wait before they could again stroll through the echoing, draughty cavern.

The brightening of the tunnel was probably for the benefit of a large party of distinguished visitors, including William Huskisson, who were taken by the directors and George Stephenson to view the Sankey Viaduct, Rainhill Bridge and Olive Mount Cutting on Friday 21 August. The party, about 135 in number, rode part of the way behind *Twin Sisters*, and arrived at Edge Hill, where a train of waggons awaited them. According to Stephenson, 'Many of the first families in the County were waiting here to witness the procession which, accompanied by a band of music occupying one of the waggons, descended in grand style through the Tunnel...'[1]

The tunnel was reopened to the public from September, but it was decided that no further visits would be permitted after 27 November and that persons would not be allowed to walk along the line after the end of the year. On 30 November Mr Statham, Town Clerk of Liverpool, took Francis Giles and his pupil Joseph Hekekyan through the tunnel on what the latter described as a private opening. Giles soon detected various faults in the work which he pointed out to young Joseph, who wrote in his diary that '... some of the cement facing was giving way ... like a bad plastered ceiling would do, falling off in large sheets.' He then rode in a waggon from the top of the tunnel at a speed, estimated with the aid of a stop-watch, of 95 mph, a calculation which suggests that either his eyesight, mathematics or stop-watch needed attention.[2]

A party from Knowsley attended the trials of a locomotive on 16 December 1829, and the next day the tunnel was lit up for Lords Harrowby and Sandon; James Hornby, Adam Hodgson and 'Scoresby of the Arctic Regions' were in the group of twenty who rode down to the Wapping yard in what was described as 'a kind of German post-waggon.' One of the party regretted his fate at being 50 years old at the beginning of such things.[3] It seems that private visits to the tunnel continued, for Stephenson complained that they were hampering work there in August 1830, when it was ruled that only visitors accompanied by a director would be allowed in future. Visitors to other parts of the line were so numerous at this time that severe interference was experienced by the engineers preparing for the opening day, and no further tickets were given, except by the Chairman.

With the regular arrival of new locomotives, and the works approaching completion, the Board was able to turn its attention in the summer of 1830 to the final arrangements for opening the line; on 21 June the decision was taken to open on 15 September. A few gaps remained, but it was decided to commence trial runs carrying passengers in order to gain favourable publicity for railway travel and to give the drivers some experience. It had been hoped to start between Liverpool and Newton on 24 May, but the first journey of inspection was made by the directors on Monday, 14 June. The train consisted of seven waggons carrying 80 stone blocks, the Bolton Close Coach and an open carriage carrying 20 persons; six people rode on the tender, and the total weight was about 33 tons, drawn by the *Arrow*.

'The train started from the Engine House, Edgehill, at twenty minutes before nine, and proceeded to the bottom of the Whiston Inclined Plane, being met a Quarter of a Mile on this side by the "Dart" Locomotive, which was attached to the "Arrow" for the purpose of assisting the train up the incline. The whole ascent was effected in 12 minutes; the speed for the first ¼ of a mile being 17 miles an hour, which, however, gradually decreased to about 4 miles an hour, before reaching the top. On the summit level at Rainhill, where the line is straight and level, the "Arrow" proceeded with her load at the rate of 16 miles an hour. She arrived at Oldfield Lane Bridge, Salford, Manchester, 5 minutes past eleven, having stopped at Parkside, and again near Eccles, to take in water. On the journey homewards the Load consisted of the Engine, Tender and 2 carriages and Passengers. The train started at 6 minutes before five, and arrived at the Liverpool Station at 20 minutes before seven, being 1 hour and 46 minutes on the road, including two stoppages, one at Bury Lane to set down Mr Hulton, and one at Parkside to take in water.

'The ascent of the Sutton Inclined Plane was effected at an average speed exceeding sixteen miles per hour, and the rate of movement on other parts of the road was frequently 25 miles per hour and upwards, the engine working below her power a great portion of the way.'[4]

The directors were very impressed by all they saw, and recorded their appreciation '. . . of the great skill and unwearied energy displayed by their Engineer, Mr George Stephenson.'

The first of several weekly excursions was made on Saturday afternoon, 10 July, when the directors and their friends went as far as the Kenyon Cutting and back, and then on 17 July *Arrow*, pulling three open carriages, left Liverpool at 4.00 p.m. and ran to Parkside. Each Director had at his disposal six tickets, including his own, for proprietors and guests. On 21 August the trip was to the Sankey Viaduct, and three trains were run, the *Phoenix*, *Rocket* and *Arrow*, working them in that order; among the guests on this occasion was Lord Belgrave and his family. A week later, with the same three locomotives, the trains ran to Ordsall Lane, Salford. A special train had been run on Wednesday 25 August, for a select party of 16, principally directors, but including as guests the actress Fanny Kemble and her father. After riding through the Crown Street tunnel in an open carriage, they stood admiring the locomotive, when George Stephenson invited Miss Kemble to ride with him on the footplate. Her enthusiastic account[5] of the experience has often been quoted along with her confession that Stephenson had quite turned her head. While the engine was taking water at Newton old George took her down into the valley spanned by the Sankey Viaduct, discoursing at some length on the technicalities of railway engineering, and from her subsequent recounting of the details, she seems to have been a promising pupil. A few days later the Board issued an order that no one in future was to ride on the tenders except the enginemen and directors; the latter must have been considered a poor substitute for attractive young ladies, but were probably less of a distraction to the younger drivers who might have been encouraged to follow Stephenson's example.

The trips on 4 September were made by *Dart*, *Phoenix* and the newly-arrived *North Star*. These were probably the last as the Board had ordered that all engines '. . . except the *Sisters* should be taken off the Railway on 1 September for overhaul and requisite experiments prior to the opening day.'

The invitations to the principal guests were sent out in July, and the Prime Minister, the Duke of Wellington, agreed to open the railway. Lord Derby was among those invited but, being over 80, he felt unequal to the strain of a strenuous day on the railway. In a most gracious letter to the Chairman he wrote:

'. . . I am obliged to decline the honour of joining their party . . . At the same time allow me to assure you and the committee that although at the commencement of this fine work I thought myself fully justified in opposing it, I am now so well satisfied of the public benefit likely to accrue from its progress as sincerely to congratulate the committee on the accomplishment of their object, and to offer them my best wishes for its complete success.'[6]

Three special carriages were built for the opening ceremony, the most magnificent being that prepared for the Duke. It was 32ft long by 8ft wide, and ran on eight wheels. Fitted out by Edmondson's,[7] its sides were in the form of Grecian balustrades with gilt scrolls, bearing the heavy hand-rail which extended

38 *Commemorative medal engraved by Halliday. The reverse side bears the inscription 'Entrance to the Liverpool Station and Tunnels', the latter being visible through the Moorish Arch, and in three lines below, 'Published by T. Woolfield, Bazaar, Liverpool.' (The actual diameter of the medal is 48 mm)*

all round the carriage. The doors were in the centre, and around the pillars crimson curtains hung in festoons; these could be drawn all round the carriage to screen the occupants from the weather. Along the centre was a large ottoman providing seating for 30 passengers and overhead was a 24ft canopy supported by eight gilded pillars, and so arranged that it could be lowered by a windlass mounted on the floor for passing through the tunnel. The drapery was of rich crimson cloth, lavishly adorned with tassels, and the whole was surmounted by two ducal coronets. The carriages in the Duke's train were coupled by long poles – an early version of combined central buffer and coupling – to prevent the jolting experienced when chains alone were used. The other carriages were smaller and less ornate, but constructed on the same lines. Lace for the coaches and silk for the flags that each train was to carry, were purchased shortly before the opening.

B. Faulkner of Birmingham approached the Board with a suggestion that a commemorative medal be struck, and at least two designs were on sale in Liverpool by early September. Thomas Jones, Silversmith, advertised his medal showing Stephenson and the Newton Bridge in 'Silver, Bronze and Metal' (the metal was in fact pewter), while Thomas Woolfield of the Fancy Bazaar offered one depicting the Moorish Arch and Sankey Viaduct in the same metals for 21s., 8s. and 1s. respectively; the latter were also on sale in various parts of Liverpool and Manchester.

Elaborate plans for the entertainment of the Company's guests were made; Mr Lynn, the proprietor of the Waterloo Hotel, was to prepare the *déjeuner* in an upper storey of the Manchester Warehouses, where a broad wooden staircase had been erected to form a temporary entrance. Mr Radley of the Adelphi Hotel was entrusted with the arrangements for the dinner to be held at the Wellington Rooms on the return to Liverpool. A separate dinner arranged by several engineers and others '. . . interested in the success and promotion of STEAM-POWER . . .' was to be held at the Adelphi Hotel on Wednesday evening, the tickets for which were two guineas.

During the weekend before the opening the railway presented a scene of feverish activity as the final preparations were made. On the Sunday the locomotives, having been thoroughly overhauled, were freshly painted, and at several places along the line the hammers of the carpenters rang out as they erected stands and booths. These were private ventures and several were advertised in the *Albion* of 13 September; for the very large one at Edge Hill, approached from Crabtree Lane and within 20 yards of the chimneys, the entrance fee was 2s. 6d. to the stand, and 1s. for standing room. The booths and tents were set up in fields for innkeepers who intended to transfer their activities from the empty town that day, and one, William New of the London Tavern, Richmond Street, took over a farmhouse at the Wavertree Lane crossing for the purpose. Ale and porter by the cartload was delivered to these establishments during the next couple of days.

Each locomotive had its regular driver and fireman, as distinct from the director, and these men and boys wore the new blue livery of the Company, faced with red. In the case of the latter, the word 'Fireman' and the name of the engine to which they were attached appeared around their caps in red letters on a blue cloth ground. Engineers, contractors and some who were later to hold important positions in the Company acted as Train Directors, flagmen and brakesmen that day (see Appendix A). The extent of actual driving done by the director was probably limited to starting the engine at Edge Hill. A printed leaflet headed 'Orders for Engine Men' was issued to all concerned setting out a simple system of flag signals and defining the speed limits and distances to be maintained between trains.

The Company had reckoned upon 1000 guests, but the number was reduced to 700 after the failure of Braithwaite and Ericsson to deliver two new locomotives. There were to be about 100 persons in each of seven trains, excluding the Duke's, and each passenger was issued with a numbered ticket corresponding in colour to that of the flag distinguishing his train. Printed notices were also given to each passenger warning of the possible dangers, particularly that of alighting from a train that had stopped. Two days before the ceremony a Liverpool stockbroker was offering tickets for the opening to purchasers of shares.

On 9 September the 4th (King's Own) Regiment had disembarked from Ireland, and four companies were held back in Liverpool to assist the police in maintaining order at that end of the line; the Regimental Band was engaged to play on the Duke's train.

As a precaution against accident or mischief, all the switch-plates but one were removed; apart from those at the extremities of the line, only the points at Huyton were left in position. It was thus practically impossible for any of the seven trains that would use the north line to cross to that on which the Duke's train was to run.

JAMES RADLEY'S
ADELPHI HOTEL.

BILL OF FARE.

First Course.

Turtle and Turtle Fins.	Chickens and Purée of Almonds.
REMOVE WITH	Raised Pigeon Pies.
Turbots and Dee Salmon.	Fricandeaus, Veal, and Sorrell.
REMOVE FISH WITH	Larded Fillets, Fowl, and
Twelve Haunches and Ten Necks of Venison.	Tomato Sauce.
	Stewed Partridges and Cabbage.
Braized Beef and Spanish Onions.	Larded Sweetbreads and
Do. Turkeys and Celery Sauce.	Stewed Peas.
Do. Hams and Tongues.	Souteé of Lamb and Cucumbers.

Second Course.

Roast Black Game.	Citron Souflies.
Grouse.—Snipes and Partridges.	Fried Oysters.—Apricot Tartlets.
Noyeau Creams.	Stewed Mushrooms.
Grapes in Jelly.—Chantilly Baskets.	Fondieus.
Italian Salads.—Apricot Tourts.	Ratifia Puddings.

DESSERTS.	WINES.
Pines.—Grapes.—Melons.	Hock.—Champaigne.
Peaches.	Sparkling Burgundy.—Moselle.
Nectarines.—Egg Plumbs.	Sauterne.—Sherry.
Green Gages.	Silleray Champaigne.
Plumbs.—Pears.	East India Madeira.—Old Port.
Apples.—Filberts.	Claret.—Red Burgundy.
Preserved Apricots.	Constantia.

LIQUEURS.

Curaçoa.—Marisquino.—Marisquino Punch.

Wellington Rooms, 15th Sept., 1830.

39 *Menu for the banquet on the evening of Opening Day. The charge to the Company was two guineas per guest, but as very few attended, Radley was paid on the basis of the profit he would have made*

Orders for Engine Men.

Every Engine-man must be provided with all necessary tools and implements for the immediate repair of accidents.

He must also be provided with three signal flags, viz.—*white, red* and *purple:* the white flag signifying "*Go on*"—the red flag, "*Go slowly*"—"Hold down the brake"—the purple flag, "*Stop.*"

When the signal flag is held aloft it is meant to be observed by the Carriages or Engine of the immediate train to which it belongs. When it is held horizontally it must be considered a signal for the next Engine and train to *fall back* or to *come forward,* as may be required.

When moving at a slow speed, the different trains must be kept 100 yards apart from one another; when moving at a quick speed, say 12 miles per hour, or upwards, they must be kept 200 yards asunder. The Engine-men are charged not to exceed a speed of 18 miles per hour *down the inclined planes.*

By Order,
GEO. STEPHENSON,
Engineer.

40 *Orders for the enginemen on Opening Day*

Opening

OF

THE LIVERPOOL AND MANCHESTER RAILWAY,

WEDNESDAY, 15TH SEPTEMBER, 1830.

CHAS. LAWRENCE, CHAIRMAN.

THE BEARER OF THIS TICKET IS ENTITLED TO SEAT No. 34.
NORTH STAR'S TRAIN.

YELLOW FLAG.

ENT.D

THE OPENING OF THE RAILWAY

The final preparations were not completed until Wednesday morning, when strong paling was erected along the top of the precipitous walls of the Edge Hill excavation, and the station was generally tidied up. George Stephenson mounted on his horse was early on the scene directing operations.

The Duke attended a great dinner in his honour at Manchester on Monday evening and travelled to the Marquis of Salisbury's seat at Childwall on Tuesday afternoon. His programme in Liverpool included several functions apart from the opening of the railway, among them a long-standing engagement to receive the freedom of the Corporation. This ceremony was arranged for Thursday, 16 September, to be followed in the evening by a great ball. Charles Lawrence as former Mayor was closely involved in all these activities, as were other directors of the railway.

There is no doubt that the events of 15 September 1830 received more newspaper coverage than was ever accorded to the opening of a railway, before or since. Journalists gave full rein to their talents, and their combined efforts have left an account of that memorable day which, a century and a half later, still conveys all the excitement and gaiety that marked its first few hours and the sorrow and apprehension that brought it to a close.

For several days before the opening the roads approaching Liverpool had been crowded with visitors converging upon the town from all parts of the country; steam vessels brought others from Ireland and Scotland, and by the weekend there were more strangers in Liverpool than ever before in its annals. One observer,[8] after being awakened by heavy rain at 4.00 a.m., records that by 7 o'clock all were up '... basking in the full sunshine of hope as its rays glanced upon the early breakfast table.' By this time the streets of Liverpool were already becoming choked by the crowds making their way to selected vantage points along the railway, for no work was done that day; all wore 'their best and brightest apparel', and soon the whole country seemed alive, with every lane filled and every field by the line sprinkled with spectators. At Edge Hill depot not only was every space

41a *Invitation tickets to the opening of the Railway; upper, printed on yellow card; lower printed in gold on blue-tinted card, for special guests travelling in the Duke's train*

41b *Instructions on back of invitation ticket*

**The Doors of the Station in Crown-street, Liverpool, will be open at Nine o'Clock in the Morning, and the Company are requested to assemble not later than Half-past Nine.

Carriages to approach by way of Crabtree-lane, and to set down with the Horses' Heads towards the Botanic Garden.

⁂ Please to show the Ticket at the Door, but not to part with it.

On the return, the Procession will move down the great Tunnel to the Company's Warehouse-Station in St. James's-street, from which Street Carriages must enter the Yard, and be in waiting at Four o'Clock with the Horses' Heads towards Wapping.**

ORDERS OF THE DAY.

LIVERPOOL, SEPTEMBER 15th, 1830.

The Directors will meet at the Station, in Crown Street, not later than Nine o'clock in the Morning, and during the assembling of the Company will severally take charge of separate Trains of Carriages to be drawn by the different Engines as follow:—

NORTHUMBRIAN	*Lilac Flag.*	Mr. Moss.
PHŒNIX	*Green Flag.*	Mr. Earle.
NORTH STAR	*Yellow Flag.*	Mr. Harrison.
ROCKET	*Light Blue Flag.*	Mr. A. Hodgson.
DART	*Purple Flag.*	Mr. Sandars.
COMET	*Deep Red Flag.*	Mr. Bourne.
ARROW	*Pink Flag.*	Mr. Currie.
METEOR	*Brown Flag.*	Mr. David Hodgson.

The men who have the management of the Carriage-breaks will be distinguished by a white ribbon round the arm.

When the Trains of Carriages are attached to their respective Engines **a Gun will be fired** as a preliminary signal, when the "Northumbrian" will take her place at the head of the Procession; a second Gun will then be fired, and **the whole will move forward.**

The Engines will stop at Parkside (a little beyond Newton) to take in a supply of water, during which the company are requested not to leave their Carriages.

At Manchester the Company will alight and remain one hour to **partake of the Refreshments** which will be provided in the **Warehouses** at that station. In the farthest warehouse on the right hand side will be the Ladies' Cloak Room.

Before leaving the Refreshment Rooms a Blue Flag will be exhibited as a signal for the Ladies to resume their Cloaks; after which the Company will repair to their respective Carriages, which will be ranged in the same order as before; and sufficient time will be allowed for every one to take his seat, according to the number of his Ticket, in the Train to which he belongs; and Ladies and Gentlemen are particularly requested not to part with their Tickets during the day, as it is by the number and colour of the Tickets that they will be enabled at all times to find with facility their respective places in the Procession.

42 *Leaflet issued to each guest who travelled in the trains on Opening Day*

43 *The scene at Edge Hill on the morning of Opening Day*

occupied, but several men had climbed up the inside of the newly-built chimneys of the engine house and sat on the rims, whilst others were perched on a nearby windmill.

From before 9 o'clock until 10 o'clock the carriages of the guests were arriving at Crown Street Station, soon to be thronged with groups eagerly searching for their places in the waiting trains, to the accompaniment of music from the Wellington Harmonic Band and that of the King's Own Regiment. At length the Duke of Wellington arrived; after striding down between the carriages, recognising friends and laughing heartily when the trumpeters attached to each train played 'See the Conquering Hero Comes', he took his place in the special train which had been brought out of the tunnel on to the centre line of rails. 'In the midst of this din of harmony, a gun was fired within a few yards;[9] at the sound of which, as its smoke curled above the walls, the leading carriages were slowly launched away, each set following at a short interval, till the whole, gliding from the area, entered the smaller tunnel, with a low rumbling sound, as the iron wheels revolved on their iron beds.'

Emerging from the dimly lit tunnel into the broad daylight of the Edge Hill excavation, the trains were greeted by the cheers of thousands while the 'eight fine engines' which had been waiting with steam up, were coupled to them. George Stephenson, not yet 50, but now white-haired, stood erect on the footplate of *Northumbrian*, a proud man in this, his moment of triumph. *Northumbrian* took the Duke's train on the southern track while the others, headed by *Phoenix*, ran on the northern line, waiting at Wavertree Lane until the procession was ready. The Duke's train meanwhile ran up and down its own line to afford the spectators a glimpse of such a gathering of the nobility and the illustrious in other spheres as they were not likely to see again for many a year. Along this part of the line the police and soldiers managed to keep the line clear of sightseers; as the *Albion* put it, 'But Liverpool has no mob and, therefore, even in times of great excitement, the task of managing myriads of our townsmen is not very difficult.'

At about 11 o'clock the signal gun was fired again when, with the coloured silken flags fluttering in the breeze, and '... amidst clouds of steam, while the rocks re-echoed with the deafening shouts of the myriads above and about us', the procession started, led by *Phoenix* pulling three open and two closed carriages; the reporters appear to have been placed together on this train. One of them wrote:

'Our speed was gradually increased till, entering the Olive Mount excavation, we rushed into the awful chasm at the rate of twenty-four miles an hour. The banks, the bridges over our heads and the rude projecting corners along the sides were covered with masses of human beings past whom we glided as if upon the wings of the wind.'

Into the open country at Broad Green and beyond the train ran between vehicles of every description drawn up in the fields on either side with thousands of spectators lining the way. Slowly up the Whiston Incline and gathering speed past Rainhill Bridge, the trains passed the Duke's Car, stopped there for the benefit of the sightseers, and for the other trains to pull ahead. At some point *Phoenix* had become derailed, one wheel ploughing along the ballast, which, with the application of the brakes, brought the train to a stand so suddenly that the one following could not quite stop before hitting it. The passengers had braced themselves for the impact which followed, but little harm was done, and the trains were soon on the move again.

From the trains rushing down Sutton Incline and across Parr Moss it became '... difficult to recognise or distinguish the countenances of the long continuous lines of spectators, as they seemed to glide away, like painted figures swiftly drawn through the tubes of a magic lantern.' At the foot of the incline stood the grand-stand erected by the St Helens and Runcorn Gap Railway for the shareholders and their friends, while that for the proprietors of the Wigan Branch Railway was near Parkside. One of the largest, holding 1000 persons, stood near the Sankey Viaduct. Admission was by ticket at 10s. 6d., including 'conveyance to and from certain places, and a handsome collation'. A band was provided and it was intended to occupy the time between the outward and return journeys of the trains with a ball.

A lady who watched the proceedings from one of the grand stands recorded her impressions of that day in her diary. Her party

'... approached the rail-road, which lay in a hollow, looking something like the bed of a canal before the water is let in. We got places on the form prepared, for which we paid three shillings and sixpence each. Though we had to wait some time, we found sufficient occupation for eyes and ears, for there was not a little scolding and gossiping in the broad Lancashire dialect among the ladies who sat near us, and no small elbowing and threatening among the persons below us, who gave their sixpences for a standing. In the meantime the people came pouring in by hundreds and thousands, from all quarters, and even up to the rail-road, not allowing themselves to be persuaded to leave it even by the police, till the guns from Liverpool informed them that the procession from the town was on the move.

Soon after this notice came a string of carriages, all bedight with scarlet and gold, and filled with gallant gentlemen and gaudy dames (for all the carriages were open), and there was such a flying of flags, and such smiling and bowing, that I was fain to think myself very small, sitting on my bench, and of no more consequence that day than a fly at a coronation procession. In the most magnificent of these carriages stood no less a person than the hero of Waterloo, who was saluted as he passed (for the carriages were sufficiently observant of courtesy to go somewhat slowly before the stands) by shouts from men, and screeches, and waving of handkerchiefs from the Lancashire women. The Monsters, being very civil monsters, not only relaxed their energies in passing the stands, but actually backed to give us time to see more of them ... At length, however, the whole pageant disappeared in double quick time.'[10]

Thousands had gathered in the Sankey Valley to see the trains glide over the great viaduct, and the vessels in the stream beneath lay idle while their crews gazed upwards. The trains were now approaching Parkside where they were to stop for water, the journey so far having taken just under an hour. The engines were filled from several tanks, and then moved their trains off before waiting some distance down the line. After three trains had passed that of the Duke, waiting on the southern line at Parkside, passengers started to alight and walk about the track while the remaining engines were filled. Members of the Duke's party also descended from the grand carriage, but into the narrow space between the tracks because there were at this point large pools of water on either side of the line; several trains had still to pass this point on the other line, and as the next one came on, drawn by *Rocket*, there occurred the tragedy, for which this day has always been remembered.

E. J. Littleton – later Lord Hatherton – was in the Duke's car, and from his letter to Lord Palmerston on 18 September the following extracts are taken:

'*My Dear Palmerston,*
'The papers will have conveyed to you the intelligence of the horrible catastrophe which has taken Huskisson from his friends and the public.

44 Parkside watering station, 1831

'As I was present with him from the moment he entered the car till that of the accident, of which I was an immediate eye witness, you will perhaps feel a melancholy interest in having some of the details. We were at a place when the Railroad goes through a quarry on a narrow dam in the centre – the sides being full of water – about 50 persons were walking about while the Engine took in water, when it was observed that another Engine was coming along at speed on the parallel line. Everybody entered as soon as they could, or stood still between the cars – I had just time to enter through the wicket. It was difficult because the car was 4 feet from the ground and there were no steps. I pulled in Esterhazy, who was after me. I then saw Huskisson seize the wicket, which was about 4 feet long, and in great trepidation try to get round it into the car – instead of standing still as he ought. It was too late – the Engine had come up and either knocked him down or he fell on its road in front, on his back, in trying to get across its line out of its way. His left leg and thigh . . . lay across the rail – the whole passed over him – he was then seen lying with his leg and thigh reduced to pulp . . . a more horrible spectacle was never witnessed. Mrs Huskisson hearing at the moment a general shriek, and her husband's name, became frantic. We held her in the car till the thigh could have a tourniquet made of a silk handerchief and a cane applied by Lord Wilton and the limb be covered. The papers tell the rest correctly. He was carried to Eccles, a place within 4 miles of Manchester by the Railroad at a speed of 35 miles an hour. Granville and Lord Wilton and four medical men stayed with him till his death. I was in the train part of the time. His shrieks were horrible, when the intermittent spasms was on him – In the intervals he was composed – drew the ears of those he wished to speak to down to his lips – made an alteration in his will, favourable to Mrs H, and took the Sacrament. He died a quarter before 9 having survived the accident exactly 9 hours.

'At the moment that the fatal engine was coming up he was talking, with much apparent cordiality on both sides, to the Duke of Wellington – who was standing in his car at the leading corner – Huskisson was standing on the ground outside. Everyone was getting in or into a place of safety to allow the Engine to pass, when the Duke, observing a stir said (I was close by and heard it): "We seem to be going on – you had better step in"!!! Had Huskisson stood where he was he would have been safe. The Duke's last words were, accidentally, the cause of his misfortune. The Duke was certainly greatly affected – and behaved excellently – so did Peel.'[11]

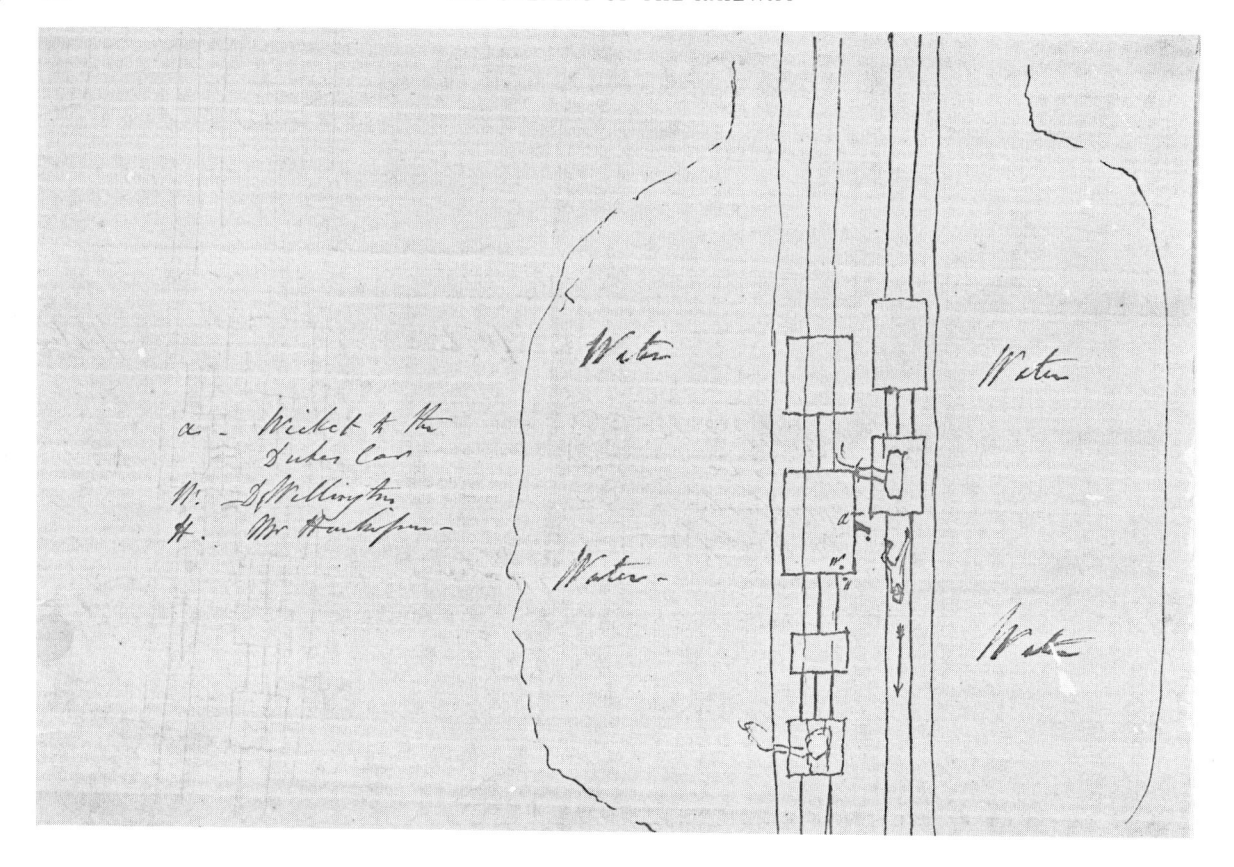

45 *Sketch accompanying Littleton's letter to Lord Palmerston of 18 September 1830*

The *Rocket*'s director, Locke, was very distressed by the occurrence. Lady Frances Sandon, who had seen the accident, wrote that night from Knowsley 'I am afraid there was some degree [of] blame attached to the Director of the Carriage who it is thought ought not to have gone at such a pace where the crowd was so great around the Carriages.'[12] The engine had no brakes, and although the valve-gear could be thrown into reverse while it was still travelling forward, the operation took an experienced driver several seconds to manipulate the levers.

The careful plans of the directors which, up to this point, had gone without a hitch, were now thrown into confusion. The *Northumbrian* and the musicians' carriage were uncoupled from the Duke's train, and Huskisson with a small party were driven on to Eccles, where they were left at the vicarage in charge of the Vicar's wife. George Stephenson then drove on to Manchester with Lord Wilton who collected four surgeons and returned with them riding on the tender to Eccles.

Meanwhile Wellington, Peel, the Directors and others considered whether or not to abandon the proceedings. The Duke was in favour of returning but there was some degree of uncertainty until Bulkeley Price, the Boroughreeve, urged that the trains go on to Manchester; to disappoint the vast crowds there might lead to some disturbance, he argued, to which the Duke replied 'There is something in that', and consented to go.[13] It was agreed that all further festivities should be cancelled and the military bands were left to make their way back as best they could. The first two trains were coupled together, with *Phoenix* at the head and *North Star* somewhere in the middle, and from the combined train a long chain was attached to the Duke's car, which was then drawn along the other line. The other trains followed, '. . . but the buoyant exhilaration of the morning was past, and the whole now wore the sombre aspect of a funeral procession.' To deepen the gloom, the morning sunshine had gone and the clouds gathering over Chat Moss brought the first heavy showers; soon a steady downpour had set in to continue intermittently for the rest of the day.

The still large crowds cheered wildly as the trains passed, wondering at the delay but ignorant of its cause, and no doubt puzzled by the lack of response from the passengers. Halfway across Chat Moss *Northumbrian*, returning from Eccles, met the procession and took what remained of the Duke's train onwards. As they drew nearer to Manchester the character of the crowds changed; an increasingly large minority were determined to make the occasion one of political protest, and an underlying chorus of hooting and hissing was audible as Wellington rode past. A ragged weaver sat at a hand-loom by the lineside near Eccles, the tricolour flag of revolution hung from some bridges, cries of 'Vote by Ballot' and 'No Corn Laws' were heard. A stretch of line near Eccles had been left unguarded, and on a report that a mob was approaching from Oldham, about 50 men who had been special constables, but whose licences had probably expired, were assembled, armed with staves and clubs, and dispersed along the railway. A rumour that the railway was being torn up by another mob sent a troop of dragoons in full trot from Manchester who, returning drenched and angry at their fruitless errand, were more than ready to deal with anyone who crossed their path.

Near the town the crowds were no longer in detached masses, but had closed in upon the trains on every side, causing many of the passengers some anxiety. The engines were now travelling very slowly, their path being cleared by police and soldiers, and into the dense mass of humanity rode the Duke, grave and impassive, standing with folded arms, his military cloak around him. Across the Irwell Bridge soldiers of the 59th Regiment were drawn up on either side and presented arms as his Grace passed along. Beyond the bridge the trains stopped and the guests hurried off to the warehouses for refreshments, all except Wellington who stayed in his carriage with a few of his party and for over an hour and a half, shook hands with the thousands for whom he, rather than the railway, was the main attraction.

The Manchester authorities were terrified however, not by the multitudes who had waited 15 years to honour him as the hero of Waterloo, but by the roughs thronging the railway and insulting any guests of the directors within earshot. The Duke was quite unperturbed, but the head of the police establishment, not wishing to have the injury or assassination of the Prime Minister on his hands, urged that the Duke's train be sent off while it could still get through the thickening concourse of people, and at about 4.30 p.m. it slowly moved out, fortunately without accident to anyone. Another train that was on the same line had an engine attached, and it followed the Duke's train.

Just clear of the Manchester suburbs they met three engines returning from Parkside, where they had been sent for water. These were anxiously awaited at Manchester where six trains were ready to leave for Liverpool, but unfortunately they were on the wrong line and there were no points for crossing between the terminus and Huyton Quarry, a distance of over 25 miles. Since there was no question of the Duke's train being allowed to return to Manchester there was no alternative but for the three locomotives to run ahead of it to within 6½ miles of Liverpool, there to cross to the other line. The Duke, after stopping at Eccles to enquire after Huskisson, went on to Roby where he left the railway with the Marquis of Salisbury's party and returned to Childwall.

Two of the three engines had been shunted on to the other line at Huyton and were ready to start back towards Manchester; the third had evidently developed some mechanical trouble and had gone forward to Liverpool. The Duke's train was coupled to the one that had followed it, and the combined train of nine carriages with nearly 300 passengers started for Liverpool, the spare engine having gone back with the other two. Rumours of a major disaster of which Huskisson was only the most prominent victim, had already reached the town and a vast crowd occupied the line making progress very difficult. As the train edged its way through so the masses fell back, to close in again behind it, and much of their earlier good humour had evaporated. The train eventually arrived in Liverpool at 7.00 p.m.

Meanwhile at Manchester it had become apparent what had happened to their locomotives, and the engineers marshalled the 24 carriages of the six stranded trains into one, coupled the three engines that were there to the one long train and started for Liverpool at 5.20 p.m. The crowds had dispersed with the departure of the Prime Minister and the onset of soaking rain, and in the gathering darkness the train '... finally cleared the suburbs without running over or being assailed by a single radical.' Before long the coupling chains began to give way under the strain, and ropes were substituted. At Newton the other three engines came up and two were coupled to the front of the train, making five in all; the other was used as a pilot engine, running a short distance ahead of the train and signalling back by the swinging of the lighted end of a tar-rope. Contrary to expectations the train now went at a slower rate, the extra engines apparently retarding its progress.

A short distance up the Sutton incline the train

stopped and then fell back under its own gravity, its engines proving incapable of getting it up the gradient,

'... and the gentlemen accordingly dismounted, in number about 400, to walk the ascending mile. There was something more striking, perhaps, than agreeable in this part of the days' work. The five engines throwing out jets of sparks into the air, which were carried far away by the wind, while the roadway was sprinkled with fiery particles falling from the furnace grates, the flames casting a bright golden light on the clouds of condensing steam which were constantly escaping – all combined to produce a strange but sombre illumination, gleaming partially on the long train of carriages, succeeded by such a numerous escort.'

Hardly had the men resumed their seats when a further delay was caused by the pilot engine running into a wheel-barrow maliciously placed on the line, and at Rainhill a shower of missiles from the bridge fell upon the passengers.

The train stopped at Broad Green at 9.30 p.m. and several passengers alighted to make their own way home. When it reached Liverpool, the train was sent down the long tunnel to Wapping, where the private carriages were waiting; it finally rolled safely into the station, amid cheers of relief from anxious friends, at 10.30. For many the ordeal was not yet over, as they were in a remote part of the town, far from their inns and hotels; many had not even booked accommodation, never dreaming of such a delay. As one of the passengers wrote five days later,[14]

'Strange adventures must have fallen to the lot of some, in such a scene of confusion, unpalatable enough at the time, though now, when nought is left but retrospection, leaving pleasant as well as painful reminiscences of a day whose counterpart they can never expect to see again.'

The Engineers' banquet that was to have been held at the Adelphi Hotel that night was cancelled, as was the Ball, arranged for the following evening. The Company's dinner at the Wellington Rooms, prepared for 219 guests, was held, but only 47 attended; Lawrence presided, and the company dispersed as soon as Huskisson's health had been drunk.

The next day Lord Salisbury's party, including Wellington who attended incognito, met Stephenson and were conducted through the Wapping Tunnel. Some mishap caused them to be left in total darkness for a while, and Lord Ellesmere thought they had acted rashly in going at all. All public festivities in Liverpool, including the presentation to the Duke of the Freedom of the Corporation, were postponed. Wellington had to return to London before the funeral of William Huskisson, which took place in Liverpool on Friday, 24 September. Following two mutes on horseback, 1100 inhabitants of Liverpool walked six abreast before a great number of carriages bearing the nobility and other distinguished mourners. After the body came more coaches, the Mayor's State Carriage, another 900 gentlemen inhabitants and nine more coaches.

The diarist[15] who with such delight had watched the trains go by in the morning, on learning of Huskisson's death, wrote of the engines, 'Can it be that these terrible Monsters will ever come in to general use?'

CHAPTER FIVE

Travelling on the Railway

MANY EARLY TRAVELLERS on the L&MR have left descriptions of their experiences in letters or diaries, often with expressions of respectful awe at the magnitude of viaduct, tunnel and cutting. When all the earthworks were new it was an impressive sight, running across largely open country. A feature that intrigued the first passengers was the illusion of the ground appearing to close in on them as the train travelled along cuttings and then to fall away when it ran over the embankments; accustomed to road travel at ground level, they now enjoyed for the first time distant views of familiar towns and villages unfolding before them.

Olive Mount Cutting inspired a great many writers, one of whom even noted the appearance of moss on the south side, untouched by the rays of the sun. The spectators on the bridges watched the trains below, while the noise reverberating against the rocky walls was '. . . calculated to produce sensations of delight and astonishment' in watcher and traveller alike. In March 1831 the Chairman referred to '. . . the quiet and almost deserted appearance of nearly the whole Line of Railway, even on the busiest days', adding that the passage of 4000 tons of goods would not occupy any one part of the line for more than 15 minutes a day.

In a long account of his impressions of the railway soon after it was opened, Dr James Johnson, MD, wrote of the locomotive:

'. . . this magic automaton darts forward on iron pinions, swift as an arrow from a bow; unerring, undeviating from its destined course. Devised by science but devoted to industry; unwearied as rapid in its toils and movements; harmless as the dove if unopposed, but fatal as the thunderbolt if encountered in its career. . .'

On riding in an open carriage he wrote:

'The projections or transits of the train through the tunnels and arches are very electrifying. The deafening peal of thunder, the sudden immersion in gloom, and the clash of reverberated sounds in confined space, combine to produce a momentary shudder or idea of destruction – a thrill of annihilation – which is instantly dispelled on emerging into the cheerful light. The meetings or crossings of the steam trains flying in opposite directions are scarcely less agitating to the nerves than their transits through the tunnels. The velocity of their course, the propinquity or apparent identity of the iron orbits along which these meteors move, call forth the involuntary but fearful thought of a possible collision, with all its horrible consequences. The period of suspense, however, though exquisitely painful, is but momentary; and in a few seconds the object of terror is far out of sight behind.'[1]

Most contemporary writers refer to the concussion caused by loose coupling chains on starting and stopping. One Colonel Phipps of the Hon. East India Company, in his diary of a tour in 1831, says:

'The ends of the carriages have strong leather mufflers to soften the force of the blow when they come in contact with each other, which frequently occurs when the engine stops. We stopped for water at a half-way house, and once to regulate something out of order. The speed was by no means uniform, but varied considerably. At every mile a watchman is stationed to keep the way clear from stones, and to prevent any tricks being played to injure the railway. We first passed on the road a string of carriages like our own, coming from Liverpool. The velocity with which both bodies are moving, separated only by a space of two or three feet, gave a terrific appearance to this occurrence, although, in reality there is no danger, when each person keeps his seat, and does not put the head out of the window . . . The last carriages we passed were platforms laden with merchandise and poultry. A gentleman's carriage was conveyed across on one of these platforms.

'On arriving at a tunnel near Liverpool the steam-carriage was taken off, and the coaches slowly moved under the rocky arch by ropes turned by steam, and on clearing the dark passage, omnibuses were in readiness to convey the passengers to their inns. No fees of any description are taken, and the whole is very well managed.'[2]

On 9 June 1833 H. Crabb Robinson travelled to Manchester in a 2nd Class carriage and noted the event in his diary. The train was not full but he had been told that a train had once taken 1000 passengers to Newton Fair and concluded that there must have been two engines pulling it. He compared the noise made by engines passing the other way to '... the whizzing of a rocket.'[3]

Another diarist who had travelled from Manchester on 18 July 1833, rode in the last carriage but one of a 10-coach train, and found the '... motion greater than I had expected – *trembling and rocking*'. Returning by second class train the next day he refers to the frequent and tedious stoppages, and to '... some derangement of our steamer' which necessitated the train being assisted from the rear by a following heavy goods train.[4]

Matters had improved by the time that Thomas Moore, the Irish poet, travelled on the line two years later:

'To Liverpool by the railroad; a grand mode of travelling, though as we were told, ours was but a poor specimen of it, as we took an hour and a half to do the thirty-two miles ... The motion so easy that I found I could write without any difficulty *chemin faisant*.'[5]

Miss Kennedy, a young lady who made her first trip on the railway in July 1833, confided her impressions of the experience to her diary:

'At half past one we drove down to the famous railway, by far the most interesting thing we have seen. One engine came up hissing exactly at 2 o'clock, and was attached in front of the string of carriages. There were six mail coaches, each capable of containing 18 persons, in the train, the Adelaide, the Sovereign, the Clarence, etc., all shut up just like other coaches. We preferred a more open one, that had only curtains to the sides, and took the two front rows, sitting opposite to each other.

46 *Engraving by Henry Heath,* The Pleasures of the Rail Road: Showing the Inconvenience of a Blow-up, *1831. The Liverpool & Manchester Railway inspired a number of such cartoons, the subject usually being some kind of catastrophe*

Louis was perched up in high style in our carriage, which was fixed on a machine with hollowed wheels like all the rest of the train, and of a sudden the engine was worked, and with a little jerk we were all put in motion, and ran rattling along the iron bars. We had no baggage or animals in our train but we met several on the road that passed us like lightning, steaming on from Liverpool to Manchester.

'Sometimes we went faster, sometimes slower, where the roads were bad, or they were busy putting down new iron bars. Every now and then there were tiny huts by the road where the men lived who picked up the stones and otherwise kept the way clear and in order.'

On reaching Crown Street,

'All the passengers got out and drove away in omnibuses; a postillion with two horses was waiting to be engaged, and after our britska had come down from its carriage we got in and drove to the Waterloo Hotel, much to the grief of poor postillion who belonged to the Albion . . .'[6]

Greville in his *Memoirs* describes a journey from Birmingham to Liverpool in 1837 in which he found nothing disagreeable '. . . but the occasional whiffs of stinking air which it is impossible to exclude altogether.' After an initial feeling of '. . . being run away with . . . a sense of security soon supervenes and the velocity is delightful . . . it certainly renders all other travelling irksome and tedious by comparison.'

This was not the view of all writers, particularly those reminiscing a few years later. One asked of the old stage coaches:

'Where are they now? . . . We are all for speed . . . We are, as it were, shot forth from station to station at a speed becoming the spirit of the age. But one consequence of all this is that the rising generation know nothing of the old high-ways and by-ways of their country – its shady lanes, its lovely nooks and corners, the sudden turns in our old lines of road which used unexpectedly to open to us the most charming prospect, and then as suddenly to hide it . . . These were exquisite treats to us old travellers. We miss them, but we are not regretting. We like to keep up with the pace of the age.'[7]

A writer in 1865 recalled the day when as a boy of nine, his father lifted him up to see the arrival of the Duke in Manchester. In the following year, 1831, he was taken by train to Liverpool, apparently travelling in a 2nd Class carriage for his cap was blown off on Chat Moss. Of these carriages he said 'a more odious contrivance to ensure discomfort the wit of man surely never conceived.' Umbrellas were a necessity in wet or snowy weather; the sides of the carriage reached to the neck of a full-grown man when seated. He remembered the journey as having taken between two and three hours; '. . . Being a first-and-second-class train, time was of no consequence', and there was the advantage of refreshments:

'At Eccles trays were "poked" at the passengers filled with the cakes then famous, and at Newton, where an hotel of note was situated near the line, the same attention was paid; "home brewed" and sandwiches were carried by waiters along the length of the train, an imitation of the stage-coach custom.'[8]

A gentleman who rode from Darlington to Stockton in October 1830 complained that the railway was too slow, taking over two hours for the 11 miles, although it often took more than three hours. A fortnight later he travelled from Manchester to Liverpool in $2\frac{1}{2}$ hours complaining now that 'The speed was too great to be pleasant, and makes you rather giddy . . . The road itself is ugly, though curious and wonderful as a work of art.'[9]

Apart from the mile-by-mile descriptions of the route in the numerous guide books to the railway, many short articles appeared in the periodicals of the time, extolling the beauty of such features as 'The noble viaduct across . . . the valley of the Sankey, with its slow-plodding barges urging their tedious way'.[10] Few had a good word to say for Manchester:

'From Patricroft into Manchester there is scarcely anything to attract notice. The train stops on an eminence, just above the junction of the Irwell and the Medlock, whence there is a pretty extensive view over the townships of Hulme and Chorlton. The prospect is anything but cheering. Forests of chimneys, clouds of smoke and volumes of vapour, like the seething of some stupendous cauldron, occupy the entire landscape; there is no sky, but a dark gray haze, variegated by masses of smoke more dense than the rest, which looks like fleeces of black wool, or clouds of sublimated ink . . . There is little in the Liverpool-road to dissipate these gloomy illusions; it is not until the traveller reaches Mosley-street, that he begins to think that Manchester is a place which may possibly be inhabited from choice.'[11]

This aspect of Manchester impressed a French observer[12] who visited the Railway in 1835; the sun appeared through the layer of smoke as a disc without rays, and in the half-light the ear was assailed by the constant shriek of steam from the boilers, the incessant beat of the looms and the continuous heavy rumble of carts.

In those far off days there must have been many curious and amusing incidents on the railway. A traveller in 1842 recounted an episode which occurred when he was travelling from Liverpool in a carriage with three merchants, a butcher and a blind woman engaged to shampoo the Earl of Derby:

'The Liverpool gentleman shaded his conservative importance behind a Tory paper, the shampooing rib entertained the butcher, Runcorn and St Helens were talking about coals and soda, and I was looking on. At the Broad Green Station we lost the butcher .... a female of an enormous obesity, quite an African Venus, made her appearance to fill the empty stall. The guards being occupied somewhere else, the Liverpool gentleman next to the door took hold of the hand that was stretched in for assistance; the task, however, was above the limits of his dragging power; the lady with a good grasp and a heavy pull, tumbled back, taking her cavalier with her, on a heap of snow, where both were safely extended, no serious mischief being the consequence. Now, three men backing her centre of gravity, she was at last hoisted into the vehicle, and all was right save the loss of ten minutes.[13]

For those unable to enjoy the experience of railway travel at first hand, there was, at the Baker Street Bazaar, London, what was described as the Disyntrechon; this 'mechanico-graphicoramic view of the Liverpool Rail-road' was a model railway with trains moving against a 10,000-sq. ft canvas background upon which the prominent features of the line were painted. Admission to the Bazaar, later associated with Madame Tussaud, was one shilling.[14]

CHAPTER SIX

Relations with Other Railways

IN THE COURSE of its independent existence five railway companies effected junctions with the L&MR; three of these, the Wigan Branch Railway, the Warrington & Newton and the Manchester & Leeds, were each to form the nucleus of major railways a few years later. The Bolton & Leigh and the St Helens railways, like the L&MR itself, eventually became constituents of the London & North Western. In addition to these railways, a number of private branch lines, principally from collieries, fed traffic on to the L&MR.

The first powers granted by Parliament for a railway in Lancashire were given to the Leeds & Liverpool Canal in their Act of 1819, for a line from the Wigan & Leigh branch to Low Hall colliery, but the first full railway Act in the county was for the Bolton & Leigh Railway in March 1825.[1] This, the thirty-fourth railway Act passed since 1801, was based on the canal and turnpike Acts of that time of which there had been 80 for Lancashire alone during that period.

Of the 48 original proprietors, William Hulton, coalowner, was one of the most active. George Stephenson was the Engineer, and two plans were submitted for his consideration, one prepared by his own assistant Hugh Steel and the other by Robert Daglish.[2] It would appear that the plan adopted was a combination of the two, but during construction several alterations were made, apparently on grounds of economy, to which Stephenson strongly objected when he inspected the line in February 1827. His report of 10 February was, in fact, extremely critical of Daglish, Steel[3] and of the whole work; his brother Robert was, incidentally, one of the engineers.

A section of the line from Lecturer's Closes, Bolton, to Hulton's Collieries at Chequerbent, was opened on 1 August 1828; the ceremonies included naming the *Lancashire Witch*, the free distribution of the eight waggon-loads of coal brought down and a cold collation at the Commercial Inn. The public were given free rides for the rest of the day.

The B&LR terminus at Leigh was on the canal but several feet above it, and it was always the intention of the proprietors to join the L&MR. To this end the Kenyon & Leigh Junction Railway was launched, largely by L&MR Shareholders, and was authorised in 1829 to build the 2½-mile connecting link to Kenyon Junction, three miles east of Newton.[4] The two lines together totalled about 10 miles, and apart from half a mile near Bolton, was of single track with passing places; the severe Chequerbent Incline, worked by a stationary engine, was on the B&LR section. Later, near Kenyon Junction, a lodge and waiting room were built, together with a locomotive and carriage shed.

On 6 April 1830 another opening ceremony took place when the directors, riding in a coach drawn by *Sans Pareil*, declared the line open for goods between Bolton and Kenyon. Goods traffic on a small scale started to come on to the L&MR at Kenyon Junction in January 1831 and the lines were officially opened to passengers on 11 June. Two of the B&LR First Class coaches, with the unlikely names *Elephant* and *Castle*, formed the first through train to Liverpool, drawn by their engine *Union*, on 13 June.

Arrangements had been made in April 1830 for the B&LR to work their trains between Bolton, Liverpool and Manchester on payment of toll and on condition they found their own locomotives, waggons and carriages. A further stipulation was that every vehicle be fitted with springs and every waggon a brake.

In April 1831 the B&LR notified the L&MR that the working of the line was about to be let under contract to the carrier John Hargreaves of Bolton, and he was introduced to the Board. This was John Hargreaves Junior, whose father was a well-established carrier on the Leeds & Liverpool Canal, operating mainly in the Wigan area. The arrangement was obviously satisfactory to the contracting parties since it was maintained until 1845, when the B&LR amalgamated with the GJR. There were differences between Hargreaves and the L&MR from time to time, usually concerning the condition of his rolling stock or the rate of tolls charged, but they were resolved, despite occasional threats that he would abandon the contract. The Company generally made concessions to enable Hargreaves to compete with the canals when they cut their rates drastically, but when he attempted to increase his charges to the coal owners, he was reminded that the maintenance and encouragement of the coal trade formed part of the agreement between the two railway companies; such action, it was hinted, might lead to a modification of this agreement.

47 *The Liverpool & Manchester Railway and associated lines, 1838*

In the summer of 1831 the Company provided a wharf, shed and cranes at Wapping for the B&LR at a charge of £150 a year; it was situated between the railway and Crosbie Street. Hargreaves' engine stopped at Edge Hill and the L&MR brought the trains through the tunnel at 6d. per ton. At Manchester the B&LR were given the use of part of the coal staithe and the whole of the small warehouse.

The Company agreed in December 1831 to hire locomotives to 'Mr Hargreaves Jnr', but a month later decided to let him have one on order from Bury and to sell him one of their old engines.

At this time Hulton sought the assistance of the L&MR in persuading Hargreaves to charge him less than the maximum tonnage rates on his coal, as he could not otherwise send it to Liverpool or Manchester. In March 1832 he decided to operate his own coal trains and the L&MR agreed to provide locomotives until he had his own, but could not spare any waggons.

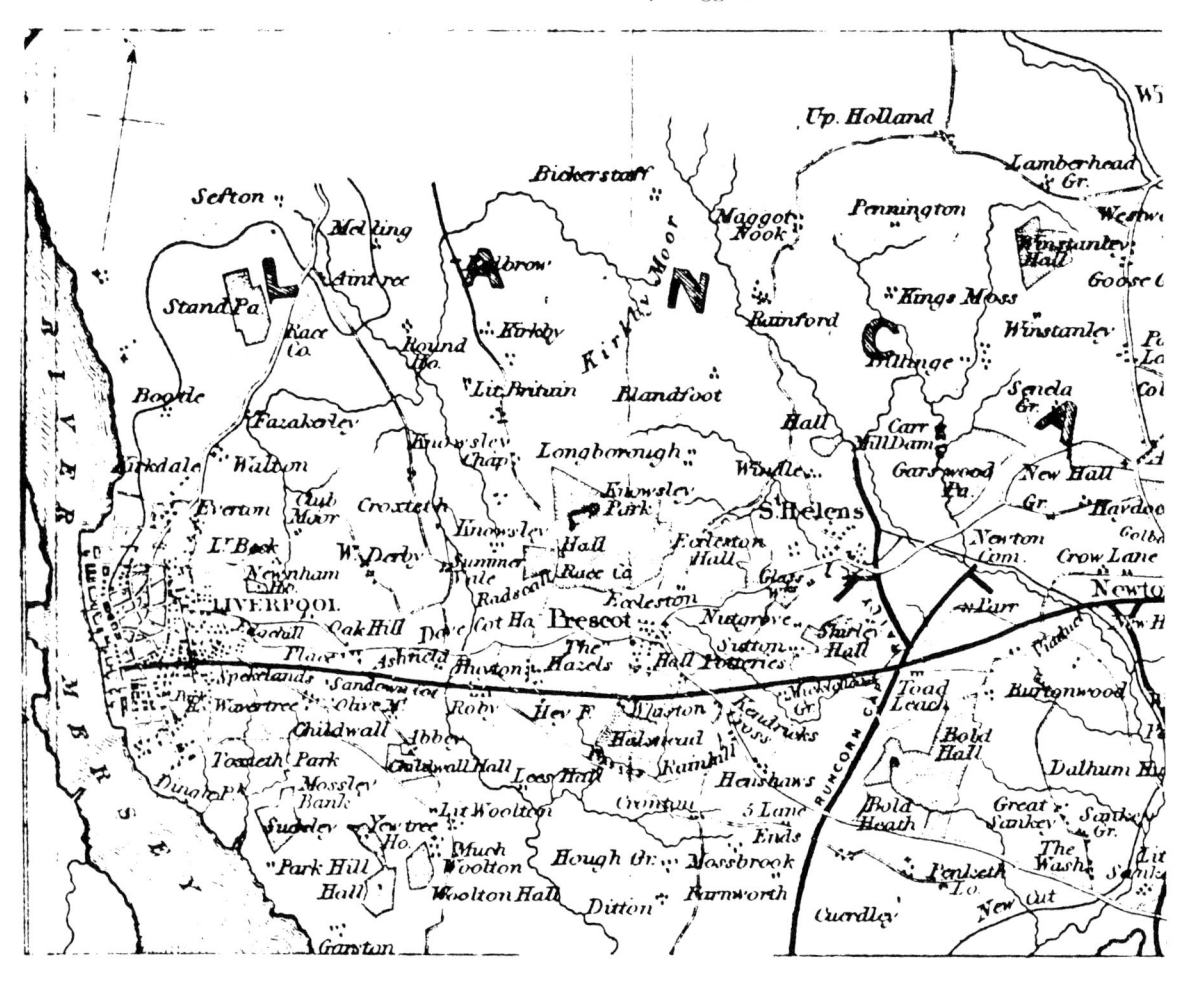

Kenyon Junction was laid out facing Liverpool for most of the B&LR traffic was in that direction and Hargreaves ran a regular passenger service between Bolton and Liverpool, usually attaching carriages to coal or luggage trains. In June 1832 arrangements were made for Bolton passengers to be booked at Manchester and transferred to B&L carriages from Liverpool at Kenyon Junction; in the other direction they were to be taken on to Manchester by the Company's Blue (2nd Class) trains. The fare was fixed at 2s. 6d. 1st Class and 2s. 2nd Class to any point on the B&LR, the L&MR receiving two-thirds of the gross receipts.

Hargreaves operated six 1st Class carriages built by Cooper of Bolton at £400 each. The bodies and wheels were painted green, and the Company's arms were displayed on the panels. There were eight 2nd Class carriages and about 300 waggons, some with iron bottoms; they were used for coal one way and merchandise the other.

By 1840 he had 14 locomotives of a variety of designs and supplied by eight different makers; two were 8-wheeled engines[5] and Hackworth's old *Sans Pareil* was still in service.

At first trains from Kenyon were drawn up the 1 in 30 Chequerbent Incline by a 50 hp condensing engine and allowed to run down the Daubhill Incline by gravity. In descending the inclines the rope was attached to the train and the drum, thrown out of gear, was retarded by a brake. Horses took the train the half-mile from the bottom of the gradient into Bolton. This arrangement was superseded later by having the stationary engine haul locomotive and train up the inclines. The signal for starting the stationary engine was to back the train after attaching the rope, causing a spanner balanced on the rope or winding drum to fall off.

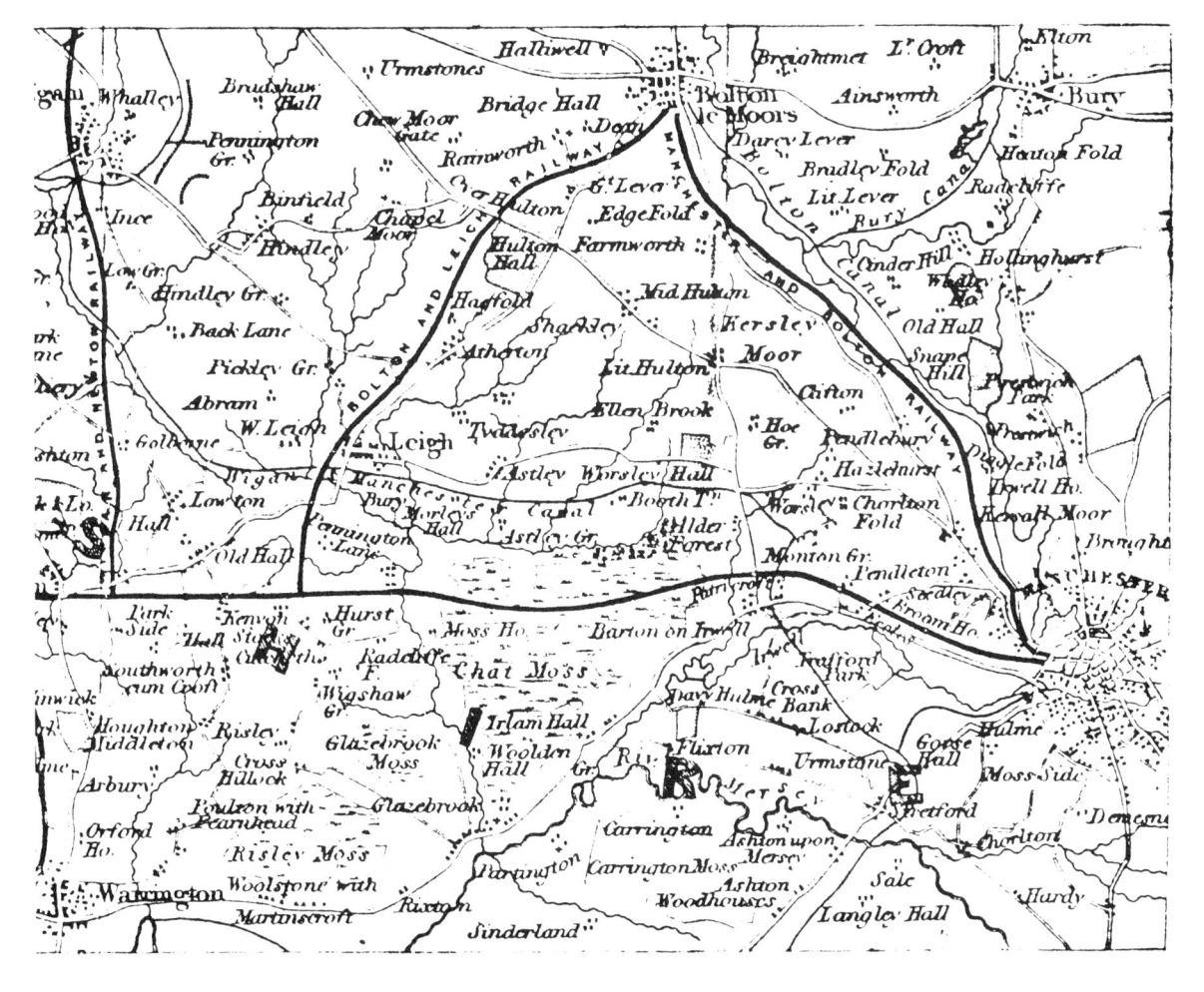

Allcard was sent to Bolton in March 1833 to warn Hargreaves that many of his waggons had defective brakes and that the L&MR would detain any such waggons arriving at their stations, notwithstanding the inconvenience to the B&LR.

Hargreaves does not appear to have exercised that control over his enginemen to which those on the L&MR were accumstoned and many of them seem to have been singularly irresponsible. On the morning of 23 December 1835 serious delays occurred on the main line towards Manchester when one of his coal trains was left on the line, the driver having abandoned it while he took his engine to Eccles for water. Coming back, he ran into his own train, smashing several of the coal waggons. That evening the same man stopped on Chat Moss without sending a signal behind, in consequence of which the Haydock coal engine ran into his train, smashing several more waggons and knocking others off the road. Two more L&M passenger trains were delayed for hours and '... strong representations were made to Hargreaves on the subject.'

Eight years later Hargreaves still had some wild men in his employ. One William Markland was brought before the Magistrates and fined £5 in August 1843 for passing Parkside at full speed in fog with a heavy luggage train, while the early morning mail was standing there.

The St Helens & Runcorn Gap Railway was authorised in 1830[6] to construct a line from the St Helens coalfield to the Mersey at Runcorn Gap, where Widnes was later to develop; the distance was about eight miles with an additional five miles of branches to collieries. By 1845 new branches had brought the total to 16 miles.

Vignoles was the Engineer, and his plans for crossing the L&MR by the 'Intersection Bridge' were submitted to the Board in January 1831 and sent to Stephenson for approval; the crossing was at the foot of the L&MR Sutton Inclined Plane. From a point just north of the bridge, where several branch lines from collieries joined the main line, a spur facing towards Manchester connected the two railways; the line between here and St Helens was completed by the end of 1831 and the L&MR lent the locomotive *Jupiter* and a few carriages for the opening on Monday, 2 January 1832.

Construction of the rest of the line continued during 1832, some of Braithwaite & Ericsson's locomotives being used on the works. There were two inclined planes, the first of half-a-mile at 1 in 30 up to the Intersection Bridge. This was worked by a

48 *The Intersection Bridge carrying the St Helens & Runcorn Gap Railway over the L&MR near the foot of Sutton Inclined Plane, 1832. The St Helens train is drawn by one of Braithwaite and Ericsson's locomotives; to the left of the Liverpool line are some L&MR railwaymens' cottages*

stationary engine erected by Robert Daglish Jnr about 200 yards south of the bridge. After a level section of four miles, a self-acting inclined plane descended towards Runcorn, again at 1 in 30, after which the line levelled off to its termination on the banks of the Mersey.

The first train ran from Broad Oak collieries to the Docks, then under construction at Runcorn Gap, on 28 November 1832; this train was run to settle a wager between a coal owner and the engineer of the Sankey Canal, and the line was not in full operation until 29 August 1833.

A very considerable coal traffic soon developed and the method of operating it involved three locomotives. The waggons were brought to the foot of the Sutton Incline by one locomotive and were then drawn up the incline by the stationary engine; a second locomotive drew them to the top of the southern plane, which they descended by gravity on the self-acting principle, drawing up by a rope the empty waggons returning from the Mersey. At the foot of this second incline a third locomotive was attached to convey them over the last mile to the river.

With this system it was found impracticable to cater for many passengers, and they were not encouraged. In September 1833 two Blue (2nd Class) coaches were hired from the L&MR at £1 per month, one to run between St Helens and Sutton and the other between Sutton and Runcorn Gap; in each case they were attached to coal trains. Passengers walked the intervening distance of the Inclined Plane and this primitive arrangement lasted until 1845; when there were only one or two passengers they were made to ride on the tenders of the engines. The L&MR agreed in principle to one of its 'close' (1st Class) carriages being taken along the St Helens Railway for the convenience of passengers between Manchester and Southport, to start in the summer of 1835, on the '... proper understanding that the Company's carriages should be properly taken care of at St Helens ...' In 1839 Robert Daglish and John Smith contracted jointly to work the St Helens Railway, an arrangement that continued until 1848.

A St Helens engine might well have been involved in a serious accident on 5 August 1841 but for the vigilance and courage of a L&MR porter at Newton Junction. The driver had brought his locomotive on to the main line in order to shunt some carriages before returning to St Helens, when he saw a L&MR ballast train coming down the Sutton Incline a few hundred yards away and on the same line. Alarmed at the inevitable collision, both drivers jumped off their engines, the St Helens man failing to shut off the steam on his. With the L&MR engine slowing down and the other accelerating, the actual collision was slight, but the St Helens engine ran the several miles to Newton Junction with no-one in charge, until the porter there jumped on to the footplate and stopped her. Green, the policeman at St Helens Junction, was fined 40s. for neglecting to signal to the drivers there, and the St Helens Company was told not only to deal with their driver, but also to put in a siding for shunting and to keep their engines off the main line in future.

On amalgamation with the Sankey Brook Navigation on 21 July 1845 the name was changed to St Helens Canal & Railway and after extensions to Garston, Warrington and Rainford in the 1850s the Company was absorbed by the L&NWR on 29 July 1864.

The Manchester & Leeds Railway was incorporated in 1836[7] to construct a 50-mile line from Oldham Road, Manchester, to a junction with the North Midland Railway at Normanton; it would then run the last ten miles to Leeds over the metals of the NMR on payment of toll.

Opened in sections from 4 July 1839, it had no effect on the L&MR until the two systems were joined by the Hunts Bank extensions in May 1844, when through rail communication was established between Liverpool, Leeds and, via the York & North Midland, Hull. The M&LR by amalgamation became an important part of the Lancashire & Yorkshire Railway in 1847.

The Wigan Branch Railway was authorised in 1830[8] to construct a line from the L&MR at Parkside to Wigan, a distance of seven miles. It was launched by the coal proprietors of Wigan; Hardman Earle was the Chairman, Captain James Chapman, RN, late inspector of works on the L&MR, the Secretary, and Vignoles the Engineer.

In July 1831 Chapman intimated that his Company was ready to make the junction with the L&MR but it was not actually laid until June 1832. A month later discussions were held to determine the best method of operating the line and it was decided that the L&MR should take over the working experimentally for three months, sharing with the Wigan Company any profit or loss that might attend the trial.

The Wigan Branch Railway was opened on 3 September 1832 and a passenger service of three trains daily in each direction was maintained by one of the older locomotives and four carriages; certain L&MR trains were stopped at Parkside to take the passengers on to Liverpool or Manchester, the fare to either from Wigan being 5s. 1st Class and 3s. 6d. for 2nd. The Wigan branch being single track, the L&MR insisted on the exclusive use of the line for passenger trains for three 2½-hour periods daily between 7 a.m. and 7 p.m.; the other user was Evans, whose coal trains ran down the line. On the morning of 6 November 1832 one of these coal trains, while running during a prohibited period, hit a Wigan passenger train near Parkside, hurling it back 30 yards, fortunately without casualties.

After three months working the Board discovered that the Wigan Company was receiving only 1s. per ton carried on its line against the L&MR share of 5s., and they voluntarily reduced their own share to 4s. In the meantime John Hargreaves Senior had offered to take over the Wigan traffic between Liverpool and Parkside, and arrangements were made under which he became increasingly involved; eventually he entered into a contract to lease the Wigan line, and in October 1834 an agreement was made whereby the traffic between the railway and Chorley, Burnley and other places on the Leeds & Liverpool Canal was transferred from Leigh to Wigan. The L&MR continued to work the trains over the Wigan line but from December 1835 all goods were carried in Hargreaves' waggons.

The 15-mile Preston & Wigan Railway, a project of the cotton spinners of Preston, was authorised by an Act of April 1831,[9] but construction did not start until 1834. In May of that year it was amalgamated with the Wigan Branch Railway to form the North Union Railway, the first recorded case of a railway amalgamation under Parliamentary powers.[10]

The L&MR put in hand the construction of eight new 1st Class and four 2nd Class carriages in October 1837 in readiness for the opening of the Preston & Wigan line in 1838; four other recently built 2nd Class coaches were also appropriated to this traffic, which the L&MR had agreed to work.

The NUR was opened through to Preston on 31 October 1838, prematurely Captain Chapman said, in order to satisfy the public and the GPO. Waiting rooms were built on both sides of the line at North Union Junction, Parkside, in 1839; as they were for the benefit of NU and GJ passengers, those companies paid three-quarters of the cost. Parkside Station was gas-lit in 1841, the gas apparently being produced on the spot, for the three Companies shared the cost of £150 for pipes, retorts and gasometer.

The Preston traffic increased rapidly and in February 1840 additional horse boxes and trucks to

49 *Parkside Station, c. 1848. Built in 1839, 17 chains east of the original station, at North Union Junction; view looking westward with North Union line diverging on the right*

the value of £2000 to cope with it were ordered by the L&MR Directors. That summer they received invitations to attend the Official Openings of the Lancaster & Preston Junction Railway on Thursday, 25 June and the Preston & Wyre Railway on Wednesday, 15 July; within a short time these were contributing their quota of traffic over the NUR and L&MR.

Arrangements for operating the NUR were extremely complicated; within a few years, Hargreaves, continuing as lessee, had six engines working his goods trains, seven were at work for various coal owners and the NU Company eventually had 17. In addition to these, L&MR engines were often on the line. The NUR worked the passenger trains to Parkside, where the passengers for London had to change to a GJR train and re-book here and again at Birmingham. In 1841 it was a common occurrence for three or four trains from Preston to accumulate at Parkside. Passengers for Liverpool or Manchester were taken on in NUR coaches, either attached to L&MR trains or as complete North Union trains. A special meeting of the L&M and NU Boards was held in October 1844 when it was agreed that a better system of working was necessary in the public interest; it was decided to have completely separate trains for the Preston service, with the possible provision of three engines to work them over the L&MR.

While the Preston extension was under construction the original Wigan line was being converted to double track. In January 1836 an accident occurred when *Vulcan* was derailed about two miles from Wigan, where the contractor's men had left an over-rail wrongly set at the points. The locomotive was 'completely upset' and extensively damaged, while a colliery boy riding on the tender was badly injured.

The NUR acquired its first locomotives in 1837, but occasionally hired one of the smaller L&M engines at the rate of 5s. per mile. On 28 December 1838 their newest engine, No 8, was damaged near Wigan by the *Cyclops*.

On 17 August 1840 a NU train had been started down the Lime Street tunnel with only one carriage brake, and that one defective. With much difficulty the train was stopped by scotching the wheels with bricks and the incident led to a L&MR rule being issued that half the vehicles of all coach trains to Lime Street were to have brakes '... of the best construction and made to the satisfaction of this Company.'

The NUR confided to the L&M Board its anxiety at the imminent opening, in June 1843, of the Bolton & Preston Railway. This Company was incorporated in July 1837[11] and by December 1841 was already open between Bolton and Chorley. The NUR had tried unsuccessfully to arrange a division of traffic with the B&PR and now feared that a price war would ensue. The final portion of the new line between Chorley and Euxton Junction, where it joined the NUR for access to Preston, was opened on 22 June 1843. However, by 1 January 1844 all differences between the two concerns appear to have been resolved, for on that date they amalgamated, some four months before the Act was passed entitling them to do so.

Relations between the Boards of the L&MR and NUR were very cordial and from July 1844 the latter were allowed the singular privilege of meeting in the Lime Street Board Room.

The Warrington & Newton Railway, 4½ miles long, was incorporated on 14 May 1829[12] and opened on 25 July 1831. It was agreed in April that the Company should provide its own engines and rolling stock but the L&MR promised to help in the meantime. Just before the opening arrangements were concluded under which up to 12 1st and 24 2nd Class passengers would be booked by each Blue Train from Liverpool and Manchester to Warrington and that through bookings from Warrington could be made to either; there was to be no travelling on the Warrington line on Sundays.

At the time of its opening the Company had only one locomotive, No 1, *Warrington*, and the L&MR provided additional engines and rolling stock so far as could be spared. Two further engines, 2, *Newton* and 3, *Vulcan*, had arrived on the line by the end of 1831; all were built by Stephenson & Co. and were of the 'Planet' type.

An accident occurred on a section of the line where the platelayers were working on 21 January 1832, when an engine taking coal waggons to Haydock Colliery was thrown off the track; the engineman, James Hope, became entangled with the valve handles and was killed.

The future Locomotive Superintendent of the Midland Railway, Matthew Kirtley, after a spell as fireman on the L&MR and labourer at the Vulcan Foundry, became an engine driver on the Warrington line; his brother William, also a W&NR driver, was appointed Locomotive Engineer to the London, Chatham & Dover Railway in 1875.

Traffic on the new line did not come up to expectations, and its Chairman, Holbrook Gaskell, approached the Board in October 1834 requesting that locomotive power should be provided by the L&MR, but the Company did not wish to extend its responsibilities in this direction.

On 6 May 1833 the Grand Junction Railway Act received the Royal Assent;[13] this was for a line from Birmingham to Warrington which, in conjuction with the London & Birmingham and W&N Railways, would establish a through route between London, Liverpool and Manchester. John Moss was Chairman and the Boards of the GJR and L&MR had many members in common. Most of the capital was raised in Liverpool.

Negotiations for the purchase of the W&NR were opened in 1833 but the price demanded was such that the GJR surveyed an alternative line, crossing the Mersey at Fiddler's Ferry and joining the L&MR at the foot of Whiston Incline. As most of the traffic was expected to be between London, Birmingham and Liverpool, this route would have saved six miles and avoided not only the W&NR but the two inclined planes as well. However, with the prospect of the sale failing to materialise, the Warrington Company came to terms and the GJR absorbed the line on 12 June 1835 under an Act of that date.

The agreement under which the GJR trains were to work over the L&MR had been under discussion since 1833 and was eventually signed in 1835, with the completion of the line still two years distant. In the meantime arrangements were made for George Stubbs, former agent of the W&NR, to take over the working of that line as lessee.

In 1837 engine sheds were built at Brickfield Station, Edge Hill, Liverpool, for 12 locomotives, and at Charles Street, Manchester, for four. The first trial trip was made by the Directors from Liverpool to Wolverhampton on 1 June and a more ambitious one, with separate trains from Liverpool and Manchester that were coupled together at Warrington and taken on to Birmingham as one, on 24 June. During that month the GJR guards and conductors rode on the L&MR trains in order to gain experience.

The GJR was formally opened on 4 July 1837, with little ceremony, to become the first trunk line in Britain. At the end of the month free passes for each other's Engineer and Treasurer were exchanged, and the L&MR Board was presented with two medals commemorating the opening of the GJR by their maker, Promoli. With the opening throughout of the L&BR in September 1838 a great deal of extra traffic came on to the GJ & L&M lines, and arrangements were made to provide more accommodation for the GJR at Liverpool and Manchester. In June 1840, when the L&MR were about to erect new store rooms, offices and sheds, they learned of the possibility of the removal of the GJR locomotive establishment to Crewe and work was suspended.

The GJR trains for Manchester stopped at Parkside to connect with the NUR and from October 1838, a month after the opening of the L&BR, Preston was linked by railway with London. In 1839 through carriages ran between London, Liverpool and Manchester, the journey taking $11\frac{1}{2}$ hours from the capital to either of the northern destinations.

With the opening of the Manchester & Birmingham Railway between London Road, Manchester and Crewe on 10 August 1842, the GJR Manchester services were transferred to that line and the tenancy of the L&M premises in and around Liverpool Road was given up in 1843. Some Manchester mail trains, however, continued to use the Newton – Warrington route.

In 1839 the GJ Company appointed William Buddicom as Locomotive Superintendent and Alexander Allan as foreman of the workshops; on Buddicom's resignation in 1841 he was succeeded by Francis Trevithick. At this time two other officers of the Company resigned: J. R. Chorley, the Secretary, and Captain Cleather, Outdoor Manager and Assistant Secretary; they were replaced by Captain Mark Huish from the Glasgow & Greenock Railway. The Crewe Locomotive Works were officially opened on 23 December 1843, with more ceremony than had attended the opening of the railway itself.

On 9 September 1837 a GJR 1st Class train was involved in an accident at Kenyon Junction. At 7 o'clock on this Saturday evening the L&M 2nd Class train from Manchester had stopped at the junction for two Bolton coaches to be attached at the rear, when the GJ train crashed into them, completely wrecking both carriages. The passengers leaped out in time, all except one woman who was killed; the driver and fireman were subsequently charged with manslaughter.

By March 1839 some rivalry had developed between the enginemen of the two Companies; arguments occurred as to whether the L&M or GJ luggage train should follow first after the 7 p.m. coach train, and the Company ruled that its own should go first. In August James Scott, the L&MR superintendent at Manchester, complained to the Board of the reckless manner in which GJ drivers frequently took their trains along the L&M '... regardless of signals made to them to stop, or proceed carefully, on certain parts of the road ...', quoting a collision on the Whiston Inclined Plane where a GJ engine ignored the signals and ran into a waggon.

In the early hours of Sunday morning, 8 March 1840, a GJR night watchman drove one of that Company's engines into the wall of the north engine house at the top of the Lime Street tunnel, causing damage to the masonry; how this man came to be moving an engine was not explained.

On occasion the GJR had cause to complain; Captain Mark Huish referred to a case in August 1841 of a freight train being taken on to the Whiston Incline in front of a GJ mail train; the danger had been so serious that the L&MR Managing Committee referred it to the magistrates under Lord Seymour's Regulation of Railways Act, 1840.

Three collieries were linked to the L&MR. Near Huyton Quarry a branch on the south side went to Willis's Collieries in the Whiston area; and about ten miles from Liverpool on the north side was the junction for Bourne & Robinson's Elton Head Colliery. Both junctions were laid in the summer of 1830.

James Bourne[14] purchased a new locomotive in October 1832, but Stephenson objected to its use on the grounds of its 5ft 6in. wheels; a certificate was issued, however, but a speed restriction of 12 mph was imposed. The firm gave the railway notice in May 1841 that they were about to work the Elton Head pit under the line but, in order to avoid the risk of subsidence, they proposed to extract only half the coal and required £130 compensation for that which was left. The Company engaged a coal viewer to look into the matter and on his advice refused to allow the coal to be worked at all.

The junction for the Haydock Colliery line was opened in May 1831. Despite a previous decision of the Board that no crossing should be made on the level, it was agreed that this line should come in from the north side at Newton and curve on to the main line towards Liverpool; another curve to the south connected it to the Warrington & Newton Railway. In 1832 a direct crossing to the W&NR was laid; this line crossed the L&MR main line at right-angles.

The Haydock line was originally worked by Thomas Legh, MP for Newton, and in October 1831 the Company agreed to provide engine power to take his coal to Liverpool while he was awaiting delivery of a locomotive of his own. This engine, named after a racehorse, *Shrigley*, went into service early in 1832 and enabled him to undersell the Bolton, Bury and Oldham colliers in Liverpool and Manchester. On 13 April the *Liverpool Mercury* reported that his enterprise had offended the coal-merchants and caused '. . . so much excitement among the workmen that some serious outrages are apprehended.' A troop of hussars was sent to Haydock to protect Legh's men from violence threatened by the other miners.

When Legh's collieries were taken over by Turner and Evans they were given permission for their agents and messengers to travel in separate waggons on their coal trains at a toll of 2s. 6d., but the Board could not approve of any passengers riding in the tender with the engineman.

The Newton Junction was a particularly complicated one and several attempts were made to rearrange the lines. In January 1836 Dixon was asked to make a survey and plan of the Haydock crossing to see if it could be abolished by the erection of a bridge and in March the matter was discussed with Turner Evans & Co, who proposed to move the crossing about 30 yds to the west. In April some Directors, with Locke and Dixon, inspected the crossing where, only the previous week, an L&M train had run into a train of Turner & Evans' empty coal waggons from Warrington which was crossing the main line, and a woman, riding in one of the waggons, had been thrown out and killed.

In December 1837 plans were still being considered; the proposal now was for a crossing to the east of the existing one, which was situated at the foot of the colliery company's inclined plane – itself a source of danger. No satisfactory solution was found and in July 1838 a tall flagpole was erected at the junction and the policeman was instructed to hoist a 'distinctively coloured flag' whenever a coal train was about to cross the main line.

One of Turner & Evans' enginemen, on the evening of 22 March 1843, took an engine that had been under repair at Melling's Rainhill Works on to the L&M line, without permission, and with no red rear lamp, but with several of Melling's workmen on the tender. On Parr Moss the pumps failed and the engine had to be brought back to Melling's Works by one of the Company's bank engines. The driver was brought before the magistrates and find 40s.

Sidings were provided for firms and individuals whose works were alongside the line; the Rainhill Bottle Company were the first to request this facility, in July 1830. One was laid near the Huyton Turnpike for Lord Derby's lime, and at the request of James and George Nasmyth sidings were laid from the main line at Patricroft to the new steam engine factory they were about to erect.

With the trains of several different owners on the line, and with their own engines working on other railways, the L&MR sometimes had the delicate task of apportioning liability for damage resulting from accidents. In November 1833 the Wigan Branch

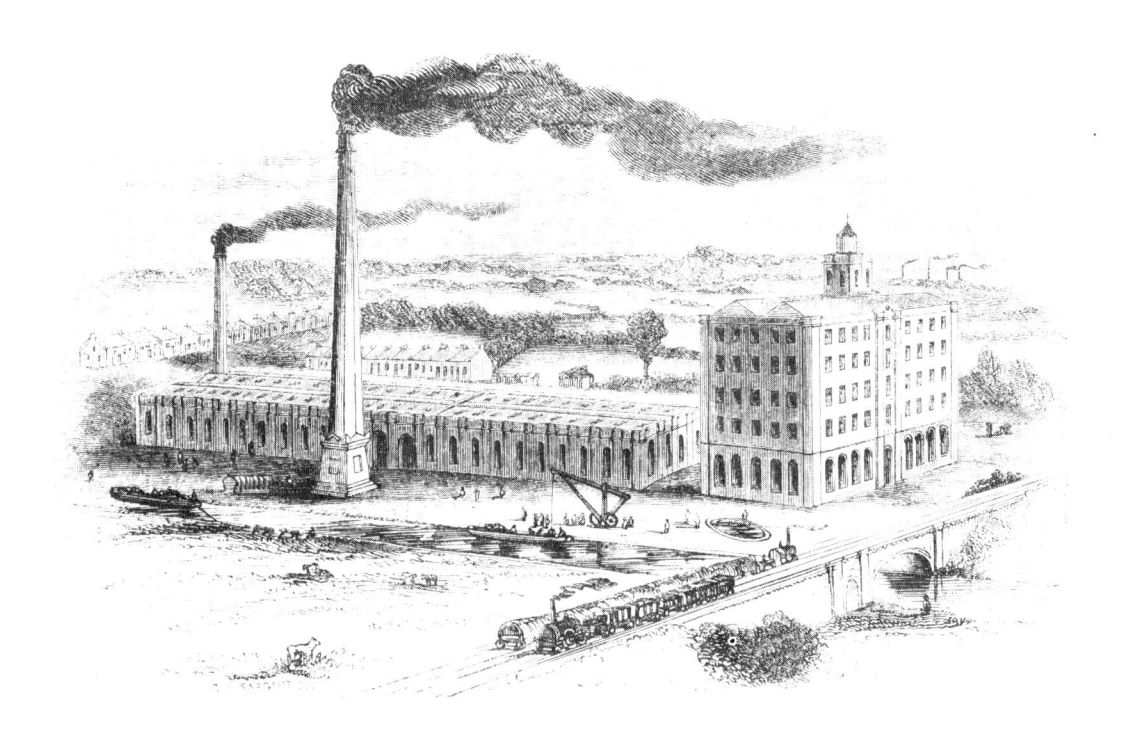

50 Patricroft; Nasmyth's Bridgewater Foundry, the Bridgewater Canal and the railway, c. 1842

Railway tried to persaude the L&MR to contribute to the cost of repairing *Rocket* which had been damaged by a Warrington engine while working on the Wigan line, but the Company decided they were in no way responsible and left the Wigan and Warrington & Newton Railways to settle it between them.

Several of the L&MR Directors were also on the Boards of other companies, and at times they must have experienced some difficulty when a conflict of interest arose between the Boards on which they sat. In December 1837 Lawrence, Moss, Hornby, Sandars, Rotherham and Hardman Earle resigned en bloc from the L&MR Board when another member, Theodore Rathbone, suggested that as they were also directors of the GJR, matters concerning the two companies should be discussed by a committee of which they were not members. A week later they withdrew their resignations on receiving an assurance that no reflection on their honour was imputed. Rathbone himself was also a director of the NUR and possibly felt some embarrassment when either Board was in dispute with the other. In those days there was rarely any suggestion that the directors of the L&MR, or any of the companies associated with it, were other than men of unquestionable integrity.

There was at this time a movement, led by James Loch, for the amalgamation of the L&M and GJ Railways, but it was premature by some years.

From an early date a number of plans were put forward for junctions between the L&MR and proposed lines, usually in the Manchester area. In the autumn of 1828 plans were seriously considered for constructing a Stockport Junction Railway to connect the L&MR with the Cromford & High Peak Line, while in Feburary 1831 the Manchester & Sheffield Railway proposed to join the L&M on, of all places, the Irwell Bridge. The Board refused to consider this, but informed the M&SR that if they built a bridge of their own, they could join the L&MR between it and Ordsall Lane.

A railway from Manchester via Stockport to the Macclesfield Canal, projected in 1834, received assurances from the L&MR that a junction would be favourably considered when the plans were nearer maturity.

Towards the end of 1833 a second route between Liverpool and Manchester, known as the 'North Line', was projected and Stephenson was consulted on the best grounds for opposing it. A year later the Manchester, Bolton & Bury Canal Navigation and Railway Company announced its intention of applying to Parliament for a similar line and the Board commissioned Locke and Vignoles to examine the deposited plans and make a survey. The intended railway was to run from Williams Street, near the Fort in Liverpool, for about 1½ miles along the North Shore and then via Bootle, Rainford, Windle Township and Downall Green to join the MB&BR at Park House Farm, near Irlam-o'th'-Heights. Walker and Burgess were the Engineers and Comrie the surveyor, and their line involved massive earthworks. Locke and Vignoles reported to the Board in January 1835, and their observations were ordered to be printed as a pamphlet;[15] Hodgson and Sands went to London and on 6 April it was reported that they had successfully opposed the rival line, the Bill for which had been thrown out on 30 March.

The MB&BR line, originally authorised in 1831,[16] was built by Jesse Hartley, whose partiality for the use of stone led him to lay the rails on continuous walls of masonry with disastrous results in broken wheels and axles. The line was opened between Salford and Bolton on 29 May 1838 and absorbed by the M&LR in 1846.

Early in 1836 a proposal was made by the Rochdale Canal Company to construct a tunnel to the Old Quay on the Irwell via Charles Street and the L&M goods station, with facilities for transferring freight between the canal and railway. Two years later the project was still under discussion but nothing eventually came of it.

The prospectus of a company that could have been of only academic interest to the Board was received in February 1834, that of the first projected London underground railway. The line was to run in a tunnel under the metropolis from Paddington to the vicinity of London Bridge.

Plans for the west coast route to the Border came before the Board in November 1837; two proposals for lines to run north were examined, '... one by Penrith, the other across the sands of Morecambe Bay to Whitehaven. The Directors would be glad to see a good railway communication from Lancaster northwards', but were not prepared to express an opinion on the merits of either. Subsequently the L&MR gave the Board of the West Cumberland & Morecambe Bay Railway £50 towards the survey.

Little progress had been made by November 1841 when the Committee for promoting the West Coast Route invited the railways south of Lancaster to raise the money for a survey; by this time the L&MR said

51 Sir Hardman Earle (1792–1877). After his early opposition to the railway, he became one of its most active Directors, going on to serve on the Board of the L&NWR until, at his death, he was the oldest railway director in the country. He was created a Baronet in 1869

they were not sufficiently interested to join in, but Captain Huish managed to persaude them otherwise and wrung £50 from a reluctant treasurer. The Company's contribution towards the preliminary survey of the 'Caledonia Railway' in November 1843 was £47.

In April 1845 the Board recorded its concern at the possibility of the GWR extending the Broad Gauge from Oxford to Birmingham, '... into the heart of the Narrow Gauge system ... of which the Liverpool and Manchester forms a part, and from which it emanated, and must be fraught with the utmost inconvenience to the Public.'

Further proposals for the amalgamation of the L&M and GJ Railways were made to the Board by the Chairman on 26 August 1844; he stated that the GJR were willing and it was agreed if 'mutually fair terms' could be arranged. About this time the L&MR had several plans for extensions and improvements under consideration; the enlargement of Lime Street Station, more accommodation for coal and merchandise at Edge Hill and Crown Street, Crosbie Street and Wapping, a new tunnel to the Waterloo Dock and a branch from Patricroft to join the Bury & Rossendale Railway near Clifton on the Manchester, Bolton & Bury Railway. There was also a rather nebulous plan for a line from Roby through the coalfields to St Helens, Rainford and Southport. George Stephenson recommended a line from Kirkdale via Walton to Rainford and surveys were ordered for an application to Parliament.

The GJR was planning to cross the Mersey at Runcorn and to join the L&MR near Huyton to provide a shorter and more direct route to Liverpool. During discussions between the two Boards on 18 September 1844 the GJR suggested joint ownership of the lines from the point of junction, and of the stations. While accepting the argument that if the GJR did not make the Runcorn crossing another company would, the L&M Directors were less than enthusiastic at the prospect of joint lines and stations; alternative arrangements were examined, including a 1000-year lease of part of the L&M line to the GJR.

By the autumn of 1844 a spate of new railway projects threatened the L&MR; this was the beginning of the great railway mania which was soon to cause serious concern to all the established companies, and it lent urgency to the negotiations with the GJR.[17]

In November a possible amalgamation with the NUR was discussed and in January 1845 Woods reported on the B&LR, suggesting a 3½-mile branch to join the NUR and thus avoid the steep Chequerbent Incline.

Early in 1845 a Bill was prepared for the amalgamation of the L&MR, GJR and NUR and the absorption of the Bolton & Leigh and Kenyon & Leigh Junction Railways. The L&MR Board recorded the decision reached by the companies involved that there should be 15 Directors, with the possible addition of two from the NUR who must reside on that line; this was '... to secure the acknowledged beneficial superintendence of Local Directors until the different component parts of this concern were made into one great whole and sectional differences were forgotten in the general prosperity.' In the event the NUR withdrew from the arrangement, after the introduction of the Bill in Parliament. The shareholders, at a meeting called to confirm the Board's decision to amalgamate, were strongly opposed to it, partly because of the delay on the part of the GJR in introducing the Bill.

Once it was presented in April 1845, the Bill met with little opposition and made rapid progress, receiving the Royal Assent on 8 August 1845, just before the adjournment.[18] It authorised the amalgamation of the two major companies under the title of the GJR and the absorption of the B&LR and the Kenyon Junction line. The NUR, which logically should have formed an integral part of the combine, was leased jointly to the GJR and the M&LR on 1 January 1846. On 16 July 1846 the GJ, L&B and Manchester & Birmingham Railways amalgamated to form the London & North Western Railway which, through its connection with the historic Liverpool & Manchester Railway, was proud to call itself 'The Oldest Firm in the Business'. It also enjoyed the distinction for many years of being the greatest joint-stock company in the world.

CHAPTER SEVEN

Stations

THE HEART of the Liverpool & Manchester Railway was at Edge Hill, 1¾-miles east of the Mersey and, in 1830, on the eastern extremity of Liverpool. Here the tunnels from Crown Street and Wapping terminated, the stationary engines for working those tunnels were established and the principal locomotive sheds and repair shops were set up; the locomotive sheds and works were known collectively as the Brickfield Station or 'Melling's Shed'. In course of time, as the railway developed, so the importance of Edge Hill increased.

The original Edge Hill station area was 22 yds wide by 68 yds long, at the bottom of a cutting 40ft deep, hewn from solid rock. About two-thirds of the way up was a string course of stone and above this a strong inclined brick wall surmounted by another string course topped by coping stones; flights of steps cut in the rock led down to the line. Although early prints show visitors on these steps, they were not the passenger entrances to the railway, but were for access to the engine houses.

At the western end were three tunnel portals, the larger central one leading to Wapping; the right-hand or northern tunnel was that to Crown Street and the left-hand portal was added for the sake of symmetry, the excavation extending only a few yards. In October 1832 this blind tunnel was cleared out and used as an engine shed during the winter; later it became the waggon repairing shop and remained as such until, in May 1845, it was decided to drive this tunnel through to the Crown Street coal depot. It was excavated to the same dimensions as the Wapping Tunnel so as to carry two tracks, and in order to provide sufficient clearance the cutting wall on the south side was cut back a couple of feet. The rock above the tunnels was streaked with red and white in variegated grain, and a contemporary writer[1] expressed the hope that no paint or whitewash would profane its natural beauty.

High above the tunnels at the western corners of the area towered the two chimneys of the boiler-houses. Over 100ft high, they were built of one course of brickwork, ascending spirally, and they were finished to resemble Doric columns with pediments and capitals of stone. At the eastern end were the two engine houses designed by John Foster in the form of towers on either side of the line, which was spanned at this point by the famous Moorish Arch. On 14 September 1829 the Board approved Foster's two designs for the '... different fronts of the Engine Houses and Gateway at the top of the Tunnel'; intended to have been of stone, by the time building started at the end of June 1830 there was a shortage of this material and stuccoed brick was used instead. The engine houses were 35ft long by 18ft wide and stood about 29ft apart.

On either side of the cutting vaults were excavated from the rock for use as boiler houses, engine sheds and coke stores; others were fitted up as passengers' waiting rooms and offices, there being no room in the cutting for ordinary buildings. Both the cutting and the Wapping Tunnel were liable to flooding and in September 1831 a culvert was made to drain the cutting; in the tunnel, water that had percolated through the rock could be heard constantly flowing in the drain beside the track.

The provision of stationary engines to work the trains through the tunnels was discussed on 27 April 1829, when it was agreed that Robert Stephenson & Co. should construct one for £1600 under a contract to be prepared. The engine was sent from Newcastle at the end of September but on 5 October reports reached the Board that the vessel carrying it had been wrecked off the coast near Aberdeen and was a total loss, although it was thought the engine would be salvaged. George Stephenson reported on 16 November that the Tunnel Engine was ready at Newcastle – whether the original or a new one was not stated – and he was told to have it sent through the Forth & Clyde Canal. At the same meeting the Company's Solicitor was directed to claim a penalty of £500 from RS&Co. as the engine had not been put up by 4 November according to the contract. The firm appealed but the Directors refused to release them from the penalty clause, and ordered that the amount be deducted from the next payment due to them; the £500 was recovered on 25 January 1830. Meanwhile the tunnel engine had arrived at Liverpool Docks.

About three weeks after the opening of the railway it became apparent that a second tunnel engine was needed, and on 6 December RS & Co. contracted to supply one in four months for £1800. They appear to have been of similar design, with cylinders of 24in. diameter and 6ft stroke; the beams were 13ft 4in. long and the flywheels 20ft in diameter. Normally the engine on the north side worked the Crown Street tunnel and the southern one the Wapping traffic; the new engine came into service about the time when the Company announced that the line was open to carriers and goods traffic was starting in earnest.

Steam was supplied from return-flue boilers, two on each side, set in excavations in the sides of the cutting near the engines. Smoke was carried to the

52 *Edge Hill; Moorish Arch looking towards tunnels, 1831*

chimneys by flues running some distance through the rock. In 1832 a steam pipe connecting the boilers on either side was installed so that either set of boilers could be used for either engine, and at the same time an underground passage was made between the two engine houses to avoid the need for men to pass 'within the moving machinery'. Through this subway a connecting shaft was put in '. . . to enable the South Engine to work the Little Tunnel rope without putting in motion the Big Spur Wheel.'

The winding mechanism for both tunnels was supplied by William Fairbairn and that for the small tunnel was comparatively simple, the rope being wound on a reel 3ft 4in. in diameter and 3ft wide. When the train reached Crown Street the rope was detached and the end brought back to Edge Hill by a small four-wheeled carriage, called a pilot, drawn by one horse in readiness for the next train; the reel was put out of gear, allowing the rope to unwind easily and the whole operation was completed in about five minutes.

The Wapping Tunnel was worked by an endless rope running down the centre of one track and back along the other. The main pulley, driven by cog-wheels from the shafting, was 10ft in diameter and

53 *Edge Hill; Moorish Arch and Engine Houses from Tunnel, 1831*

placed horizontally below rail level, its centre being exactly between the two tracks. In line with it, and on the tunnel side were two 5ft pulleys also set horizontally, at distances of 11ft, to sustain the tension on the rope. The rope passed twice round both the large pulley and the centre one, and once round the second small pulley; the latter was mounted on a tightening carriage which ran on a small track, and to which was attached by a chain a counterweight of $2\frac{1}{2}$ tons suspended in a well 100 yds deep. If atmospheric or other conditions caused the rope to stretch the weight fell, moving the carriage farther away to take up the slack; when it shrank it pulled the carriage closer against the pull of the weight.

With the extension to Lime Street a new passenger station was required at Edge Hill to the north of the original area. Referred to at first as the 'New Wavertree Lane Station', the plans were approved in December 1834 and in March 1835 a contract was let for the building of the new engine houses and offices for £1981. The new station was about 500ft by 100ft in area; the approach was by two inclined carriage roads descending from gates above and in line with the tunnel portal. Stone platforms ran the length of the station and, set back 19ft from the edge, were the waiting rooms, offices and other accommodation in two-storey stone buildings of uniform classical design. On 29 August 1836 the Board recorded that the Edge Hill Coach Station was now in use and the Wavertree Lane stopping place for 2nd class trains was to be discontinued.

Edward Bury assisted with some experiments on the old tunnel engines in May 1833 to determine the best specification for the new engines to be ordered for the Lime Street Tunnel, and in the early months of 1834 several tenders for these engines were considered. The Board had asked Dixon if the new tunnel could be worked by shafting from the existing engines, but were assured that this was impracticable. Both George Stephenson and Dixon advised the purchase of two engines as a precaution against the failure of one, and a pair were ordered of Mather, Dixon & Co. in April 1834; with the rope gearing they cost a total of £2880.

Designed by John Grantham, MICE, they were two-cylinder non-condensing engines of the side-lever type, similar to the paddle steamer engines of the period. The cylinders were 25in. in diameter with a 6ft stroke, and they worked the connecting rods downwards to the 18ft beam, situated in a vault cut out of the sandstone rock; the beam pedestals were fixed to the rock floor of the pit.

The engine houses were built at the eastern end of the new station, one on each side of the line; they

54 *Edge Hill Passenger Station, 1836; new engine houses in foreground*

projected 6ft farther across the platforms than the other buildings and were connected by a series of underground chambers in which the winding machinery was situated. The engines were connected by the main shaft which ran beneath the line and upon which was mounted the 21ft drum wheel; this was in effect a flywheel and its shaft could be rotated by either engine.[2]

The endless rope, 4800 yds long, 6in. in girth and weighing 8½ tons, ran in a 10in. groove round the circumference of the drum wheel. A series of six horizontal and vertical sheaves 5ft in diameter guided the rope on to the drum wheel; one of these, mounted on a tightening carriage, maintained the tension. The rope ran in a covered channel past the station buildings and over 474 sheaves set at 8 yd intervals

55 *Rope and tightening-carriage machinery, Edge Hill*

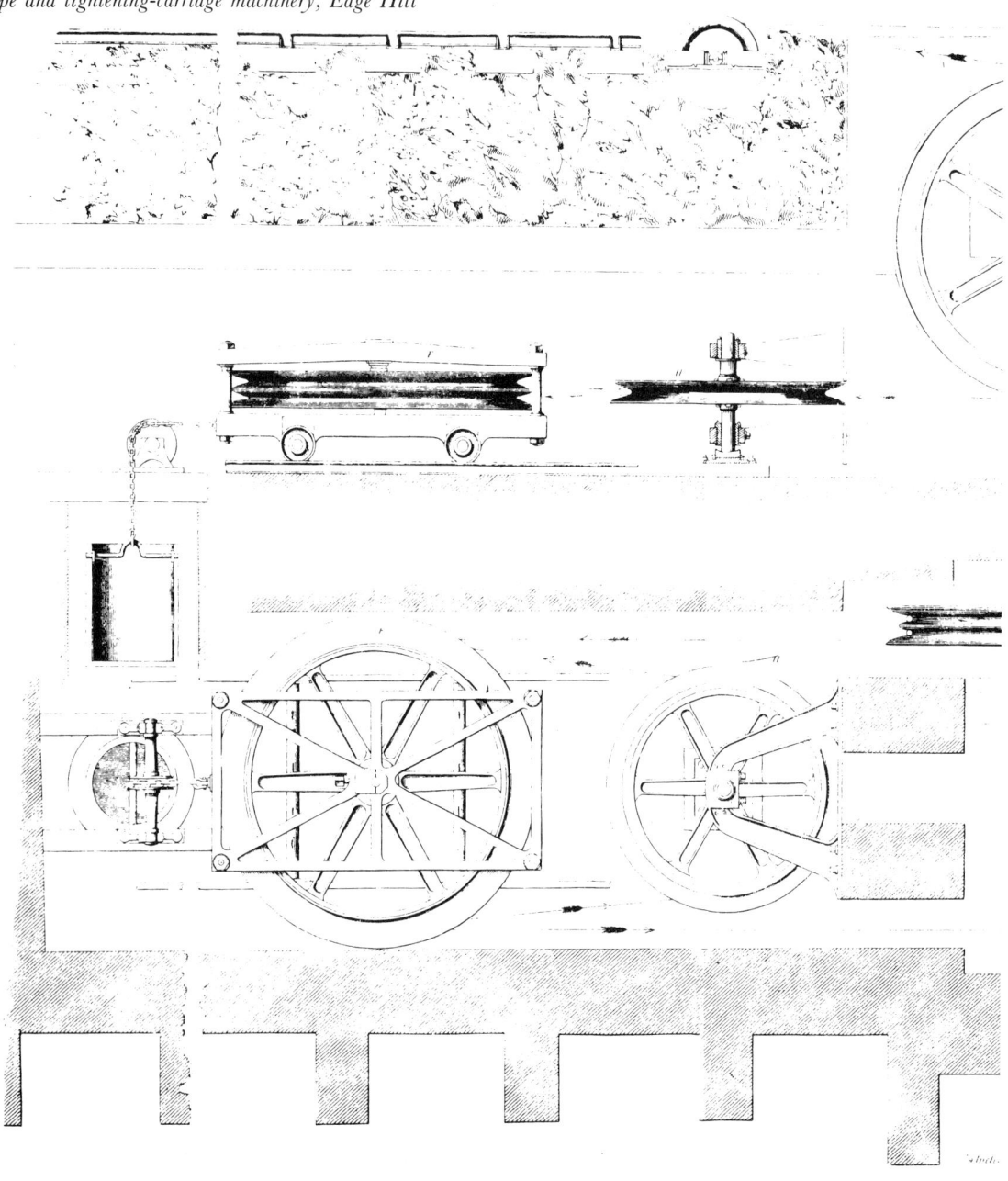

down to Lime Street and back, passing round a 5ft horizontal pulley at the bottom.[3] This hempen rope, tarred to the point of saturation, stretched nearly 500 yds in the first few weeks of operation. The bank from Lime Street was 2370 yards at varying gradients, but with a mean rise of 1 in 92; 2230 yds of the incline was in tunnel. The engines, when run in, could draw a 55-ton train up in six minutes.

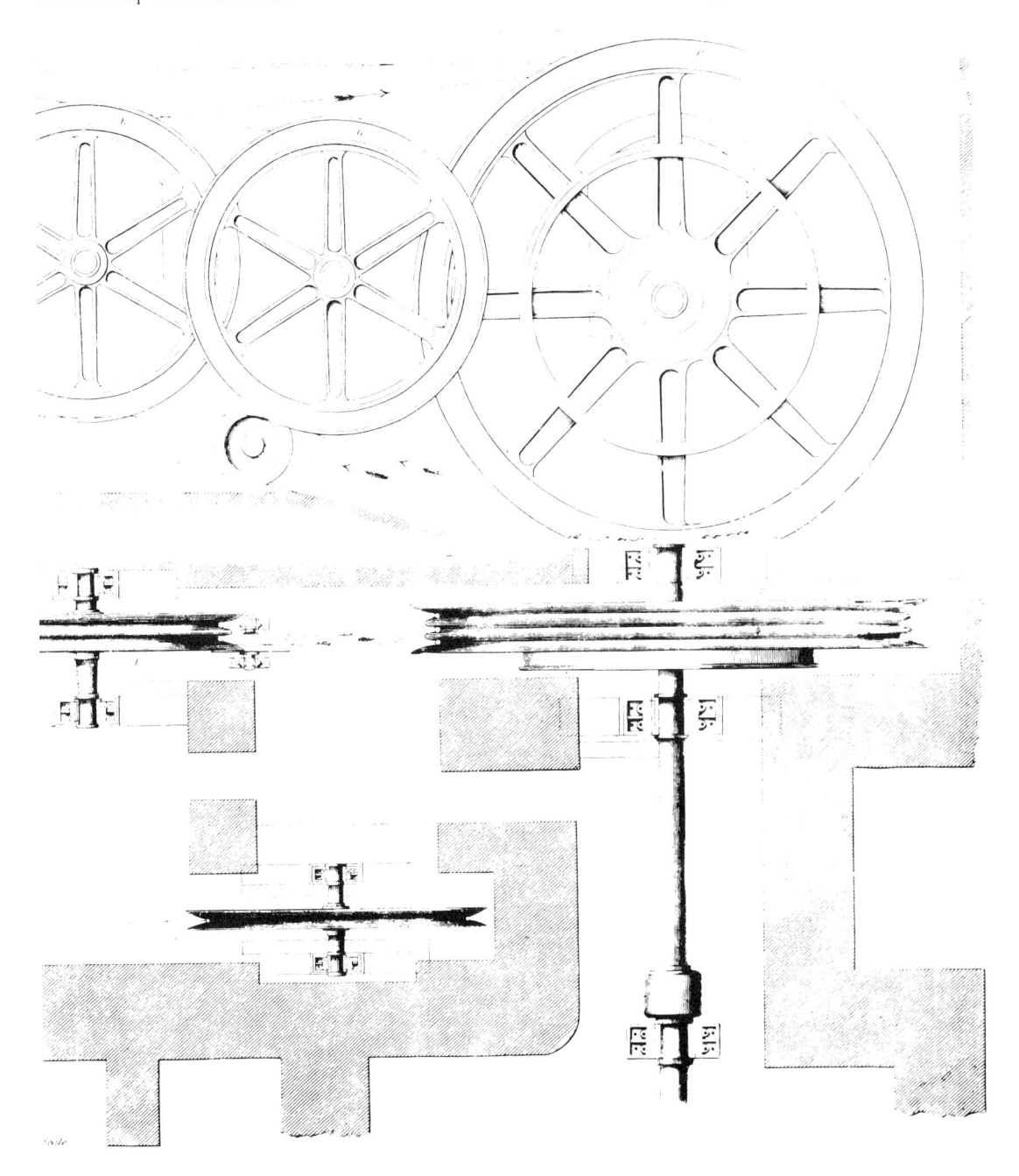

Two additional boilers were required for the new engines, and were supplied by Thomas Vernon of Liverpool for £1120 the pair; they were multi-tubular, with 3in. tubes. They could not be erected close to the engines, however, and were sited near the old boilers, 448 yds distant, the steam being conveyed through 10in. pipes laid in a small bore tunnel excavated through the rock. The steam accumulated in a reservoir near the engines, but there was a serious loss of pressure between the boilers and the reservoir, together with a great deal of condensation. Stephenson had foreseen this and had suggested having one of the boilers near the engines and taking the smoke back to the chimneys through a flue, along which a steam pipe from the other boiler would have been laid; the hot gases would have reduced the condensation in the steam pipe, but the plan was presumably regarded as too complicated, for it was not adopted.

In 1840 a set of coke-fired tubular boilers was erected on the north side of the line close to the engines, producing greater efficiency on half the fuel consumption – 15 tons of coke per week.

Parliament's restriction on smoke from locomotives did not extend to the original stationary engines and boilers and for years they ran on cheap coal. By 1839, however, the six boilers constantly fired were producing a volume of smoke objectionable to the surrounding neighbourhood, and coke was mixed with coal for the Wapping Tunnel boilers in an attempt to abate the nuisance.

The signal to start the ropes in the old tunnels was by bell; the wire running along the side of the tunnel was often broken, causing heavy delays to traffic and the engineman, Robert Kirkup, was reprimanded in October 1833 for failing to get it repaired quickly. On the completion of the Lime Street Tunnel a pneumatic signal was installed for communicating between the station and engine house. It consisted of a ½in. gas tube with a 'gasometer' at each end, supplied and laid by the gas company. When air was forced either way it sounded a whistle at the far end. Shortly afterwards the Old Tunnel bell wire was replaced by a similar system.

The first tunnel ropes were made in Sunderland and cost £60 per ton; they were of 5½in. circumference, 2000 fathoms in length, and lasted little over a year. In September 1832 a 'New Patent India Rubber Rope' was installed in the small tunnel to deal with the ten-waggon coal trains going through to the Crown Street depot. The short 'messenger ropes' by which the trains were attached to the main haulage ropes were also described as being of rubber.

The ropes broke occasionally, the first instance being on 30 August 1832, when a train had reached the 70th lamp, near the top, and ran back down the tunnel to Wapping. The tunnel engineman knew, when the engine speed suddenly increased, and was able to give warning, but the brakesman could not stop the train and managed to get off just before it reached the lower pulley wheel. The Lime Street

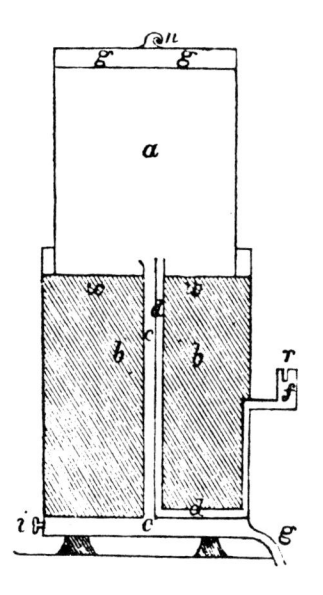

56 *'Gasometer' for operating pneumatic signals in Lime Street and Wapping Tunnels. The air-chamber* a *is suspended by a rope from a beam, attached to hook* h. *When released, the air-chamber, weighted at* g *with lead, gradually sinks into the water vessel* b, *forcing the air through the tube* c *and the tunnel pipe* g *into a whistle or organ-pipe in the distant engine house, to produce a sustained note. On being hoisted by the rope, the air-chamber is refilled through the valve* r *and the tube* d

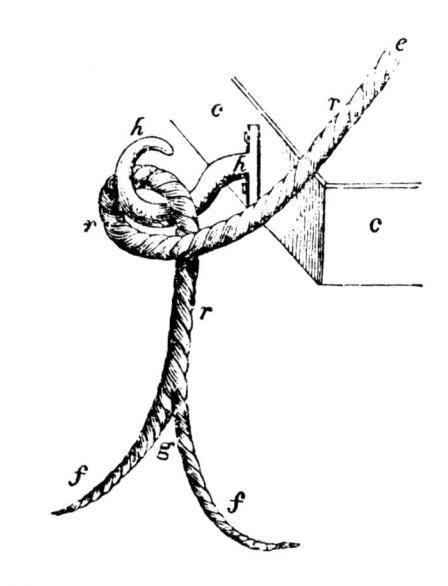

57 *Messenger rope, attached to the tunnel rope by the tapering ends* f. *It was hand-held at* e *by the guard until the train reached the top of the tunnel, and then released*

tunnel rope had been maliciously cut several times, and in August 1845 some handbills offering a £50 reward for the discovery of the offender were distributed. Wire ropes had been used in the Crown Street tunnel from 1842 and the Board were considering their use in the long tunnels at that time, but as the less flexible wire would have involved the replacement of the pulleys by larger ones, the idea was shelved.

In July 1832 one of the engines was damaged by cotton waste having been '... knowingly placed for an evil purpose' in the valve box; John Melling, the Superintendent, could find no evidence as to the culprit.

About the time when the Lime Street tunnel engines were coming into service two fatal accidents occurred at Edge Hill. In July 1836 one of the enginemen was scalded to death and some others injured when a steam pipe on one of the old Tunnel engines broke, and in August during the first week of the opening of the New Tunnel, one of the original Wapping Tunnel boilers blew up. On this occasion one man was killed outright and two others died later from their injuries.

On 8 September 1836, as the 3 p.m. train from Lime Street was about half-way up the tunnel the chain of the balance weight broke and the slackened rope suddenly stopped. The train returned to Lime Street and two locomotives were sent down to draw it up the tunnel; they continued to haul the trains up to Edge Hill until the rope was working again at 10 a.m. the next day. By 1839 the chain by which the weight was suspended had been replaced by a rope.

Steam whistles, arranged to blow automatically when the water level fell below three inches, were ordered to be fitted to the boilers in December 1836, after the flue of one of those on the south side had been burnt out; the failure of the clack valve caused the water to be forced back through the feed pipe unnoticed by the engineman, Robert Weatherburn, who was attending to some waggons at the tunnel mouth.

Apart from the main engines and boilers at Edge Hill, other equipment was added as occasion arose. In October 1832 the old boiler from the locomotive *Phoenix* was installed as part of a water-feeding apparatus for the large boilers and in September 1835 an additional engine was bought from Banks & Co. for the dual purpose of pumping water to the new boilers and drawing up coal through the small tunnel. It was a compact high-pressure engine of $13\frac{1}{4}$in. cylinder and cost only £250; installed in No 1 Engine House, it enabled the two large engines to be used solely for working the Wapping Tunnel. In May 1837 a hot-air smoke-consuming apparatus was completed with the erection of four 30ft cast iron pipes.

In December 1838 the Board decided to replace the boilers at the Old Tunnel mouth, south-side, and Booth was asked to inspect the smoke-consuming apparatus used at Royle's factory in Manchester with a view to its adoption for the new boilers. These were made in the Company's yard, the first being reported as nearly ready in August 1839.

As the trains for Lime Street arrived at Edge Hill, the locomotive was uncoupled and driven forward into a dead-end siding between the station and the tunnel-mouth. Lighted oil lamps were then hung outside the sliding window of each carriage door and the train pushed by hand to the tunnel, when it started to descend by gravity.

About 400 yds east of the Moorish Arch the lines from Wapping and Lime Street converged, and for some distance there were four tracks and numerous sidings. To the south were the locomotive shops of both the L&MR and the GJR and opposite these was a carriage shed 140 yds long.

In 1845 the Company obtained powers to drive yet another tunnel from Edge Hill, this to the North Docks near Waterloo Road, and to extend and improve its installations at Crown Street and Edge Hill. The works were started after the amalgamation of the L&M and GJ Railways, and were completed by the L&NWR. Edward Woods, the L&MR Chief Engineer, was in charge of the work and remained with the Company until its completion in 1851.

The Victoria Tunnel, two miles long, was started in 1847 and finished two years later. New engine houses for working the tunnel were built at an angle to the older buildings, but in line with the new tracks, and a boiler plant was erected south of the station. This contained six boilers, and was capable of supplying steam for the new engines then installed for working the Wapping Tunnel and the new tunnel to the Crown Street coal yards. During these alterations at Edge Hill an iron-and-glass overall roof was erected over the passenger station.

The Company's Liverpool terminus at Crown Street on the eastern edge of the town, was a two-storey building of elegant design, housing the booking offices, waiting room, counting house and Board Room. A verandah ran the length of the building, and its 12 iron columns also supported one side of the wooden overall roof, the other side resting on a curtain wall. There were three lines of rails, the centre one with the tunnel rope being the arrival road; they were connected by points near the tunnel portal and by wooden turnplates beyond the other end of the station. In common with the other stations, Crown Street was completely devoid of platforms. The 'Inspector of the Coach Wheels' was stationed here and his duties included attending to the points and the signal bell at the top of the Little Tunnel. In 1831 a separate ladies' waiting room was provided.

No locomotives entered the station and the trains at different times were manhandled or drawn by horses to the tunnel, where they were 'let off', to descend by gravity to Edge Hill.

Alongside the passenger station, but screened from it by the wall, were large goods and coal yards, and the Millfield Works. The yards were extended in 1832 to deal with the rapidly increasing traffic, and over the years further extensions became necessary. The whole area was enclosed by high walls.

It soon became apparent to the Directors that Crown Street was too far removed from the centre of Liverpool ever to serve as the town's principal station; it was so remote that several of the approach roads, including Crown Street itself, were unpaved until some time after the railway opened. On 9 May 1831 the Sub-Committee recommended that a survey be made with a view to bringing the railway into the town somewhere between Dean Street, Charlotte Street and Ranelegh Street, and in June Stephenson produced a plan for a line from Edge Hill to Dean Street, to be followed by one for a tunnel from the Cattle Market at Haymarket to a point near the Engine Shops. At a Special General Meeting on 28 September the Shareholders were in favour of the project and some in fact wanted a third tunnel driven to Princes Dock. The Common Council had already approved the scheme subject to the extension being restricted to passengers only,[4] and in October Swanwick drew up the detailed plans for the approach to Parliament. The estimates for the tunnel and station, to face on to Lime Street, totalled £100,000, but when completed 30 minutes would be saved on the first 1½-miles of the journey, and the saving on the expensive and inefficient buses, provided by the Company to convey passengers between Crown Street and Central Liverpool, would equal the interest charges on the additional capital.

The Bill received the Royal Assent on 23 May 1832[5] and a loan to cover the cost of the new works

58 *Edge Hill Station, c. 1848. View shows a 'Bird' class locomotive preparing to take the train on from Lime Street Tunnel, porters stowing luggage on the carriage roofs and the stationmaster watching from a pulpit-like balcony*

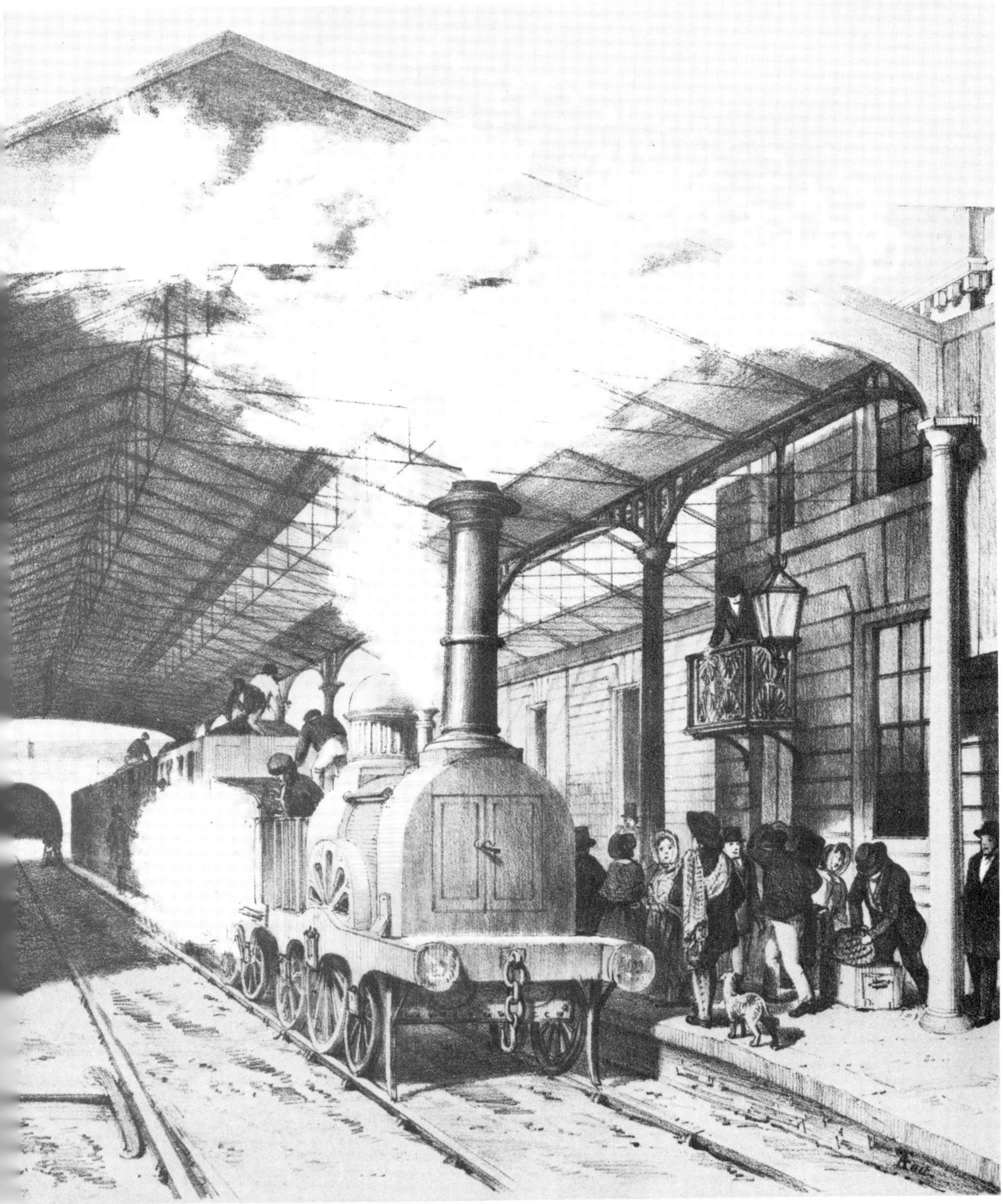

was raised with the Exchequer Loan Commissioners.

In anticipation of the Act, arrangements were made in December 1831 for the purchase of the Old Botanical Gardens and two fields east of Crown Street for dumping spoil from the tunnel and Stephenson started to prepare the specifications for advertising the contracts. In July several shareholders were having second thoughts about the necessity for a new tunnel and suggested making an open cutting from the Wapping Tunnel to a passenger station in Park Lane at the upper end of the Goods Yard.

By the end of October the tenders had been received and that of Mackenzie, Longworth & McLeod at £38,156 was accepted, for completion of the work in two years. For some reason, probably the time limit, Mackenzie's partners withdrew, and he signed the contract with Henry Haydock as his surety. Work started immediately under the direction of Allcard; Stephenson spent little time on the undertaking and after about six months the Board asked Joseph Locke to make an independent survey of the workings. They must have had some doubts about the accuracy of the alignment, and these proved to be well-founded, for when Locke's report was read on 24 June it was revealed that several sections of the tunnel would never have formed a straight line; in one instance the two portions would have passed each other without meeting at all.[6] The report had previously been shown to Allcard and Dixon for their comments, and on 8 July Stephenson attended the Board to account for the errors. He regarded the deviations as trifling and claimed that they would be 'scarcely perceptible' when the tunnel was finished. He said that no blame attached to Allcard, and that an error of 2ft 2in. between the Crown Street and Asylum shafts was caused by the needles of the compasses being deflected by an iron pump used to drain the Asylum shaft; this was only discovered when the new Pembroke Street shaft was sunk. His explanations for the more serious errors were not recorded, but his resentment against Locke began at

59 *Crown Street Station, Liverpool, 1833*

this time and the final breach between the two engineers was not long delayed. Two weeks later Allcard resigned and Dixon assumed responsibility for the tunnel.

By a series of drifts and widenings of the excavations, the alignment was corrected, but at the cost of delaying the eventual completion of the work. In September 1834 the tunnellers struck an underground spring sufficiently large to warrant a Mr Etches being allowed to pump the water to his slaughterhouse at Browntree Hill.

It had been decided in 1832 that the new tunnel should be lighted and warmed, and in October 1834 plans were produced to warm part of it from a boiler in the yard at the bottom; the hot water was to be carried by a pipe up one side for 400 yds, and back down the other side to the boiler, the rest of the tunnel being warmed by the heated air thus produced rising up to Edge Hill. Directions were given in May that the temperature of the old tunnel be taken on different days and times, and compared with the open air, the Board presumably having had second thoughts on the necessity of warming the Lime Street tunnel. At this time it was decided not to light the tunnel with gas, but to hold trials, 'carrying the lamps with the trains' in Wapping Tunnel on Saturday, 2 May.

On 3 January 1835 the last joining of the tunnel sections was made under Edge Hill, and a few days later the directors walked through the whole length of 2230 yds; it was 17ft in height and 22ft wide, and like the Wapping Tunnel, was on a falling gradient from Edge Hill.

The first step taken towards building Lime Street Station was the purchase of the Cattle Market from the Common Council for £9000 in October 1833;[7] consideration of several plans followed in May 1834 when it was decided to have two 'departure wharves', '... to effect a classification of passengers'. The station was, in fact, planned piecemeal, fresh sets of drawings appearing every few months, first for the general offices, then for the parcels office and coachmakers' workshops fronting Great Nelson Street, the train shed roof, the carriage house workshop and dwelling house on the south side by Gloucester Street, and the façade in Lime Street.

John Foster produced some drawings for the front elevations accompanied by estimates ranging from £3700 to £6120, the latter to include ashlar-worked ornamental columns. A deputation of directors waited upon the Mayor in February 1835 to follow up an invitation to the Council to contribute to the cost of building the station. Their argument that '... the great public entrance into Liverpool should not be inferior in style and design to the most approved Public Buildings of the Town' persuaded the Council to offer half the extra cost of '... erecting the proposed façade above the sum of £2100 ... the estimated cost of a plain building', up to an amount of £2000, and subject to approval of the designs. In May the Council promised to pay £2000 as soon as £6123 had been expended and the work completed to their surveyor's satisfaction, and the next month the site was at last cleared, after over 18 months' delay.

The offices, workshops and various other parts of the station were designed by Cunningham, a Liverpool architect, and he in partnership with Holme, designed the wooden, partly glazed overall roof. All the drawings were submitted to Foster for approval. Several contractors were involved in the construction of the station, John Kilshaw undertaking most of the building with Samuel and James Holme erecting the roof; George Robinson of Toxteth Park built the façade. Another contractor paved and flagged the station area, and two gas companies, the 'Old' and the 'New', were invited to tender for the station lighting.

Lime Street Station was opened on Monday, 15 August 1836 while still unfinished. At the east end was the lamp room and in September another room was ordered to be built to correspond with it in appearance, to be used for the tunnel signalman, and for the storage of axle grease, screw chains and other stores. Work on some of the ancillary buildings did not start until 1837, and when completed they were let immediately to the GJR. In May 1837 the iron palisade and gates in front of the façade were erected by James Monro of New Scotland Road for £148, and the station frontage now being completed, the Company formally applied to the Mayor for the Council's contribution. Plans for a suite of offices at the south-west angle with Gloucester Street were prepared for Foster's approval in July 1837, and in February 1838 he was paid £200 for his professional services.

The exterior of the finished station was of very elegant appearance, as is evident from the engravings made at the time, and the interior had most of the features to be found in the termini soon to be constructed all over the country. Low platforms were provided on each side of the station, and tracks in between the arrival and departure lines were used for shunting and carriage storage. Turnplates, 20 in number, connected the lines at various points for the transfer of carriages; these could accommodate vehicles with an 8ft 6in. wheelbase.

Traffic increased to such an extent that the Board considered the enlargement of Lime Street in September 1842, and a station improvement committee was set up; in May 1844 the first suggestion of an iron roof was made. The general plans for remodelling the station were produced in 1846 by Joseph Locke and the work eventually took four years to complete; it proceeded without interfering with the growing traffic, and with only occasional inconvenience to the passengers, as when the refreshment rooms became temporary booking offices.

The tunnel entrance was cut back and Hotham Street, which had passed over the tunnel, was carried across the railway on a cast iron bridge supported by Tuscan columns, designed by Edward Woods. The platforms were now extended to the tunnel face, giving a length of 500ft.

A new block of offices with a frontage of 270ft along Great Nelson Street on the north side of the station, was designed by William Tite FRS. The façade was of brick faced with millstone grit quarried in Darley Dale, the same kind of stone as was used in St George's Hall; the plinths of the columns and of the building generally were of Devonshire granite. The ground floor consisted of booking offices, waiting rooms, refreshment rooms and various other offices; the Board Room and Secretary's department were on the first floor and the ticket department was housed on the second floor. Kitchens, third-class refreshment rooms, staff rooms and offices of various kinds occupied the basement. The contractor for the building was John Jay of London Wall, and the cost about £30,000.

The Company originally intended having an iron roof similar to that at Euston, consisting of a number of ridge roofs supported by rows of iron columns between the tracks, but were persuaded by Richard Turner of the Hammersmith Iron Works, Dublin, to consider his plan for a single curved roof, principally on the grounds of safety. The single span roof had become a possibility following the introduction of the wrought iron deck-beam in the building of iron vessels. The Company agreed to a trial and Turner erected two bays of the roof at his Dublin works, where they were subjected to stringent tests by Locke; after some modifications Turner was awarded the contract and he erected the roof over a period of ten months in 1848–9. In the meantime the disadvantage of the pillar-supported roof was illustrated at Euston,

60 *Lime Street Station, 1836*   **61** *Lime Street Station, interior, 1836*

62a *Lime Street Station, 1849; elevation of new offices in Lord Nelson Street designed by William Tite, FRS*

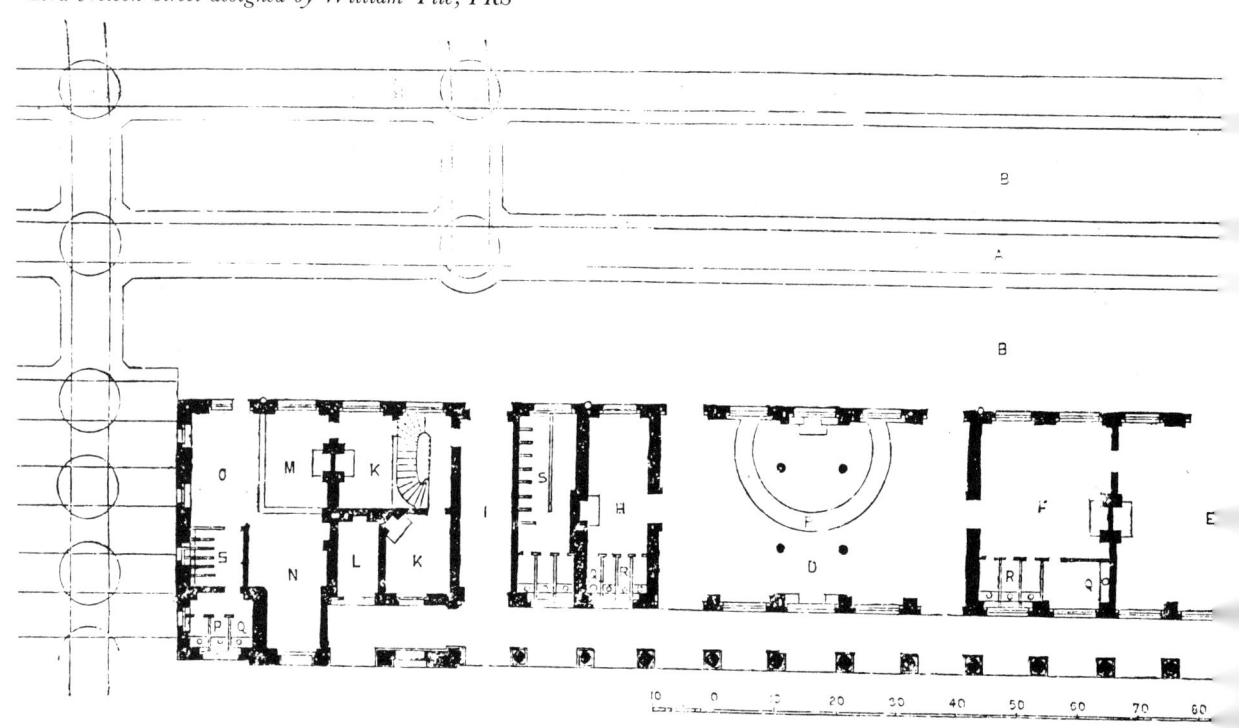

where a derailed train knocked away one of the supporting columns, bringing down a portion of the roof.

When completed the roof was just over 120 yds long from the Lime Street frontage to the Hotham Street bridge. It was supported on one side by the inner wall of the new offices in Great Nelson Street for most of its length, the last 63ft resting on a massive box beam of wrought iron made by William Fairbairn; on the south side the supports were 17 cast iron columns of Roman Doric design, 23ft in height and set in a row 50ft away from the trains.

The roof covering consisted of corrugated galvanised iron and rough plate glass in sheets 12ft 4in × 3ft 6in.;[8] the latter were arranged in three rows running lengthwise and covered rather less than a quarter of the whole area.

The roof was the first of its kind to be used in railway station construction, and the largest iron roof in existence for any purpose at that time. The total cost of the roof and its supports was about £15,000.

The passenger station at Liverpool Road, Manchester, was a modest building, but it appears to have satisfied the inhabitants of the town. The two-storey exterior in stone was of late Georgian style, presumably to the designs of the Company's architect, John Foster. The line, coming in off the Irwell Bridge, was level with the upper part of the building and here were the booking office and waiting rooms; a wide flight of wooden stairs led down to the entrance hall. There were never any platforms and the space between the trains and the building appears to have been open to the elements until in October 1834 it was decided to erect a roof '. . . over the area . . . in front of the Coach Office at Manchester, where the trains of carriages start.' The roof, of wood and slate, was supported along its outer side by a row of

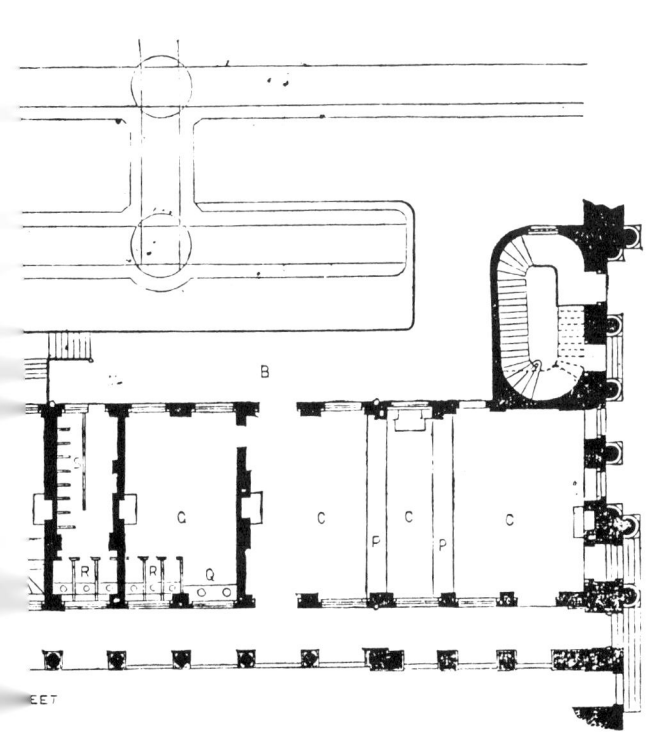

62b *Lime Street Station, 1849; plan of new building, Lord Nelson Street*

References to Plan.

A Great shed.
B Departure platforms.
C Booking-office for Manchester, Bolton, and Preston.
D Booking-office for London and Birmingham.
E Refreshment-room.
F Ladies' first-class waiting-room.
G Ladies' waiting-room.
H Ladies' second-class waiting-room.
I Entrance gateway.
K Superintendent's rooms.
L Bullion-office.
M Left cloaks, umbrellas, &c.
N Porters'-room.
O Lamps.
P Counters,
Q Wash.
R Water-closets.
S Urinals.

iron columns. Early in 1832 a spare Coach Office at the Water Street end was converted into a house for Scott, the Chief Superintendent, and in 1834 a wall was built to enclose the station. This range of buildings included an engineers' office, a workshop and a shed to hold 20 carriages.

Passengers arriving at Manchester left the trains between the Irwell and Water Street bridges, and for their protection a shed was erected over part of the Irwell Bridge in 1833. Two years later it was decided to build a new station on the site of the dye works to serve as an '... arrival station for railway coaches from all quarters.' The plans, prepared by Messrs Haig and Franklin, included stables in Water Street and a new warehouse; meanwhile £720 was spent on alterations to the original station, including the provision of booking offices on the ground floor.

William and Henry Southern built the new arrival station and other works in the latter part of 1837, and the passenger station was opened on the morning of 4 December; with the completion of the boundary wall and gates in 1838 the cost had been about £8600.

The new arrival shed on the north side of the line between the river and Water Street covered an area 150ft by 50ft, and the roof rested on iron columns at intervals of 13ft along the side next to the railway. At the west end was a loading dock for common road carriages, and an inclined road led down to Water Street. Beneath the station were stables for 60 horses and vaults for general storage, while under the inclined road a kitchen was provided where the men could have their meals.

Before the L&MR obtained its Act, a company had been formed to build a line from Manchester to Leeds; strong opposition from the Rochdale Canal delayed the survey, and it was not until 15 November 1830 that the report of George Stephenson and James Walker was published. On the same day the L&M Board agreed to a junction being made with the M&LR. The original company failed to obtain its Act in 1831 and it was 1836 before an amended line was sanctioned.[9] With Thomas Gooch as Resident Engineer, construction started in 1837 and the Manchester (Oldham Road) to Littleborough section

63 *Lime Street Station, 1849; section of iron roof*

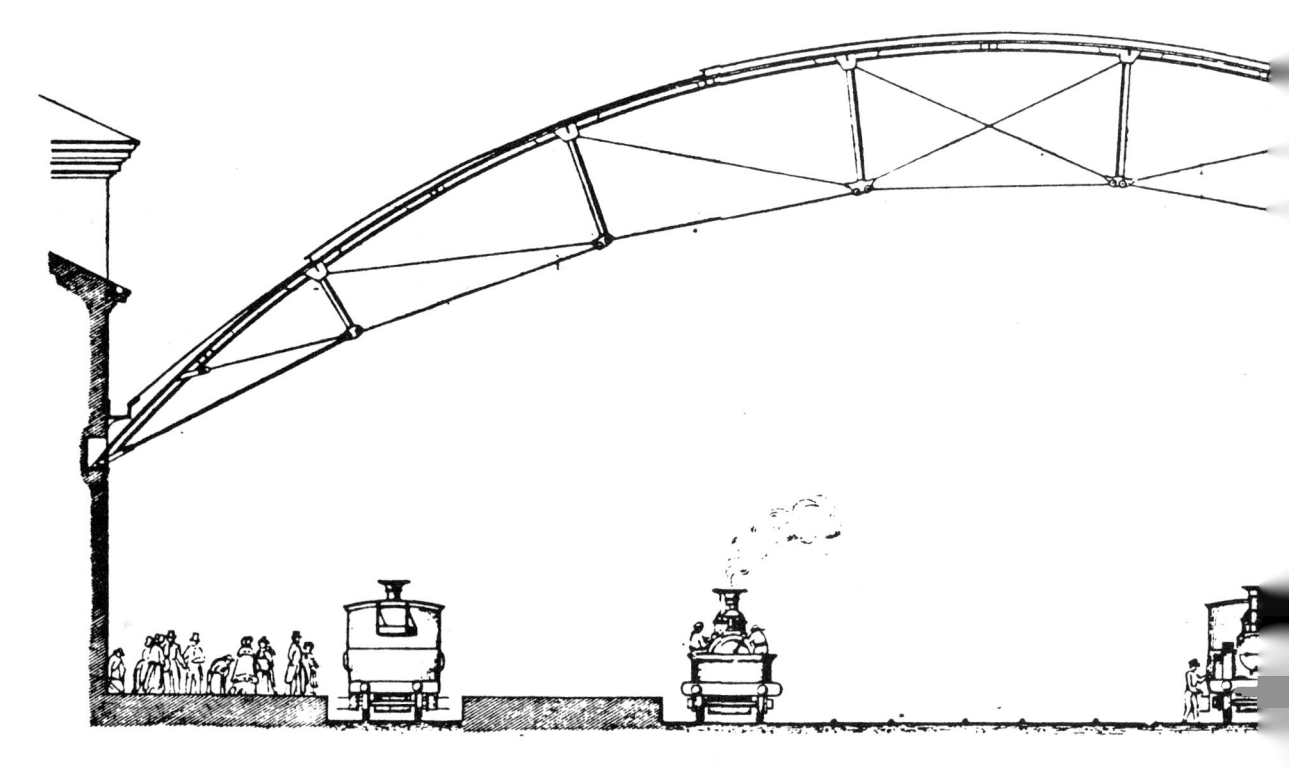

was opened on 4 July 1839; the line was opened throughout on 1 March 1841.

Meanwhile in November 1835 William Brown, referring to the revival of the M&L project, suggested it afforded an opportunity of forming a junction between the MB&B, M&L and L&M Railways near Salford, and four months later Hartley's plan for a junction with the Bolton line near Cross Lane Bridge was approved.

In July 1838 the M&LR raised the question of a connection with the L&MR, and the Board enthusiastically pressed forward with the plans. In June 1839 the Leeds Junction Act[10] was passed for powers to build a line in collaboration with the MB&BR to join the Leeds Railway at Hunts Bank, where a large new station was planned.

Several influential shareholders were uneasy about the project and in August 1839 R. T. Cadbury of Birmingham asked that the proprietors be given full information before the Company exercised its new powers. Then difficulties arose with the MB&BR and with the canal companies, and the Company considered abandoning the plans for a line through Salford in favour of a southern route with a tunnel connection to the M&LR and incorporating junctions with the Manchester & Birmingham and Sheffield, Ashton-under-Lyne & Manchester Railways. For three years the powers remained in abeyance while the Board negotiated and manoeuvred and the M&L Directors' impatience turned to desperation. Eventually, under the threat that if it did not complete the link the M&LR would seek powers for an independent line to Liverpool, the L&MR secured another Act[11] for a line completely independent of the MB&BR, and by the autumn of 1842 work was proceeding.

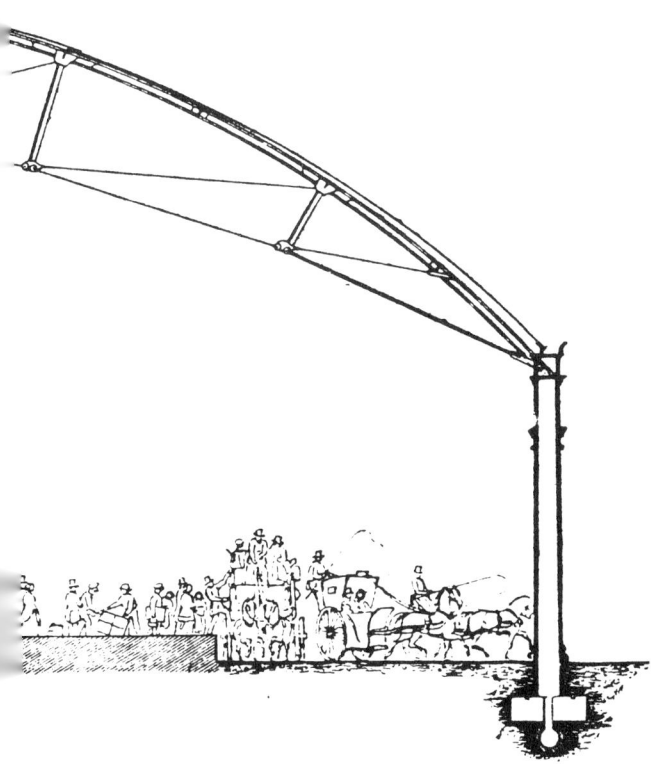

Edward Woods planned the line and designed the bridges and viaduct on which it was carried over the streets of Salford, curving to right and left for more than half of its one-mile length. There were 76 brick arches varying in span from 22ft to 43ft; most of those crossing streets were of oblique construction and the piers of the larger of these included stonework for strength and appearance. The contractors were Pauling & Henfrey of Manchester. Cast-iron girder bridges were erected at five points; the River Irwell was spanned by a 120ft bridge with lattice work on each side, Chapel Street and Gravel Lane by iron skew bridges, and Ducie Street, where the line widened before entering the station, by one 62ft wide with closed iron side parapets; the fifth iron bridge spanned the Bolton & Bury canal.[12]

For a distance of 250 yds along Upper Booth Street, between the Manchester & Bolton Railway and the boundary wall of the New Bailey Prison, the railway ran on an iron colonnade supported by massive iron columns in pairs along the centre of the street. There were 22 bays, and the permanent way rested on brickwork arches built between the girders. The viaduct was finished with

'... an iron entablature above the columns. These are in the Ancient Egyptian Style and are very massy, with grotesque figures of two non-descript animals in alt relief upon each of the compartments above; and if this colonnade could be seen from a distance, instead of being between two walls, it would have an imposing appearance.[13]

The tracks on this section were 5ft apart; on the rest of the branch 6ft separated them. The brick arches were covered with several coats of coal tar and layers of broken brick; 75 lb. rails were laid on pine sleepers.

Major-General Pasley inspected the new works on 3 May 1844, riding with Lawrence, Booth and Woods in a special train. With the assistant engineers and

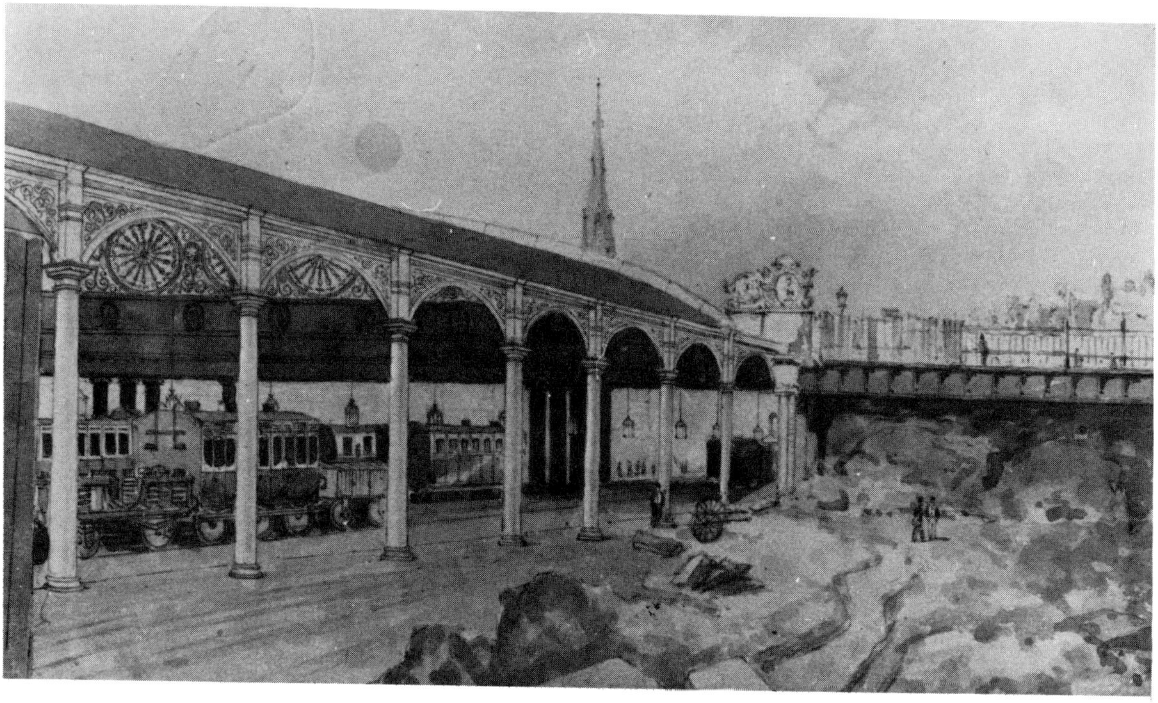

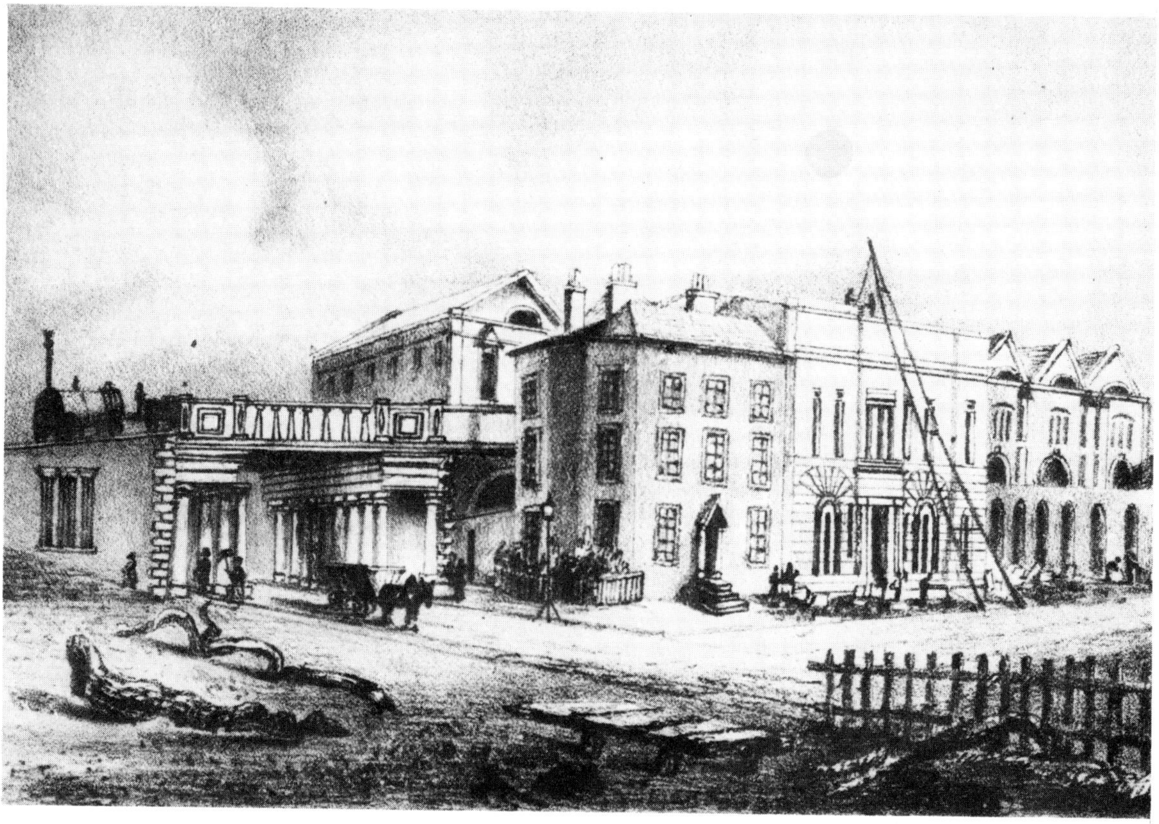

contractor the party then walked along the line and the Inspector found it all highly creditable to Woods and the contractor. The next day the line was opened without ceremony, except that the engines were dressed with flags during the morning.

When the L&MR extension line was opened, Hunts Bank Station had already been in use for a few months by the M&L company. In November 1843 the Board agreed to leave the running of the station to the M&LR and on 8 January 1844 they concurred in that Company's proposal to change the name to Victoria. When opened, it was the largest station in the kingdom being over 850ft in length and 130ft wide. Its iron roof, in three compartments, supported by the side walls and intermediate iron pillars, covered 80,000 sq. ft; it was supplied by Fox, Henderson & Co. Skylights, glazed with Chance's patent 'strong, thick and cheap glass', provided ample light, and the other parts of the roof were boarded to conceal the slates. By night the station was gas-lit by Hall's new 'Rose Light' lamps, consisting of several tubes radiating like wheel-spokes, each with a number of perforations into which flat-flame burners were fitted. All the lamps in train shed, offices and outside the building were controlled by a master valve and were only turned on to full pressure when a train was arriving or departing.

One platform 852ft long and on the south side was sufficient at first for all the traffic, the L&MR using the western half and the M&L the eastern; the station building housing booking offices, waiting and refreshment rooms was similarly divided. Among other unusual features were the outside canopies supported by 9ft brackets instead of iron columns and, in the basement, a 3rd Class refreshment room '... with a bar and every convenience and accommodation suitable for that class of passengers.'[14]

The L&MR put up engine and carriage sheds near the station; over the engine shed was a new type of water tank supplied by Fox Henderson, which contained a watertight partition, enabling one half to be emptied for repair or painting. Goods traffic was kept away from Victoria, each company dealing with it at its old station, but the L&MR arranged for the North Midland Railway to build them a warehouse at Leeds.

On the opening of the new line William Green the engineer was given the post of L&M Stationmaster at Victoria.

The Board were undecided on the question of through bookings and thought that if allowed, they should not be between intermediate stations; later they agreed to permit the M&L to book through to Liverpool from their stations. By September 1844 through bookings to Yorkshire were being made but

64 *The Lime Street Station of 1849 during the preparation of the ground for the enlargement on the south side, 1866*

65 *Manchester, Liverpool Road Station and warehouses, 1830*

66 *Manchester, Liverpool Road Station in 1880, the Jubilee year of the L&MR*

the passengers had to change at Manchester. After six months, complaints about the inconvenience of changing reached the Board, and the M&LR was asked '... was the railway in a safe state as to the *Gauge* of their rails to admit the Liverpool carriages', and if not, would they allow theirs to come through to Liverpool. The problem arose from the gauge of not only the M&L, but the NMR, Y&NMR, Midland Counties and Hull & Selby Railways all being 4ft 9in., but it was found that no difficulties ensued from running L&M, GJ or L&BR trains through to Hull, nor those of other companies to Liverpool.

There were about 25 roadside stations or stopping places on the line, situated at the level crossings where a policeman or gateman was permanently on duty. Passengers wishing to alight at a wayside station told the guard when joining the train, and if any were to be taken up, the policeman signalled the driver to stop; these stations also served as goods depots, where the 'picking-up trains' stopped, if required, to collect or discharge small consignments. There were no platforms or buildings apart from the gatekeeper's cottage, and this served as a waiting room for passengers in cold or wet weather, and at night. At Rainhill, one of the busier stopping places, the gatekeeper was allowed an extra ton of coal to provide some comfort for his customers; a larger cottage and separate passengers' room was built here at a cost of £127 in 1832. A permanent cottage was built at Broad Green at this time and the temporary wooden one re-erected at Cross Lane, near Manchester. As the need arose extra rooms were added to existing cottages for use as waiting rooms, as at Birchall's cottage, St Helens Junction, in February 1835. Some of the stopping places were in use for only a short time; one of these, Gorton's Buildings, was in existence in 1831, and another at Barton Moss was temporarily abandoned in favour of Lamb's Cottage in November 1832. This was one of the stations on Chat Moss, and in 1836 the Company agreed to a request from local farmers to stop the trains at McGrath's Farm instead; when the farmers protested at the fare of 1s. 6d. to Manchester the Company refused to reduce it, having been put to the expense of providing the station to 'accommodate McGrath and friends.' Other requests for stopping places included one in the Olive Mount Cutting.

67 *Bridge over the River Irwell on the approach to Victoria Station, Manchester, 1845*

STATIONS

THE HUNTSBANK STATION
ON THE LIVERPOOL, MANCHESTER, AND LEEDS RAILWAYS.

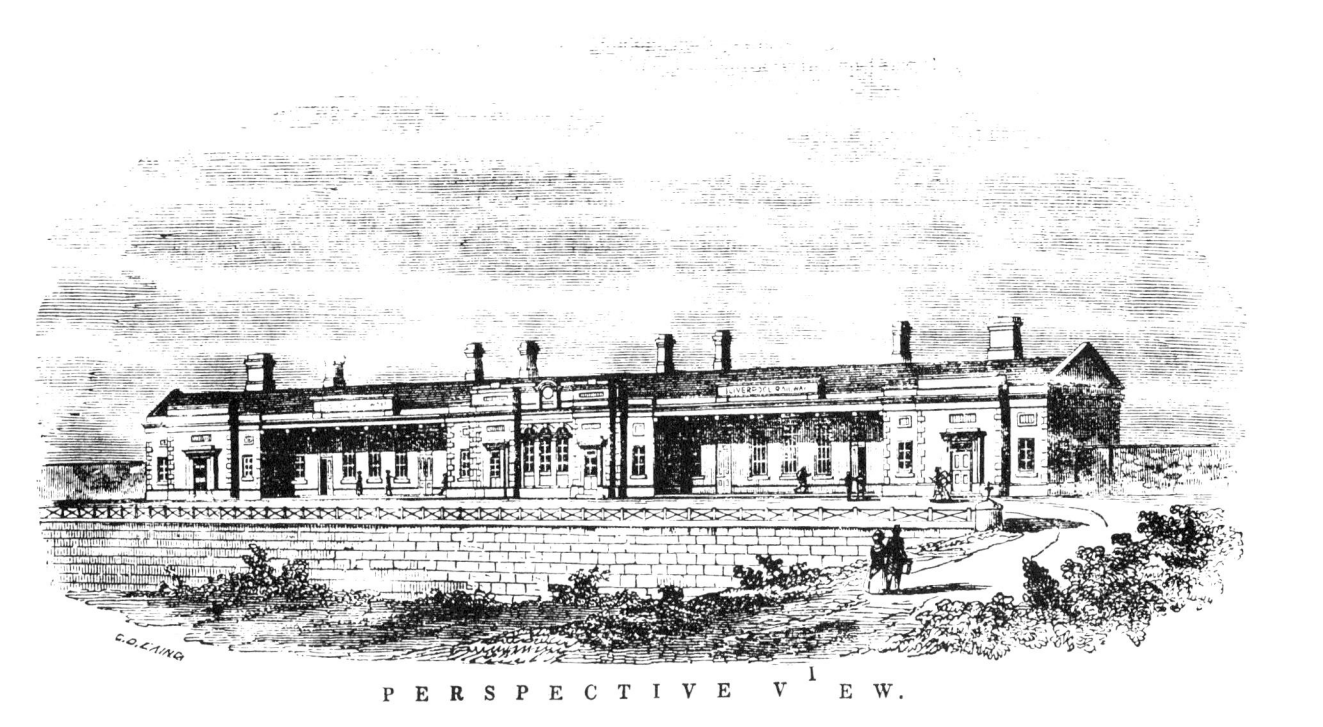

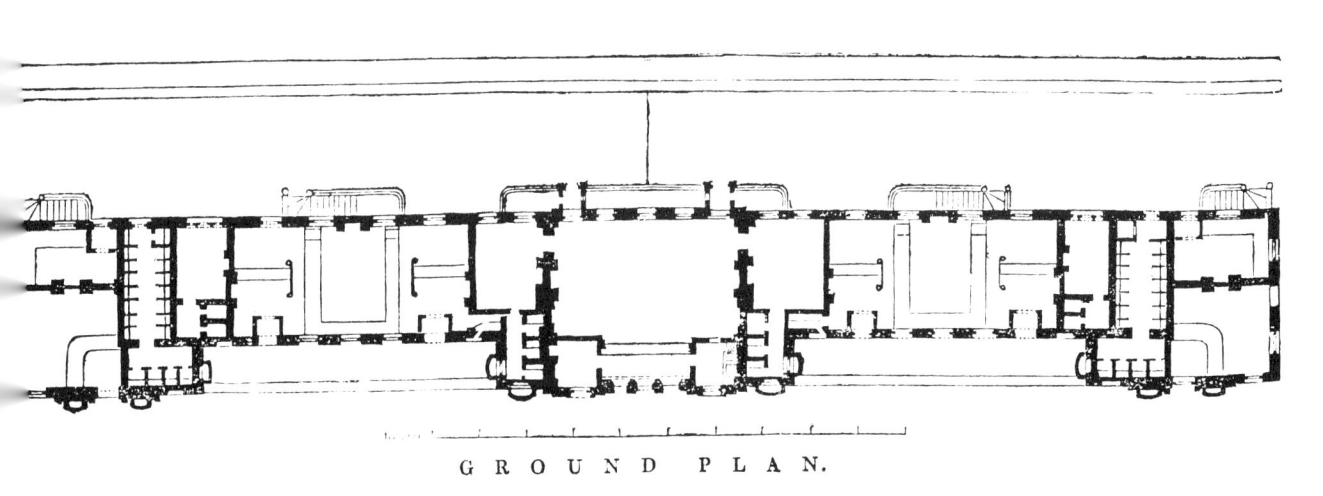

PERSPECTIVE VIEW.

GROUND PLAN.

68 *Hunts Bank (Victoria) Station, elevation and plan, 1845*

69 *Manchester, Victoria Station interior, 1847*

When it was decided in 1838 that a waiting room was required at Bury Lane, the owner of Chat Moss Tavern was asked if he would let one room for the purpose, '. . . such room to have no communication with the rest of the house'; not surprisingly, Woods was unable to make an arrangement on these terms and the wooden hut from Patricroft was moved there, to be replaced by a brick structure. At this time permanent waiting rooms were provided at Flow Moss and Kenyon Junction.

With the opening of the branch lines, the stations at the junctions assumed greater importance. Parkside, the principal watering and re-fuelling station, became the junction for the Wigan Branch Railway, and in October 1832 the L&MR contributed £35 towards the cost of building a waiting room, and agreed to an amended plan to erect it on '. . . the sunny side of the road, instead of under the rock on the south side of the cutting.' By 1840 the line was five tracks wide at this point.

Additional waiting rooms and sheds were built at Kenyon Junction in 1840, and on each side of the line at Newton a cottage was built containing a waiting room and booking office.

Although Henry Booth said in 1841 that 'The intermediate stations are of so little importance on our line, we have there few but policemen', the Board was aware that facilities were very inadequate, and in August they carried out a special inspection of the line and stations. At the next Board Meeting the Directors resolved that arrangements for the comfort of the passengers must be improved, and large waiting rooms were ordered to be built at Rainhill, St Helens Junction, Bury Lane and Patricroft. Platforms were provided at the stopping places where there were no stations and large name boards of uniform design were erected at those places. The men in attendance on passengers at these minor stations were provided with uniforms and caps, and in some cases, booking clerks were engaged; where it was thought necessary, clocks were installed.

The stopping places at Flow Moss and Lamb's

70 *Manchester, Victoria Station, 1847*

Cottage ceased to be used for 2nd Class trains from October 1842, but Barton Moss, where a policeman was required, was kept open. About this time the Home Secretary ordered a copy of the *Police Gazette* to be sent to each railway station in the country.

On the opening of the Hunts Bank line, Ordsall Lane station was closed, but was reopened for setting down passengers after a petition had been received from the public. Early in 1845 a policeman's cottage, waiting rooms and sheds were built at Astley Station on Chat Moss, and stone was being brought along the line by platelayers for the new Patricroft Station then under construction. At Newton Bridge new booking offices and waiting rooms were being built at a cost of £400, and at several of the road stations assistants were appointed; by the end of 1845 about 15 of the original stopping places had emerged as permanent stations, each with its buildings and staff.

Six tenders were considered on 19 April 1830 for the construction of five warehouses at Manchester. These were to accommodate 10,000 bags of cotton 'or equivalent other merchandise', and the contract went to David Bellhouse Jnr, of Manchester, at £12,250; two of the buildings were to be finished by 31 July and the other three by 15 August. The Board recorded on 31 May that work on the warehouses was proceeding rapidly, and they were ready in good time for the opening in September.

The warehouses at Manchester were found to be inadequate within two months of the commencement of goods traffic and additional buildings were under construction by July 1831, when the plans were altered to include a third storey. About this time a coal depot was established at right angles to the end of the line; by 1839 there were five tracks, two of which were arranged over coal shutes for the loading of road vehicles. At Hulton's request a weighing machine was installed and a charge made for its use. Another part of the area was fitted up as a timber wharf, after the Company had received an assurance from the Liverpool timber merchants that the traffic would justify the estimated cost of £3000; four years later, in

ODSALL LANE near SALFORD.

71 *A typical wayside station, Ordsall Lane, 1833*   **72** *Wapping Goods Station and tunnel entrance, 1833*

December 1835, a separate office was built for the timber business.

In 1837 the third large warehouse built on the river side of Water Street brought the total floor area of warehousing, including one or two smaller buildings, to about five acres, and the capacity to over four million cu. ft.

The principal warehouses were three storeys high in addition to the cellars and vaults below. Rails were laid on the first floor and eventually over 60 turntables were installed to enable waggons to be rolled in and unloaded under cover. The hoists in the original building were worked by John Hague's pneumatic engine, installed in August 1830; steam-operated cranes and hoists were employed in the other buildings, and jiggers[15] were used extensively. This equipment, used in conjunction with trap-doors in the floors and loop-holes in the walls, facilitated the rapid handling and despatch of goods. A weighing machine, also capable of weighing 20-ton locomotives, was provided for the 'Manchester Luggage Station' at a cost of £100 in 1839. Apart from the L&MR installation, another warehouse was built for the GJR to the north of the coal depot, in Charles Street.

The Liverpool goods station at Wapping extended from near the north end of Queen's Dock to Crosbie Street, where the main entrance was situated. The railway, emerging from the tunnel, was in a cutting here, and the warehouses, about 100ft long, were built over it. The floor was supported by cast iron pillars and it contained a number of hatches under which the waggons were placed by means of turnplates. There were four tracks running on a slight incline down to the tunnel mouth, passing through an open area where the tunnel rope terminated and where the offices were located.

The station was reported to be near completion in July 1830, but in November it was ordered that arched recesses be excavated in the side walls of the cutting to accommodate empty waggons. Additional sheds were built near Crosbie Street in 1831, some of them for the B&LR, and a further shed and offices were added in June 1838;[16] sidings for empty waggons were laid between Wapping and Ironmonger Lane in 1833.

The railway was at a disadvantage compared with the canals, in that all merchandise had to be brought from the docks across to the station, whereas barges were loaded direct from the ships, often while they were still lying out in the Mersey. Oats and grain were discharged in bulk to the barges, while these and similar products could only go by rail if in sacks. To overcome these problems the Company established a coal yard in King's Dock in October 1832 and received the Council's permission to lay rails across Wapping and Ironmonger Lane to reach it; only four waggons were to be drawn at a time, and the depot and tracks were ready by the end of 1833.[17] Meanwhile the Company proposed a line along the Dock Quay to Clarence Dock, then at the northern extremity of the system and two miles distant from Wapping Station, but after prolonged discussion the Council ruled that no party had the authority to grant the powers required. However in October 1835 permission was given for a line to the Company's timber yards in Brunswick Dock to the south of the station and work on it started a few weeks later. It was originally laid between Parliament Street and Stanhope Street, then taken up and relaid along the Quay past Queen's Dock. In March 1838 the Docks Board wanted it moved again, but the Company referred the matter to Hornby, who was a director of both concerns.

The increasing traffic from the GJR led to further extensions to Wapping southwards across Crosbie Street; a ropewalk and most of the street had been bought by 1838, and cleared of old buildings to make way for waggon sidings and more warehouse accommodation. By 1842 following extensions eastward the name Park Lane Station was adopted and in that year Bramah, Fox & Co. erected an iron-framed roof over the cotton loading shed. Early in 1844, in anticipation of the extra traffic from Yorkshire and Hull when the Leeds Junction line was opened, further encroachments were made into Crosbie Street for the enlargement of the depot. During the rebuilding of part of the station that summer conditions were chaotic and as much traffic as possible was transferred to Crown Street.

By 1840 the Company had plots of land on the docks side of Wapping, that thoroughfare and Ironmonger Lane both intersecting its property on the level. Some of this land near the docks was roofed over in 1844. There were six tracks through part of the station, and about 80 turntables for the shunting of waggons; larger ones had to be provided for the GJR rolling stock in 1844.

Towards the end of 1839 a steam engine was installed for working the numerous hoists, the engine house being situated near the junction of Crosbie and St James's Streets. Near the tunnel entrance the Company erected what was probably the first loading gauge; it consisted of two upright posts with a cross-timber set at a height of 12ft 5in., its particular purpose being to regulate the loading of cotton waggons. From St James's Street an inclined passage ran down to the railway at the point where cattle trains were loaded. Pigs constituted the bulk of this traffic and an observer refers to the '. . . singular sight to see these animals driven into the waggons.'[18]

The tunnels were lit continuously by gas at first, but in October 1831 stop-cocks were fitted to the pipes in the Small Tunnel to prevent consumption when carriages were not passing through. Even so, the cost of gas for the tunnels, stations and offices at Liverpool alone amounted to £800 in 1832, and the Board decided in April 1833 to make its own gas; the gas company was informed, and the assistance of their engineer in planning gas works for the railway was requested. It is unlikely that this received very favourable consideration, and the reduced expenditure on gas reflected in the accounts for the next few years probably resulted from a reduction in the gas company's charges.

The wayside stations were lit by oil lamps until 1843, when naphtha lamps replaced them. In August 1845 Nasmyth, Gaskell & Co. were asked to lay pipes and supply gas from their gasometer to the new Patricroft Station opposite their works.

CHAPTER EIGHT

The First Railwaymen

For the first few months of its existence the railway was run by the men who, as Stephenson's assistants, had built it. Locke had left the Company's regular service before completion, but was to be closely associated with it in years to come as Consulting Engineer. Of the other Resident Engineers, Thomas Gooch left early in 1831 to assist George Stephenson with the survey of the Manchester & Leeds Railway and then to work with Robert on the London & Birmingham, while Frederick Swanwick joined George Stephenson in 1832 to survey the Whitby & Pickering Railway.

George Stephenson ceased to be the Company's Principal Engineer on 1 February 1831, but was appointed Consulting Engineer from that date at 300 guineas for 30 days of his time per annum. He became Chief Engineer for the new Lime Street Tunnel, the survey for which was made in the autumn of 1831, and his account for professional services that year came to £690; Allcard was responsible for the construction of the tunnel. On 6 May 1833 the Board received letters from Stephenson, Allcard and Dixon, all tendering their resignations; although no reasons are given in the Board Minutes it was about the time of the discovering of the errors of alignment in the Tunnel and the appointment of Locke to check the survey. Lawrence saw Stephenson and persuaded him to retain the office of Consulting Engineer at 100 guineas a year, the business to be conducted mainly by correspondence; he was also to remain responsible for the unfinished tunnel with Allcard as Resident Engineer. Allcard's salary was increased by £100 to £400 a year, giving him parity with Dixon, which evidently satisfied him; Dixon withdrew his resignation and resumed his job at the Manchester end without achieving any apparent advantage. The arrangement was short-lived, however, for on 22 July Allcard resigned, soon to become Assistant Engineer to Locke on the GJR, and Dixon took over the tunnel works in addition to his other duties for an increased salary of £500.

He informed the Company on 7 October that he had accepted an engagement under Robert Stephenson as a resident engineer on the L&BR at £600 a year. The Board quickly offered the same amount plus travelling expenses if he would stay, and at his request, Lawrence secured his release from his undertaking to Stephenson. In July 1835 he was given leave to value the locomotives of the S&DR, and probably received an attractive offer while there, for he was soon asking the Board about his salary and how much notice of resignation they would require. He eventually gave three months notice of resignation on 12 September 1836 and, when he left at the end of the year, was the last of Stephenson's original team of Resident Engineers.

Anthony Harding's career on the L&MR, which started with such promise, had ended in disgrace. On 30 April 1833 at a Special Board Meeting evidence of several cases of dishonesty was brought against him by Mr Rigg,[1] including the drawing of greater amounts than he actually paid out in wages to the men, fraudulent entries in the Company's pay bills, and that he had contrived favourable terms for a contract awarded to his brother. The charges were proved and he was immediately discharged from the Company's service, his appeals for reinstatement or recommendation to another railway being firmly rejected. A week later his other brother, John, resigned his situation at Edge Hill.

Two of Dixon's superintendents resigned in December 1833 having accepted a contract to maintain the permanent way, and on the recommendation of Cropper, the young Edward Woods[2] was appointed to the Liverpool end at £60 a year, rising by £10 a year; similar terms were arranged with Thomas Forsyth at Manchester, whose brother and father also worked for the railway.

73 John Dixon (1796–1865)

Cropper was a shrewd judge of character, and his protégé served the Company well. Woods knew the railway from 1831, having visited it frequently while on holiday from his engineering studies at Bristol, and on 1 January 1834, while not yet 20, he assumed responsibility for the line from Liverpool to Newton, including the new tunnel, to supervise and pay the permanent way contractors and police, and to attend the Board Meetings. On the resignation of Dixon, he was promoted to Principal Engineer at a salary of £250 rising to £400 in three years; he was to reside in Manchester, with William Buddicom appointed as his assistant at Liverpool. Buddicom, aged 20, had just finished his apprenticeship with Mather Dixon & Co., and it was upon J. P. Mather's recommendation that he was engaged on a 2-year contract at a salary of £100 to £125. On the expiry of his contract in October 1838, he went to the Glasgow, Paisley & Greenock Railway, returning to Edge Hill as Locomotive Superintendent of the GJR in 1840.[3]

In January 1837 Woods engaged George Scott as a sub-engineer at Manchester, on an apprenticeship basis, for which he was to receive £10 for the first year, increasing by £10 yearly, for five years. After 15 months he wished to leave, but the Company would not release him, and on Buddicom's departure he succeeded him at the Liverpool Works.

Alexander Fyfe,[4] who had been with the Company from the early days of construction, was appointed foreman of the Manchester Engine Shops in March 1832, and among other early appointments were those of William Gray and his son John, employed at Millfield Station and Workshops, and John Melling who was superintendent at the Brickfield Station, Edge Hill; his son Thomas was with him until 1837, when he left to join the GJR. The Grays were given notice in July 1832 but for some reason it was rescinded, and in October 1833 their offer to engage, at a joint salary of £270 and the house they occupied, was accepted. John Gray was in charge of the Waggon Department and with the other engineers, attended the Board Meetings to receive the Directors' orders each week.

The Grays had been in trouble in June 1833 when charges concerning engineering stores and supplies were brought against them by 12 witnesses. The enquiry lasted from 18 to 29 June, involving four Special Board Meetings, two of them on Saturdays, at each of which at least seven directors were present. In the end it was resolved unanimously that there was 'no sufficient evidence to impeach their character as zealous and well-intentioned servants of the Company.'

In July 1836 their contract was renewed at a joint salary of £550 for a further three years. John Gray mentioned that he had received a much higher offer to superintend a railway on the Continent and the Treasurer was '... instructed to write to The Chevalier Gerstner[5] expressing the Directors' surprise that he should have proposed to any of the Company's servants to leave their present employ, upon the inducement of a higher salary on the Continent.'

John Gray left the L&MR in January 1840 to become Locomotive Superintendent of the Hull & Selby Railway. John Melling was in charge of the locomotive repair shops, involving heavy work and long hours of duty. When the bulk of the work from

74 John Melling

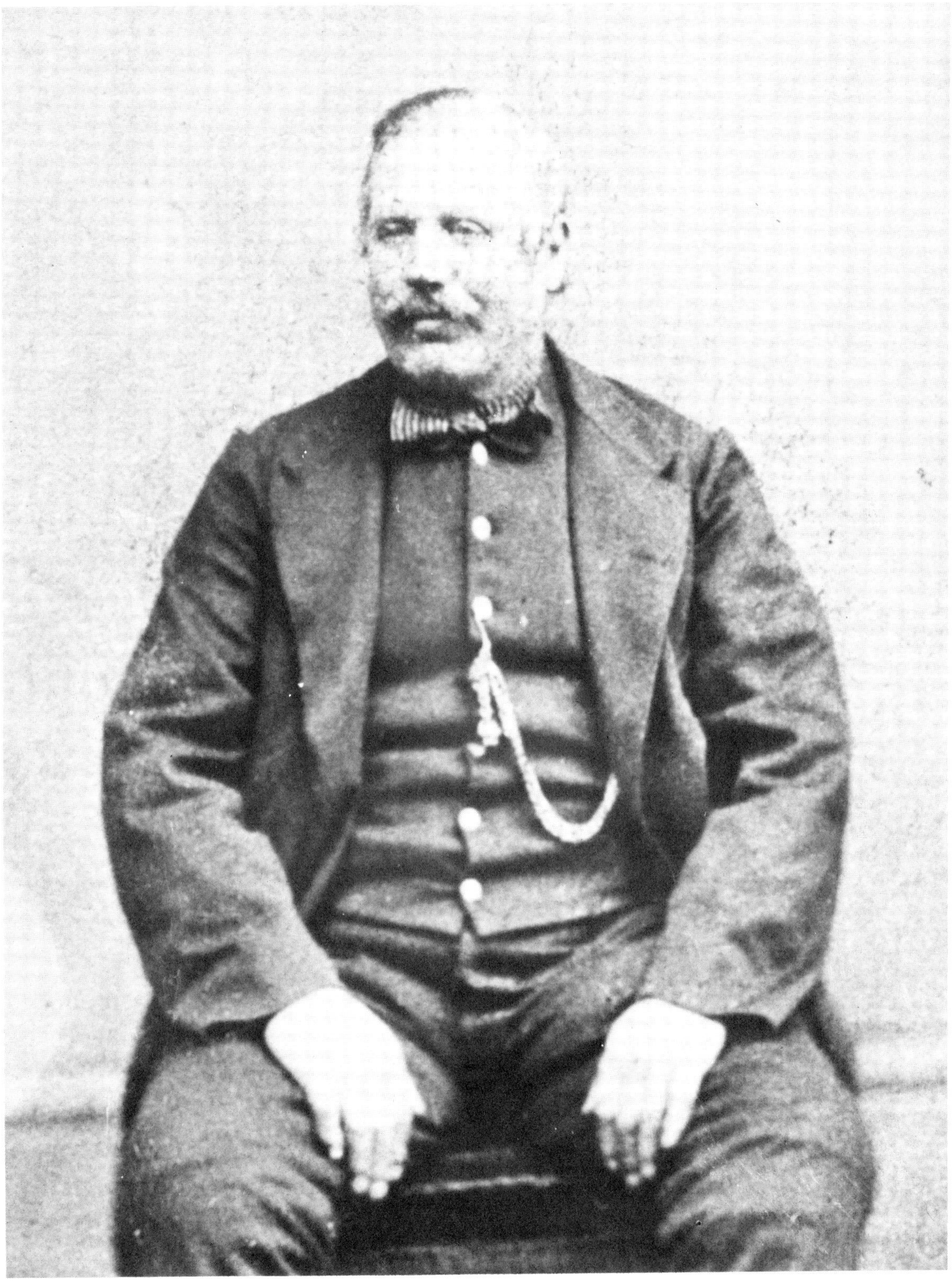

Manchester was transferred to Liverpool in May 1837, Melling was put in complete charge at six guineas a week, but with the reorganisation of the Locomotive Department in 1840 he was replaced by John Dewrance. His son was discharged from the GJR at the same time, and together they established the Rainhill Iron Works.

Dewrance was an experienced engineer who had been with the Stephensons at the time when the *Rocket* was built, and he had already made several improvements in locomotive design. He joined the Company at the mature age of 37 and remained their Chief Locomotive Superintendent until the amalgamation. The Edge Hill Works, under his control, built the standard 'Bird' Class locomotives of his own design, that met all the Company's future requirements. In a short time his zeal and ability in improving the department brought a salary increase of £50 to £300 a year.

The Carriage Building Department, established in 1828, was in the capable hands of Thomas Clarke Worsdell, a London coachmaker who, with his three sons, settled in Liverpool in 1827. The excellence of his coachwork brought him to the notice of James Cropper, a fellow Quaker, leading to his engagement with the Company, and to that of his eldest son Nathaniel. Thomas Worsdell left the L&MR in January 1837, writing to thank the directors for their encouragement and kindness 'for so many years', and was succeeded as Superintendent of the Coach Building and Repairing Shops by John Pownall. Nathaniel was appointed superintendent of the GJR Carriage Department.

Charles Ritchie was Superintendent of the Waggon Shops at Millfield Station and he was brought before the Board in March 1845 when a man from the Crown Street Yard who had been dismissed informed the Board that he had employed one of the joiners to make a piece of furniture for his own use from the Company's materials; although the directors were sceptical when Ritchie explained that he had kept an account of the joiner's time and materials used, intending to credit the Company with the amount, they took no action beyond warning Ritchie not to indulge in such an irregular practice again under any pretext whatsoever.

Joseph Green and Andrew Comber were the Company's Chief Agents at Manchester and Liverpool respectively. Both were engaged on 1 March 1830 at £400 a year, Comber having been Pickford's local agent for ten years at £200. Green's duties were particularly arduous since he was responsible for the warehouses, goods and passenger traffic, the cartage department and the general management of the terminus 30 miles away from the Head Office; in 1834 his salary was increased by £100 and his house put in repair. Comber occupied a similar position at Liverpool, where his office was above the Company's stables in Park Lane. In January 1845 he gave notice of his intention to resign at a time convenient to the Company, and in fact remained in its service until the amalgamation, as did Joseph Green.

The Superintendents[6] at Lime Street and Liverpool Road Stations were Thomas Ilbery and James Scott respectively. With the coming of the GJR traffic the arrivals and departures, particularly at Lime Street, became so numerous as often to be either simultaneous or in very quick succession; salary increases were given, assistants engaged and both Superintendents received presents of £20 from the GJR each Christmas.

Two superintendents were engaged in July 1830 at an annual salary of £80 each, to examine and oil the carriages as they arrived at each end of the line. The one at Crown Street was referred to as the 'Inspector of the Coach Wheels', and although the method they employed is not stated, they may well have been the first wheel-tappers. In 1836 it was reported that the carriages were thoroughly inspected, cleaned and the axle-boxes greased after every trip.

Even the Company's higher officers received few privileges; the Minutes for 27 March 1833 record that Worsdell was granted 8–10 days leave to attend to some family business in London but that he was '... not to be allowed wages during his absence.' On the other hand, Ilbery was loaned £40 in October 1836 to meet the expense of illness in his family, and Simpson of the Liverpool Road station, who asked the directors' help in paying a debt of £20 contracted when his salary was £65 a year, was given the money.

No records of the number of men employed in building the railway have survived, if in fact there ever were any. Hundreds of men were employed by the various small contractors, and almost as many day men who were paid by the Company; in addition there were the Resident Engineers and a small permanent staff of clerks, enginemen and mechanics.

When the Works were nearing completion Stephenson was asked to select men for training as drivers and mechanics, and these were invariably men who had been with him in the north-east. From among the labourers, gatemen and platelayers were selected for employment by the Company, and soon after the opening there was a pool of semi-skilled labour available from the declining coach industry:

some booking clerks, guards and porters came from this source.

When the Railway had been opened for about two months the Board found it necessary to ascertain exactly who it did employ and asked for a return of all employees showing what they did and where they were doing it. Further lists were prepared in April 1831 when it was decreed that each engineman and fireman should be responsible for a particular engine, and should not change without the directors' approval. It was not until April 1832, however, that the Board discovered that there were too many firemen at the Tunnel Engines and discharged one of them; he had been employed erecting the engine and '... ought not to have continued in the Company's service.'

At the end of March 1832 the average number employed was 706 including 73 salaried staff. A little later the number of enginemen was reduced from 17 to 12. George Stephenson agreed to take one for his colliery in Leicestershire and the others were given the option of becoming firemen; nine firemen were dismissed at the same time. Twenty policemen also went, bringing the total down to 32, and soon their chief, Captain Brook, was also to go.

Over the years the number of employees gradually increased until in June 1841 there were 1180; by 1843 the number had fallen by about 100, reductions having been made in the engineering departments.

In March 1843 16 employees were listed as being 'incapable of any very active service.' Four of them had been with the Railway from 1826 when construction first started, one being a labourer 73 years old, although 'old age' was the reason for the inclusion of another who was only 50.

The railway was very much a man's world; the 1100-odd employees in 1843 included just one woman, the office cleaner Cath Donally, who also had the unenviable distinction of being the lowest-paid at 3s. 6d. a week.

After the amalgamation most of the staff were retained first by the GJR and then by the L&NWR. In 1865 the directors of the L&NWR were asked to head a subscription list with £100 on behalf of John Thompson, described as the oldest railway servant in England, who served on the L&MR in 1826 and retired from its successor in 1861 when his health failed.[7]

On 3 October 1842 Edward Robinson and Samuel Burgess were each given a silver watch on leaving the company's employment after 12 years' service; this is the first recorded instance on the L&MR of what was to become a tradition on the railways, although with a considerably longer qualifying period.

Most of the staff were appointed by the individual directors, who took their turn in a set order of rotation to engage all employees from porter upwards; from 1839 they agreed to nominate their candidates leaving the Sub-Committee discretion as to whether to make the appointment.

At first there was no particular system of progression or promotion on the L&MR; engine cleaners could become porters or guards, and fitters from the workshops were just as likely to become enginemen as firemen were. When the gatekeeper at Huyton died, his job went to a platelayer, and his widow was allowed '... to carry out the parcels for the Derby family and the Rector of Huyton.'

Wages fluctuated for various reasons – trade depression and the falling cost of living bringing small reductions, increased work or longer hours resulting in increases. In 1835 wages in the Manchester cotton-spinning factories averaged 11s. a week; the lowliest labourer on the railway earned nearly twice as much.[8]

Houses and cottages for certain of its employees were provided before the line was opened. In July 1830 six cottages and a smith's shop were built on Chat Moss and more were to follow a year later. By 1832 several groups of cottages existed at Rainhill and Sutton and one at the Watering Station at the top of Whiston Incline. Six more were built at Sutton this year at a cost of £430; these had gardens and were let at 3s. 6d. a week, the wooden cottages along the line going for 2s. a week. There were others at Edge Hill where a large proportion of the men were employed. As most of the enginemen lived in Liverpool, there was always a shortage of locomotives at Manchester on Monday mornings, and in February 1832 Dixon was instructed to ensure that there were sufficient engines and men to work them, even if it meant enforcing residence in Manchester. He offered to build some houses in Manchester as a private venture if the Company would sell him the land cheaply, but the Board did not approve of its officers being landlords to any of its other employees, and it provided the houses itself.

An amenity provided in August 1843 was the reading room for enginemen, mechanics and other employees, established at Edge Hill, '... the books and periodicals to be approved by the Board before being circulated to the men.'

The first enginemen, as drivers on the L&MR were called, were already experienced men, having been brought from the north-east by Stephenson to work the ballast trains during the construction period.

Mark Wakefield, Robert Hope and John Dunn ballasted with *Lancashire Witch*, Thomas George and Robert Creed with *Twin Sisters*.

Wakefield drove the *Rocket* at the opening, and his brother John the *Phoenix*; Thomas George and Robert Creed were in charge of *North Star* and *Northumbrian*, and Creed ran the first regular passenger train after the opening. As new and more powerful engines arrived on the line, they were allocated to these drivers, George taking over *Planet*, Wakefield *Mercury* and Dunn the *Sun*.

These men in turn trained others, and for some years the Company had in its employ the most experienced and skilful locomomtive men to be found anywhere. Most had gone by the 1840s, some to other railways, some abroad; several attained responsible positions with other companies.[9]

The drivers were paid 1s. 6d. a trip, but in the summer of 1831 Anthony Harding was instructed to pay 2s. a trip for those exceeding four a day. The day before this order was made *Etna* had performed six trips. A year later the higher rate for extra trips was withdrawn, and in February 1833 the standard rate was reduced to 1s. 3d. for drivers and 10d. for firemen; payment for working on Sundays was 4s. and 3s. respectively. Working the banking engines counted as five trips and a day's work on the Wigan Branch as four.

A deputation of enginemen attended the Board Meeting on 1 March 1833 and presented a letter objecting to the reduction in their wages. The drivers, Scott, Dunn and Fenwick, proposed that they be allowed to work the engines, pay their firemen, provide oil, tallow and hemp, pack their own pistons, but not clean the engines, for 4s. a trip. The Directors said that they could not agree to this arrangement without much consideration, and certainly not at present. The reduction was then discussed, which would make the average wage 32s. a week, '. . . and the enginemen admitted that in all probability they could not do better anywhere else.' The Board agreed to their request that those who had to work on Sundays should be paid 5s., and also that all the drivers should take turns at working the banking engines on the inclined planes; this was considered to be very hard service owing to the long hours. Various other small grievances were aired, and the deputation withdrew, but not before the Chairman had told them '. . . that the letter which they had written was an improper one, and cautioned them not to write another such letter in future.'

In recognition of the long hours worked by the goods train drivers, Dixon, on his own responsibility, paid them 1s. 6d. a trip on four trips instead of 1s. 3d. on five, an arrangement accepted by the Directors on 16 October 1834. The concessions made to the drivers did not extend to the firemen and when they protested the Company decided, in May 1833, to replace them with 'stout boys' at 15s. a week, but to allow the existing firemen to stay on at the new rate until they could find other employment. The first two boys taken on to fill vacancies were paid only 10s. a week. At this time the two Tunnel Engine firemen had their pay reduced from 25s. to 21s. a week.

The first and most serious strike[10] on the L&MR occurred among the enginemen in February 1836. Although not a cause of the strike, a decision taken in November 1834 was to have serious consequences for some of the strikers; in that month the Company's solicitors drew up a new agreement to be signed by all newly appointed drivers to give three months' notice to leave and to deposit £10 'good conduct money' with the Company (the amount to be paid by weekly instalments). The object was to stop drivers who had gained their experience on the Railway from going off to other lines now opening, where trained men were being offered higher wages. Two drivers resigned for this reason, in May 1835; one of them, John Wakefield, went to the L&BR.

In September 1835 the Management Committee looked into the question of enginemen's pay compared with that of firemen, and reported that the former were frequently paid up to £2 per week against 15s. for firemen;[11] it considered that '. . . enginemen's wages were far too high' and recommended the Board to reduce them, '. . . and perhaps to raise in some degree the firemen's wages.' On 18 September the following rates were announced, to come into effect after three months notice:

	Enginemen	Firemen
Per trip with coach or picking-up trains	1s.	8d.
Per trip with luggage trains	1s. 3d.	10d.
Sundays	5s.	2s 6d.
Waggons picked up as at present, each	1d.	½d.

A fortnight later the Committee received notice that the enginemen would quit the Company's service on 1 January if the directors enforced the reductions, and the men were then given a fortnight to reconsider their decision, after which time they would be replaced and never again employed.

Three drivers, William McCrie, Barned Rice and Charles Callan attended the Management

Committee meeting on 29 October 1835 and urged the directors to abandon their resolution to reduce wages. The principal arguments advanced by the men concerned their long hours on duty and the destruction of their clothes from the nature of their work, but the only concession they could secure was a guarantee that their wages should not fall short of 30s. a week. This did not meet the drivers' demands, however, and on Monday, 30 January 1836, when the new rates were about to be introduced, several of the enginemen gave verbal notice of their intention to leave on the following Friday evening. On Wednesday morning, 1 February, the Treasurer asked John Hewitt, one of the oldest enginemen, if he persisted in that notice and Hewitt, answering that he did, was discharged instantly. Thereupon the regular drivers came out on strike and were replaced by engineers and fitters from Melling's Shed and Gray's Yard, and by a few firemen and newly-appointed drivers. Although there were delays to luggage trains at first, by some miracle only one accident occurred; there was, however, 'much damage to machinery'. In recognition of their service in the face of 'persuasions and threats' the Board awarded premiums of £5 and £3 to each driver, with half those amounts to the firemen.

Agreements of service had been signed by four of the enginemen, Henry Weatherburn, Charles and Peter Callan and George Massey, and these were taken before the Magistrates who sent them to Kirkdale Gaol, each for one month's hard labour. The court 'considered the offence of so grave a character, that if these men or any others were brought before them, and convicted of similar misconduct, they should commit them to prison, to hard labour, for not less than three months.' It is probable that the sentences were harsher than the Board had anticipated, for when it was learned that the men were kept at the treadmill for six hours a day immediate steps were taken by the Directors to relieve them of this part of their punishment.

The chief concern of the directors was to avoid yielding to threats from their employees which would impair their authority in future and the Chairman believed '... that the strict measures adopted in this first display of insubordination will tend powerfully to secure discipline and good conduct hereafter.' Whether their method of adjusting differentials was the wisest one is another question, but their offer of a guaranteed minimum wage must have been unusual, if not unique, in those days.

It appears that the drivers who had been imprisoned may have been reinstated; in August 1836 driver J. Greenall assaulted one Callan after the latter had taunted him with his alleged lack of skill. Some time later a Callan was off duty for two months with fever; recommended by Melling as a useful and valuable man, he was awarded £5. There is no evidence that the Company ever had more than two drivers of this name.

Whether as a result of the strike, or because drivers were now in great demand for the new railways, the attitude of the directors when dealing with accidents or breaches of the Company's regulations was far more lenient than in the years when the L&MR was virtually the only employer of engine-drivers. Offences which then would have brought instant dismissal now attracted a reprimand or nominal fine, and only in the most serious cases of endangering the lives of passengers were men discharged. From April 1836 up to £10 a month was distributed among those enginemen with the best time-keeping records.

An engineman from the Company's early days was Ralph Thompson, then driver of the *Mars*, whose name appears in the records on several occasions. Suspended in February 1832 for refusing to take out the *Arrow*, he was reinstated a month later, and in August 1834 he was fined 5s. for leaving his engine while it was in motion to talk to the coach guard. He is last mentioned in the Board Minutes of 2 March 1835; two days earlier he was driving the Horseley Iron Company's ill-fated *Star* with the 2 p.m. train from Liverpool. At St Helens Junction the points had been left in the wrong position and the engine '. . . was jerked off the rails and ran across to the other side of the road when she came into collision with the *Caledonian* engine and tender. Ralph Thompson, the engineman, was thrown off and killed . . .' The Company paid his widow £5.[12]

By September 1834 the practice of appointing firemen from Melling's workshops had been established, although not always strictly observed; Melling complained of 'improper persons' being engaged as drivers and firemen at Manchester, and Dixon then protested that it was none of Melling's business. The Board's view was that

'In appointing firemen it was desirable to look forward to their becoming enginemen, and with this in view it must be an advantage to a man to have been employed in a fitter's shop. They wished, therefore, that when vacancies occurred, that the firemen should be supplied from the repairing sheds at the different stations.'

When Jonathan Marsh, who worked an engine at a ropery, decided he wanted to be a railway fireman, he was engaged at 4s. per day on coach or picking-up trains with the stipulation that he take charge of an engine whenever required, without extra charge.

In December 1835, when the pay dispute was becoming serious, William Daniels was discharged for refusing to take a train because of an alleged error in his wages; the train was delayed several minutes while another engine was found, although Daniels was there. His fireman, Wainwright, who was also an occasional driver, was severely reprimanded for 'getting out of the way and hiding himself' instead of going in Daniels' place, and he lost his turn for promotion to engineman.

Joseph Armstrong, later to achieve fame as the Locomotive Carriage and Wagon Superintendent of the GWR, was engaged as a driver by Edward Woods in 1836 at the age of 20. In October 1837 he requested the Board to free him from the obligation to give three months notice as he had been offered a situation by Edward Bury who, when questioned, said his agent had offered 'employment when an opening arose, but it was a solitary case.' Armstrong was told to give the stipulated three months notice.

In September 1837 several enginemen gave in their notice, this time to earn higher wages on the GWR. The Treasurer wrote to the Secretary of the offending company on the '. . . impolicy of Railway Companies outbidding each other in the wages of enginemen', to which Saunders replied that the GWR was careful not to indulge in the practice.

An attempt was made in June 1837 to get all the enginemen to sign the Company's agreement of service, but two years later there were still some who refused to do so; with the demand for experienced men increasing as the new railways were opening, the Company was in no position to enforce its ruling.

The increasing traffic of the GJR, particularly its luggage trains running late into the evening, threw a great strain on the crews of the banking engines who worked a 14-hour shift. In 1839 their pay was increased to 7s. a day for enginemen and 4s. 4d. for firemen. At the Management Committee's meeting on 11 February 1841

'. . . in testimony of the Directors' approval of their care and attention in keeping clear of accidents, and of their general steadiness and good conduct during a winter of extraordinary severity . . . it was resolved that £2 be presented to each engineman and £1.5.0 to each fireman.'

After the railway had been open for ten years, it was decided to keep staff records at the head office of all enginemen and firemen, giving their age, by whom recommended, etc., and at the same time, to have the printed rules and regulations read to them by the Principal Engineer or the Chief Superintendent of Locomotive Engines.

The men in the locomotive sheds and workshops worked from 6 a.m. until 8 p.m., an 84-hour week; they were allowed half-an-hour for breakfast, one hour for dinner and another half-hour for 'bagging', a local term for tea-time.

The railway police were on duty from 14 to 16 hours a day, most of them being stationed along the line at junctions, sidings and any potentially dangerous places. When the line opened they numbered nearly 60 and their pay was 17s. 6d. a week; this was increased to 21s. in the autumn of 1831, when they were also given winter coats and provided with watch-boxes. It was reported at this time that although they were supposed to be on duty before the first engines with goods passed along the line, few of them were actually to be seen. In April 1832 the force was substantially reduced, the men being given a fortnight's wages on discharge. Unfortunately among those retained was the Elton Head Junction policeman, Owen O'Neil, who in July was arrested for a 'brutal assault on a young woman'.

The introduction of improved points in the late 1830s relieved the police of the more laborious part of their work; according to Baxendale of the L&BR, '. . . the great misfortune as to policemen is that they have so little to do.'[13]

The incorrect setting of switch plates usually resulted in the policeman being fined; one Turner lost a week's wages for this offence in 1835.

The Newton Junction policeman, Bates, left the points incorrectly set for Liverpool and then fell asleep. In consequence a GJR train got on to the wrong line, and in being backed over the points, some waggons were derailed; Bates was charged with misconduct before a Magistrate in March 1841 and fined £3.

Gatekeepers were appointed at all the 21 level crossings; one of the first to be employed was the keeper of the Wavertree Lane gate, at 15s. a week and a rent-free cottage. These men were on duty from 5 a.m. until 10 p.m. and in recognition of their 'long hours of attendance', their wages were increased to £1 a week in November 1832.

The earliest gatemen were selected by Stephenson from among those who had built the railway, and although no particular educational standard was required, it was decided that Birchall, of Kendrick's Cross gate, should be changed for one who could read and write; he was sent to Norman's Lane gate.

The gatemen were exposed to some risk as their

cottages were accessible from the roads. In July 1838 one was attacked and injured by two drunks who then broke into his cottage and assaulted his wife and daughter; the Company took immediate action against them. At about the same time another gateman was discharged for allowing a drunken man and a child to get on to the railway.

There were two categories of porters, goods porters at Liverpool and Manchester, nearly 250 in all, and those at the principal passenger stations, Liverpool, Newton and Manchester. The goods trains were loaded and unloaded by the porters, who stored the merchandise in the warehouses or loaded it on to the carriers' carts. The passenger porters had various duties around the stations, and were responsible for securing passengers' luggage on the carriage roof. In 1839 an order was made that no porters over 40 years of age were to be employed.

During the busy summer months of 1831 a number of unofficial porters made their appearance at Crown Street; they charged passengers a fee for their services, and while the Company found this objectionable, there was little they could do as these porters were not on railway property. These outdoor porters increased in number with the opening of Lime Street Station, and often interfered in the working of the station yard. An attempt was made in July 1839 to bring them under some control by appointing an assistant superintendent to Ilbery and James Woods, and by arranging for them to wear distinctive badges.

The Company's own porters were often at a disadvantage compared with the outside men. In November 1843 it was discovered that they were acting as lodging house keepers for emigrants, to the detriment of those who did not have access to the yard or Lime Street Station. On the grounds that the practice might interfere with their ordinary duties, the Company ordered it to cease, but were not prepared to make regulations covering the outside porters.

After lengthy consideration the head porter at Newton Bridge Station was allowed to officiate as Parish Clerk at Newton Church between the hours of 10 a.m. and 5 p.m. on Sundays, on the understanding that he attended to any GJ trains at the station within those hours.

Where supervision was not very strict, the porters appear to have discriminated against some of the customers; a merchant complained to the Board that he could not get his coke forwarded from Parkside without bribing the porters there.

In the summer of 1844 the goods porters at Wapping appealed for a reduction in their working hours, which were 6 o'clock in the morning to 10 o'clock at night, and often to midnight. The maximum wage was £1 a week, with an additional bonus of about 3s., but the basic pay of the majority was only 19s. They were willing to give up part or all of the bonus for shorter hours, and Comber said that an additional 30 men at a cost of £1500 a year would be required, half the amount being met by the men, whose bonus would be reduced to 1s. 6d. There were 130 porters at Wapping, and Comber was authorised to engage as many extra men as would be needed to effect the new arrangement. In early September Comber reported that the men were still working excessive hours, owing to the building work in progress at Wapping, some being on duty from 6 a.m. to 9.30 p.m. and others from 8.30 a.m. to near 11 p.m., for a total of 20s. 6d. a week. The Company decided to give up their portion of the bonus while the building work went on, giving the men an extra 1s. 6d., which Comber thought was satisfactory. In June 1845, however, he had to report a '. . . Turn-out among the Porters at the Wapping Station'; they had gone on strike over the bonus system and a lack of accommodation at the station, resulting in their working longer hours for less money. The Board agreed with Comber that the bonus system was too complex, and a fixed wage was introduced.

The goods guard was responsible for ensuring that the porters had loaded the waggons properly, and he then tied down the tarpaulin sheets. Referring to this latter duty an early authority on railways, Lieut. Lecount,[14] says, rather ambiguously, 'steady seamen make the best goods guards, being accustomed to lashings.' The guard then found himself a perch, as best he could, on the last waggon.

The primitive and complicated method of booking passengers led to countless instances of cash deficiency, most arising from genuine mistakes. The Company held the booking clerks responsible for any shortage of cash, usually making a deduction from salary but often refunding the amount after the end of a trouble-free period, or, as in the case of a senior clerk at Crown Street who, on obtaining a position with the Bank of Manchester, was repaid £20 of the sum he had had to meet for one of his assistants.

In the early years of the Company four or five clerks were employed in the General Office at Crown Street; their salaries ranged from £100 to £130. In January 1833 the Chairman reminded the Board of the arduous duties of the Crown Street Coach Office, the long hours and the responsibility of handling large sums of money, and Williams, the Chief Booking Clerk, was presented with £21. At the end of that year he left to become Principal Superintendent of the Leeds & Selby Railway at £300 per annum.

A few years later, with the increased traffic coming on to the railway from other lines now opening, those in responsible positions were given increases in salary; among these were James Knox at the Edge Hill Luggage Station and McCormack, the Lime Street Chief Booking Clerk.

A lapse of concentration by a booking clerk could prove expensive. McCormack could not remember two passengers paying for 1st Class tickets, and declined to issue them unless they paid again, on the understanding that if on balancing the cash they were found to have paid (which subsequently proved to be the case) the money would be refunded. The passengers refused to pay again, were left behind, and took a post-chaise to Manchester, the cost of which, being £7 0s. 11d., McCormack was ordered to pay.

Henry Mitchell, a booking clerk at Lime Street, had his salary raised from £8 to £10 a month so that he might maintain his family in respectability and to cover the unavoidable losses in small sums to which a booking clerk was exposed.

A burglary occurred at Crown Street Station on Christmas Eve 1833 which illustrates the primitive security arrangements in force at that time. John Kyle, now chief booking clerk, had the day's takings, about £57 in gold and silver, put in a locked tin box which was in turn locked in an iron safe, and the key was handed over to him. His usual practice when he finally closed the office was to remove the tin box from the safe and take it home, but being tired that night he was already resting at home, and his wife locked up; he remembered afterwards that he had not removed the cash, but thought it would be safe. On Christmas morning, before 6 o'clock, he gave the key to the gateman who opened the office and lit the fire, and at 6.30 he began to book passengers for Manchester. It was not until the afternoon that he had occasion to go to the safe, when he discovered that the tin box together with a parcel thought to contain money had been stolen. A police enquiry failed to trace the thief, and Kyle was admonished for failing to keep the money in his bedroom at night according to his orders. Iron safes fitted with Chubb locks were then provided, one for the Crown Street office, and one for Joseph Green to keep in his bedroom, since he also often held large sums overnight. As the Company's Manchester Agent, he collected the freight charges which, in those days, were usually settled in gold and silver coin.

By the summer of 1831 the Board was rigorously enforcing staff discipline, particularly among those employees who came into direct contact with the public – guards, porters and the omnibus crews. During August porters and guards were discharged for insolence, and engineman Robert Hope was dismissed by Harding for drunkenness. The policy was strictly adhered to, drunkenness, neglect of duty, improper behaviour and the accepting or demanding of tips almost invariably bringing dismissal; less serious offences were usually dealt with by the imposition of fines or by the offender paying for part of the damage caused by his negligence. Even complaints by one employee against another were dealt with by the Sub-Committee; one Lionel Dove protested about the very improper and insulting language used by engineman Dunn resulting in the offender being reprimanded and fined 5s. Engine driver Murphy and Williamson, a porter at Parkside, were reprimanded over an incident in October 1837; Williamson had loaded bad coke on to the engine and Murphy threw it off, whereupon the porter became abusive and Murphy struck him. At the enquiry Williamson was alleged to have 'demanded silver' from Kennedy, Bury's partner, when the L&BR engine No 1 was undergoing trials on the L&MR.

The Board took a serious view of drunkenness, and very few of those discovered to have been drunk on duty escaped dismissal.

In May 1831 Thomas Blackburn, fireman of the *Majestic*, was discharged for 'drinking and neglecting his duty', and in August 'Simon Fenwick, Engine Man of the *Goliah* had assaulted the workmen when in a state of intoxication – it was not the first time he had been drunk – [and it was] ordered that Simon Fenwick be discharged.' He was an efficient and intelligent driver, however, and was either reprieved or subsequently re-engaged for on 5 December 1832 he was up before the Board for taking the *Vulcan* with a passenger train from Liverpool to Manchester in 1 hour 8 mins, but as there was a strong west wind behind the lightly loaded train, and he did not strain the engine, he got off with a reprimand. *Vulcan*'s original driver, Percival Hall, had been dismissed in March after having driven from Manchester to Liverpool while drunk; McCrie and his fireman were suspended for the same reason.

Mr Hulton wrote to the Board in October 1841 expressing 'regret and mortification' that one of his agents had treated a considerable number of the Company's enginemen at Vidler's Hotel. The reason for this generosity was not given, but there was an election pending.

The Superintendent at Edge Hill Station was so drunk one night in January 1836 that he was taken into custody by one of his own watchmen, but was later offered an inferior job at Wapping '. . . if he would abstain altogether from fermented liquors.' He reappears about 18 months later when, having fallen off a ladder, he was awarded £1.

Police, gatemen, guards and platelayers were discharged over the years for being '. . . found in drink'; their dismissal was usually immediate if seen by a director. Not surprisingly, the Company turned down a request for the grant of an ale allowance to its employees in 1834.

Men who were discharged often appealed to the Company for reinstatement, producing a document signed by persons supporting their case. Where drunkenness was the reason for their dismissal, the appeal usually failed, as in the case of the Patricroft gateman, James Faulkner, whose petition was sponsored by Sir Thomas Jos de Trafford and Lord Francis Egerton, among others. When James Smith, a guard, was suspended for being intoxicated on duty, he was able to produce a certificate from his doctor that medicine prescribed for him would increase the stupor induced by any liquor; a novel defence at that time, it saved him his job.

The Broad Green policeman Thomas Young appeared before the directors on a charge of having been drunk on duty, and although he 'prayed for forgiveness', the Board ruled that no exceptions could be made and he must go. On petitioning for any employment with the Company, the compassionate Cropper and his friend Hodgson moved that he be found work as remunerative as the job he had lost, but they were outvoted by the other three directors on the Management Committee. However, a few weeks later the Committee awarded him £5 for information he had furnished relating to the charges against Anthony Harding. He is last heard of in July 1833 when he asked if the Company would pay the passage to America for himself and his family, but their decision is not recorded.[15]

The Company's rule against the accepting of gratuities was rigorously enforced, porters and guards almost invariably being discharged if unlucky enough to be observed receiving money. Porter No 12, seen by the Chairman to 'take a fee from a passenger' in July 1839, was discharged, and a notice setting out the circumstances of his dismissal was displayed in the yard. A porter who ran through the Crown Street tunnel to hand a hat box to a passenger in a GJ train at Edge Hill was rewarded with sixpence by the grateful passenger, but fined 5s. by the Board, with a warning of dismissal if he was again caught accepting a gratuity.

The Board considered itself responsible for dealing with offences committed outside working hours and off the railway premises. On one occasion a labourer was dismissed for poaching on Parr Moss and the Roby gatekeeper, Hunter, was threatened with dismissal if he persisted in annoying his neighbour.

The derailment of *Goliah* at the top of Sutton Inclined Plane in April 1831 through the 'switch wrong placed' cost McDonald the policeman and James Twist the Sergeant of Police their jobs, although the constable was later reinstated.

The driver of *Majestic* was ordered to pay for the damage to his engine from a collision near Manchester in August and the Collins Green gateman was discharged for failing to prevent his gate being broken through by an engine. William McCrie, the *Majestic* driver, was in trouble again in November, when he and another driver were discharged for failing to observe the Whiston Incline orders, but he was reinstated a week later, after being interviewed by the Board, and the arrangements for working the inclines were revised.

One of the Company's senior drivers, Martin Weatherburn, was suspended in June 1832 for running his engine *Victory* too close behind the *Comet*, a coal engine, and colliding in Olive Mount Cutting.

Phoenix, while running with a goods train near Broad Green on 26 March 1831, was derailed by a plank carelessly left on the track by three platelayers, and the fireman, who jumped off the engine, was killed. When the Board discovered that the three men were being held in Lancaster Castle awaiting trial for manslaughter, they ordered immediate steps to be taken to bail them as they had not previously been in trouble. A few weeks later a former employee was before the Prescot magistrates on an assault charge, arising from his having helped one of the gatekeepers '. . . to prevent some rough people passing along the Rail Way. Mr Pritt [the Company's solicitor] was instructed to do the needful at Prescot on his behalf.' This was not the only instance of the Company assisting employees in trouble with the Courts.

With the passage of the first Regulation of Railways Act in 1840, the Company tended to refer more serious cases of negligence to the courts.[16] Thus the engineman David Fletcher was taken before the Liverpool Magistrates under 'Lord Seymour's Act' for driving the *Buffalo* down the Whiston Incline on the wrong line and nearly colliding with an ascending GJR train, which he knew to be due. He was fined £5 and lost his job.

Perhaps the most glaring example of irresponsibility was that on 8 November 1841, when one of

Hargreaves' early morning luggage trains arrived at Manchester with only one man on the footplate of the locomotive, *Marquis of Douro*, and he was asleep. A serious disaster was prevented by the prompt action of some L&MR porters who jumped on to the engine and shut off the steam. Booth brought the driver before the Manchester magistrates, who fined him £2 for culpable negligence, and he, the fireman and the two brakesmen concerned were prohibited from coming on to the L&MR again. The porters who had stopped the train were given 'suitable recompense'.

At 5 a.m. on the morning of Christmas Day 1841 the early mail train from Parkside, consisting of two carriages, emerged from the Lime Street tunnel at full speed and crashed into two 2nd Class coaches, practically wrecking them. There were only three passengers on the train, and they escaped serious injury. The guard, William Davidson, was ordered to appear before the Board, but failed to do so, and was ordered to be brought before the magistrates on a charge of culpable negligence, since evidence suggested that he had been asleep in the 1st class carriage. He was duly sentenced to two months in the Borough Gaol, and on his release, he asked the Company for a character testimonial; he was told that if he could get one from the magistrate who sentenced him, he could bring it to the Treasurer. The carriages had belonged to the NU and Lancaster & Preston Companies, and their repair cost the L&MR £82, apart from the damage to its own vehicles.

At times, when employees were brought before the directors, the Board Room assumed the aspect of a court, and something akin to a trial ensued. In July 1837 one of the town policemen appeared with three porters and a gateman accused of fraud and disobedience; two were found guilty and dismissed, the others were acquitted and returned to duty for want of conclusive evidence.

Four guards were found to have defrauded the Company by allowing passengers who had not been booked, to travel at a reduced fare, which they pocketed. When brought before the Board, the Chairman told them that they were to be discharged but that the Board had decided not to bring them to court on criminal charges. On their protesting they were given the option of being charged before a magistrate but reminded that if the case against them were proved it would mean committal to Kirkdale Prison. The next day Booth reported that none wished to go before a magistrate; they were then dismissed.

Collectors, booking clerks and others who handled money had to find sureties for various amounts from £200 to £1500, according to the degree of responsibility attaching to their position. They were rarely able to balance their books, and from a resolution in October 1831 to increase their pay, it appears that at the time they balanced their cash and paid it over to the Company monthly. After this time they had to pay the deficiencies themselves before receiving their salaries.

In some cases collectors and clerks absconded with the Company's money, and the surety was then called upon to make good the amount involved, the London Guarantee Society being one of them.

Roby, the Chief Clerk at Liverpool Road Station, was discharged in 1833 after two guards had reported him for entering less road money in his books than they had brought in. This was the money collected by the guards from passengers who joined the trains at intermediate stations.

Comber discovered in November 1837 that an assistant collector had gambled away £170 to £200 of the Company's money. Comber said the lad, 'who was very penitent ... might be reclaimed' and his mother had offered to pay the deficiency by instalments if the Company would let her son redeem his character by retaining him. This they agreed to do, but he was to have a job with no responsibility, and Comber was to watch him carefully. The boy's senior collector, himself £100 deficient, was dismissed, and replaced as Principal Collector by a man with an impeccable reference from a local firm of distillers.

One of the Manchester warehouse clerks was convicted of embezzlement of the Company's property in 1831, and was sentenced to 12 months hard labour at Lancaster Castle. He had been stealing cotton and the two men who detected him were given 1 guinea each. The Superintendent of the Manchester Corn and Flour Depot was prosecuted for embezzlement of £160 collected and unaccounted for in January 1843.

One of the arguments advanced for the railway was that the pilfering of goods in transit, so prevalent on the canals, would be eliminated, but it was soon discovered that the Wapping Tunnel provided an opportunity for oranges and oysters, among other small items, to be spirited away from the trains travelling slowly through it.

A platelayer caught stealing a keg of butter from a train climbing slowly up the Whiston Incline was convicted and sentenced to six months' imprisonment.

Some of the Company's police were not entirely blameless, and one Jennings displayed a degree of ingenuity when an occasion arose in September 1835. The last waggon of a Saturday evening luggage train became detached at Broad Green, and Jennings put it into a siding where it remained until Monday morning, when it was discovered that he had drawn off several gallons of wine from a cask on the waggon by removing the bilge hoop, spiking the cask underneath and then replacing the hoop, '. . . a work that must have taken considerable time to accomplish.'

The Company's own property was by no means inviolate. Until it ordered specially coloured candles to be made in March 1832, it was buying far more than were needed to light the warehouses, stations and offices.

A weighman was accused by a firm of coal merchants of recording greater weights than their waggons contained, and after checking some returns, the Company decided he should be discharged as soon as someone else could be found to do the work. It is hardly surprising that inaccuracies crept in as the weighbridge men kept their accounts on slates.

Under the general heading of misconduct a great variety of offences came before the Board. Several porters were discharged in August 1831 for 'rude behaviour to passengers', while other cases of impertinence, often by gatekeepers, attracted reprimands or fines.

The operating staff of the railway seem to have accepted the risk of injury or death as a normal hazard and not one to be taken too seriously; there can be no other explanation of the casualty figures remaining just as high in 1844 as in 1830, when accidents to employees were attributed to inexperience. Enginemen, firemen, guards and brakesmen thought nothing of walking along the roofs of swaying carriages, picking their way around the luggage and jumping to the next coach, or performing a similar feat on a train of lurching goods waggons, the tarpaulin covers of which provided an uncertain and treacherous foothold. For every man who slipped between the vehicles to death or certain injury, hundreds must have taken such risks with no dire consequences. An order was made in 1839 forbidding the brakesmen to pass over loaded waggons except in case of emergency, but this was for the express purpose of protecting fragile goods and the waggon sheets from being trampled on.

The fireman of the *York* lost his foot from slipping under a train running down an incline while he was attempting to pin down several waggon brakes. Another fireman, James Green, after hooking on some waggons at Broad Green Cattle Station, passed along the moving train, fell and died a few days later from his injuries. In July 1831 *Mercury*'s fireman was killed when attempting to detach the engine from the carriages at the foot of Whiston Incline before the train had stopped and the coupling chains had slackened, and yet another, Daniel McIvie, fireman of *Patentee*, was killed at Manchester in April 1838; he fell between his engine and *Thunderer* while trying to uncouple them while in motion.

William Wood, engineman, was killed between Newton and Parkside on Friday evening, 11 June 1841, when taking the extra train from Newton Racecourse to Manchester. He had stepped from the tender to the first coach, and on returning to the engine, slipped and fell under the train.

Peter Dean, a luggage brakesman, lost a leg through attempting to jump on to the tender of the 7.30 blue train on the morning of 8 April 1840, and falling beneath it, while another, named Purdie, died at this time from the effects of an accident some weeks earlier.

Tragedy struck the Jones family in July 1837. The father and two sons worked on the railway, and while both sons were 'laid up with accidents', Jones Snr, a tunnel brakesman, had his leg cut off by a passing train; the Company ordered full wages to be paid until further orders.

Although some of their decisions appear to be somewhat unfeeling towards the staff, the directors did take a personal interest in the welfare of their men and their dependants. John Cropper brought up the case of the family of William Formby, a coach porter who had died on 3 February 1841 '. . . in consequence of a cold taken when going out as occasional guard'; it was resolved that £5 '. . . be placed in Mr Cropper's hands, to be disposed of for the benefit of Formby's family.' There were many similar instances over the years of financial help to the widows of men killed on the line.[17]

In June 1837 a fitter was crushed to death between the buffers of a locomotive and a tender when a fireman, in the restrained phrase of the Minute Book, 'inconsiderately backed an engine' against the one upon which he was working. The Parkside pointsman sustained some broken ribs in a similar accident, having '. . . placed himself between two luggage waggons just as the engineman backed the train a little'. This seems to have been his own fault, as in the case of a coal porter at Crown Street yard, whose arm was crushed between the buffers when he tried to unloose the coupling chains before the train had stopped. A proportion of the accidents then, as always, arose from completely unforeseen circumstances; such was the case of a porter at Wapping, who was killed by a windlass handle flying round when the brake failed on a crane lowering timber.

June 1845, a few weeks before the end of the Company's separate existence, was a bad month. A policeman was run over at the foot of Whiston Incline, dying later, and another man fell from a train near Newton while passing from one carriage to another; the Board noted that his leg had been amputated, but that he was '. . . doing tolerably well under the circumstances'. Yet another employee, Sullivan, a brakesman, was killed in the Wapping Tunnel by falling from a waggon while adjusting the brake; the Treasurer was asked to enquire into the circumstances of his widow and family.

The tunnels were particularly dangerous places, many men having been killed or injured in them; others narrowly escaped on the frequent occasions when 'waggons running amain in the Old Tunnel' crashed at Wapping. In July 1841 a porter went up the Wapping Tunnel with a train and in attempting to get off while it was running, fell to his death under the wheels. Hossick, a tunnel brakesman, died in 1842 whilst trying to loose the messenger rope from a goods train at the top of the Old Tunnel, although there was a regulation against disengaging the rope while the train was moving. The brakesmens' job was made more difficult by the presence of the open drain in the tunnel, and it was not until May 1844 that it was filled in.

While a goods train was being hauled up one day in April 1845, the messenger rope broke when near the top, and the brakesman, probably not realising in the darkness that the train had changed direction, allowed it to run down to the bottom. Another brakesman named Davies on hearing the train approaching, attempted to get a horse out of the way, but actually put it in the path of the train descending on the wrong line, and both he and the horse were killed.

At Lime Street Station a coach porter was strapping luggage on a carriage roof when the train started. Instead of observing the general practice of riding up to Edge Hill, he jumped off the carriage about a hundred yards inside the tunnel, and straight in the path of a train from Manchester which killed him instantly. At Edge Hill in September 1842 a coach porter was crushed to death between two horse-boxes by attempting to hold back one vehicle while the other was being shunted into a siding.

A common and dangerous practice by platelayers was to hook their lorries to passing trains and ride in them along the wrong line. Fireman Ogden of *Cyclops*, on a goods train to Manchester in November 1837, leaned over the side of the tender and with his fire rake, attempted to pull a lorry from Chat Moss Tavern to Patricroft. Catching the corner of it, he pulled it off the rails, and one of the platelayers was thrown under the train and killed. At the subsequent enquiry the directors did not think much blame attached to anyone, but they told Ogden and the engineman James Thompson to be more careful in future. A similar incident occurred when four men from the Salford engine shed attached a trolley to a Liverpool-bound goods train, intending to ride home to Eccles. Near Weast Lane the truck was upset and one man broke his thigh; a few days later, they were all dismissed. The platelayers were allowed to attach their trolleys to the rear of 2nd Class passenger trains, but in July 1841, after another had been killed when a trolley was derailed, the Board of Trade Inspector wrote that he would be glad to hear that the practice had been discontinued.

From the time of opening certain grades of staff were provided with, or expected to purchase, uniforms or livery. Whether the blue and red caps worn by the firemen on opening day were replaced is not recorded, but top coats were supplied to drivers and firemen. In 1841 each man was given £2 10s. to buy a new winter coat of a pattern approved by Edward Woods.

The guards of the 1st Class trains were issued with green livery, hats and badges in 1830, and in June 1831 similar uniforms were given to the guards of the Second Class trains. A fine of 1s. was imposed on any who failed to wear his brass badge. In the winter the guard, buttoned up in a huge drab overcoat which came down to his heels, huddled in his seat on the carriage roof. Policemen on duty wore blue frock-coats and top hats; in September 1831 they were issued with great coats.

At Lime Street the head superintendent wore a blue frock coat with the Company's buttons and the assistant superintendents similar coats but with braid on the collar; similar arrangements were made for the superintendents at Manchester and Newton stations. The first suits were issued free but thereafter they had to be paid for. These uniforms were based on the patterns of those used on the L&BR and Eastern Counties Railway. A traveller in April 1842 remarks on the blue and gold livery of the travelling inspectors, evidently a reference to the police superintendents.

Until 1838 the coach porters appear to have had no distinctive uniform, for it was then decided that they should wear a fustian jacket with brass buttons and a brass badge on each arm bearing the wearer's

75 *Guards on a 1st Class train in Olive Mount Cutting, 1831. The brake handle can be seen by the guard's right hand*

number, these jackets to be purchased and worn while in the Company's employ. When it was discovered that some porters wore their badges loose, so that they could be slipped off if the occasion arose, it was ordered that they be sewn on.

In October 1839 it was decided 'That in order to make the porters clean and respectable in their appearance, the Company should provide them with two suits per annum, with badges and numbers'. Olive and drab jackets for the station and yard porters respectively, with moleskin trousers and caps, were ordered for issue in April and October, and about half the cost was recovered by a deduction of one shilling a week from the man's wages for six months from April each year. The badge was now worn on the cap.

As early as June 1831 an annuity fund for the Company's employees was discussed, but no steps were taken at that time to establish one.

The practice of paying half wages to men under medical care was discontinued in 1837, and all the Company's employees were urged to join a reputable benefit club; membership of a club would be made a condition of employment for new men. After this time the Company made a cash grant in exceptional circumstances, such as prolonged illness, usually reminding the recipient that he would have been better off had he followed the Board's advice and joined a club. The practice of paying the clerical staff half or in some cases, full pay during periods of illness was continued however.

A return presented to the Board on 14 June 1841 showed that of 1180 employees, 833 were in sickness benefit clubs. The proportion at Manchester who were members was only about 50%, however, and Green was told to remind them that the directors did not accept an obligation to assist men who had not joined a benefit society. The Secretary of the North Midland Railway was trying to organise a General Benefit Society for railwaymen at this time.

The Company paid surgeons who attended its employees after accidents, although it expected any prolonged treatment to be carried out by the Infirmary unless the Board gave specific instructions. This ruling resulted from a doctor's bill for over £11 for attendance on a fireman who, while leaning from his engine, knocked his head on the pier of Platts Bridge, Whiston, and was paid on the urgent recommendation of Melling.

In December 1831 the Company paid the surgeon who had attended workmen injured on Olive Mount and other excavations £21; he had claimed £70 for his five years' service.

Rewards and bonuses were paid by the Company to its employees on many occasions, sometimes as incentives, more often in recognition of some special service or prolonged effort under trying circumstances.

In May 1833 Cropper recommended that prizes of £3 or £5 be awarded to those enginemen who took most care of their engines over a period of six months, but the Board could foresee difficulties arising when it came to adjudicating, from the differing age and construction of the locomotives; instead they placed £25 at the disposal of the Management Committee to be allocated at its discretion, and the following March £20 was distributed in bonuses. Resulting from this scheme, each driver had, so far as possible, to keep to one engine.

The severe winter and prolonged frost of January 1838 imposed a severe strain on the railway, largely from the increased traffic thrown on to it from the ice-bound canals. The Board recorded that it was all dispatched without delay, and the men who kept the trains running received gifts ranging from £21 for Woods to 6s. for each fireman.

When the Midland Counties Railway was given permission to send a prospective manager to spend a few months in the booking and parcels offices to learn the job, it was suggested that a small fee should be paid, to be distributed among the office clerks.

On Queen Victoria's Coronation Day, Thursday 28 June 1838, all the Company's employees not required for duty were given the day off with pay; those who had to work received double pay.

CHAPTER NINE

Locomotives and Rolling Stock

At the end of the Rainhill Trials the L&MR possessed three locomotives, *Twin Sisters*, *Rocket* and *Sans Pareil*; *Lancashire Witch* was still working on the line, but its owners, the B&LR, were pressing for its return. A week after the award of the £500 premium, the Board placed an order with Robert Stephenson & Co. for four engines similar to *Rocket*, to be delivered in three months.

At this time the Company received several offers of locomotives; the Board promised Mr Price of Neath who was building an engine on Braithwaite and Ericsson's plan, but with alterations and improvements, that they would give it a full trial and purchase it if satisfactory. Alexander Christie & Co. of Sheffield submitted a plan for working the tunnel by locomotive and W. Parkinson of Boston Waterside wrote concerning his compressed air locomotive; both schemes were referred to Stephenson, who evidently did not recommend them. An engineer named Gale asked the Company for £1000 to build a 'new locomotive carriage', and Mr Gurney who had 18 or 20 steam carriages 'building for the common roads' asked if they would be suitable for railways. It would seem that the Company offered to let him convert and try one on the railway, for on 7 December 1829 it is recorded that Gurney would supply an engine only for 'an immediate compensation over and above the price of the engine'. At the end of March 1830 William Crawshay wrote to the Company offering a new heavy locomotive, and in May Timothy Burstall was preparing a locomotive for the railway, but nothing further is heard of either.

The first of Stephenson's new engines, *Wildfire*, arrived on the line on Monday, 18 January, and was tried that same afternoon near Edge Hill when it is said to have attained 30 mph. On Friday and Saturday extended trials were held at Rainhill where it hauled over 30 tons, and further trials followed on subsequent weekends. The locomotives incorporated several improvements over the *Rocket*; the 10in. × 16in. cylinders were nearly horizontal, the driving wheels were of 5ft diameter and the boiler contained 90 two-inch tubes. It was said to run faster and more smoothly than *Rocket* at a 20% saving of fuel; she and her sister engines cost £600 each.

On 1 February the second engine arrived and the Board then established the policy of choosing their own names for the locomotives. The first engine originally named *Wildfire* by the makers, was renamed *Meteor* and the second *Comet*. *Dart* and *Arrow* arrived, in that order, during the month. Meanwhile a further two engines were ordered from RS & Co.

Of the other Rainhill engines, *Novelty* was back on the line, having been rebuilt by Fawcett, Preston & Co., and was undergoing trials by 5 January 1830, for on that day the Company's overlooker at Sutton, Towlerton, was killed by falling off a waggon being propelled by this engine. The Company paid his widow £50 and ordered that no further trials be held except under the personal supervision of Ericsson with a limit of 4 mph when propelling trains. The full trials took place on 26 January and the Directors were sufficiently impressed to order two locomotives on the same principle, but larger, at £1000 each for delivery in Liverpool by 15 June. In August *Novelty* was being refitted in Manchester by Ericsson, and appears to have been used by Vignoles on construction work; but she never saw regular service on the L&MR.

In 1833 *Novelty* was rebuilt by Robert Daglish, who fitted a new copper-tube boiler, cylinders, axles and cranks; the locomotive went into service on the St Helens & Runcorn Gap Railway on Saturday, 3 August 1833. Daglish gave the original cylinders to Melling, and from his Rainhill Iron Works they passed into the possession of the Prescott & District Gas Co., who subsequently occupied the building. There they remained until 1903, when one was given to the Science Museum; the other was presented to the LMSR in 1929. Mounted on a plinth at Rainhill Station, it was the last remaining relic there of the Trials. *Novelty* ran across the Ribble Viaduct on the NUR on 30 May 1838, the day before the opening of the line, being driven by Vignoles' son, Hutton, then aged 14; this is the last mention of the engine in Vignoles diary.[1]

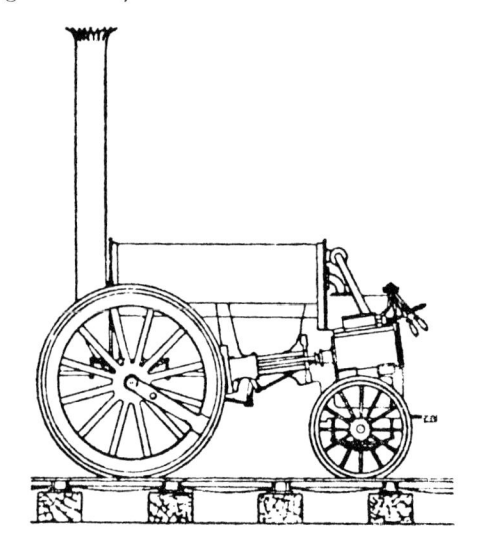

The Company lent *Sans Pareil* (the 'Darlington Specimen Engine' as they called it) to the B&LR on its return from Hackworth, and in January 1830 it was again being repaired by Hackworth's man at Bolton. The B&LR was now becoming impatient for the return of its own *Lancashire Witch*, but in March they agreed to hire *Sans Pareil* at £15 per month. It remained the property of the L&MR until September 1832, when it was sold for about £100 to the B&LR, where it remained at work until 1844; it then worked until 1863 as a pumping and winding engine at Coppull Colliery near Chorley, and the following year John Hick of Bolton presented it to the South Kensington Museum (now the Science Museum).

At the end of June the first of Robert Stephenson's two additional engines had arrived from Newcastle and was named *Phoenix*; its sister engine, *North Star*, was on the line by 23 August. These engines were the first to be fitted with smokeboxes, and the cylinders were slightly larger than in the preceding four, being 11in. × 16in.; in other respects they were similar and the price, £600, was the same.

In the meantime RS & Co. had been working on a new locomotive, referred to in a minute of 5 July:

'... after the next Locomotive Engine, which they expected shortly to despatch from Newcastle, and which was proposed should be called the 'Northumberland' [sic] the price, in consequence of the increased quantity of copper, and superior workmanship, of the engines, as now made, would be £650 each.'

76 Meteor *(3)*

77 Northumbrian *(7); drawing shows rectangular smokebox*

When it arrived on 9 August it was named *Northumbrian*, presumably as a personal tribute to George Stephenson, with whom the Board was well pleased at this time, the opening of the railway being at last in sight.

The *Northumbrian* incorporated several improvements on the earlier designs, the most revolutionary being in the firebox which now became an integral part of the boiler. The number of tubes was increased to 132, their diameter being reduced to 1$\frac{5}{8}$in., and it was said that the boiler and chimney were made of copper instead of iron. It is likely that it was just the outside casing of the boiler that was of sheet copper, as the Company's engines are described at this time, September 1830, as having boilers 'cased with wood or copper',[2] and the others certainly had wooden cladding of $\frac{1}{2}$in. deal timber secured by iron hoops. The frame was of much stronger construction, being built up from bars and plates arranged vertically instead of flat as in former designs. The smokebox was probably rectangular in its original form, from the evidence of the original maker's drawings and subsequent illustrations. Attention was also given to the tender, which although small, had a built-in water tank.

At its trials on 16 August, it is reputed to have approached 40 mph. *Northumbrian* was the last locomotive to be delivered before the opening of the railway, and being by far the best, was allocated to the Duke of Wellington's train on that occasion. Two more engines of the same class, *Majestic* (No 10) and *Mercury* (No 11), were ordered; but so rapid had been the development of the steam locomotive at this time, that the design of *Mercury* was modified during construction to incorporate later improvements.

It appears that about June 1830 the Company decided to number its locomotives and starting with *Rocket* (No 1), *Arrow*, *Meteor*, *Dart* and *Comet* were numbered 2 to 5 respectively, although this was not the order of delivery. From then onwards the engines were numbered strictly in order of their arrival on the line, thus *Phoenix* was No 6, *Northumbrian* 7 and *North Star* 8.[3] The numbers ran on consecutively and when an engine was scrapped the number remained blank in the list. Several of the early engines had their names transferred to replacements, but the name *Rocket* was never used again. The engines had their names on the

78 Northumbrian *(7); sketch by James Nasmyth, who appears to have confused it with* Rocket. *Other contemporary drawings also show chimney stays*

boiler barrel and, with the first few, also on the tender water-cask; the numbers were on the front buffer beam and high on the front of the chimney, the latter probably in the form of separate brass numerals.

RS & Co. seem at this time to have devoted part of their factory to the development of new designs, for even while *Northumbrian* was building, a yet more advanced type was being evolved. The prototype arrived on the L&MR on 4 October and was named *Planet* (No 9). It was about the same size as its predecessor and incorporated the improved smokebox and firebox; the cylinders were the same size and the multitubular boiler was of a similar pattern. The radical departure from previous practice, however, was in the placing of the cylinders inside the frames, and under the smokebox, where they were kept warm. The 5ft driving wheels were at the rear, and the drive was through a cranked axle in front of the firebox. The main frames were outside the driving wheels and a series of internal frames provided, in all, six supports for the crank axle. The technique of forging crank axles had not advanced very far at this time and the multiple frames, later known as sandwich frames, were provided to reduce the chances of the engine becoming derailed in the event of axle breakage. The engine weighed about eight tons, of which the driving wheels carried over five tons, considerably increasing the power over that of previous engines; the price was £800.

At the engine's trials on 23 November it ran from Liverpool to Manchester in one hour, including a stop for oiling and examining the machinery about half-way. On Saturday, 4 December, its trial took the practical form of working the first goods train to Manchester, consisting of 18 loaded waggons, a total of 80 tons, and including some passengers. It did the journey in six minutes under three hours, including stoppages for water, oiling and assistance up the Whiston Inclined Plane.

The Directors were very impressed with the performance of *Planet* and ordered six similar engines; it was also arranged that three engines still

79 Planet *(9)*

outstanding from previous orders should be modified, making nine in all. Stephenson promised, on 6 December 1830, to deliver one a fortnight, but it was not until the following November that the last of the batch arrived on the line. Their names, allocated by the Company, were:

Mercury (11)	*Saturn* (16)	*Etna* (20)
Mars (12)	*Sun* (17)	*Victory* (22)[4]
Jupiter (14)	*Venus* (18)	*Vesta* (24)

Within a week of the opening of the railway, the Board decided to order two powerful engines for assisting trains up the inclined planes, and Stephenson produced a modified version of the 'Planet' class with four coupled wheels 4ft 6in. diameter and larger cylinders, 14in. × 20in. in *Samson* (No 13), and 14in. × 16in. in *Goliah* (No 15). The locomotives were delivered in January and March 1831 respectively, at a cost of £1000 each.

These engines were used on goods trains at first, and on 25 February *Samson* took a train of 30 waggons, 120 yds long and weighing 151 tons, to Manchester in 2½ hours. At Whiston Incline, 14 waggons were detached and *Samson* took the remaining 16 up unaided; the others were propelled to the top by *Mars*, *Mercury* and *North Star*. On 2 April the two engines took 1000 bags of cotton to Manchester, *Goliah* leaving its train at the foot of Whiston Bank to assist *Samson*; it then took its own train of 27 waggons up in three parts, unassisted.[5]

At this time Stephenson recommended that the passenger trains should take 1½ hours for the journey and the goods train 2½ hours; the load for 'Planet' class engines was 10 waggons, and 'for *Meteor* and engines of her size', seven.

The two engines ordered from Braithwaite and Ericsson reached Manchester on 21 September 1830 and started their trials at Liverpool two days later; they were *William IV* and *Queen Adelaide*, the names being given by permission of the King. On 24 September, *William IV*, when returning to

80 Goliah *(15) (always spelt this way in the Company's minutes)*

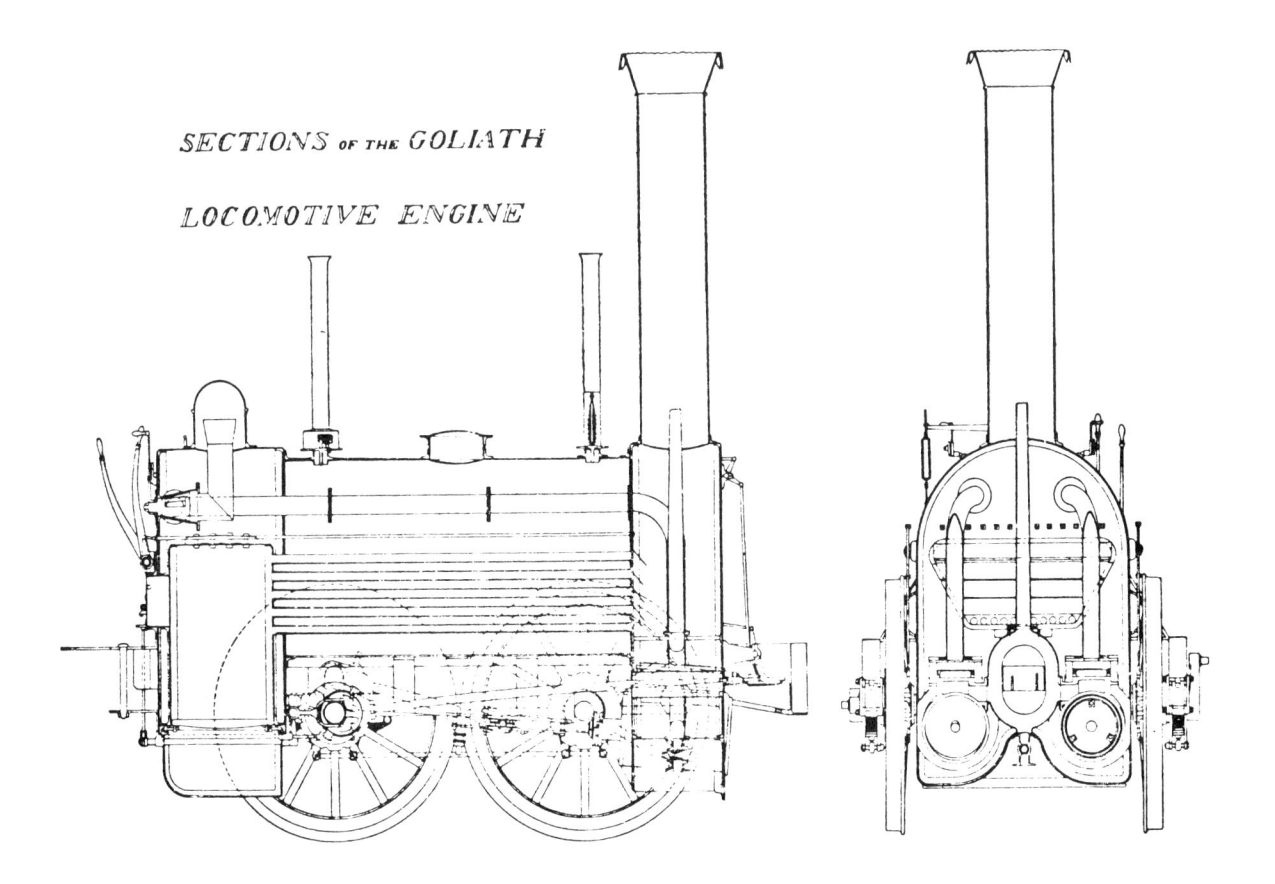

Manchester, slipped off the railway on the Sankey Embankment, being saved from rolling to the bottom by the soft earth into which it plunged. Secured overnight by ropes, it was rescued the next day by men who rode to the spot in a horse-drawn railway waggon.[6] After further trials in October both engines were modified, and were again tested in February 1831. *William IV* set off from Manchester without a load, but was overtaken at Newton by *Mars* which had left with eight waggons 30 minutes later, and was pushed all the way to Liverpool.[7] Unlike *Novelty*, these engines were provided with separate tenders propelled in front. The Company declined to purchase them and they were used for a time by Vignoles. Their failure on the L&MR was stated by the Directors to have caused the delay of several months in starting goods traffic.

In July 1832 Hardman Earle wrote:

81 William IV

'... it is now two years since the Planet was laid down, and upwards of twenty engines have since been launched from the Newcastle and other manufactories, and yet she comes nearer to what we consider perfection (relatively of course) than any which have succeeded her; her wheels and axles have been strengthened, but her form and general construction has never been improved upon.'[8]

The Board expressed its disappointment at the delay in receiving new locomotives from RS & Co. in November 1830, and informed the makers that it required 'some specific contract' in future.

In December 1830 RS & Co. came to an arrangement under which Murray & Wood of Leeds would build engines from their drawings, and by May 1831 the firm, by now Fenton Murray & Co., had delivered the first one, *Vulcan* (No 19); this was followed by *Fury* (No 21) in August, and in January 1833 the third and last built by this firm arrived, *Leeds* (No 30). All three were passenger engines of the Planet class, and cost £780 each.

Two more 0-4-0 'Luggage Engines' were ordered from RS & Co., *Atlas* (No 23) delivered in October 1831 and *Milo* (No 25) of February 1832. Each had 5ft coupled wheels and 12in. × 16in. inside cylinders. The Company declined to accept *Milo* until a stronger axle than the $4\frac{1}{8}$in. one originally fitted had been substituted. *Atlas* was the first engine to be fitted with piston valves. Both engines were reported to be of 'defective construction', and although new, had undergone frequent repair by April 1832, when the Board informed the makers that it expected reimbursement. RS & Co. were debited with the cost of 'extraordinary repairs' to *Vesta*, *Atlas* and *Milo* in June.

Gore's Advertiser of May 1831 carried an advertisement inviting engine makers to tender for the supply of two locomotives '. . . equal or superior to the best engines at present in use on the . . . Line' and promising liberal treatment '. . . by the Directors, whose object is to obtain the most improved Locomotive Engine that mechanical skill and experience can furnish.' This brought offers from the Manchester firms of Sharp, Roberts and Fairbairn and from the Liverpool engineers Edward Bury and George Forrester. Fairbairn's price was too high, and owing to some misunderstanding with Henry Booth, Forrester withdrew. Bury received an order for two engines, and Sharp Roberts, at their own request, for one only.

It was arranged in January 1832 that Hargreaves should take Bury's first engine for the Bolton & Leigh Railway (*Bee*), and in April the second one arrived and was accepted by the Company who named it *Liver* (No 26). Both engines were on Stephenson's plan except that they had round fireboxes, a design to which Stephenson strongly objected on the grounds that, having no stays between the outer and inner shells, they were unsafe. A defect developed in *Liver*'s firebox shortly after delivery and orders were given that it was not to be employed on coach trains. As Bury's engines were used on the L&MR by the B&LR and Bourne & Robinson, the Board decided to consult a number of engineers on the merits of the circular firebox, but while awaiting their reports Bury was given permission to try his latest locomotive, *Liverpool*, from the Bolton line with as many waggons as she could take from Liverpool to Manchester, the Company replacing her with one of its own engines for the day. In another series of experiments towards the end of June comparative trials between *Liver* and *Planet* took place over a six-day period; the result showed that *Liver* consumed less coke for the same amount of work. During these trials it was discovered that Anthony Harding had ordered the coke fillers to pick good coke for the Newcastle engine and fill the other bags by shovel, marking them with a cross and a chalk line respectively. Dixon discovered the trick in time and Harding was severely reprimanded by the Board for '. . . a proceeding so reprehensible, and quite at variance with that fair and impartial conduct which alone the Directors could sanction.' Some time afterwards it came to light that the safety valves of *Planet* had been screwed down to enable her to take as heavy a train as *Liver*.

The reports from Farey and Field was eventually delivered in January 1833 and gave a decided preference for square fireboxes. Edward Bury was unconvinced, however, and since he would not adopt the square pattern, he received no further orders from the L&MR. He continued to repair the Company's locomotives until December 1834, when he wrote declining any more engine repairs '. . . on account of the difficulty of giving satisfaction to the foremen and enginemen on the Rail Way.' Hardman Earle said of his locomotives, '. . . they are specimens of excellent workmanship and perform as well as any of the same power upon the road.'

Sharp, Roberts, an old-established textile machinery firm, built their first locomotive for the L&MR and went on to become one of the leading manufacturers in the country. On 15 August 1831 Sharp attended on the Board for orders and was given the same specifications as Bury. He offered an engine with outside vertical cylinders, and it is referred to in the Board's Minutes of 17 October as 'then building'. Over a year elapsed, and on 29 November 1832, Sharp Roberts sent drawings of the engine, which had an overall width of 8ft; it was rejected on the advice of Robert Stephenson, who thought the plan 'very objectionable'. On 16 May 1833 Sharp reported that their engine had been 'working well for a week now' and offered it for £1000. The Board agreed to give the engine, named *Experiment*, a trial, but after protracted tests under the supervision of John Dixon, they refused in October to buy her since she consumed too much coke.

The engine, with its vertical cylinders working through bell-cranks to impart a horizontal motion to the connecting rods, was a prototype of the same makers' *Hibernia* for the D&KR. The Company, pressed by Sharp, Roberts to accept the locomotive, offered £800 for it if they would exchange the cylinders for new ones fitted with spring pistons and replace the steam valves with a more efficient set admitting of easy adjustment. It seems that Sharp, Roberts were unwilling to comply, and in February 1834 sold the engine for £700 to the L&MR, who carried out the conversions themselves, fitting new 11 in. × 16in. cylinders and motion; it became *Experiment* (No. 32).

The existence of the L&MR set many engineering firms in those towns thinking about entering the field of locomotive building; one of these was Galloway, Bowman & Glasgow, of the Caledonian Foundry, Manchester, who completed their first machine, the

Manchester, in the summer of 1831.

-It underwent trials at the end of August, and under the heading 'New Engine on the Railway' the *Manchester Courier* of 3 September referred to it as of 'peculiar construction' but added that it had been employed on the line for the past week 'with great success'. The following extract from John Galloway's Memoirs throws some light on the hazards and excitement that attended locomotive trials in those early days.

'I passed a great deal of my time at the railway terminus in Ordsal Lane, being very intimate with Fyfe, the Superintendent ... The Railway Company proved very good customers to us, because an engine seldom came in without requiring some repairs, and they had no workshop of their own, though Mr Fyfe later on got a lathe or two and a few men about the place. We then determined to make a locomotive, *the first made in Manchester*, which was not the heavy and trim looking piece of mechanism of the present day. It was named the "Manchester". The cylinders were vertical, and the whole affair was kept very light ... The wheels were of wood, made by John Ashbury himself, a young man just out of his time, who afterwards founded the great waggon works at Openshaw bearing his name – on to these we shrunk iron welded tyres. When we had completed it in the shop in Bridgewater Street, we were met by the serious difficulty of getting it down to the station. We could not put steam on, nor was there a wagon which would take it, so we had to "bar" it down to Ordsal Lane, which took a gang of men with crowbars from 6 p.m. to 9 a.m. The road was not paved with sets as now, but very poorly and irregularly. The news got about that it was going to be tried, and a lot of friends gathered round to take part, so I got about half a dozen third-class carriages to run up to Chat Moss and back ... We started off about noon, about 200 in number, as every one was anxious for a ride, and pulled up at Chat Moss tavern – this was usual in those days and was continued for a long time afterwards, being sanctioned by the Company. We pulled up at Parkside, where we unhooked the waggons, the

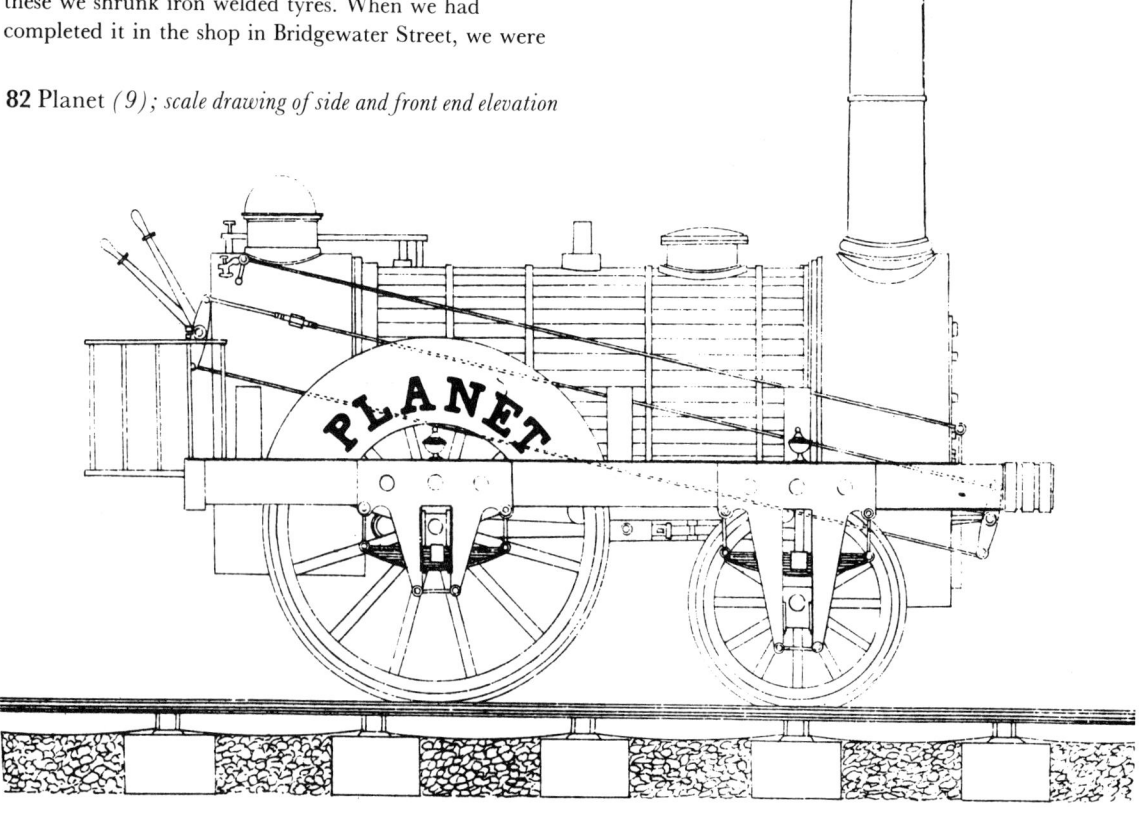

82 Planet *(9); scale drawing of side and front end elevation*

occupiers of which had quite a holiday in the country, while eight or nine of us ran a few miles further on the engine. We turned back on the same line, a proceeding which would not be countenanced for a moment now, as signalling was unknown, but we knew from the small number of engines and trains in existence that there was little danger of meeting another. A train from Liverpool on its own line was coming up and we ran alongside it for some distance, when, without expecting it, we ran against the points. One wheel remained on the line but the other ran off, straining the crank axle. The engine was quickly pulled up, and the passengers jumped or tumbled off in great excitement; – fortunately no one was hurt. It took us an hour or two to get back to Parkside, as the crank shaft being crooked, the engine "wobbled" very much. The party were waiting, thinking we must have run on to Liverpool, and the question arose how to return. Old Fyfe . . . was with us and we waited for a train from Liverpool, which took him, and he brought another train back to take the party. Some had however gone on foot and walked the whole way, probably thinking it was safer, and as it was summer time it would not be disagreeable. I and a few others remained all night to get the engine back, which we accomplished by taking out the bent axle. We had no more trouble with this engine, nor with any other, but we did not make more than 4 or 5 altogether, as the trade did not seem likely to be remunerative, and we certainly did not foresee the immense possibilities of the railroad.'[9]

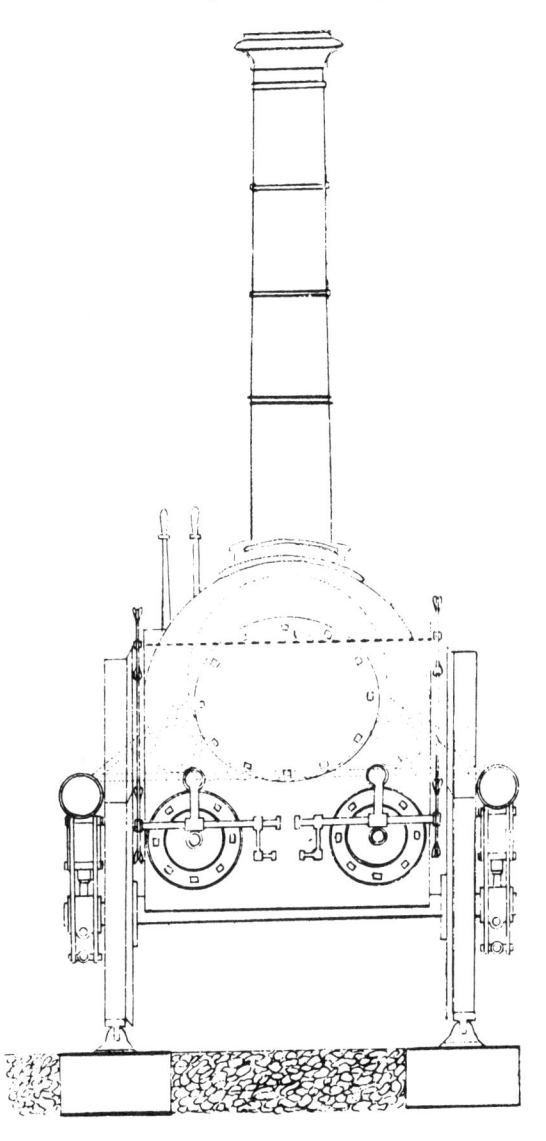

The Company did not purchase *Manchester*, but allowed Galloways to hire her to the Haydock and the Hulton Park collieries to work their coal trains over the line; the Company also hired her during periods of crisis for working goods trains. While so employed on 2 March 1833 she was involved in a fatal accident when it was stated that she was never safe at a high speed since there was no reverse motion and the brakes were inefficient. At the Coroner's Inquest evidence was given that any engine with vertical cylinders was unsafe when propelled down an inclined plane with a load behind it, and Stephenson, reporting on the fitness of the engine for further work on the L&MR, said that the centre of gravity was too high in locomotives of this type. This was the last engine he examined for the Company, as he was relieved of this duty, at his own request, soon afterwards.

Galloways' second engine, *Caledonian*, was completed in the late summer of 1832 and ran trials on the railway in September. It was a goods engine of the 0-4-0 type and although of more orthodox appearance than *Manchester*, it had vertical cylinders placed outside the boiler and between the 5ft wheels, working on to a crank shaft which in turn actuated the coupling rod at its centre. This obsession with vertical cylinders arose from the belief that the cylinder walls were less likely to suffer wear than with horizontal ones, where the weight of the piston bore on the lower half of the cylinder.

On 20 September, *Caledonian* took 25 loaded waggons to Liverpool in about $2\frac{1}{2}$ hours, taking 12 minutes to ascend the Sutton Incline assisted by *Goliah* and on that day the Company sought to hire her for a short time to work one of the inclined planes, *Samson* and *Goliah* both being in need of repair. However, she was purchased outright on 29 October, the makers accepting the Company's offer of £800; she retained her name and was numbered 28.

160　　　　　　　　　　LOCOMOTIVES AND ROLLING STOCK

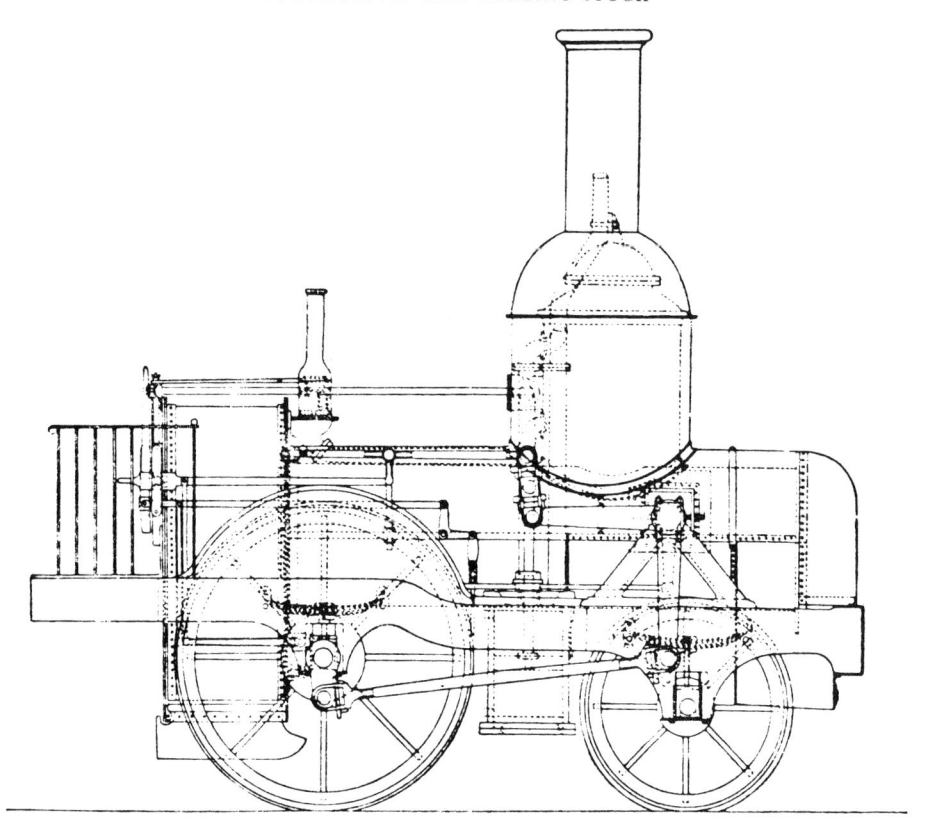

83 Experiment *(32)*

84 Manchester

Another firm that engaged in locomotive construction for a short period was the Horseley Iron Co. of Tipton, Staffs. They had supplied three engines to the St Helens Railway early in 1833 and on 31 October a new locomotive for this railway was tried on the L&MR with a goods train. In November 1833 Horseley offered to make one for the L&MR to the Company's specification and a Minute of 15 December 1834 refers to 'the new Horseley engine now putting together on the Rail Way' having inside bearings and outside cranks. The engine, named *Star*, was of the 2-2-0 type, designed by Isaac Dodds and incorporated a number of new features. It was claimed to be the first locomotive to have its boiler secured at the front end only, allowing for expansion and contraction without injury or stress to itself or the frames.

The engine had been working for only a short time on trial when, on 28 February 1835, she was involved in the fatal collision with *Caledonian* and sustained heavy damage to her frames, cylinders and steam pipes. As she was still the property of the Horseley Co., and the accident was directly attributable to the negligence of the Railway Company's servants in setting the points incorrectly, the Company offered to pay for the repairs; the builder's agent, John Pollock, countered with an offer to sell the engine for £970, but this was declined after John Dixon had reported on the *Star*'s performance. Eventually *Star* was sold to the D&KR for £700 and the maker's claim for £492, including £275 loss on sale went to arbitration; the award in June 1836 was £179.

In the meantime RS & Co. continued to build 'Planet' class passenger engines and *Pluto* (No 27) was delivered in August 1832. The Board directed that 'a pair of strong wood wheels be put under the new engine *Pluto*, the axle shafts to be reduced in size as far as Gray might think necessary or advantageous'. *Ajax* (No 29), with iron wheels, followed in November and *Firefly* (No 31) in April 1833; all still cost £800 each.

During 1833 RS & Co. were developing a larger engine that would run steadily at 30 mph over the light track of the L&MR and the result was their 2-2-2 Patent Locomotive delivered on trial from the works of Charles Tayleur, where it was probably assembled or finished, in December. A week later it had '. . . been along the line, but its wheels rubbed against the check rails and wooden switches'. RS & Co. priced the engine at £1050, but the Company offered £1000 if the flanges were removed from the driving wheels, new cylinders fitted and the frames strengthened.

With the stipulated alterations made the engine came back from Tayleur in September 1834 and was taken into stock as *Patentee* (No 33), the name allotted by the Company. This was the last locomotive ever supplied by RS & Co. to the L&MR; their offer of two engines at £1200 each in April 1836 was declined.

There was a growing reaction in some quarters against the Stephensons, father and son, at this time, both in England and abroad. Cropper, who had never concealed his dislike for them, contrived in 1835 as a director of the London and Birmingham Railway, to ensure that since Robert Stephenson was the Chief Engineer, he could have no financial interest in the supply of locomotives, or in any other contract. Dr Lardner had strongly criticised the L&MR for its apparent favouritism towards the Stephensons at a time when all but four of its locomotives had been supplied by RS & Co., and two of these were to the Stephenson specification. He claimed that there was a widespread impression, both in Liverpool and Manchester, that any competitors had to face capricious objections from the Engineer, who was at the same time a 'manufacturer of engines, and arbiter of the fitness of all others which may be proposed for the road.' It was also suggested that as the assistant engineers and practically every employee in the locomotive department had been appointed by George Stephenson, they tended to regard him as their employer rather than the Company, and out of a misplaced sense of loyalty to a 'kind patron', had prevented, by various means, a fair trial of rival engines.[10]

The Stephenson's influence extended in a great degree to the Continent, and when the Chevalier von Gerstner emigrated to the USA in 1838 he told the Engineer to the B&ORR that he wished to escape from '. . . this system of England, where George Stephenson's thumb, pressed upon a plan, is an

85 Caledonian *(28)*

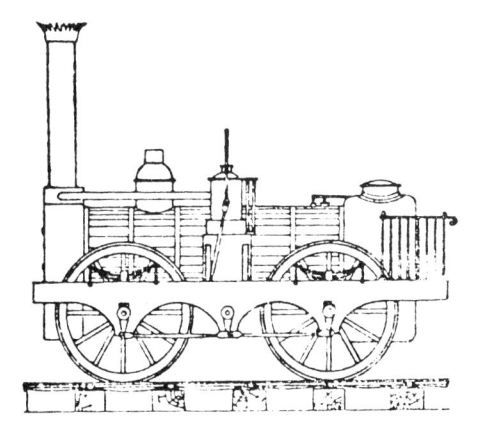

imprimatur, which gives it currency and makes it authority... In England it is imitation – in America it is invention.'[11]

In locomotive construction, as in railway operation, the first decade from 1830 was one of experiment, of trial and error; RS & Co. had countless problems to overcome and their early products were not notably durable. By 18 January 1837 only 11 of the 27 locomotives they had supplied to the Company were still in service, 16 having been sold or broken up. *Milo* (No 25) ran for only two years eight months and many of the others had lasted only a little longer. In just over six years the Company had purchased 51 locomotives, and had a working stock of 34 (Sharp's *Experiment* also having gone); of these several were soon to become unserviceable, others were already laid aside and a number were fit only for ballasting duties.

At least half of the Company's locomotives had been involved in accidents by 1833 and were out of service for varying periods; *Rocket, Goliah, Mars, Venus, Victory, Comet, Fury, Saturn, Liver, Etna* and *Pluto* all fell victims either to the inexperience or recklessness of their drivers, or the incompetence of other workers on the line. In November 1832, after the Rainhill accident, orders were given that the men were to work night and day on *Mars* and *Fury* '... until they are ready, probably about three days'.

The Company adopted the practice of sending engines needing major repairs – new boilers or fireboxes – to outside engineering firms; Bury repaired *Venus* in November 1832, the Vulcan Foundry, Galloway, Bowman & Co. and Forrester all received orders for similar work. In November 1832 *Victory* was sent to Foster & Griffin of Liverpool for a new firebox lining, the tubes and other repairs being done 'in Mr Melling's shed'. The firm's charges were considered exorbitant, however, and there is no record of their having secured further orders.

A further batch was sent in October 1834 when Earle said that unless a double set of good working engines was established costly night work in the Company's shops could not be avoided. *Saturn* went to the Vulcan Foundry, but when dismantled was found to be too far gone to be worth repairing, and Forrester, to whom *Milo* had been sent, found it to be so defective in its firebox, chimney-end, cylinders, wheels and axles, that a new engine would be cheaper; *Milo* was then only just over $2\frac{1}{2}$ years old.

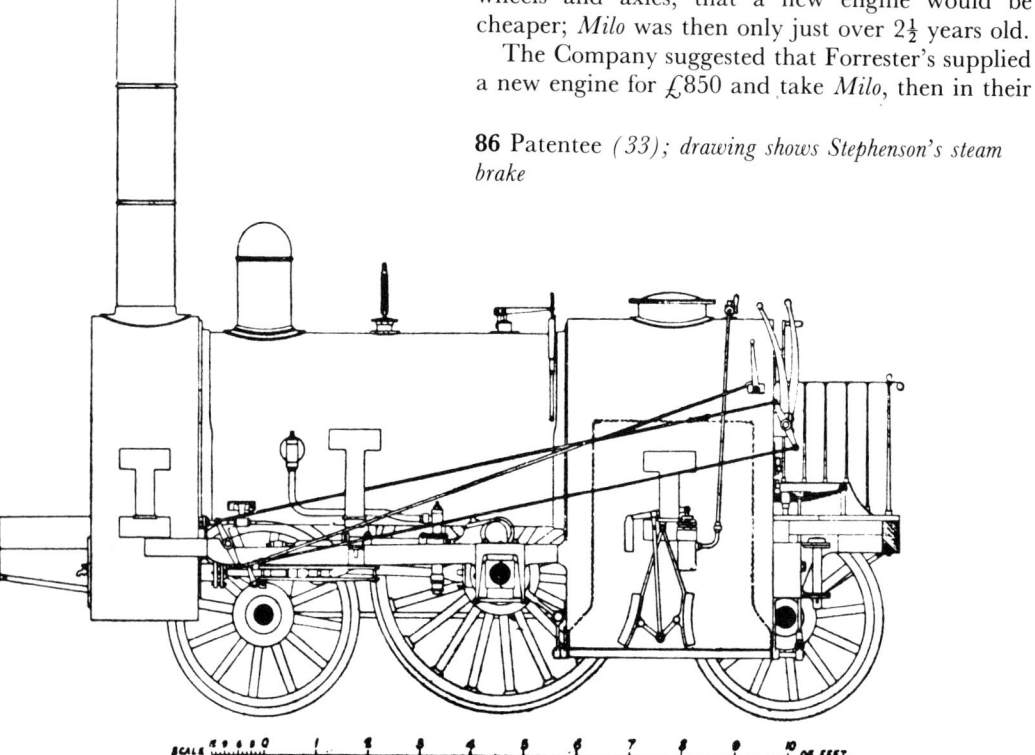

The Company suggested that Forrester's supplied a new engine for £850 and take *Milo*, then in their

86 Patentee *(33); drawing shows Stephenson's steam brake*

yard, in part exchange for £250, a proposal that the firm declined; five months later, *Swiftsure* (No 36), a 2-2-0 passenger locomotive with outside horizontal cylinders, was bought from G. Forrester & Co. for £860, *Milo* having been scrapped. *Swiftsure* had outside plate frames and bearings, 5ft driving wheels, 3ft 6in. leading wheels, and 4-eccentric valve gear; it was of similar design to locomotives already supplied to the D&KR, with which the L&MR was familiar, having allowed Forrester to try one of them on the line in June 1834.

The first suggestion that the Company should build a locomotive in its own workshops was considered on 23 December 1833 but, presumably owing to pressure of work, the idea was abandoned. In February 1834 two 0-4-0 luggage engines were ordered of Tayleur & Co. at £950 each. These were delivered in September and October 1834 and named *Titan* (No 34) and *Orion* (No 35).

On 15 December 1834 a new specification for *Planet* class passenger engines was produced, specifying 12½in. × 16in. cylinders, and two were ordered from Tayleur & Co., '... both to be made to one pattern, that a duplicate of any part may suit both'. This first attempt at standardisation seems to have gone wrong somewhere, for when delivered in May 1835 *Rapid* (No 37) had 11in. × 16in. cylinders, while those of *Speedwell* (No 38) of June 1835 were 12½in. × 16in.

At the same Board Meeting a new specification for banking engines capable of taking 100 tons up the inclines was considered, but pending a decision Dixon was sent to the Leicester and Swannington Railway to observe the new heavy 0-6-0 *Atlas*, built by RS & Co. Following his report on 8 January 1835 that the engine was 'very slow, and did not appear to be much approved on that line', the Board decided on a modified version of the 0-4-0 *Samson* type, but with 15in. × 16in. cylinders. Mather Dixon's tender of £880 was accepted and two were ordered; *Hercules* (No 39) was delivered in December 1835 and *Thunderer* (No 44) in the following spring.

When ordering '... an additional pair of wheels to be immediately placed under the heavy end of *Orion*' on 11 May 1835, Melling was asked to '... devise some plan for making the small pair of wheels under the *Atlas* bear their proportion of weight while the fire-door is open for coking.' The result was a device whereby the trailing wheels could be lifted off the rails by an auxiliary steam cylinder, presumably to throw the whole weight of the engine on to the coupled wheels for increased adhesion. The device must have

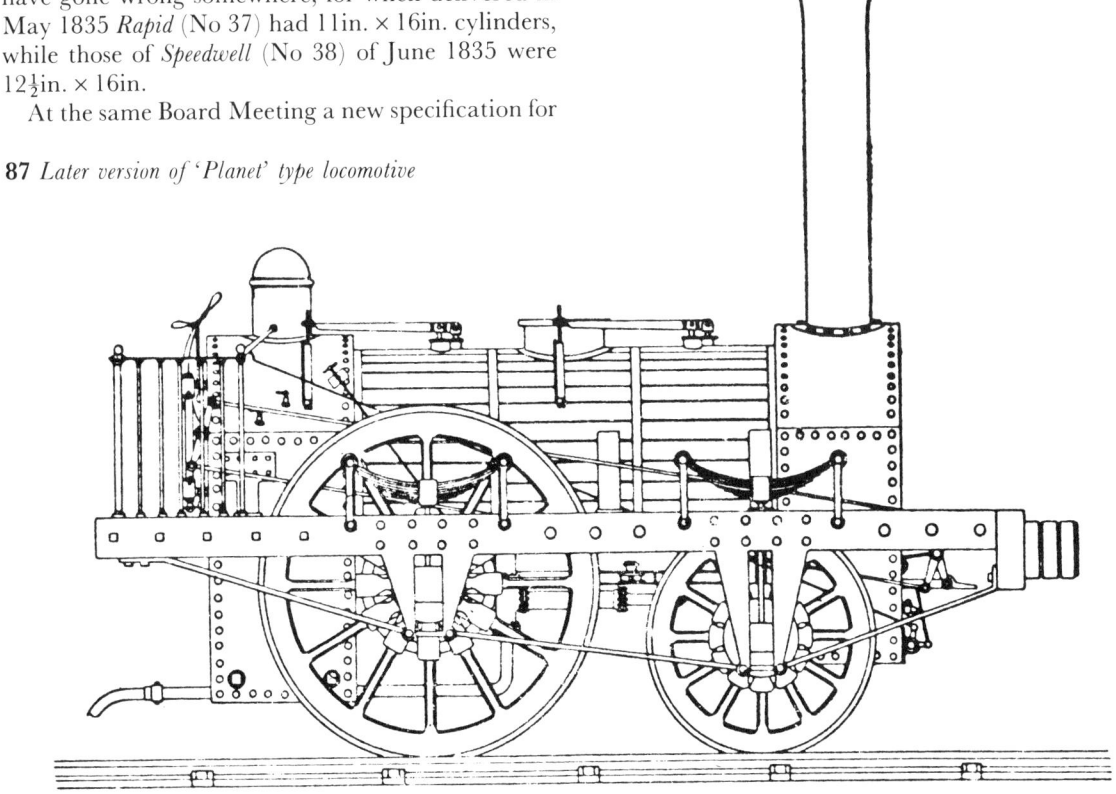

87 *Later version of 'Planet' type locomotive*

caused trouble, however, for on 11 June 1835 the engine was ordered to be taken off the line '... until the springs of the hind wheels were so adjusted as to make it impossible for her engineman to put them in and out of play.' Incidentally, the fire-door must have been of massive proportions if opening it threw the engine out of balance.

Four new passenger engines were required in August 1835 to replace those worn out, and Booth recommended a shorter stroke to diminish the reciprocating motion of the machinery. On 10 August the Board considered experimenting with two of 16in. and two of 12in. stroke and on 31 August the Haigh Foundry tender for two of the normal type incorporating '... the latest improvement in every respect' at £850 each was accepted; the order was later increased to three locomotives. Tayleur & Co. were given the order for the fourth, with 14in. × 12in. cylinders at £1050, and as *Star* (No 41), it was delivered in February 1836; it was a 2-2-2 engine, the first of the 'short stroke' type.

Back in December 1831 the Board 'Read a notice from Mather Dixon & Co. that they were about to bring a new locomotive engine on the line and hoped that it would be approved. Referred to the Engineer'. This was probably *Black Diamond* which was purchased by the Haydock Colliery. In January and again in February 1835 another engine, *Everton*, was offered to the L&MR for £850 but declined as of unsuitable design. At this period William Buddicom, later to become Assistant Engineer on the L&MR, was serving his apprenticeship with the firm.

The Company arranged in November 1835 to take two luggage engines that Tayleur & Co. had nearly finished and wished to dispose of. These were 12½-ton 0-4-2 locomotives with 5ft coupled and 3ft trailing wheels; the cylinders were 12in. × 18in. and they cost £1050 each. *Eclipse* (No 40) was delivered on 28 December 1835 and *York* (No 42) a month later. These were the first 0-4-2 locomotives built as such, although several others had already been converted by the addition of trailing wheels.

The engines from the Haigh Foundry were of the 2-2-2 type, with 3ft 6in. leading and 3ft trailing wheels; the driving wheels were the usual 5ft and the cylinders 12½in. × 16in. *Vesuvius* (No 43) arrived at the same time as *Star*, *Lightning* (No 45) and *Cyclops* (No 46) following in June 1836. They were not quite identical, differing in heating surface and weight.

Star appears to have impressed the engineers and directors alike at its trials for between April and June 1836 ten more engines, the 'same size and description as the coaching engine, the Star', were ordered, four

from Tayleur at £1150 each, four from Mather Dixon at £1120, and two from R. & W. Hawthorn at £1150. By distributing the orders among three makers the Company ensured that completion would be fairly rapid, and in fact most of the locomotives were delivered over a period of about four months, the first to arrive being *Milo* (No 47) from Tayleur on 21 November 1836; *Dart* (No 48) and *Phoenix* (No 49), from Mather Dixon and Tayleur respectively, came a few days later, and Tayleur delivered *Majestic* (No 50) and *Etna* (No 51) in December and January, thereby completing their order.

Mather Dixon sent *Arrow* (No 52) in February 1837 with *Meteor* (No 54) and *Comet* (No 55) following later; Hawthorn & Co. supplied *Sun* (No 53) in March, but in April asked '... to be released from their contract for the second engine like *Sun* at £1150'; the Board refused to rescind the contract and the engine *Vesta* (No 56) was delivered in July. These were all 2-2-2 passenger engines and all but two had 14in. × 12in. cylinders. At the Board Meeting of 9 June 1836 'The Treasurer asked that some of the coaching engines lately ordered might be of 13" instead of 14" cylinder as being more economical with small and moderate loads', and it was agreed that two should be of 13in. diameter; these were *Phoenix* and *Majestic*, both built by Tayleur. All these new engines bore the names of earlier locomotives which had been sold or broken up.

The short-stroke engines were not a conspicuous success in service; they used more coke and water than the standard locomotives, and Edward Woods attributed their modest performance to the valves, which at that period had no lap, and to the fact that the steam was not used expansively.

The Sub-Committee recommended the purchase of ten new engines in August 1837 and two months later orders were placed with various makers.

Two Luggage Engines of 0-4-2 type, two 2-2-2 Coaching Engines and two 0-4-2 Banking Engines were ordered of Todd, Kitson and Laird for delivery between April and September 1838. 'Ben Hick of Bolton' secured an order for two 0-4-2 Luggage Engines and Rothwell & Co. of Bolton two Coaching Engines of 2-2-2 type. Melling was instructed to inspect the engines from time to time during their construction. The prices ranged from £1060 to £1350 each.

Todd, Kitson & Laird's Luggage Engines were apparently delivered on time for they were paid for in July 1838; they were *Lion*[12] (No 57) and *Tiger* (No 58) and were the first locomotives produced at the Railway Foundry, Leeds. The passenger engines,

Leopard (No 62) and *Panther* (No 64) were completed at the end of the year and were the first L&M locomotives to have 5ft 6in. driving wheels; their Banking Engines, *Elephant* (No 65) and *Buffalo* (No 67) arrived on the line early in 1839. Rothwell's two passenger engines, *Rokeby* (No 59) and *Roderic* (No 60) were not received until October 1838 and Hick's *Samson* (No 66) and *Goliah* (No 68) arrived early in 1839, well over a year after the order had been placed.

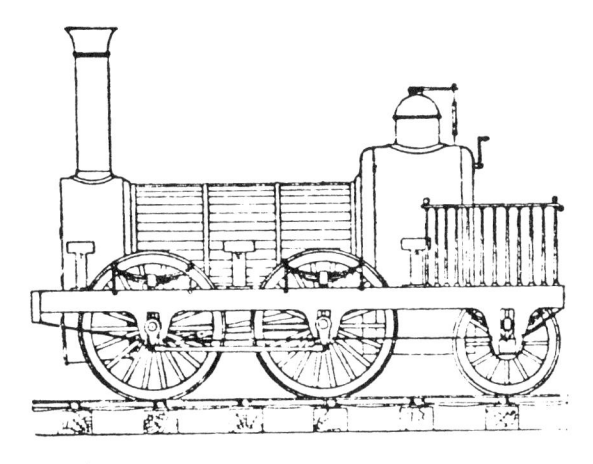

88 Lion *(57)*

Thomas Banks, Engineer of Manchester, who had built his first engine *Alpha* in 1835 for construction work on the London and Southampton Railway, was reported on 16 April 1838 to have '... sent a locomotive engine with oscillating cylinders to the Railway, and wanted leave to try it'. The Board declined this request, but in December Banks was allowed to try another engine and it was purchased on Edward Woods' recommendation for £1305; at the same time a second similar engine was ordered, and this was delivered almost immediately. They were 0-4-2 goods engines with 12in. × 18in. cylinders, *Mammoth* (No 61) and *Mastodon* (No 63). These were the last engines to be ordered from outside firms.

When four new engines were thought to be required in October 1838 it was decided that they be partly made in the Company's works; however, no new engines were made or bought at this time. Nasmyth Gaskell offered the Company locomotives at £1000 to £1200 each in June 1840 and Booth was authorised to buy two if he thought it prudent; evidently he did not, for the time was approaching when the Company hoped to build its own.

In June 1837 the Company had made an abortive attempt to find a contractor for the Locomotive Department, and the draft contract[13] specified that the Company's locomotives and fixed engines should be taken over at valuation, along with the Engine Shops, machine tools, pumping engines at the watering stations and all other installations concerned with operating and maintaining the locomotives; he was also to assume responsibility for the enginemen and other staff of the department, but men and machines were to revert to the Company on the termination of the contract, which was envisaged to run for three years in the first instance. At the closing date in August no tenders had been received.

As an alternative a form of common user arrangement was discussed with the other companies for the use of each other's locomotives, with safeguards against their being taken off their regular duties on insufficient grounds, but nothing came of it.

By the autumn of 1839 both the GJR and the L&BR had been in full operation sufficiently long for a comparison of their operating costs to be made and in the locomotive department the L&B Company's costs, as a percentage of receipts, were considerably lower than those of either the GJR or the L&MR. The published accounts of the L&BR were carefully analysed by Henry Booth, who was also given access to the unpublished details in order to ascertain whether the discrepancy was attributable to management or to factors beyond economic control, and he reported to the Board on 16 September 1839. On the same day a committee was appointed to consider the whole question of locomotive power, particularly the system of working and repairing engines at both ends of the line. On 25 September the L&MR and GJR considered whether to employ a contractor to provide power for both lines, but it was decided that at first each Company should appoint a first class superintendent of locomotives in the engineering department, to take complete responsibility and to examine costs. Before the post could be advertised, Tayleur & Co. wrote offering to contract for locomotive power. They had made a similar offer back in October 1833 but the Board could not consider it, '... while so many changes were taking place in the mechanical operations of the Company which might still be considered experimental.' They submitted no tender in 1837 when they had the opportunity. In the meantime Henry Booth had been preparing a report on the management of the locomotive department.[14]

Among the factors which increased the cost of working the L&MR compared with the longer trunk lines were the high consumption of coke and the wear and tear on the locomotives; trains often made 20 stops in the 30 miles and travelled at as high a speed as possible over the intermediate distances. To maintain the numerous departures to suit both the public and the Post Office, many engines had their fires burning for up to 17 hours a day, although they were actually running for only six or seven hours. The consumption of coke on the L&MR was 57 lb. a mile in 1839, compared with 39 lb. a mile on the L&BR.

Booth was impressed by the uniformity of design of the L&BR engines, all of which had been built by Edward Bury; only two types existed, 2-2-0 passenger engines and 0-4-0 goods. Over a dozen different types were running on the L&MR for, he said, it would have been unwise to refuse a trial to alterations that promised an advantage, adding 'The stock has grown up with our growing necessities'.

In November 1839 Booth was authorised to reorganise the Locomotive Department by consolidating the separate workshops into one establishment at Edge Hill. The works there were to be enlarged and Edward Woods was to assume responsibility for the mechanical departments and to continue as the Company's Civil Engineer. His salary was increased to £800 a year and George Scott was re-engaged for three years as Engineering Superintendent at £150 a year, rising to £250. John Melling and the Grays at the Liverpool end, and Fyfe at Manchester, were given three months notice of the termination of their engagements, and John Dewrance, from Peel, Williams & Peel of Manchester, replaced Melling as Foreman of the engine shops at £250 a year and Melling's house. Charles Ritchie, Mather Dixon's engineering draughtsman, was engaged as Foreman of the Crown Street Yard at £130 a year and a house on the premises.

With the advent of the GJR, engine sheds and repair shops were provided by the L&MR at Edge Hill, at first on the south side of the line and extended in 1838 to the north side. In January 1839 the Company bought 10,000 square yards of land beyond the engine sheds at Wavertree Lane for further extensions.

Over the years the Company had acquired units of plant and machinery necessary for the repair and maintenance of its locomotives, but in May 1840 new equipment was ordered for the Edge Hill Works, where a programme of major repair and rebuilding was started. From January each job was numbered, and in 1840 one coaching engine and two ballast engines were thoroughly overhauled.

The reorganisation programme was carried out in close co-operation with the GJR and their Chief Engineer Locke made contributions to the discussions which were of great value to both companies. He argued that the machinery necessary for repairing locomotives was precisely that required for their construction and that since '. . . the mechanics who repaired the engines saw their defects, and consequently were better able than others to guard against them, in the construction of new ones', it could be only to the advantage of the railways to build their own.

It was at this time that the GJR Board decided to remove its locomotive department from Edge Hill, some 20 miles off its own line, to Crewe, but in the meantime Locke persuaded William Buddicom to leave his post in Scotland and become Locomotive Superintendent to the GJR at Edge Hill.

By 1841 the Works were fully operational, and in that year four old engines were repaired, eight were rebuilt and five entirely new engines were constructed, the first locomotives built by the Company. Woods, in a report to Charles Lawrence, described the three categories as follows:[15]

'The "New" Engines are those which have been built entirely by the Company, and which, from the uniformity observed in their construction, rank *first* in value.

'The "Rebuilt" Engines are such of the old Engines as have had all their parts renewed with the exception of perhaps the boiler, firebox and framing, and rank *second* in value.

'The "Repaired" Engines are such of the old Engines as have undergone thorough general repair without altering the cylinders, gearing etc. to conform with the most approved models, and rank *third* in value.'

The repaired engines were expected to give about another three years' service.

The new locomotives were designed by John Dewrance and the first, *Swallow* (No 69) went into service on 8 September 1841 to be followed by *Kingfisher* (No 72) on 18 September, *Heron* (No 71) on 30 November, *Pelican* (No 73) and *Martin* (No 70) on 24 and 30 December respectively. Known as the 'Bird' class, they were 2-2-2 passenger engines of identical design, and over the next four and a half years 13 more were built at the Edge Hill Works. The goods version differed only in its 2-4-0 wheel arrangement and in its 13in. × 20in. cylinders instead of the 12in. × 18in. fitted to the passenger engines. The first of these, *Owl* (No 75) appeared on 29 April 1842; 17 more were built in the next four years.

From the fact that from 1840 until 1845 there is virtually no mention of the locomotives in either the

LOCOMOTIVES AND ROLLING STOCK 167

89 Ostrich *(74); 2-2-2 passenger engine of the 'Bird' class built at Edge Hill Works, 1842*

90 *2-4-0 goods engine, 'Bird' class*

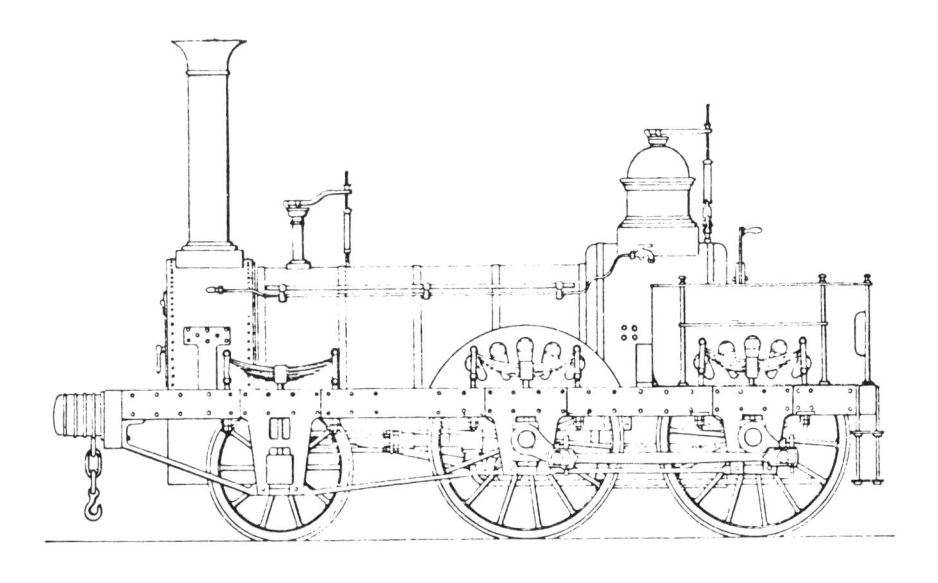

Minutes of the Board Meetings or those of the Management Committee, it is evident that this department under Woods and Dewrance caused the Directors no anxiety. There was increasing co-operation between the Company and the GJR, and for a fortnight in July 1842 trials were held between the *Stork* and the GJR *Hornet* on regular coach trains between Liverpool and Birmingham. Coke consumption among other things was analysed and the performances of the two locomotives were about equal, and in both cases, very good.

The Manchester Locomotive Department, which had employed 120 men in 1839, was reduced to 40 by 1843, but at Edge Hill and Millfield there were 262 at this time.[16]

In 1841 a seven-year apprenticeship scheme for training in the workshops was started and 20 boys were taken on. In the expectation of attracting gentlemen's sons the Company prepared a programme of more extended training in the mechanical arts over a period of five years at a premium of £100; this was the recognised form of training for professional engineers. In 1842 the 20 apprentices at Edge Hill were paid from 6d. to 2s. per week.

The records of the L&MR contain many references to the Locomotive Department during the earlier, more hectic years of its existence, when the experience upon which its later efficiency was built had to be dearly bought.

The first engine sheds were built in the summer of 1830, at Wavertree Lane near Edge Hill and at Manchester near Ordsall Lane on the south side of the line. On the opening of the Railway these sheds became the first workshops, but it soon became clear that larger and properly equipped shops would be needed to maintain the engines in working order, and plans were prepared in July 1831; at Salford these were built on the north side of the tracks, just west of the Irwell, and at Liverpool they were near the sheds, in an area known as the Brickfield Station. The carriage and waggon shops were established on land adjoining Crown Street Station, and this area, officially called Millfield Station but generally known as 'Gray's Yard', became the stores depot. On the closure of the passenger station in 1836 the works here were greatly expanded.

As the need arose a variety of machine tools and the engines to drive them had been installed in the various shops, and in August 1832 Hodgson recommended the concentration of the work into a single establishment at Brickfield Station. On the advice of Stephenson and Dixon, heavy repair work was sent there but the Company could not dispense with the other works. By now the pressure on the repair shops was such that additional specialised machinery was required, including a hydraulic wheel-press at Brickfield Locomotive Depot.

Melling suggested the Company purchase a punching machine to enable boilers to be made and the Board considered 'It was a question whether the Company would become boilermakers – if so, the requisite machinery should be got.' The boiler shop was built in Gray's Yard, where an iron foundry and other works were established. Here springs, forgings, screws and a great variety of components were made for use in the locomotive and other departments. The engines could not be brought to Gray's Yard as they would not pass along the 12ft high tunnel, and the engineers and fitters worked on them in Melling's Shed, where, in November 1831, troughs had been provided between the rails for the men to work in.

The years 1832 and 1833 were critical in the Locomotive Department. The early engines were now becoming worn out faster than the workshops could repair them, despite working day and night, and at Melling's Shed the machinery never stopped. At the end of 1832 only six or seven engines were actually working at any one time out of a total of 29, and it was often necessary to use coaching engines on goods trains. A number were already beyond repair and others fit only for occasional duties. *Comet* had been relegated to working coach trains between Sutton and Liverpool in December 1831 and by the following September was ordered to be kept at Parkside with steam up, ready for emergencies. *Phoenix*, which the Company had intended rebuilding in its own works as a 'Planet' type with various other improvements, was broken up early in 1833, as was *Dart*.

Eventually nearly 200 men were employed in the workshops and engine sheds. The cost of locomotive repairs was £10,582 for the first half of 1832 and £12,000 in the same period of 1833; this was calculated at the time to represent £500 a year for each mile of railway, 10½d. to 1s. 1d. per train mile or the equivalent of the cost of replacing the Company's 20 workable locomotives with the same number of new ones.

In the last six months of 1834 the wages account for repairing locomotives was six times as much as that of drivers and firemen together, £4892 against £815.

Stephenson was firmly of the opinion that the wear and tear sustained by the locomotives was the result of running them faster than railway engines had ever been run before, and urged maximum speeds of 8 mph for goods trains and 16 mph for passengers, '... the latter speed yielded to satisfy the public's wish for rapid travelling'; the Company accordingly decreased the speed of its trains in 1832 as an economy measure. At about the same time the Board ordered the engineers to contrive some method of preventing the waste of coke from its falling between engine and tender. They discovered years later, however, that the firemen deliberately threw dust and small coke off the engines in order to avoid spoiling the fire. They also directed that the brightly polished hand gear and other working parts of the engines were to be coated with black varnish. The engineers were instructed to keep the engines thoroughly cleaned, however, and to employ extra men for the purpose.

The engines were divided about equally between the engine sheds at Liverpool and Manchester, and '... on coming in at night the steam is blown off and the machinery is thoroughly cleaned.' The earlier engines with 1in. tubes were unpopular with the cleaners as these small-bore pipes became choked with soot and ashes. Each night almost every engine was in need of some small repair or adjustment; on one occasion a Manchester driver complained to the Board that Fyfe had neglected to repair his locomotive during the night and in consequence he had lost part of his earnings the following day.

In 1831 some of the older engines were hired out to the B&LR, *Arrow* and *Meteor* in August, *Planet* and *Atlas* a few months later. Vignoles hired *Majestic* and *North Star* with their drivers in November for the St Helens Railway, and the Company lent *Jupiter* for the opening of that line. Other companies were occasionally supplied with tenders and miscellaneous equipment and their engines were repaired in the Company's works until, in March 1832, all owners of engines running over the L&MR were asked to provide themselves with sheds and repairing shops.

Generally by 1831 there were eight or ten engines at work, each of which made four trips a day; on 22 January *Majestic* ran six trips, a total of over 180 miles. On one occasion *Fury*, with 12 loaded waggons, about 45 tons, ascended Whiston Incline unaided; running at 30 mph on the level, her speed was down to 2 mph at the top.

Within the first few weeks of operation, it was found that the engines were too weak for the work expected of them, and they required strengthening in almost every part. Heavier axles, piston rods, frames and the substitution of iron for wooden wheels sent the weight up to over seven tons, and in November 1832 Stephenson recommended adding a third pair of wheels behind the firebox to avoid having $5\frac{1}{2}$ tons on the driving wheels; this increased their total weight to nearly 10 tons, on a track designed for $4\frac{1}{2}$-ton locomotives. *Mars* and *Atlas* were the first to be converted, to be followed by *Titan*, *Mercury*, *Orion*, *Hercules*, *Thunderer*, *Firefly* and *Planet*.

With the introduction of the inside cylinder locomotives the problem of crank axle failure arose, and after *Etna* ran off the Brosley Embankment with a passenger train following the fracture of the axle, in September 1831, axles of larger diameter and made of Swedish iron were ordered. A few weeks later the axle of *Vulcan* failed; Fenton Murray reported that it had been carefully made of the best scrap iron. At about the same time *Planet* was relegated to working goods trains as her axle was of 'inferior iron'.

When the 2-2-2 passenger locomotives went into service flangeless driving wheels were employed to reduce the strain on the axles at points and sharp curves.

In October 1831 the Company received offers for some old locomotives; Legh of Haydock Colliery wanted *Rocket* and the B&LR enquired about *Arrow*, but the Company would not part with either as they were essential for ballasting. They were prepared to sell *Sans Pareil* to the S&DR '... as this engine will not work with coke, and is therefore unfit for the Liverpool and Manchester line'. An offer of two 'Planet' class engines from the Darlington line was declined by the L&MR, and *Sans Pareil* was sold to the B&LR.

The old construction engine *Twin Sisters* remained in service, although it was never numbered with the regular locomotive stock. Much slower than the other engines, it was used only at night on heavy goods trains. On 8 February 1831 she arrived at Manchester with 27 loaded waggons at about 2 a.m., and while being run backwards and forwards to work the boiler pumps a guard was thrown off the tender and killed. She was broken up about December 1831 when Galloway, Bowman used one of her cylinders in a pumping engine.

Incapable of much heavy work and outclassed by the newer engines, *Rocket* practically went into retirement soon after the line was opened, although improvements carried out after Rainhill enabled her to take 40 tons at 14 mph – three times the weight she pulled at the trials.

For a few weeks there was still some ballasting and general clearing up to be done, and on 28 October, while engaged on this work, the axle of *Rocket*'s tender broke while running in reverse, apparently causing the firebox end of the engine to rear up and tip the

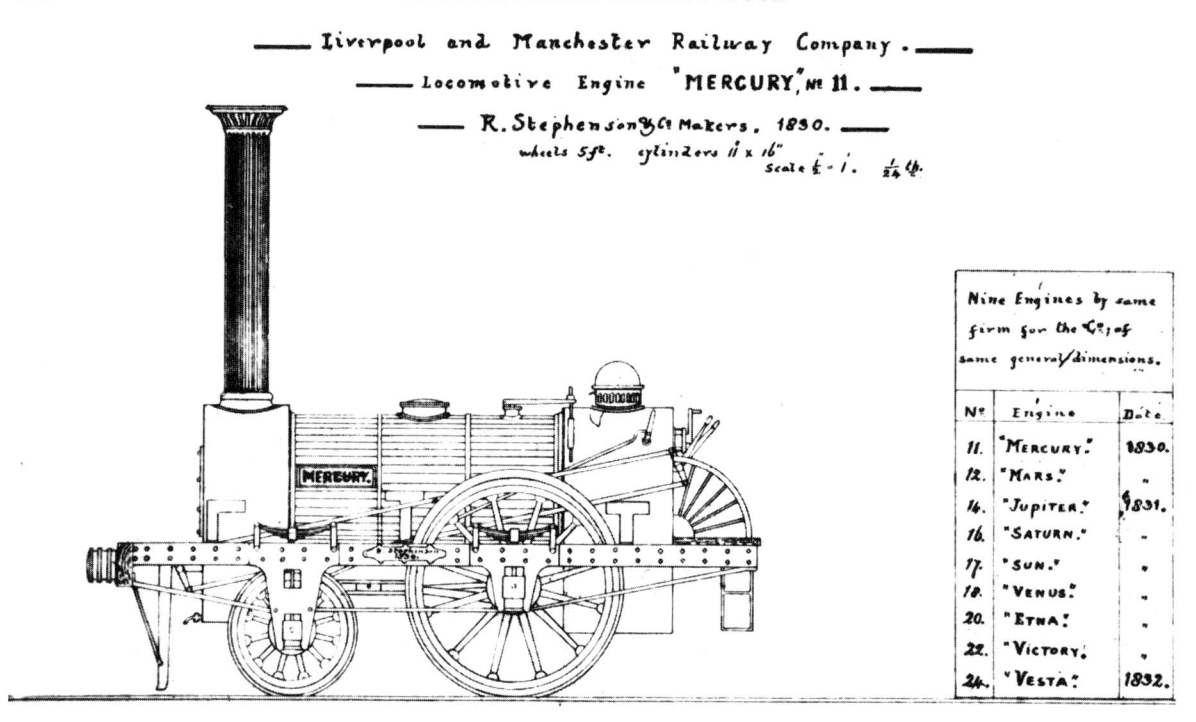

91 Mercury *(11); 2-2-0 as originally built, 1831*

92 Mercury *(11); as converted to 2-2-2, 1833*

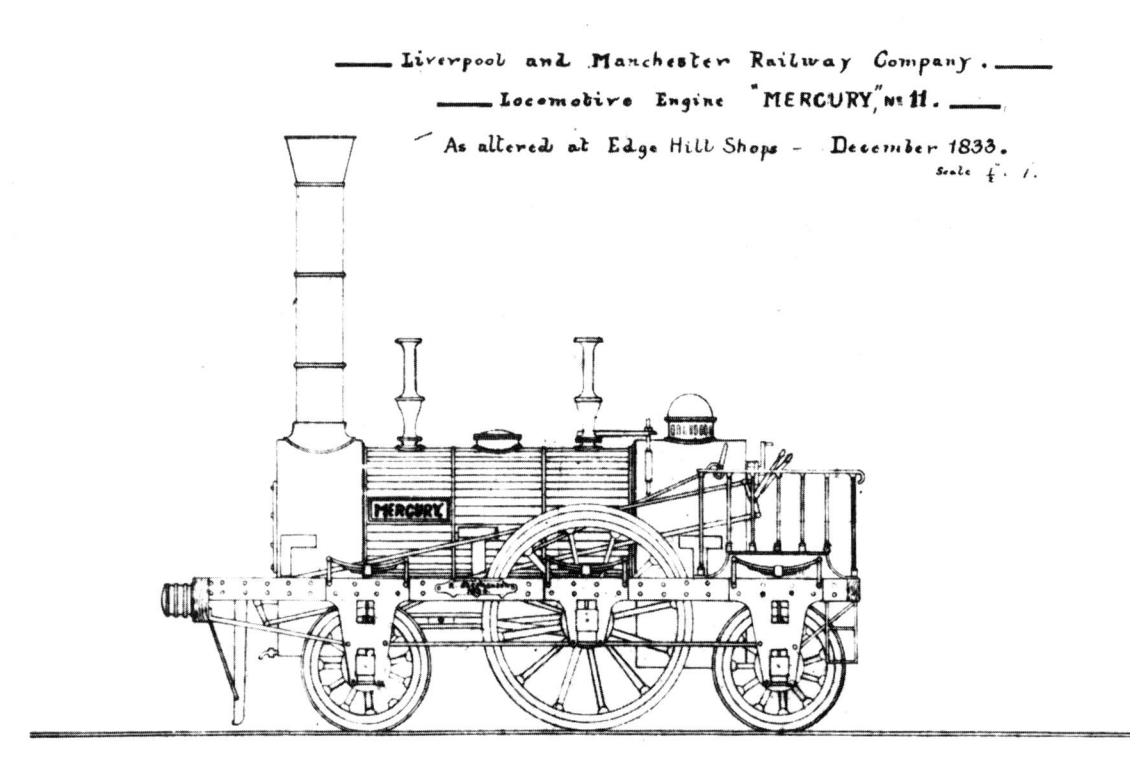

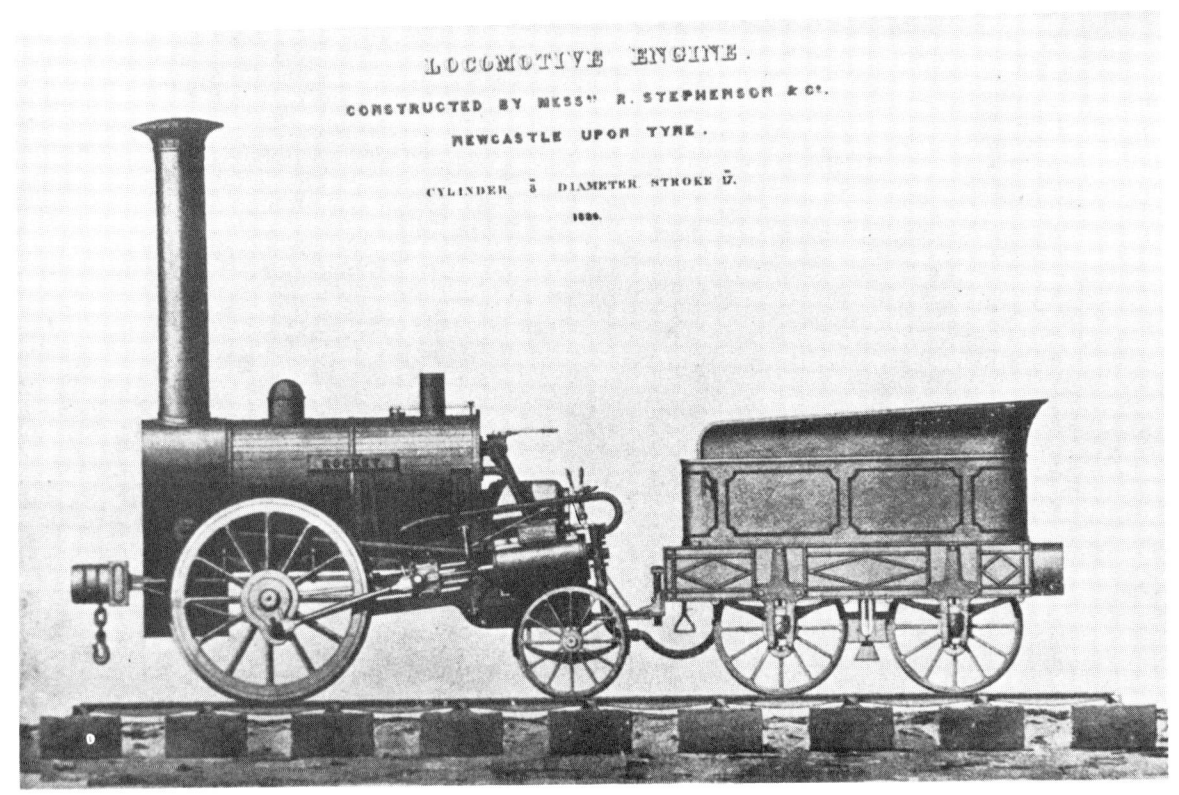

heavy chimney end downwards on to the track. A publican named Hunter from Eccles, who had been riding on the tender, was killed. It was evidently during the repairs to *Rocket* that the old chimney was replaced by a smokebox and chimney similar to that of the *Planet*.[17]

By December 1830 she was used as a pilot engine to coach trains, with orders to keep 400 yds ahead, but as traffic increased, this became impracticable, and she went back to ballasting work. On 25 January 1831, while running in Olive Mount Cutting, she struck the points and was overturned. From September 1832, she worked the light Wigan traffic, until on 6 November she was badly damaged in a collision with a Warrington engine drawing a coal train. While she was under repair Allcard drew attention to the 'great deal of unnecessary ornamental brasswork put on the *Rocket* engine without authority', and the Directors' disapproval of such expenditure was conveyed to Melling, although no order to incur further expense by removing the decoration was given. She reappears briefly in 1833 for Badnall's experiments, and in the late autumn of 1834 for those of Lord Dundonald.[18]

On 22 June 1836 Booth reported that he had received an enquiry for the purchase of *Rocket* if the

93 Rocket *as rebuilt with smokebox, lowered cylinders and fitted with new style tender. The drawing is probably the one made by order of the Board before the locomotive was sold in 1836*

Board was disposed to sell her; they agreed, subject to a fair price being obtained, and ordered that 'a good drawing should be made of her to exhibit the form and construction of the first engine employed on the Railway.' Having made this gesture to the unique place in history *Rocket* already enjoyed, she was sold to James Thompson of Kirkhouse, Cumberland, for £300 in October 1836, to work on the Brampton Colliery Railway. Laid aside after three or four years, she was eventually returned to Stephenson's works, originally to be restored for inclusion in the Great Exhibition of 1851; the restoration of the now derelict engine was not carried out until several years later, however, and then only imperfectly. Fortunately she was sent to London in 1862, where she found a well-earned place in the Science Museum.

In a report presented to the Board in 1834,[19] Booth remarks on the fact that the Company's position with regard to locomotives was still one of experiment, and likely to remain so for some time. The experiments could not be made in the calm surroundings ideal for scientific work, but '... amidst the bustle and responsibilities of a large and increasing traffic', with the Directors not knowing how long each engine would last,

'... but compelled to have engines, whether good or bad; being aware of various defects ... which it was impossible at the time to remedy, yet obliged to keep the machines in motion, under all the disadvantages of heavy repairs, constantly going on during the night, in order that the requisite number of engines might be ready for the morning's work'.

About this time Charles Lawrence, addressing the shareholders, referred to the many new schemes and inventions offered to the Company, adding 'Past experience forbids any very sanguine anticipations'. Nevertheless the Board patiently examined every plan and contrivance sent in and dealt courteously with the inventors whose ideas usually had to be rejected.

In February 1831 I. K. Brunel submitted a sketch of a disengaging hook for carriages and Stephenson was ordered to have a pair made for testing between two coal waggons. Brunel attended the trials which were apparently successful, for he was paid £35 for the idea.[20] In April the Company agreed to inspect a locomotive being built by E. Rawlins when completed, and the plans eventually arrived in November. G. H. Palmer offered a new invention, a great improvement on the locomotive, for £28,000, in May 1831, and was told that the directors would await the securing of the patent and see the improvement in operation. At that time Mr Dockray wrote to the Company of a scheme for working and repairing locomotives, and Stephenson was sent to inspect General Viney's boiler at work in a Manchester factory. There is no record of George Stephenson ever recommending any invention referred to him.

Edward Evans's model of a disengaging apparatus and Bywater's anchor for holding a derailed engine appeared in January 1832, and in June the Directors received notice from Baron Drais of his invention to protect passengers from the locomotive smoke nuisance, for which he would 'expect a pecuniary reward'. Earle and Booth, when in London that month, called on the Baron and learned of the startling simplicity of the plan, which was to push instead of pull the carriages. At the same time Alexander Gordon of London made exactly the same suggestion, but coupled with an arrangement that made propulsion safer.

A new locomotive and machinery, the initial cost of which would be up to £50,000, was proposed by Kersall Wrigg of London in August 1832. Although a reduced maintenance cost was promised, the Board '... would require very satisfactory evidence before hazarding such an amount'. February 1833 brought plans for a steamless locomotive from James Wilson of Manchester and a Rotatory Engine patented by J. Reynolds of London; the Board offered to examine the detailed drawings of the latter, and if approved, to build a locomotive at their own expense on being guaranteed free use of the patent. This was the era of rotary engines, an early form of steam turbine, and it is known that Stephenson was opposed to them.

Two years later it was reported[21] that the engine was expected to be tried on the L&MR in June 1835 but there is no record that it ever was.

Jacob Perkins, an American engineer, sought permission through A. H. Houldsworth MP to try one of his patent circulators on an engine and the Board agreed, subject to no cost falling upon the Company. On 25 September 1832 some directors met him at the engine shops and arranged for his device to be fitted to *Vesta*; later, other engines were converted. The effect of the apparatus was to deposit mud in the bottom of the boiler, with a consequent saving of fuel and maintenance costs, it was claimed, and the trials lasted for six months. The terms of payment proposed by Perkins were too complicated for the Board to consider and apparently the modification was not adopted, for on receiving a letter in October from Houldsworth containing '... some extraordinary reflections on the conduct of the Directors', they refused to hold any further correspondence on the subject.

In February 1831 John Ward of London had been given permission to try Gurney's Steam Carriage on the railway but it was May 1832 before the offer was taken up. Booth gave him particulars of a recent performance by *Victory*, load, speed and coke consumed, and said that if he thought Gurney's engine could compete with *Victory*, the Board would discuss the matter, paying his return coach fare to Liverpool. Ward appeared in July and, declining the Company's offer to allow Gurney's boiler to be fitted to *Dart*, then laid aside, proposed to build a new engine which, if equal in performance to *Victory*, the Company agreed to purchase. Six weeks later the contract remained unsigned by Ward or Gurney, who could not agree with the Company on terms of payment, and the project was dropped.

Nathaniel Ogle, engineer and patentee of a steam coach for turnpike roads, informed the Company in May 1832 that he would shortly be bringing it to

Liverpool. It appears to have been demonstrated to the Board some months later for in October Ogle and his partner Summers offered the use of their Patent for £10,000. The proposal was to adapt the coach for working over the railway and the Board was willing to purchase one for £1000, but only if it was satisfactory. The engineers declined this offer and made a counter proposal to run the coaches themselves on the railway at a toll lower than that specified in the Act, but the directors would consent to no reduction. Claiming that he would rather co-operate with the Railway than accept any of the several proposals he had received from coach proprietors, Ogle urged the Board to give an unconditional order for a coach; this they refused to do, electing to face the remote possibility of competition from the turnpike roads.

In June 1832 another steam road carriage was inspected, Hancock's, at Stratford-le-Bow, but although only at the experimental stage it did not appear to the directors as suitable for the railway.

Badnall's Undulating Railway was briefly considered in May 1833 for the branch to Whiston Collieries, but owing to the uncertainty of its operation it was not adopted. In principle it was a kind of switchback railway, the momentum gathered by a train running down one gradient being used to carry it up the next. Badnall was, however, allowed the use of *Rocket* one day in September, followed by more extensive experiments with *Firefly*, *Pluto* and a train on the Sutton Inclined Plane on 27 October, and the Board received Dixon's report the following day. In their astonishment that the trials had taken place on a Sunday, they omitted to note in the records any details of the results, nor any suggestion as to how such trials could have been held at any other time.

The Board did not always wait to be approached by inventors; having read an account in the *Staffordshire Mercury* of a Patent steam engine by a civil engineer named Witty, the directors asked Stephenson in July 1833 to investigate its possibilities. The announcement must have been premature, for the plans did not reach the Company until May 1837.

Captain Ericsson appears again in November 1833 when his Patent Caloric Engine was discussed, and arrangements were made to inspect it during February 1834, when some directors would be in London.

The year 1834 brought consideration of Russell's Patent Steam Carriage, then running between Glasgow and Paisley, and practical experiments with Harsleben's double-crank locomotive carriage, worked by manpower. Hodgson and Earle rode on it to Huyton and back on 9 September when, worked by 12 men, it carried six passengers from Edge Hill to Huyton Quarries at 13 mph, the road being slightly downhill, and at 11 mph on the return journey; they considered it hard labour for the men and of no advantage to the railway. Any hopes the Board might have entertained on the adaptation of steam road carriages probably faded when an account was read to them of the blowing up of one built by Sharp Roberts in Oxford Road Manchester on 4 April.

At the invitation of Lord Dundonald, some of the directors when in London in January 1834 inspected his rotary engine. Developed primarily for use in steam paddle boats, one engine was used to drive a circular saw at Seaward's Engineering Works, Limehouse, the makers of the rotary engine; the inventor was anxious to apply the principle to the railway locomotive.

In February Lord Dundonald sent a copy of a report on the engine from the Engineer of Woolwich Dockyard, and in September a pair of rotary engines arrived which were to be fitted up as a locomotive. The Board offered to lend wheels and other materials but did not wish to become involved in any expense, nor did they want the work done in the Company's workshops. However, they were persuaded that the cost of fitting the engines to the *Rocket* could not conceivably cost more than £30 and they agreed to expend this sum on the understanding that Lord Dundonald would defray any expense beyond that amount. On 20 October Booth reported that the cost of fitting the rotary machinery to *Rocket* already amounted to nearly £80, and that it was still not ready for any conclusive trials; however, it appears

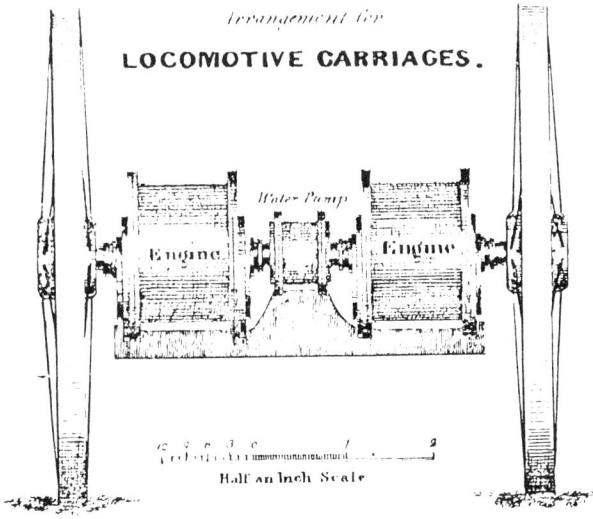

94 *Lord Dundonald's Rotary Engine as fitted to* Rocket, *1834*

that the trials were carried out in the next couple of days with disappointing results.

The modifications to *Rocket* would appear to have involved the removal of the connecting rods, eccentrics and gear levers and the mounting of the two rotary engines on the front axle. Their dimensions are given as 21in. in diameter and 15in. wide, and in appearance they resembled two small electric motors; as they projected only about 9in. above the top of the axle, there was space enough for them without any major alteration to the locomotive. Steam pipes from the boiler would have been required to supply the engines, but probably little else in the way of modifications, apart from some means of anchoring the casing to the locomotive frame.

The rotary engines propelled the *Rocket* light at slightly over 10 mph, but were not powerful enough to start it when a train was attached.

Henry Booth, writing to Lord Dundonald on 23 October, said:

'I regret that so much difficulty seems to lie in the way of bringing the principle of your Engine into practical operation on the Railway. A Gentleman of mechanical knowledge has suggested to Mellings a mode of connecting the Rotary Engine with the driving wheels of the locomotive by three cog wheels – one of them fixed on the axis of the Rotary, one on the nave of the Driving Wheel and one intermediate, being on a connecting link, to allow a yielding to the motion of springs, on which the Rotary is supposed to be placed.'[22]

No further experiments were undertaken by the Company however, and the engines were taken off the *Rocket* at the end of November and returned by canal to London a month later.

William Hosking FSA sent particulars of a Patent Pneumatic Railway in March 1835, and Kersall Wrigg, now of Macclesfield, was invited to submit further details of a method of increasing 'wheel bite or adhesion to the rail' which he had communicated to the Board in July, and which after examination was rejected. Dust prevention from engine chimneys, Bergin's buffers and a watchmaker's suggested improvements to the locomotive were all considered before the year was out.

The inventors were very active in 1836; plans for new locomotives were submitted by John Manton, a gun-maker, and Peter Pickering of Dantzig whose engine required neither fire nor steam. 'Kollman's Patent Railway and Locomotive Carriage' was considered, but Sir James Anderson's proposal that the Company should pay for the Patent of his new locomotive carriage was not. He was in partnership with William James's son, W. H. James, who since 1824 had been concerned with steam road coaches; they were to be drawn by his 'steam drag', apparently the subject of the patent, and he claimed to have an order for 400 from 'The Waggon Company of England'.[23]

Among other propositions that year were Hall's Patent for burning coal in locomotives, eventually adopted in 1842, Perkins's tubular boiler and Curtis's 'contrivance for stopping locomotives by lifting up the cranked axle'.[24]

The steam locomotive having established itself by this time, there were fewer suggestions of alternative means of traction, although one Fairbairn of London did put forward a plan for using horses in January 1837. Most of the proposals now were for modifications to, or fittings for the steam engine; James Slater's plans for a smoke-consuming furnace were examined in May 1837 and in August 1838 there was 'Laid on the table a model of a contrivance for removing obstructions from railways to be attached in front of Loco Motive Engines, and called in America a Cow Catcher.' The rotary engine made a final appearance in June 1839 when the Company offered to sell an old engine to E. Rowley, on which to try his invention.

In 1843 successful trials were carried out with Babbitt's Patent Bearings and these were adopted the following year.

The first locomotives of the L&MR were only comparatively successful and the improvements, although apparently coming in rapid succession, did not usually result from genius or intuition but from the stern and often discouraging experience of its own engineers and employees. They were in the best position to recognise the shortcomings of the locomotive in service and it was to them, rather than to the manufacturers or remote inventors, that its development was due.

In September 1832 Joseph Locke designed a new boiler to be tried on one of the engines; he said he desired no profit from it, beyond what might arise to him as an engineer from the success and extension of railways.

The valve gear of the early L&MR locomotives was of the old style with hand-levers operated by the driver when starting or reversing the engine. During the next 15 years a great number of different types of valve gear appeared, many to vanish after a very brief period. Dixon produced a drawing of an improved slide valve in January 1834 but when Booth saw it he said that John Gray had proposed the same device a month or two before.

Melling had invented his link valve gear which had been fitted to the GJR engine *Lynx* (No 16) in 1837; it was tried on the L&MR and subsequently patented without the knowledge of the directors. In November he persuaded the Board to adopt it for their new engines and only then disclosed that they would require a licence, which he proposed to grant on more favourable terms than other companies would enjoy. He was informed that the L&MR should have the use of any improvements which his position had enabled him to discover or perfect on payment of 'such compliment or remuneration as they consider proper'. In December it was decided to use Melling's gear on the ten new locomotives ordered, and he said he would not charge the Company for this or any other invention. When he was finally persuaded to put this into writing, the directors awarded him 100 guineas, and agreed to pay 50 guineas each for any other locomotives fitted with the gear; this was half the charge he made to other railway companies. In March 1838 the Company contracted to fit his Patent Link Gearing to locomotives undergoing general repair, *Pluto* and *Swiftsure* being the first to be fitted.

Gray designed a new system of variable expansion valve gear, the earliest form to be used on locomotives, in 1838. The gear, known as the 'horse-leg motion', enabled the cut-off to be varied from 82% to 46%, and when applied to *Cyclops* in 1839 a 12% saving in fuel was effected.[25] Evidently various adjustments were made for in September 1841 the Board refer to the trials that had recently taken place with *Cyclops* competing successfully against four of the Company's best engines.

Important experiments had also been going on over the years in increasing the lap of the valves from 1/16in. as used on the original locomotive valves by Matthew Murray to 1in. on *Stork* (No 77) in July 1842. The small lap allowed insufficient time for the exhaust steam to escape, and back-pressure built up in the cylinder. The trials, which started in 1834 with *Vesta*, were resumed in 1838 when *Lightning* was fitted with valves of $\frac{3}{8}$in. lap; in 1840, *Rapid* and *Arrow* with $\frac{3}{4}$in. valve lap consumed 32 lb. of coke per mile instead of 49 lb. The improved valves were fitted to the new engines built by the Company, and to those taken in for repair that would admit of the alteration; together with Gray's variable expansion gear, it resulted in coke consumption being reduced from 12,600 tons in 1839 to 3100 tons in 1843; for a quarter of the amount of fuel a greatly increased volume of traffic was moved.

Gray's gear failed to withstand the daily wear and tear to which is was exposed, being of elaborate design, and it was superseded by Howe's link motion within a few years.

John Melling made other contributions to the efficiency of the locomotive, including an improved feed pump in 1834 and the fitting of some engines with pipes that were located under the frames on either side directing jets of steam or hot water downwards to clean the rails. His ingenious contrivance called an adhesion wheel was fitted to *Firefly* in February 1837; its purpose was to convert a single engine into something approaching a coupled one by bringing into play a pair of friction wheels mounted on a cross-shaft, which, by means of levers worked by a steam cylinder, could be pulled down between the leading and driving wheels making contact with the periphery of each.[26] Woods carried out a series of experiments, running the engine down the Sutton Incline by gravity, with the adhesion wheel in and out of gear; as a result the device was patented in July and ordered to be fitted to the two new engines being built by Rothwell in October 1837, *Rokeby* and *Roderic*; it was then known as Melling's Patent Coupling Wheel.

The requirement by Parliament that locomotives should consume their own smoke could only be met by employing coke, and this, of indifferent quality, cost over four times as much as the coal used in the stationary engines, which the Company bought at the pithead for about 5s. per ton.[27] In January 1832 the Board considered building its own coke ovens in order to experiment with different kinds of coal and to produce coke more cheaply, but although Stephenson had promised plans, the project appears to have been dropped; the Worsley Company in 1834 arranged to make coke from a variety of coals in order that the railway might find the most suitable type for its locomotives.

As early as May 1828, following the arrival of *Lancashire Witch*, experiments with anthracite began with the ordering of a sample cask of Llangenneck smokeless coal '... as used by the principal London brewers'. Whether this minute quantity enabled any useful tests to be made is doubtful, but in May 1831, after experiments with gas coke, a sloop-load of 'Merthyr Tidvil Stone coal' was ordered from Insole of Cardiff at 7s. per ton of 21 cwt. The next attempt with anthracite was in July 1838, when it was partly baked before use, but it does not appear to have been adopted, for in April 1840 bonuses were offered for economy and care in the use of coke.

The problem of coal-burning fireboxes kept many inventors occupied for years. John Gray and his partner John Chanter went some way towards solving

176   LOCOMOTIVES AND ROLLING STOCK

it with their double-grated firebox of 1835, the principle being to burn the smoke in the upper coke-fired chamber as it rose from the coal fire below.

The *Liver*, due for a new firebox, was fitted up with a modified one on Gray's plan and in November 1836 extensive trials were held under Woods's supervision. Coal was used in *Fury* and *Swiftsure*, both of which were damaged by the excessive heat; *Patentee* and *Star* were then tried with screened coal, and arrangements were made to experiment with anthracite. The results from *Liver* were only partially satisfactory, the smoke not being entirely destroyed, but mitigated to an extent.

Earle, who had ridden on the engine, suggested using only half coal instead of three-quarters, but before the experiments had gone very far, the hollow, water-filled fire bars between the two fireboxes burst just as the 10 a.m. Blue train was starting from Edge Hill, severely injuring the driver and fireman. The trials were not abandoned, however, and in May the

95 *Enrolled drawing for Melling's patents, showing four of his inventions. When steam is admitted to the top of the cylinder* e, *the lever* b *brings the coupling wheel* a *into contact with the engine wheels. Steam admitted to the bottom of the cylinder forces the lever upwards bringing the two small retarder wheels* ff *into operation to reverse the direction of the leading wheels and stop the engine. Valve* q *controls the steam or hot water ejected on to the rails from pipe* p. *The valve* n, *operating at 50 psi, sends steam into the tender to heat the water*

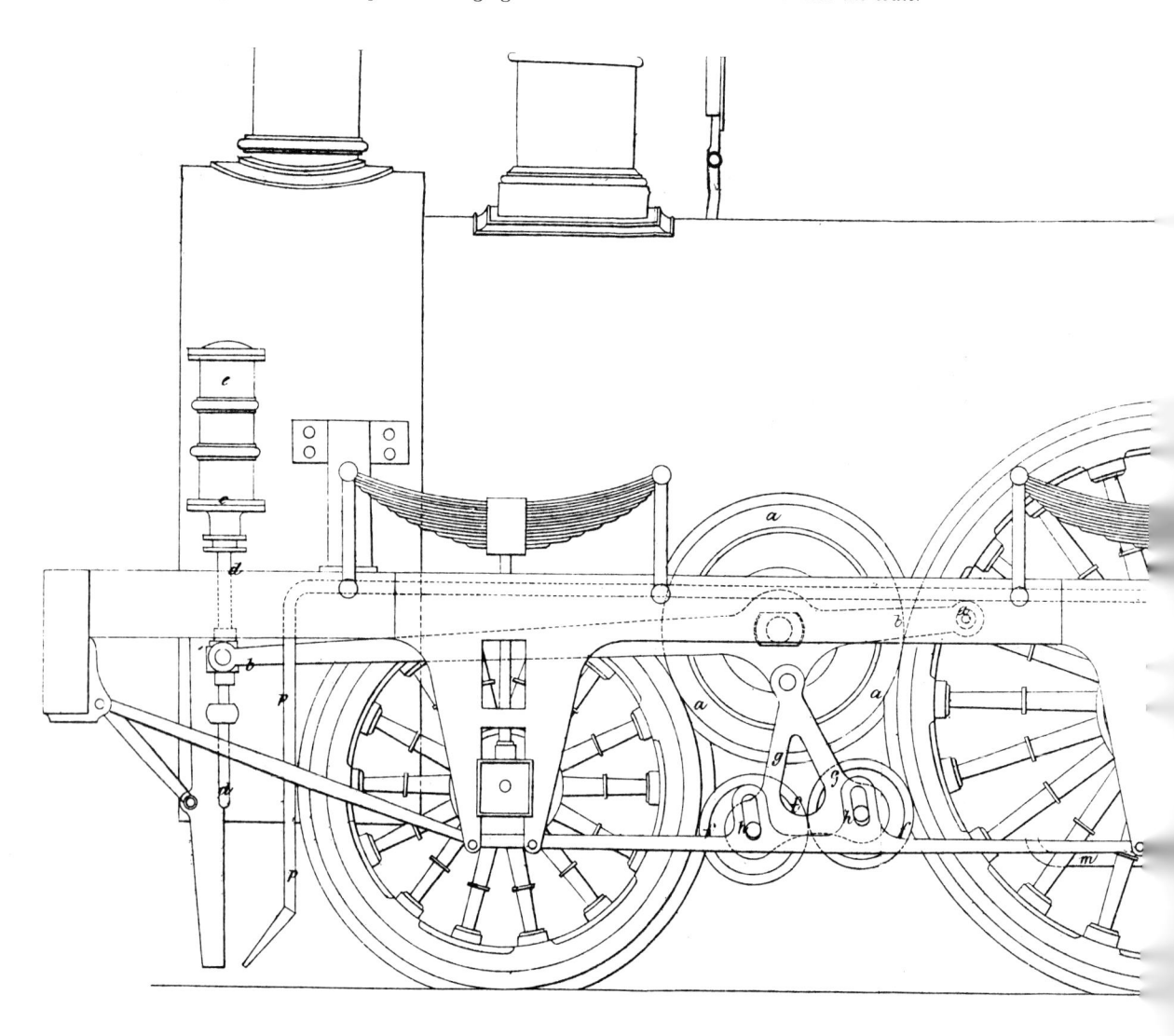

Company agreed to allow Chanter to fit another firebox to an old locomotive. John Gray was allowed to go to London in August to enrol the Patent Specification for the apparatus. The inventors then had a new locomotive built by Vernon & Co. of Liverpool, incorporating these improvements, and trials took place on the L&MR in the summer of 1838. The engine, *Prince George*,[28] was now the property of Melly Prevost & Co., exporting agents, who intended to send it abroad, but Woods considered it only partially successful and very heavy on fuel.

The problem was brought much nearer to being overcome in 1845 when John Dewrance '... burned raw coal very successfully in his engine, the *Condor*', built with a double firebox of large dimensions.[29]

Trials of Samuel Hall's smoke-burning apparatus, consisting basically of several bell-mouthed tubes running from outside the smokebox through the boiler to the firebox providing increased air for combustion, took place on the Midland Counties Railway in December 1841; Woods attended the trials and in 1842 the device was fitted to the L&MR engine *Star*. It was of limited success as it was prone to overheating.

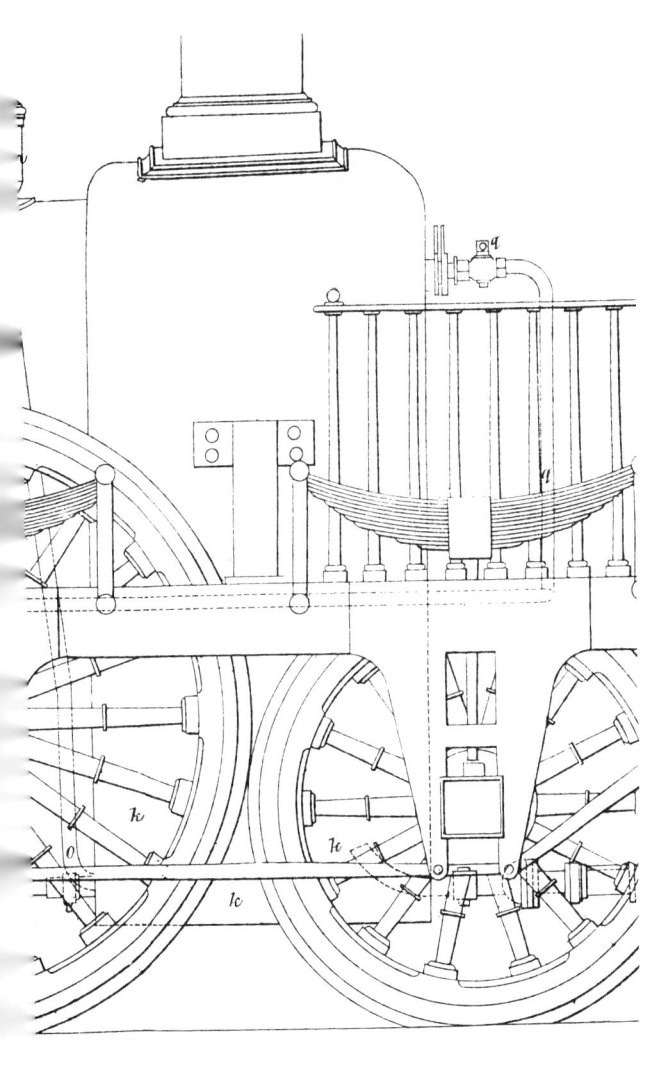

Water for the engines was pumped from wells at each end of the line and at various intermediate points; near Olive Mount it was drawn from a pond in a field and at Crown Street it was largely the overflow from a mill. The Manchester & Salford Waterworks offered 10,000 gallons a day at £70 a year in 1830, but it was of unsuitable quality and the Company installed its own boilers and pumping engines; however, in 1837, it was found that the mains water was better and cheaper at 8d. per 1000 gallons, and the Company contracted for 20,000 gallons a day.

It was fairly common practice in those early days to replenish the locomotive boilers and tenders with hot water, and for this purpose boilers were provided at Liverpool, Manchester and Parkside. Four were erected at Parkside, the half-way point along the line and the principal intermediate watering place, early in 1830, and were renewed in 1836. In 1834 an additional boiler was installed at Manchester capable of heating the water for the engines as well as pumping it, at a cost of about £60. Here there were four tanks, standing opposite the arrival shed, each of which had steam pipes running through it to bring the water temperature up to about 85°F. A reference to *Northumbrian* on the first day after the opening mentions it being filled with hot water. Water cranes with leathern hoses were used, in appearance much the same as those of recent times. Experiments of May 1831 in letting the waste steam into tanks on the tender to heat the feed-water led to several engines being fitted with the apparatus.

The wheel-spokes of the first locomotives were of wood but about 1832 RS & Co. patented an iron wheel; the spokes were wrought iron tubes arranged so that alternate spokes slanted in opposite directions, and they were cast into the boss and rim. The tires were of wrought iron. By 1833 these wheels were causing so much trouble that the Company demanded either a 12-month guarantee or that engines be sent without wheels or cranked axles. This type of wheel was also used by Tayleur & Co., who were told that they must guarantee it for 50,000 miles or change to the pattern used by Bury or Sharp, Roberts. The wheels of *Firefly* had already failed, and when in May 1836 those of both *Eclipse* and *Star* collapsed, and their springs were also found to be defective, the Company insisted on their being made good at no charge, both being new engines. The leading coupled wheels of *Orion* gave way on the evening of 2 September 1837 and the engine plunged down a 10ft slope on Chat Moss.

Improvements came about gradually over the next few years, and by 1843 steel tires were being tried on locomotive wheels.

Hand brakes, worked either by screws, levers or a rack and pinion mechanism, were fitted to all L&MR tenders from 1830 onwards, and in 1832 Stephenson

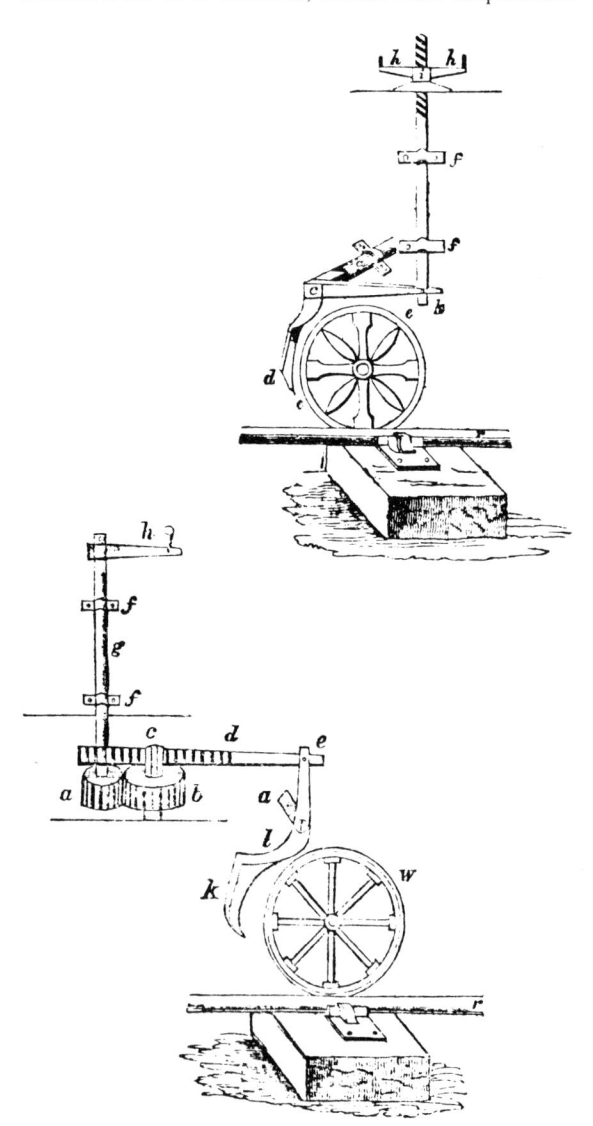

96 *Types of screw and rack-and pinion brakes used on carriages and tenders*

tried a form of self-acting continuous brake of his invention; this acted through the medium of the buffer-rods, applying the brakes to each carriage as the buffers met with any resistance. *Patentee* was the first engine fitted with Stephenson's steam brake, worked by an auxiliary cylinder and piston; when steam was applied, the piston through a system of levers brought the wooden brake-blocks to bear on the driving wheels (see illustration No 86). In 1835 it was said to have taken 40–60 seconds to stop a train, depending on the speed and state of the rails.

All the locomotives were fitted with two safety valves, only one of which was under the control of the driver. In July 1831 Allcard was ordered to test all the safety valves and to lock up and retain the key of one on each engine. Despite all precautions the valves were tampered with, and as late as 1844 it was discovered that enginemen were weighting them down with pieces of chain.

The shriek of the locomotive whistle was first heard across Lancashire about 1835 when Fyfe at Manchester was given details of the invention by Sharp, Roberts' foreman; one of the firm's workmen had been sent to Dowlais Ironworks where he had seen the whistle in use and brought back drawings, possibly supplied by the inventor Adrian Stephens,[30] who did not patent the device. It was adopted immediately by the Railway, and used also on the stationary engines as a low water level alarm.

There was nothing very scientific about the use of lubricants in early machinery; animal or vegetable oils and fats were used singly or in compounded form, sperm oil, tallow, castor oil and rape-seed oil being the most usual. On the railway oil was used exclusively at first; its application by the wasteful method of splashing it around the journals and bearings of carriages, waggons and engines by a swab on a stick resulted in heavy expenditure. In December 1834 Booth recommended a trial of grease instead of oil on coaches and waggons, and grease-boxes were fitted experimentally to one of the locomotives; in the meantime he worked on the problem and, in 1835, obtained a patent for his Axle Grease and Lubricating Fluid, a compound of Russian tallow, palm oil and rape oil, boiled with common soda and water in varying proportions according to whether it was for use on locomotive machinery or waggon axles. Booth's compounds were adopted by the Company and were in general use on railways until the introduction of mineral oil later in the century.[31]

In 1837 the Company adopted Booth's 'Patent Connecting Chain' for all engines and carriages, awarding him 150 guineas. This was his famous screw coupling, the design of which has remained practically unaltered ever since. Its two connecting shackles, drawn together by rods threaded in opposite directions, brought the buffers of adjoining carriages into contact and eliminated that jolting on the starting and stopping of trains coupled by loose chains that had caused passengers to brace themselves against the shock. It would be interesting to know how much the invention owed to Thomas Clarke Worsdell's earlier plan of using rope couplings tightened by a wooden rod, tourniquet fashion.[32]

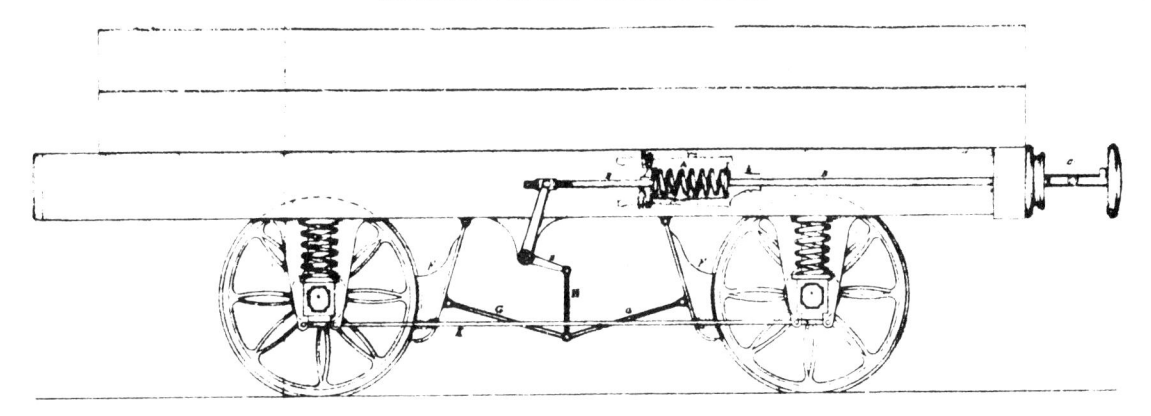

A variety of locomotives, other than its own, were constantly to be found on the tracks of the L&MR; some were the property of collieries, some belonged to other railways or in the case of the Bolton & Leigh, to its contractor Hargreaves, and others again were undergoing trials, remaining the property of their builders. For years the Railway was the only one upon which exhaustive tests of a locomotive's capabilities could be made, and the Company exercised great forbearance in the demands made upon it, consistent with the requirements of safety and the necessity of preserving its property from damage. Where extended trials were allowed, the locomotives were required to work some of the regular trains or undertake ballasting duties, and some cases they were actually hired for short periods.

Hargreaves eventually had 16 locomotives in service; they were of a variety of designs, and an old photograph of one survives.[33]

One of the first B&LR engines was Bury's *Liverpool*, a four-wheeled coupled engine with cranked axles, inside cylinders, and 6ft wheels. The hand-gearing was placed in front of the smokebox, where the driver stood, the stoker being in the usual position, at the fire-box end. The outer firebox was domed and contained a very small internal firebox, and the fire was urged by a pair of bellows working under the tender.

97 George Stephenson's self-acting brake

98 Henry Booth's screw coupling

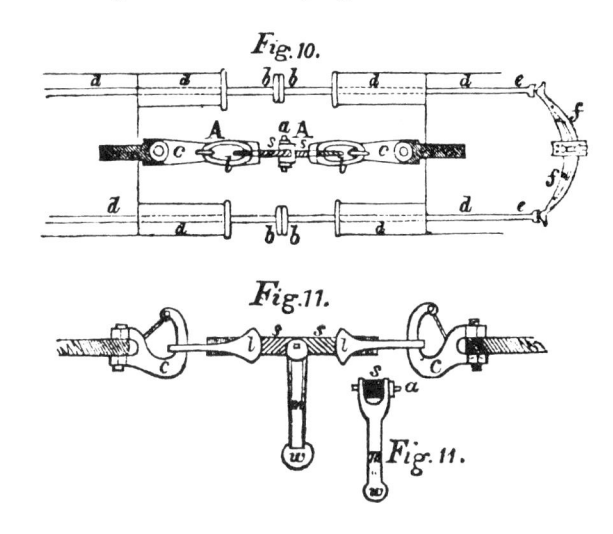

Arriving on the L&MR in July 1830, she was employed on ballasting in the final stages of construction, but was not purchased, and went to the B&LR. Here she broke a wheel, the driver and fireman being killed in the accident, but after being returned to Bury for repair, she gave John Hargreaves many years' service.

Hargreaves asked if Crook and Dean's new locomotive[34] could be used on the railway, and if so he would buy it; apparently permission was granted in October 1831. In December 1835 he was informed that the maximum weight on one pair of wheels was six tons and the Board reserved the power to require a third pair of wheels to be added to any engine where they thought it was necessary to secure steady running. The B&LR *Utilis*, weighing over 15 tons, was banned outright from the L&MR as injurious to the weak rails in February 1837, but it was subsequently furnished with eight wheels and was allowed to return.

The Company's engineers had to keep a close watch on the engines operated by coal-owners, as they did not always conform to the railway's requirements as to design and dimensions; neither did their drivers take the Company's rules and regulations too seriously. Many of the accidents on the L&MR involved locomotives belonging to collieries or other railways and they usually resulted from the disregard of a signal or bye-law.[35]

Thomas Legh of Haydock had at least two engines to work his coal trains to Manchester in 1832, *Newcastle*, which in January ran into and badly damaged *Venus*, breaking her frames, and *Shrigley*, a 'Planet' type engine, which narrowly avoided a serious accident in February when it ran at speed into Manchester station. In October Allcard signed certificates for two of Bury's engines to work on the line, one for Hargreaves (probably *Clarence*), and the other, *Collier*, for Bourne and Robinson's Elton Head Colliery. *Collier* was an 0-4-0 engine whose 5ft 6in. wheels were considered too large by George Stephenson, and it was restricted to 12 mph. Bury was notified that in future no engines with wheels larger than 5ft diameter would be allowed on the line and a bye-law to this effect was published.

Among locomotives tried on the L&MR but destined for other railways was the Horseley Iron Company's 'Improved' locomotive designed for the St Helens Railway in October 1833. The various makers were particularly anxious to ensure that locomotives for export were thoroughly tested, and Bury was allowed to try two such engines in November 1832; Tayleur & Co. tried out two of their locomotives in April 1836 before sending them to France, and the agents Melly Prevost were allowed to send two Sharp, Roberts engines for trial in 1838. In March 1838 Bury had several engines waiting on the line for eventual delivery to the L&BR, and was given permission to try one on a goods train; in May he tested two more before sending them to the Leipsig & Dresden Railway. Until this time free passage for new engines for the L&BR was allowed, but it was then decided that a reasonable charge should be made.[36]

An old book giving the performances of locomotives during 1839–40 mentions Chanter's, Smith's[37] and Nasmyth's engines, none of which was owned by the Company, since theirs were identified by their names. Neither was 'Tayleur's Engine', at work in June 1840, but 'Banks's New Engine', undergoing trials on 16 November 1839, was purchased by the Company in December. There were two *Vestas*, one belonging to Turner and Evans, and the mysterious *Asa*, a six-wheeled locomotive working as a jobbing engine in August 1840.[38] Chanter's engine was presumably the *Prince George*, still not perfected. Peel, Williams & Peel's *Soho*, designed by Dewrance while still in their employ, underwent its trials under Woods' supervision in October 1839.

There was a certain amount of unofficial trial running on the railway which might not have come to light had not a Vulcan Foundry engine collided with the rear of a train at Newton Junction in January 1837. The engine was on the railway 'without leave or notice' and the Board resolved that the matter should not be lightly passed over.

An extraordinary request was received from Bury Curtis & Kennedy in May 1842, arising from a disaster that had occurred on the Versailles Railway; in order to prove that their engines were safe, and to counter the prejudice against 4-wheeled engines they asked if one of these, with a broken front axle, might take a goods train from Liverpool to Manchester. Although generally tolerant in the matter of experiments, this one was predictably refused, either with a four- or six-wheeled locomotive.

The Company decided in 1828 to build its own carriages, and as a first step purchased a quantity of mahogany, broad cloth and small fittings. At this time Thomas Clarke Worsdell and his eldest son, Nathaniel, joined the railway and they designed and built the first carriages in the yards and buildings adjacent to Crown Street Station.

A number of vehicles were ready in time for the trial trips in the summer of 1830, and in September there were at least enough 2nd Class carriages for the seven trains that followed the Duke of Wellington at the opening. The main frames of the special cars were built by the Company and fitted out as already described; those of normal size were afterwards converted to regular passenger coaches, but the Duke's eight-wheeled saloon, after running on a few excursions, was laid up in a siding near Ordsall Lane where it remained until all the cloth had rotted away.[39]

The 1st Class or 'Yellow' coaches were basically three road coach bodies fused into one and mounted on an iron underframe running on four 3-ft wheels. They were loose-coupled with chains and a low iron railing surrounded the roof, where luggage was stowed. Each of the three compartments held six passengers; the seats, comfortably upholstered in drab[40] material, were divided into three by arm rests. Below each door was a set of folding footsteps and on the roof was a seat for the guard or brakesman who rode on the front end with his legs over the edge. The upper panels of the coaches were painted black and the lower ones yellow with the Company's name spelt out in full; to complete the resemblance to stage coaches, each 1st Class carriage bore a name. The names, apparently adopted originally to enable passengers to identify the coach in which their seats were booked, survived at least until 1842, and in all probability until the end of the Company's separate existence. No complete list has been found but from various sources it has been possible to rescue some 26 from oblivion.[41]

The number of 1st Class carriages with which the Company went into business is not recorded, but it was clearly insufficient; it is also apparent that its own works could not keep abreast of its requirements, for in February 1831 two coach bodies each were ordered of John Gorst and Richard Jones, coachmakers, at £210 each. In June, Lacy & Allen of Manchester built the *London* for £256, and the '. . , undercarriage that came as an appendage to the London Railway Coach' was returned to them at their request. An apprentice to one of these coach builders was Charles Fay who, after helping to build the L&MR carriages, remained in railway service, eventually to become Carriage Superintendent of the L&YR and, in 1857, inventor of the chain brake, standard on many lines for some 20 years.

In December 1831 Worsdell was ordered to build two new 1st Class carriages to hold 18 passengers each for the traffic expected in the summer and a month later two more were put in hand. By this time there were several types of Yellow coaches in service; the mail coaches, described elsewhere, accommodated only four persons to a compartment, a few had coupé ends with only two seats and a few others were open carriages, having curtains instead of windows. After the introduction of the latter the regular carriages were known as 'Glass Coaches'. Although all the vehicles conformed to a general specification, there were differences in detail and finish 'according to the taste of the builders'.[42]

Early in 1832 the *Royal William* and *Queen Adelaide* curtain carriages were converted to glass coaches; few open carriages were needed as they were used only in the summer and then only one to a train.

In September 1836 contracts for five or six new carriages were placed with firms in Liverpool and Manchester as the Board considered that the works could not construct them to the standard of workmanship required in time for the following summer.

100 *1st Class 4-inside coach or coupe*

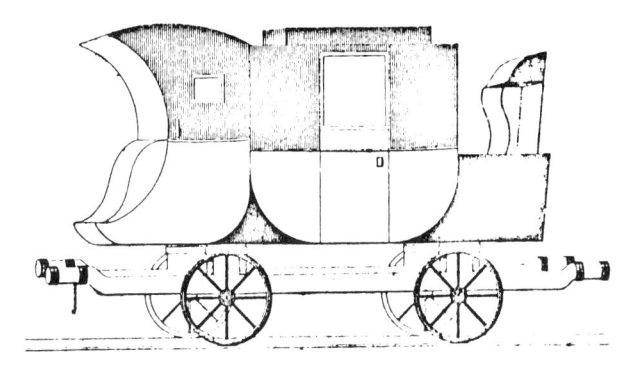

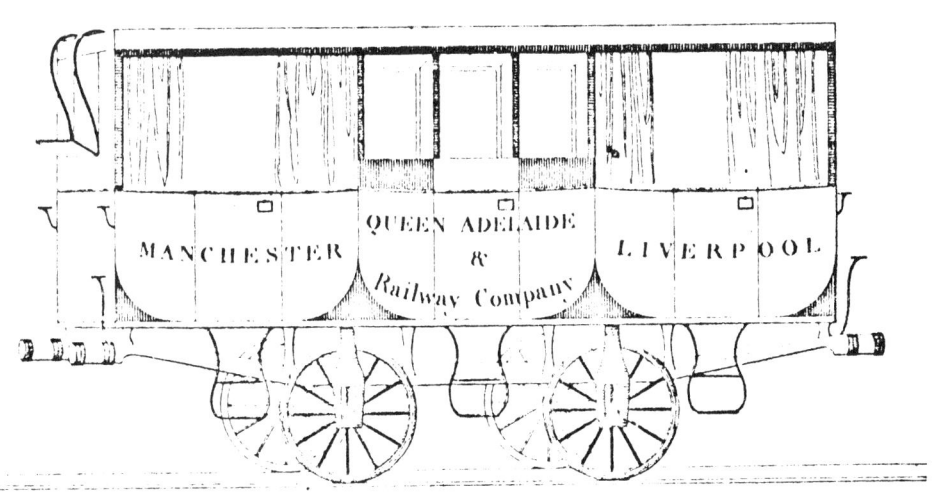

99 *1st Class carriage with glazed and curtained compartments*

The 2nd Class carriages, usually termed 'Blue Coaches' by the Company from the uniform colour of their paintwork and 'Blue Boxes' by their patrons, were originally merely open trucks fitted with seats. There were two varieties, one divided into two separate sections with an entrance in the middle; in these the passengers sat in four rows parallel with the road, the two inner rows sitting back to back with a common rail as support and the outer rows facing them on seats along the carriage sides. The other type of carriage was divided into three compartments with side doors to each and with reversible backs to the seats to enable the passengers to face the direction of travel. Some were fitted with a small railing or balustrade along the sides and ends, and each type carried 25 to 30 seated passengers. A third type, described in July 1829, appears to have been experimental as there is no record that it was adopted. It was a long carriage with doors at each end and a narrow body along the centre covered by a roof which projected beyond the body to the full width of the carriage. It carried 16 inside passengers and 16 outside, the latter sitting in rows of eight along each side of the saloon, facing outwards '... in the Irish car fashion'.

On some of the 2nd Class trains the front end of the first carriage was raised in height to diminish the force of the wind on the passengers and to afford some slight protection from soot and cinders. By August 1831 numerous complaints were coming in from passengers whose clothes had been burned by sparks while travelling in the Blue coaches, and orders were issued that roofs were to be fitted, some of painted canvas and some of wood for comparison. At the same time the B&LR notified the Board of its intention to provide tops for its 2nd Class carriages. In January 1833 a start was made in fitting draw- and buffer-springs to the 2nd Class carriages, the Yellow coaches all having been so equipped by this time.

Following experiments carried out in December 1835 on the D&KR in the presence of James Loch, when an engine was run at the rate of 15 mph into a train of coaches equipped with Bergin's Patent buffers, with neither sustaining any damage, the device was adopted by the L&MR. The new buffers incorporated coiled springs and rods which ran the length of the coach, and replaced the earlier leaf spring buffers. The buffer stops erected at Lime Street Station at about the same time were apparently on the same principle; they were described as long, strong, broad springs with beams between them and coming into effect gradually, they slowed the coaches down, but, said Booth, '... we are very angry when it is used'.[43]

In December 1833 experiments were conducted with portable gas for 'lighting the coaches in their passage through the tunnels', but they were evidently unsuccessful. At the suggestion of some corn merchants, blinds were fitted to the windows of the 1st Class carriages in 1841, and later that year the separate steps were replaced by continuous footboards on all passenger vehicles.

Booth's Patent Screw Coupling was fitted to all the carriages in 1837, adding greatly to the comfort of railway travel. Those companies whose coaches formed part of the L&MR trains replaced their loose chain couplings with the screw type, although Hargreaves had to be reminded to do so in May 1838, when it was reported that his loose-coupled coaches running in L&MR trains reduced the effectiveness of the screw couplings on the rest of the train.

The Carriage Department was responsible for the general maintenance of the coaches and in April 1831 Worsdell was reminded to pay attention to the cleaning of the Glass Coaches; in the winter of 1833 he was instructed to have all the Blue coaches freshly painted.

The carriage building and repair workshops were in an enclosed yard within the Crown Street area, to the south of the passenger and coal stations, and with rail access to the small tunnel. They were transferred to Lime Street on the completion there in 1837 of the new two-storey building adjacent to the station, designed specifically for the purpose. Four tracks were laid at ground level and the upper floor contained trap-ways through which not only components but whole coach bodies could be raised or lowered.

Thomas Worsdell resigned in January 1837 and Nathaniel took over the GJR Carriage Department. A local coachmaker, Henry Whalley, recommended one of his journeymen, John Pownall, to succeed the Worsdells and he was appointed in February 1837.

The carriages were kept under cover so far as possible and carriage sheds were built at both ends of the line. In March 1837 a 'Coach House for two carriages' was ordered to be built at Newton.

On several occasions the Company was asked to build carriages for other concerns – Tayleur & Co. and the D&KR in 1834 – but declined as their shops were fully occupied. A few Blue Coaches were sold secondhand to the St Helens Railway for £100 each and the GJR hired 20 of these carriages when it opened in the summer of 1837.

In April 1843 the Directors were invited to inspect a pair of carriages designed by Houldsworth, Chairman of the M&LR, and used the following

January for Pasley's inspection of that Company's new works at Hunts Bank. Passengers on the *Tourist* were accommodated on two levels, the centre being occupied by a raised dais, and the whole was elegantly furnished with looking-glasses and carpets. The other carriage, *Gondola*, had open ends with doors leading to the central saloon; it held 14 passengers, six on each side seated on crimson velvet sofas and two on folding seats hinged to each door.[44] The designs were not adopted by the L&MR, although the original coaches probably ran through to Liverpool on occasion. They are shown in illustration No. 69 standing in a carriage siding.

Early in 1830 the Board considered the question of goods vehicles for the line, having already allowed experiments with what purported to be waggons from which axle-friction had been practically eliminated. These were the inventions of T. S. Brandreth, whose other brain-child, *Cycloped*, has already been noted, and Ross Winans, the American engineer.

Winans' waggon had 30in. flanged wheels, the axles of which projected 2in. through the naves. The weight of the body, however, was borne by four friction wheels 8in. in diameter and with wide rims. These rims fitted over the projecting axles of the main wheels, thus hanging the load on to the main axles. The main wheels revolved several times to one revolution of the friction wheel. Brandreth's waggon worked on a similar principle although it differed in detail. Stephenson also constructed a flat truck with 3ft case-hardened wheels whose axles, after passing through the naves, were turned down to $1\frac{3}{8}$in. diameter, and worked in $3\frac{1}{4}$in. brass bearings. The three types of waggon were tested by Hartley and Rastrick in March 1830 on the Whiston Inclined Plane, the rails previously having been swept clean.[45]

The waggons were taken up the incline, and released, the test being to see which ran farthest along the level section at the foot of the gradient. The results were less than impressive and when the judges reported on 8 March, Rastrick said the small saving in friction was not worth the cost of keeping them in order, while Hartley suggested having one in regular and constant use for a year. Winans had already built ten waggons for the Company at a cost of £285 and he was paid £50 compensation for his detention in this country during the experiments. Two more on Winans' principle were built by William Brown in April for the one-year trial period, and the Company purchased Brandreth's 'friction waggons for the price they are worth'. After a time their use was discontinued and the ingenious principle had to await the invention of roller bearings to be justified.

Meanwhile the Company constructed a number of flat waggons, consisting merely of an open platform on wheels; these were used for cotton bales, and a variety of other traffic, the loads being secured by ropes and tarpaulin sheets.

Some of the flat trucks were adapted for carrying private road carriages by the addition of a low platform upon which two adjustable iron rails of channel section were fitted; the carriage wheels rested on these rails, and the vehicle was secured by chains. As the timber trade developed, special trucks were built for the purpose; used in pairs, logs of up to about 50ft could be carried. To enable them to negotiate curves, they were fitted with massive cross-timbers on a swivelling platform, to which the load was chained down.

The first special vehicles for livestock were pig waggons; these were open, with sides and ends made up of six horizontal wooden slats to a height of about three feet. In June 1831 orders for 19 sheep carriage bodies were placed with various firms at a cost of £60

101 Ross Winan's anti-friction waggon

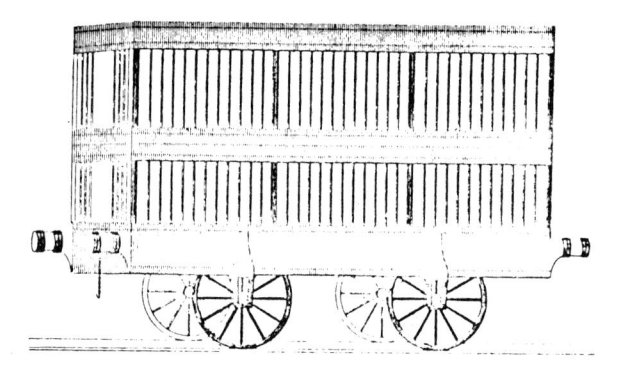

102 *Two-tier sheep waggon*

each. These were double-deck vehicles with roofs; the sides were of a light grating composed of vertical wooden rails, and four doors were provided on each side, two for each deck. At this time one 'carriage for large cattle' was ordered to be built as a pattern.

The Company had only two horse-boxes at first but in March 1833 orders were given for two more 'close carriages for horses'. They were just over 12ft long, the horse compartment occupying 9ft 6in.; side-flaps were fitted which, when lowered, became loading ramps. The interior was padded and provided with food-bins and the vehicles were among the first to be fitted with buffers; they carried up to three horses, but in later years ordinary open trucks were often used for the short journey between Liverpool and Manchester.

The coal trucks were of a variety of sizes, some being 10ft long, but only 3ft 9in. wide with a wheelbase of 4ft 8in. Some had sides tapering towards the floor and those which ran between the collieries and Manchester had bottoms through which the coal could be discharged at the staithes.

The goods trucks weighed from 1½ to 2 tons and were coupled by three heavy chains; most were fitted with buffers after 1833.

The Company's stock of goods waggons increased over the years until by 1836 there were about 460; the total for 1840 shows a slight decrease at 428. Some were built at Crown Street Works but in 1833 and 1835 large batches were supplied by outside contractors.

With the opening of the GJR difficulties arose from the differing sizes of the rolling stock, particularly of the coal trucks ranging from the 3ft 9in. of the L&MR to 7ft wide on the GJR.

For a long period before the line opened experiments were made to find the best type of wheel and axle, and to determine whether inside or outside bearings were to be adopted. Trials were conducted with both wheels revolving loosely upon a fixed axle-tree, with one wheel free and the other fixed and with both shrunk fast on to the axle. The wheels supplied by R. Stephenson & Co. from 1827 for the ballast waggons were unsuitable for the fast passenger trains and in November 1830 cast iron with forged iron tyres were tried, along with Roscoe's wrought iron wheels. Wooden wheels were used for some years, discontinued, and then re-introduced about 1839 for passenger carriages and for some goods waggons. At this time horse boxes had one pair of wooden wheels and the other pair of cast and wrought iron. The standard diameter of 3ft was adopted for the wheels of all rolling stock and was specified for private owners' waggons.

The collieries and carriers who ran trains over the L&MR under toll arrangements were expected to use their own waggons, as this enabled the Company to concentrate on building for its own requirements. Hargreaves, on the B&LR, had a large number of coal trucks, ten of which were smashed 'by running amain on the Chequerbent Incline Plane' in January 1832.

Little control was exercised over the private owners at first, and by 1832 the Company found that waggons of various patterns and degrees of safety were running over the line. Some were too heavy, others had their wheels set at 'improper distances' and a number were unsafe from having been involved in accidents. The Company published a set of regulations to be observed by private owners, insisting among other requirements that cast-iron wheels should have wrought iron tyres.

Hargreaves was ordered to install turnplates at Hulton Colliery in May 1832 so that the waggons could be turned to bring their brakes on to the left hand side and avoid the danger to brakesmen of having to work on the side on which other trains passed. In September it was reported that his waggons still returned from Bolton 'wrong end foremost' because there was no turnplate between Bag Lane and Bolton. In September 1836 directions were given that Hargreaves' unfit waggons were to be detained. Hulton's waggons were also considered to be unsatisfactory, the buffers being lower than those on L&MR stock.

The container system was operated in various forms on the L&MR for some years, mainly for the coal traffic. The principle was not new, having been in operation on Joseph Butler's Ankerbold & Lings Railway for about 40 years; there, boxes holding a ton of coke were transferred between road carts, barges and the railway trains by crane.[46] Coal boxes were used on the L&MR by some of the colliery proprietors, who sent the loaded boxes down to the main line where they were transferred to 'skeleton waggons' for haulage to Liverpool or Manchester. The boxes were made in the railway works, and an additional 12 were supplied to Bourne & Robinson's Elton Head Colliery in 1831 at £5 each. For a short time small waggons from one of the collieries were placed bodily on L&M trucks to avoid the tipping, reloading and consequent breakage of the coal. Containers for coal do not appear to have survived beyond about 1833 on the L&MR, as they soon became rickety, in the words of R. Stephenson who had tried them elsewhere, and who maintained that the strength of a railway vehicle depended on the firm connection of body to frame. Pickford's containers for general merchandise continued in use for many years.

In 1841 the Board considered a waggon made to run on railways or highways, invented by Thomas Hill of Leeds, but it does not appear to have been adopted.

In May 1831 the Board called for a return of all the Company's coaches, waggons and tenders, and at that time they were all numbered. A year later there were so many waggons running on the L&MR that the Board ordered cast-iron plates lettered 'L&M' to be fixed to its own vehicles. In July 1833 Comber

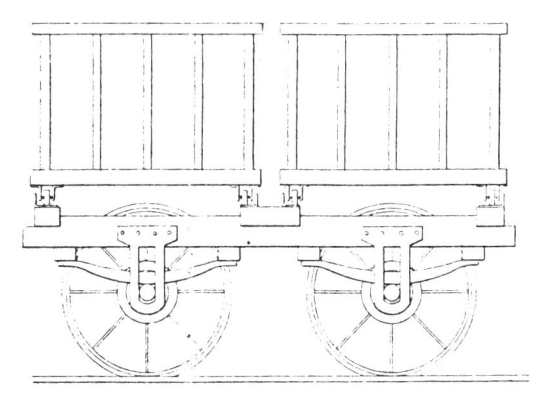

103 *Coal-container waggon*

personally searched the whole line, stations, branch lines and collieries, and found 301 waggons. The highest painted number was 312; of the missing eleven, three had been burnt, and the Board concluded that the others were waggons that had been so thoroughly rebuilt after damage as to be numbered again as new.

In the summer of 1832 there were still hundreds of ballast waggons remaining on the railway from the time of construction; 400 of these were sold to Vignoles for use on the D&KR, and the remainder were auctioned.

CHAPTER TEN

Operating the Railway

AFTER THE EVENTS of 15 September 1830 it could not have escaped anyone's notice that the railway was open, but a formal announcement to this effect appeared in the newspapers that week. On 16 September one train only went from Liverpool to Manchester and back. Drawn by *Northumbrian*, its performance was carefully timed by the Scottish engineers Grainger and Buchanan, who computed its average speed as 20 mph to Manchester and about 18¼ mph on the return trip.[1] (*North Star* the next day did not do quite so well.)

This was the first train to carry fare-paying passengers, of whom there were 130 to Manchester and 120 on the return run. The next day the regular train service came into partial operation with departures from both Liverpool and Manchester at 7, 12 and 4 o'clock; on Sundays the mid-day train was omitted. These were first class trains, the second class coming into service the following week at 10.30 a.m. and 2.30 p.m. from each terminus.

For most of its existence the L&MR provided only two classes of travel although within the 1st Class there was the superior comfort of the mail coach for which an extra charge was made. As distinct from the actual carriages, the trains were designated 1st or 2nd Class, according to whether they stopped only at Newton, or at any of the 25 or so stopping places along the line. The trains did not necessarily consist of carriages of the same class as the train, although in practice this was generally the case, the first class trains being composed of yellow or 'Glass' coaches; the second class were usually referred to as 'Blue Trains' or 'Road Trains' but at certain times a yellow carriage was attached for the convenience of 1st Class passengers from intermediate stations.

Within days of the railway opening, most of the 22 stage coaches which had plied between Liverpool and Manchester were withdrawn; they had taken four-and-a-half hours for the journey at fares of 10s. inside and 6s. outside, whereas the railway did it in less than half the time at fractionally over half the fare. At the end of the first month's working the railway was carrying 1200 passengers daily, 500 more than the total capacity of the stage and mail coaches, and by March 1831 over 130,000 had been booked for the through journey and thousands more taken up at intermediate stopping places. The number of passengers had tripled by 1833 and at summer weekends there were sometimes insufficient carriages at Liverpool for the evening trains returning to Manchester; on one occasion the Carriage Inspector at Manchester was admonished for not returning them quickly enough.

On the opening of the Railway there were two fares only; the single journey between Liverpool and Manchester cost 7s. 1st Class and 4s. 2nd Class. By January 1831 the short distance fares between either terminus and any of the intermediate stopping places had been calculated and published. About this time a new type of mail coach with only four passengers to a compartment was introduced at the original 1st Class fare of 7s., the regular Glass Coaches being reduced to 6s.; one 1st Class coach was now attached to each 2nd Class train for short distance passengers. Then in May 1831 the 4-inside, or Mail Coach fare, was reduced to 6s. and corresponding reductions made in the other rates. The practice of booking passengers at the L&MR offices through to Bolton and Warrington commenced at this time, and for a while through bookings for journeys from Manchester to Liverpool by rail and thence to Southport by Bretherton's coaches were tried, but were discontinued in June 1831. By February 1832, however, passengers were being booked through to London from the Dale Street coach office, travelling by train to Manchester and there joining the London coach.

A spare office at Liverpool Road Station was used in 1834 as a booking office for Chester and other

186

places where the journey could be commenced by train and completed by stage coach, and the Southport service was restored. This was quite popular, for although the distance from Manchester was only 38 miles by road, many passengers preferred to ride by train the 31 miles to Liverpool and take the coach for the remaining 25 miles on the grounds of speed and cheapness.

For a time another legacy of stage coach practice could be seen on the L&MR, that of carrying outside passengers. In April 1831 it was ruled that the guards seats at each end of the 1st Class carriages could be occupied, if vacant, but that only one person could ride in each roof seat, and no passenger was to ride with the guard. These places were booked at the same fare, and in the same way as inside seats.

In June 1832 some consternation was caused in the Board Room when it was learned that a new Stage Coach Bill, to apply to railways and turnpike roads, would result in the Company being taxed to the tune of about £15,000 a year. As the tax would be levied on every coach employed, whether full or empty, it would '... limit that ample supply of coach room which the Directors had hitherto been anxious to provide.' Four directors went to London to make representations and in July it was announced that the passenger duty proposed for railways would be $\frac{1}{8}$d. per mile per passenger. From 11 October the fares were increased to 6s. 6d. for mail coaches, 5s. 6d. for Glass coaches and 4s. for the 2nd Class Blue coaches, the revised rates, and the reason for them, being announced by newspaper advertisement and handbill.

The fares now remained practically unaltered for some years, and no increase was made on the opening of the extension to Lime Street in 1836. In fact, when Loch drew attention to the low fares and great numbers of passengers on the Brussels Railway, the Board pointed out that its action in bringing passengers through to Lime Street at no extra fare, but at great cost to the Company, was '... tantamount to a lowering of the fare.'

From time to time the Company was approached on behalf of various groups of passengers for reductions; neither lower fares for the working classes, sought in 1833, nor 'Seamen's Fares' between Liverpool and Hull in 1839, were conceded. Children under three years of age were carried free, but above that age full fare was payable in the early years; by 1840 however, children (probably those between the ages of three and ten years) were carried at half fare.

On the opening in 1844 of the extension to Victoria Station the fares were increased to 7s. 1st Class, with a day return at 12s., 5s. 2nd Class, with improved carriages, and 3s. 6d. for the newly introduced 3rd Class between Lime Street and Victoria, or 3s. to or from Edge Hill. In October 1844 the charges were reduced to 6s., 4s. and 2s. 6d. respectively, with 1st Class day tickets at 10s. From December, day tickets were issued from the intermediate stations.

Day tickets for 3rd Class travel were issued at weekends in the summer of 1845 between Manchester and Edge Hill at 2s. 6d. return, and enormous numbers of workers from Manchester took advantage of these cheap waggon trains to spend Sunday, their only day off work, in Liverpool. This resulted in the evening trains returning to Manchester being dangerously overcrowded and with some reluctance the Board increased the Sunday fare to 4s.; the Saturday rate remained at 2s. 6d., for return either that day or on Monday morning.

The first recorded application for what was, in effect, a season ticket was received from Mr Hornby, the Rector of Winwick, who asked if he could contract 'for a year's conveyance by the coaches'; on 25 October 1830 the Board promised to consider the proposal when the Coaching Department 'was more complete'. In January 1832 one J. Hutchinson of Commerce Court, Liverpool, offered to compound for a free passage to and from Manchester, naming his own price, £25 for twelve months, which the Board refused; at the same time several regular passengers 'expressed a wish to purchase a lot of tickets in advance, to save the trouble of paying each time', and were allowed to do so for a trial period.

An arrangement was made by Mr William Owen of Liverpool in December 1842 to contract for a limited form of season ticket entitling him to make six return journeys a week between Rainhill and Liverpool for one year at two-thirds of the 2nd Class fare, viz £31 4s. a year; the Company required only half the amount to be paid in advance.

So long as the Company operated its system of numbered seats and waybills for the 1st Class passengers, season tickets were not really practicable since places would have had to be left vacant on the off-chance of a ticket-holder arriving at the last moment. However, by 1843, when the decision was taken to change the system in six months time, the question of annual tickets was resolved; the Board agreed to issue them for an unrestricted number of journeys at the rate of £60 1st Class and at a proportionate charge for 2nd Class, the amount to be paid in advance, and the ticket to be non-transferable.

Season tickets were still subject to negotiation

between the Company and the applicant as late as November 1844, when a firm arranged for one First Class annual ticket at 50 guineas to be used by any member of the firm or its clerks, their names to be endorsed on the back of it.

From January 1845 annual tickets for unlimited travel anywhere on the railway were reduced to £40 but even at this rate the holder would reap no benefit over taking day tickets unless he made over 80 return trips a year.

The subject of fare-collection was considered some weeks before the Railway opened, when it was decided that the seats in the 1st Class carriages should be numbered and booked correspondingly. The terms 'booking' and 'booking office' were adopted from stage-coach practice, as was the system itself with minor modifications.

Separate books of pre-printed tickets were kept by the booking clerks at Liverpool and Manchester for each class and for the several branches; the classes and branches were all distinguished by tickets of different coloured paper. The 1st Class ticket from Liverpool to Manchester was pink and measured $4\frac{1}{4}$in. × $1\frac{1}{2}$in. with counterfoils of the same size; the wording was as follows:

LIVERPOOL TO MANCHESTER
No 52   12 Sep 1832
       at 2 o'clock from Railway Station
Paid 5/6   J. H. Agent
       N.B.—when seated, be pleased to hold this
       ticket in your hand till called for.
                                             (Turn over)

On the back were notices about gratuities, smoking and, from 1833, a caution to passengers to keep their seats in emergencies.[2]

The number and signature were entered in ink, the day and month by date stamp. The number, passenger's name and amount paid was entered on the counterfoil and the ticket was torn from the book against a strip of brass.

The passengers' names were entered on the waybills which accompanied every train; those for the 1st Class coaches were in the form of seating diagrams, the passenger having chosen his place when booking. These waybills also carried any special instructions for the guards.

The tickets of passengers to destinations on the L&MR were collected before the train started and were sent to the Treasurer's Office. Eventually the waybills and completed books of counterfoils were also sent there for checking, but a daily account was kept of tickets issued and collected for each train to enable discrepancies to be detected quickly. Passengers for journeys over the branch lines showed their tickets before starting, but retained them until reaching the junction. The separate waybills for these carriages were handed over to the branch company's guard at the junction and subsequently provided the information from which the various companies' accounts were adjusted.[3]

Just before the train was due to start the engine driver received a paper bearing the names of himself, his fireman, the guard and the engine together with a note of the composition of the train and the time of starting. On arrival it was given up to the timekeeper who extracted the details for the weekly summary prepared for the Board. The guard checked the passengers against his waybill, noting any who were missing. Journeys were often booked some time in advance, and if an intending passenger was prevented from travelling, or even if he arrived too late at the station for his train, he could claim a refund of half the fare.

Journeys from the termini to intermediate stopping places were by ticket with the destination written in, and the guard was responsible for seeing that the passenger left the train at the station to which he had booked; in 1839 it was said that much depended on the memory of the guard, who knew all the regular travellers, and that the system worked well.[4] Passengers joining the train at wayside halts paid the guard, who often collected their fares while the train was in motion; at first no tickets were issued, and there was no check on the amount of 'road money' handed in at the booking office by the guards. In 1836 a new system was introduced under which the gatekeepers were issued with cards bearing the name of their station and the guards with lock-up leather pouches in which there were narrow apertures to admit the cards. The pouch hung on the outside of the carriage on which the guard rode and the gateman, after entering the number and destination of the departing passengers on the card, dropped it into the slot.

On arrival at the terminus the guard put the road money in another slot in the locked bag which he then handed in at the booking office, where the money was checked against the tickets. Although small scale embezzlement was still possible, it required the collusion of too many people to make it worth while. As permanent stations replaced the old stopping places, the official in charge collected the fares and made out a waybill which he placed in the pouch when he gave the guard the money.

In 1837 tickets were still collected at the start of the journey but the directors studied the arrangements on

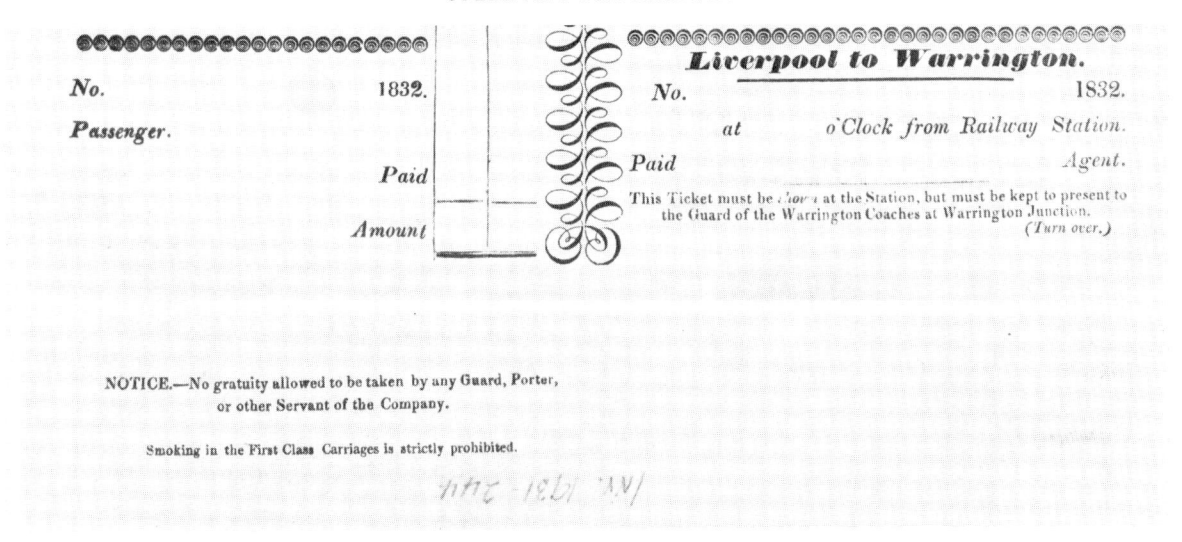

104 *Ticket, with counterfoil, Liverpool to Warrington, and notice printed on back of ticket*

the L&BR at Euston where the platforms were separated from the rest of the station by barriers, and the tickets collected there at the end of the journey. Evidently this system was introduced on the L&MR shortly afterwards. The GJR practice of collecting tickets at the top of the Lime Street Tunnel was adopted in 1838 as a greater security against fraud.

One form of ticket fraud, uncovered in September 1832, was that of booking to Newton and riding on to Manchester; to 'excite the Guards to vigilance', the Board offered rewards of two guineas to any who detected dishonest passengers. A bye-law in May 1833 prescribed a fine of £5 for knowingly travelling beyond the station to which the passenger had booked.

Early in 1840 it was discovered that two of the oldest and most trusted booking clerks had been operating a swindle over a long period; it involved the issue of a ticket at the full rate, and the subsequent endorsement of the counterfoil with the word 'child' or 'soldier', after which only half the money collected was accounted for. Another method was that practised by John Hill, discharged in October 1842. He cut the tickets from a book well in advance of the current pages and issued them without accounting for any money, having destroyed the counterfoils.

In November 1843 the Board resolved that 'Mr Edmondson's system of booking' was to be adopted on the opening of the Leeds Junction Line; Edmondson's system had been in use on the M&LR for some time, this company having been the first to recognise the value of the printed card ticket. From June 1844 it came into operation throughout the L&MR and ticket collectors were appointed at the more important stations.

At Liverpool a booking office was opened in part of the new Royal Hotel in Dale Street[5] and at Manchester passengers were booked at the Star Inn, Deansgate and the Company's office in Market St. From these offices they were conveyed to the stations free of charge by omnibuses operated under contract in Liverpool by Bretherton and in Manchester by Lacy & Allen, whose vehicles had *Auxilium* painted on their sides. Each ran four buses, and they went by three different routes, picking up intending passengers along the way; travellers arriving at the stations were taken to the town centre by these buses.

The guards on the buses were the Company's employees, and they were subject to the rules concerning gratuities; one was fined for going off the route to set a passenger down at the Waterloo Hotel, for which service he demanded a tip, and from August 1831 the penalty was dismissal.

One of Bretherton's buses overturned near Hope Street in October 1831, injuring a number of passengers, but he would not accept responsibility, claiming that the bus was overloaded, and the Company eventually compensated the injured.

There was uproar outside Manchester Station during the first week of operations. Several stage coaches had already been taken off the Liverpool run and the proprietors of the coaching inns sent coaches to pick up railway passengers and take them to their various establishments. Each had several cads and waiters in attendance, wearing ribands with the name of the inn round their hats. These men, 20 or 30 in number, shouted and fought for the passengers' luggage and custom, and at least one young lady was lifted against her will into one of the coaches and driven off.[6] The situation at Liverpool was better as the regular buses could enter the station yard but the private ones could not.

In January 1832 it was decided to increase the number of trains and to discontinue the free bus service after 15 April, the operators being notified of the termination of their contracts. Other proprietors offered to run buses on a private fare-paying basis, and the Company agreed to this, but in a short time there was confusion at Dale Street and elsewhere from the number of vehicles starting and arriving at the same time; police and porters were put on duty to control the loading of the coaches, and the sale of tickets in the street by the cads. In November the Company fixed the fares at 6d. to meet 1st Class trains and 4d. for the 2nd Class.

Lacy & Allen had the exclusive privilege of running buses between the Market Street Booking Office and the station but in January 1834 the other bus proprietors were allowed to share the business, each for a week at a time. The system failed, however, as against Lacy's four vehicles, the others, mainly hotel proprietors, had only one and could not carry the Company's parcel bags; in July the Company reverted to the old system.

The Company's booking clerks at Manchester ran a profitable sideline in booking passengers for Lacy & Allen's buses; one Baker was paid £50 a year for this service, and as he had not disclosed it, the Board felt under no obligation to release him from his liability to make good a deficiency of £22 in the accounts of one of his subordinates.

In March 1834 Taylor at Market Street was given permission as a trial, to accept ½d. per ticket for bus passengers booked, his assistant to receive $\frac{1}{3}$ of the total.

In April 1837 it was decided to close the passenger side of the Market Street office as very few bookings were made there, and the unreliability of the bus service was giving the Company a bad reputation; however, it was in use in 1844 after the opening of Victoria Station, for bookings to Southport, and the Liverpool Road office was used for the same purpose.

The Company was careful not to commit itself on the uncertain question of arrival times as these were affected by a number of factors, the most important being the various times allowed for the journey. At first these times were largely experimental, and with locomotives that were few in number and of limited power, the long and crowded trains of the summer of 1831 were often unpunctual. But by April 1832, when a more frequent service of shorter trains was introduced, 90 minutes was the time allowed for 1st Class trains and two hours for 2nd Class; the enginemen were ordered to take more time if the road was out of order or in wet weather. Several enginemen, however, cherished the ambition to be the fastest driver on the line, and with careless confidence bordering on recklessness, often brought their trains in nearly half-an-hour early. In September 1832 Robert McCrie was brought before the Board to explain how his train arrived in Manchester 25 minutes before time and in February 1835 it was noted that the 1st Class trains often performed the journey with 15 or 20 minutes to spare. At this time the drivers were reminded of the 90-minute rule and threatened with fines if they took less than 80 minutes for the journey.

By 1836 the timetable had settled down to a basic ten departures daily from each end of the line, the times being the same from each station, but with a daily service of 12 trains each way in the summer months, starting in July. Any alterations in times were made to 2nd Class trains as those of the 1st Class were 'now so well established'. In June 1837 there were 11 trains each way, the first at 7 a.m., the last, a mixed train stopping only at Newton, at 7 p.m.; the others were made up of five of each class.

Although many extra trains were run in the summer months, the basic timetable remained constant throughout the year, and adjustments were made in the length of the trains to cater for the fluctuations in traffic. Thus from November to February the average length was five coaches, from March to June eight, and from July to October ten coaches. The time allowed for the journey was now $1\frac{1}{4}$ hours between Edge Hill and Manchester for the First Class and $1\frac{3}{4}$ hours for Second Class trains; if longer than ten carriages, an extra five minutes for each additional carriage was allowed if required. In November 1837 the Board considered combining the 7 a.m. 1st Class and 7.15 2nd Class trains into one 2nd Class at 7 a.m., but had to abandon the plan as the early fast train was used by passengers to connect with the Stage Coaches from Manchester to York, Derby and Nottingham, which left at 9 a.m.

When the trains started simultaneously from Liverpool and Manchester, they usually reached Parkside (Newton) at the same time, but as the number of trains using the junctions increased with the expansion of the NUR, the L&MR train departures were staggered, generally by 15 minutes. Alterations were also made to some timings to accommodate the GJR, in pursuit of the Company's policy of maintaining good relations with that concern.

The contract waggons of the private carriers were regularly attached to passenger trains and occasionally other goods waggons were included in these trains; horse-boxes always accompanied the trucks used for passengers' private carriages.

A new timetable or 'Scheme of Departures' was sanctioned by the Board on 15 May 1843; this included the 'Parkside Mail' at 3.15 a.m. from Liverpool and 3.30 a.m. from Manchester, on weekdays and Sundays. Another Post Office train left Parkside for Liverpool at 4.20 a.m. and carried passengers.

Until 1841 the 2nd Class trains did not run to a timetable since they stopped on average at six or eight of the 20 stations, making up time on the stretches where no stops were required. A timetable would have involved stopping at every station, adding 15 minutes to the journey time, and delaying all the other traffic on the line. But the passengers from the roadside stations had to estimate the arrival time of the train, and were often left behind if it passed through earlier than usual. After many complaints the Board instructed Woods in December 1841 to calculate the intermediate times in proportion to the whole distance, and to instruct the enginemen not to start from any intermediate station more than five minutes before the calculated time; they were also to wait for any passenger seen to be approaching at such times.

The introduction of a 3rd Class was discussed by the Board on 15 January 1844, and decided upon in April. The newer 2nd Class carriages were to be closed in at the sides and have windows provided and the old open Blue carriages were to become 3rd Class. It was decided to keep the trains separate, and to charge 3s. 6d. single; this was above the penny-a-mile rate subsequently embodied in the Regulation of Railways Act. On 12 April 1845 an extra train was provided '. . . with the present engine and stock' to cope with the heavy demand.

What appears to have been a local commuter service by 'Omnibus Trains' started on 19 July 1845 between Manchester and Patricroft, the newly-built station there being sufficiently advanced to handle them.

A table of fares and times of departure was displayed at each station and regular advertisements in the press kept the public informed on these matters; this medium was also used to announce any changes in times or rates, and any additional trains or other facilities available. Printed cards bearing this information were supplied to inns, hotels and other establishments and in July 1833 arrangements were made for these to be hung in hotels at Buxton, Harrogate and other watering places.

A document dated 20 February 1831 was issued by the Directors giving the times of departure, fares, booking arrangements, omnibus routes and much other information. All the short fares were quoted, from either end to any of the stopping places, but not between intermediate stations; they were in units of 6d., with a minimum fare of 1s. Probably produced originally as a placard or handbill, it was incorporated in a 12-page pamphlet giving stage-coach and steam packet information and printed by Smith & Co. of Lord Street, Liverpool.

The Company was approached in August 1839 by John Gadsby of Manchester who sought permission to print and sell timetables of the L&M and GJR trains. The Board agreed that, published under proper conditions, this would be a great convenience to the public and the Treasurer was authorised to afford every facility to the publishers to obtain correct lists of trains as often as necessary. At about this time a timetable was published by J. Bridgen of Wolverhampton, and a revised version appeared on 18 October 1839.[7] This was the month in which George Bradshaw's first timetable appeared but whether there was any connection between them is not clear.

At Crown Street a large bell outside the station was rung five minutes before the starting of a train and a small one was placed '. . . under the verandah to ring the passengers into the coaches.' This was necessary at the Liverpool Station because the public were allowed inside, but at Manchester passengers only were admitted to the station, and the trains were started by a 'bugleman', to the tune 'I'd be a butterfly',[8] a popular song of the time.

Although the station doors were supposed to be closed at the time of departure, there were still delays for various reasons, the late arrival of a bus, the last-minute checking of the passengers against the guard's waybill and, at Lime Street, the addition of an extra coach to a train near its departure time.

Clocks were provided at Liverpool and Manchester, and, from 1831, at Newton where the clerk recorded arrival and departure times. The old sundial still to be seen on the wall of Liverpool Road Station is a relic of the early days.

The Company complained of the inconvenience to passengers from the incorrect time usually shown by St John's Church clock, and asked the

105 *Manchester, Liverpool Road Station; old sundial of 1833 inscribed with the geographical position of the Station*

churchwardens to see that it was regulated and illuminated; the tenor of their reply may be gauged from the Board's decision a few days later to pay 5 guineas a year for the clock to be kept in order by contract.

There was a steady demand for the carriage of private road vehicles by rail, and these were conveyed on flat trucks attached to the rear of passenger trains. A charge of £1 was made for a four-wheeled carriage and 15s. for a two-wheeled one; for one horse the charge was 14s. by passenger train, two cost £1 and three 24s. Normally horses were loaded into the horse boxes at Edge Hill loading dock, and these were coupled to the train when it emerged from the tunnel, but if they were accompanying a private carriage, they went on to the train at Lime Street.

The operation was carried out with great despatch and at short notice. Lord Hatherton, who arrived at Manchester at 11 p.m. on a Saturday night in August 1833, went to the Station at 8 a.m. the next morning, had his carriage mounted on the train, '. . . . the work of one minute' and was in Liverpool at half-past-nine. His coachmen retained their seats on the box of the carriage.[9]

The owners had the option of travelling in a 1st Class carriage at the appropriate fare, or of riding in their own coaches at 2nd Class rates. The latter course was attended by a certain amount of risk as the Board found out in July 1836, when an irate letter described how Lady Molyneux, riding peacefully in her phaeton, was rudely shaken up when the banking engine at the Sutton Incline ran violently against the carriage truck.

There was a free allowance of 60 lb. of baggage per passenger, but this was increased to 100 lb. in 1844 to conform to L&B and GJR practice. The 2nd Class passengers stowed their luggage under the seats as best they could, but porters packed the baggage of 1st Class passengers on the carriage roof. Hardman Earle suggested in October 1831 that a luggage waggon should run in front of a 1st Class train, but the plan was not adopted, the extra weight, equal to another carriage, presumably being the crucial factor. It appears that at one time animals were allowed in the coaches, for in April 1833 a greyhound was strangled in a carriage bound for Manchester, the owner's servant having fastened it too tightly with a length of cord.

A gentleman could not take his servant, unless he were also a passenger, on to the station platform. The servant laid his master's portmanteau or other luggage on a counter and a porter passed it through a hatch to a platform porter who put it on the carriage roof while the passenger booked. An angry Mr Toosey of Milnthorpe wrote to the Board in November 1841 concerning a black servant, in livery, being placed in the same 1st Class carriage as himself and some ladies on their journey from Liverpool to Lancaster, but the complaint was quickly passed on to the Lancaster & Preston Junction Railway when it was established that it was one of their coaches. When, in 1844, 2nd Class carriages were withdrawn from 1st Class trains, servants accompanying their masters were permitted to travel in the front compartment of the train at 2nd Class fare.

The passengers did not hesitate to write to the directors on any matter upon which they felt aggrieved and in November 1832 the Board encouraged the practice by providing Passenger Diaries at Crown Street and Liverpool Road Stations. These were sent up to the Board Room each Monday for inspection but often weeks elapsed without any observations being made. There is no record that any word of appreciation was ever written but occasionally adverse comments from the books were entered in the Minutes, such as the one of February 1833 that the '... behaviour of car-men in Crown Street to Ladies was exceedingly annoying, by several of them contending and quarrelling for their Luggage and even their persons ... endeavour to procure a constable to preserve order at the Stand in Crown St as was done at the Pier Head on the arrival of Steam Boats.'

Four passengers who were left stranded at Parkside on 31 August 1840 when the NUR coach in which they were travelling was detached from the train there, had to spend the night at Newton and claimed a total of £75 from the Company; the arbitrator's award was £8 10s. between them.

During an outbreak of cholera in Liverpool in May 1832, the Manchester Board of Health were given facilities to inspect 2nd Class passengers arriving there, in an effort to prevent the spread of the disease. In 1841 the Company was required to take a count of the number of persons of each sex who were travelling on the railway between 10 p.m. on 6 June and 5 a.m. on 7 June for the census of that year.

Although the Company made every effort to meet the wishes of its passengers, it would not permit unauthorised stops by 1st Class trains, only the Treasurer being allowed to give such authority. In September 1838 there was apparently some kind of ceremony near Patricroft, as the 1st Class trains were ordered to stop there to take up and set down Lord and Lady Francis Egerton, where they would be met by their barge, but his lordship was no ordinary passenger.

Residents near Edge Hill in August 1836 applied for permission to ride up and down the Lime Street tunnel on payment of a suitable fare and the Board thought arrangements might be made when a system to safeguard the Company against fraud had been worked out.

As it 'would be agreeable to passengers', mile and quarter-mile posts were erected in June 1836 along the south side of the railway, measured from Manchester; as they already existed along the north side from Liverpool this seems to indicate the beginnings of amateur train-timing.

The Company went to great lengths to restore lost property to its owners; £20 found in one of the carriages in December 1833 and unclaimed five months later was advertised in the newspapers, and a £10 Bank of Ireland note, found by a porter on Lime Street Station in July 1840, having been advertised twice in the Liverpool papers without result, was advertised yet again in Liverpool and Dublin.

The Directors of the L&MR, and of other early railways following their example, were determined to break the abuses of the tipping system that had become associated with stage-coach travel. Long usage had accustomed Englishmen to accepting it, but an American[10] travelling by road from London to

Liverpool was appalled to find that on reaching Coventry, where the first change of driver and guard took place, he was accosted by these individuals with "Sir, I have drove from London" and "Sir, I have guarded you from London"; the minimum tip to each was 1s., and failure to 'submit to this law of the road' would almost certainly result in the passenger's luggage being lost before he was half-way through his journey. Overnight stops at inns were expensive enough, but on leaving a 'host of privileged beggars' beset the coach windows on either side shouting "Sir, remember the Waiter", "Ma'am, I brought out your bandbox", and "Sir, I lashed your trunk".

From the beginning it was made clear to passengers that none of the Company's servants was permitted to solicit or even accept gratuities freely offered and the staff soon learned that it did not pay to be caught breaking the rule.

John Moss travelled on the 8 a.m. train from Manchester on Sunday, 20 November 1831, apparently unrecognised by most of the staff; at the next day's Board meeting he produced a list of irregularities for the sub-committee to investigate. The seven-minute stop at Newton was too long, as was the 55-minute journey time from there to Liverpool. There was only one guard as far as Newton, where the second one joined the other and rode alongside him until they reached Olive Mount, when he went to his own coach; the train should not have stopped for passengers at Kendrick's Cross or at Huyton, and it was followed much too closely by a Bolton train. At Liverpool there were no lights burning in the little tunnel and no clerk in the Crown Street coach office.

Just before the railway opened the *Albion*[11] noted with some satisfaction that it would '. . . promote the cause of sobriety, by preventing travellers from tippling on the journey. There is but one public house on the whole line . . . and it can only be visited during the stoppage of the locomotive engine'. The writer's predictions, however, did not take account of the early nineteenth century travellers' determination to obtain a drink en route, nor the ingenuity of the purveyors in ensuring that they were served.

About six months after the railway opened Thomas Legh asked the Company if they would move the watering place from Parkside to Newton as he was building an inn there. This was hardly the kind of request likely to appeal to the Board as the practice, inherited from the stage coaches, was already becoming a problem; in June it was reported that drinking at the Bury Lane Tavern, where the Blue coaches stopped, had so increased as to be a 'serious evil' and in September a passenger complained of the stoppages of these 2nd Class trains at '. . . different Pot Houses on the Road.' When consulted as to the granting of a spirit licence to a house at the Huyton Road crossing in December 1831, the Directors replied that for the good order of the railway, they would prefer that it should be refused, but that it was not their policy to interfere in such cases.

On 4 January 1832 the Board noted that the New Inn at Newton was open and serving drinks to passengers, and ordered that 'not a moment's extra time of stoppage to any of the trains' would be allowed. Two weeks later the landlord of the Legh Hotel, Newton, was warned that if the sale of drinks to 1st Class passengers did not stop, fines would be enforced against his staff for trespassing on the railway.

Following a tragic accident at Rainhill on 23 November 1832, the *Manchester Guardian* published a letter from a Mr Taylor of Eccleston stating that the 'enginemen were not unfrequently [sic] intoxicated', and on being asked for specific instances he informed the Board that he had during the last summer seen drunken drivers on several occasions. It was the 2nd Class trains which were most seriously affected as these stopped at the different public houses on the road where the men were freely plied with spirits. Dixon was consulted but he thought that it would not be expedient to prohibit altogether the bringing of refreshments to the trains, but that strict regulations be laid down to avoid delays; this the Board accepted and enginemen and guards were instructed accordingly.

In the summer of 1834 the Company discovered that its gatekeepers had gone into the business of selling ginger beer to the passengers and this trade came to an abrupt end. The owner of the public house at Kendrick's Cross gates was refused permission to supply drinks to coach trains which stopped there, on the grounds that it would be inexpedient to extend the practice.

The Board, concerned at the number of late arrivals by passenger trains in September 1836, instructed Booth to tell the 2nd Class guards that in their view much time was lost at the stopping places 'to afford opportunity for the sale of liquors to the passengers.' A year later Woods reported on the '. . . inconvenience and nuisance of the existing practice of hawking about Eccles cakes and Ale and Spirits to Railway Passengers at almost every stopping place between Warrington Junction and Manchester' and the Board ordered that the sale of all articles, especially those mentioned, be prohibited and prevented after 1 October 1837. Apparently the measures taken were effective for in November the proprietors of the Chat Moss Tavern asked if they might again be allowed to serve the passengers on the trains; their request was refused.

The seemingly innocuous Eccles cakes presumably contained some alcoholic ingredient at that time to warrant their specific banishment from the stations. They had been sold from a house next to Eccles Station, displaying a large inscription 'This is the noted Eccles Cake Shop', and at the Patricroft Tavern; in 1842 a Mrs Birch unsuccessfully sought permission to sell 'her well-known Eccles Cakes' on Newton Station.

Passengers could buy their newspapers at the main stations and a report was made to the Board in August 1839 of the arrangements at Lime Street. Here two children were allowed to sell the Liverpool papers and one man those from London; another two children sold Lacy's and other railway guides and one man periodically attended to sell the *Satirist* and other unstamped publications. Ilbery said he occasionally read these '. . . for the purpose of preventing anything of an improper character being sold on the station.' An application at this time for permission to sell 'Mr Coglan's Book' was reluctantly refused on the grounds that enough were already on sale; this was evidently Francis Coughlan's guide,[12] which might have fared better had more than five of its 180 pages been devoted to the L&MR.

Newspapers were first carried by train in early August 1831 after the Board had received a request from one of the Liverpool papers to send a parcel by the early train to Manchester. On 1 August the Directors agreed to carry the newspapers free of charge, accepting no responsibility for loss and stipulating that the parcel be collected on arrival. In response to a petition from Leigh two months later, the Board allowed the coach guard of the 5.30 p.m. train from Manchester to bring two London newspapers for the newsroom, leaving them at the Bury Lane Tavern for collection, the service to be '. . . upon trial and during pleasure, free of charge'. From November 1836 1st Class passengers found a free copy of the *Britannia*[13] in their compartment every Wednesday morning, supplied by the proprietor with the permission of the railway directors.

Smoking in the 1st Class carriages was prohibited, even if the other passengers consented, and the rule was later extended to cover all closed coaches, waggons and stations. Many passengers ignored the order, and in 1835 the guards and other employees were instructed to enforce the rule; posters and handbills were printed and eventually under a new bye-law a penalty of 40s. was imposed. Several corn merchants persisted in smoking cigars 'notwithstanding the remonstrances of the Company's Superintendents' and two of them, Maxwell and Blain,[14] were warned that a repetition of the offence would result in prosecution. Another passenger complained to the Board that he had been rudely turned out of the station yard on Ilbery's orders for smoking a cigar.

On the opening of the railway many people wished to travel on the trains purely for the experience, and to enable them to do so, with the additional privilege of riding in the 'Duke's train of carriages', the first excursion train ran on Friday, 1 October 1830. It started at 1.30 p.m. from Liverpool and ran to a siding at the Sankey Viaduct laid expressly for the purpose, at a fare of 5s. return. During the Liverpool Charity Festival a few days later the train was used on an excursion service from Manchester, leaving at 7.30 a.m. and returning at 4 p.m.

The first recorded arrangements for a privately organised railway excursion were made by Benjamin Braidley, Boroughreeve of Manchester, in May 1831, for about 150 members of the Bennett Street Sunday School to visit Liverpool during the Manchester Races of 25 – 27 May. The Company's charge for the return journey in a train of blue carriages was £20.

Special arrangements were made for excursions for small parties; thus, in the spring of 1839, a party of Friends, about 40 in number, were taken from Liverpool to Newton by special train and for the return journey their coaches were attached to a regular train. Amos Bigland, the organiser, guaranteed at least two coach-loads.

One of the earliest requests for a special train was made by the Italian Opera Company in November 1831. They required arrangements for 50 or 60 persons to travel to Manchester and back to Liverpool late at night after the performance. The Company offered to '. . . accommodate them at regular hours, but not convey them at midnight.'

Special trains were provided for the South Lancashire Conservative Association's annual dinner at Newton, usually ten or more closed coaches, returning to Liverpool at 10.30 p.m. In 1836 Dixon was ordered to superintend the operation, and especially the conduct of the enginemen on the return journey.

Periodically groups of businessmen would petition the Company to provide special 1st Class trains to meet their particular needs; the criterion was whether

106 *The Railway at Newton, looking towards Liverpool. The buildings on the right are the Conservative Hall and the Legh Arms Hotel; c. 1835. (The original print is incorrectly dated '1825')*

the numbers involved would make it worth the Company's while, 50 passengers being about the minimum. The corn dealers, dry salters and cotton dealers were successful in their applications. In January 1840 arrangements were made for a party of 60 to attend the Corn Law Dinner in Manchester, and the Company agreed to put on a special train from Manchester on 31 January 1842 for members of the Anti-Monopoly Association to return from the Corn Law Bazaar if the association would guarantee 50 1st Class passengers.

The Company itself ran special trains on numerous occasions; extra services were provided for the Liverpool Festival Week, held each autumn, and in 1836 one train left Liverpool at 5 a.m. for Manchester from Wednesday until Saturday of that week for visitors returning 'after the Fancy Ball'. Extra trains ran during Whitsun Week at a special excursion fare of 5s., leaving Manchester at 6.30 a.m. and returning at 6.30 p.m. Passengers could return on any day that

week. Many of these excursions started from and returned to Edge Hill and not Lime Street. Brunel's new ship, *Great Britain*, was in Liverpool Docks in the summer of 1845 and a special train of 1st and 2nd Class carriages left Manchester at 1 p.m. on 9 and 10 July, returning at 7 p.m., '. . . to allow the public from Manchester and places beyond to inspect the . . . steamer.'

A special train was provided every morning for a fortnight from 1 August 1842 for the Liverpool assizes; it left Manchester at 7 a.m. to enable the passengers to be in court by 9 a.m., and at Parkside on the previous Saturday special arrangements were made for the arrival of the Judges.

Requests from the Mechanics' Institute usually received favourable consideration by the Board. The first stone of the Institute's Liverpool building was laid by Lord Brougham on Monday, 20 July 1835 when a special train was provided to bring him from Manchester, and the Board meeting was postponed to enable several directors to attend the ceremony. When the Manchester Mechanics' Institute held an exhibition in the midsummer holidays of 1840 the Company agreed to transport 'models and other works of art' without charge if the public were to be admitted free. In the summer of 1844 they transported the 'Temple of Juggernaut' at 50% reduction for the Liverpool Institute; this was the rate charged at the time for agricultural and similar exhibitions. A party of 1200 travelled up from Birmingham for a Mechanics' Institute function on 7 September 1841, involving special arrangements with the GJR.

Excursion trains were becoming so commonplace by 1844, and on some lines of such inordinate length, that the Board of Trade wrote to all the railways recommending precautions for 'Monster Excursion Trains'.

The railway had been working for two months when the Parliamentary election of 22 November took place.[15] Mr Ewart's election committee hired the *Planet* and the Duke's train for the day at £21 per trip. A few days earlier the Board had received a complaint that '... some of the Freemen in the employ of the Company had been influenced by the Foreman as to the votes that they would give', and it was directed that '... every Burgess ... should vote as he may think proper.'

In July 1837 a special train took 300 gentlemen from Liverpool to Newton on Nomination Day, and for the election on 1 August each candidate wanted accommodation for about 600 passengers. The Company said this was not practicable, but it would take as many as possible, fairly apportioned between them, an arrangement that probably led to lively scenes at Lime Street. Again, a warning was given to 'Superintendents and other superior servants' not to interfere with the votes of the Company's employees.

On 25 June 1841 the Mayor of Liverpool asked the Company to be prepared in the next two days to send an express to bring a detachment of troops to the town during the approaching Parliamentary Election and to have an engine standing by with steam up ready to take a messenger at a moment's notice.

The first carriage of mail by railway started exactly a week after the Superintendent of Mail Coaches had asked the Company's terms for conveying mail bags twice daily between Liverpool and Manchester. The rate of 1d. per mile or 2s. 6d. per trip by the 7 a.m. and 2.30 p.m. trains from Manchester and the 10 a.m. and 1 p.m. from Liverpool was accepted, and the service commenced on Thursday, 11 November 1830. On that day, the first bag left Manchester Post Office at 6.50 a.m., and was taken to the station by the 'new light mail cart' under the care of a mail guard, to be placed on the 7 a.m. train; the first mails to arrive from Liverpool reached Manchester Post Office at 12 noon and were delivered by 12.15. It was thus possible for a correspondent in either town to send a letter to the other and receive a reply the same afternoon.

The charge of 2s. 6d.[16] per bag included the guard's fare by 1st Class train. He travelled in the ordinary coaches at first, as the arrangements were experimental until April 1831, when a formal agreement was entered into with the GPO, after which the Board ordered that two coaches, *Wellington* and *Lord Derby*, be converted to carry mail, and the *Fly*, a 4-inside carriage was similarly altered a few months later. The modifications involved the cutting away of the last compartment to accommodate the guard's seat, the fitting of a long box called an 'Imperial' across the carriage roof to hold the mail bags and the painting of the lower panels red; the upper panels which replaced the side windows were black. The mail guard's seat was always at the end of the train, the mail coach being the last vehicle; this enabled him to watch the mail the whole time, as his contemporaries did on the road coaches, where robbery of the posts, although a capital offence until 1835, was not unknown.[17]

In December 1831 the Post Office complained that the railway guards were conveying letters on their own account, to the injury of the Revenue; the Company asked for firm evidence.

For about four years the arrangements continued with little alteration. The Postmaster General, the Duke of Richmond, visited the Railway in September 1833 and rode through the Wapping Tunnel; and in 1834 the Company declined to carry despatches thrice daily for a proposed establishment similar to Lloyd's in London to avoid the possibility of infringing Post Office Regulations.

The Mail Service was extended to Bolton via Kenyon Junction in July 1835, and arrangements were made for mail bags awaiting conveyance along a branch line, as at Parkside, to be in the care of a responsible railwayman, paid by the Post Office; the Company agreed to this on the understanding that it was in no way responsible for their safety. In March 1837 the Director-General of Roads and Bridges, Paris, was furnished with details of the Company's arrangements with the GPO.

Heavily increased mail traffic came with the opening of the GJR, and that Company was compelled to make new arrangements with the GPO in November 1837 to reduce the number of mail trains on Sundays over the L&MR. The travelling post office was introduced early in 1838, running for the first time between Birmingham and Liverpool on 6 January. This first sorting van was a converted horse box and in May of that year it was fitted with Ramsey's apparatus for picking up and dropping mail pouches at speed. The former practice of throwing the pouches up to the guard at wayside stations had sometimes ended with pouch and contents being cut to shreds under the wheels of the train where misjudgement of aim or timing had caused the bag to fall between two carriages. Nathaniel Worsdell, now with the GJR, built the first specially constructed mail vans at Crown Street from 1838, and the L&MR made the roof-boxes for the NUR mail coaches.

The consternation among the companies caused by the proposal to confer upon the Post Office the right to put its own engines and carriages on the railways free of charge sent a deputation from the L&MR hurrying up to Euston for a meeting on 2 May 1838; here they learned that the suggestion included the carriage of passengers as well as mail in these special trains, but the opposition was so intense that the plan was abandoned.

In 1838 the mail between Liverpool and Manchester cost on average £1 per trip, or about half the stage-coach rate. By 1839 special mail trains were being provided, the 7.15 on Sunday evenings at £6 6s. per trip and from May 1841, the 4.20 a.m. Parkside to Liverpool. After the introduction of the Penny Post in May 1840 there was an extension of the arrangement under which a daily rate was paid regardless of the number of bags and in May 1844 the Company offered to carry mails by any ordinary train at £250 per quarter.

Confusion sometimes arose when the Company did not know whether the Post Office was using London or Lancashire time in arranging mail train timetables; this problem was becoming acute as the railways spread over the country, and they petitioned Parliament in June 1846 to make London time standard.

Among other special arrangements made almost as soon as the Railway opened was that with the War Office under which troops were conveyed between Liverpool and Manchester at 2s. 2d. each; the amount was arrived at by taking the government allowance of 1s. 1d. a day, the cost per man when the soldiers marched or went by canal, in either case the journey taking two days, against the two hours by rail. 'Women belonging to the Regiment' were carried free so long as there were not more than ten to every 100 men; perhaps those in excess of this proportion travelled with the Regimental Baggage at 8s. per ton. These arrangements were made on 30 October 1830, originally to meet any emergency in those days of unrest, and in August 1831 it was agreed to charge the same rates from either Liverpool or Manchester to Bolton; in June 1832 600 soldiers were taken from Warrington to Liverpool by special trains. The Passenger Tax, introduced in 1832, applied to soldiers travelling at reduced rates and brought an ultimatum from the Company to Col. Jordan, Commanding Officer, Liverpool, on 24 October: either the government remit the tax on military traffic or pay 2s. 6d. per man. The Secretary for War, to whom the matter was referred, agreed to the increase. The revised fare for officers was 6s.

No change was made in the rates until 1841, by which time other railways were conveying troops, each with its own scale of charges. A circular from the War Office indicated that the Secretary of State would be more disposed to use the railways if they would accept 1d. a mile for soldiers and 2d. for officers, and the Board, after consulting the L&BR and GWR, offered to accept the charges prevailing on those lines, $1\frac{1}{8}$d. and $2\frac{1}{8}$d. for soldiers and officers respectively, and 3d. per ton per mile for heavy baggage by luggage train. Detached soldiers were allowed 56 lb. of luggage and officers 2 cwt, free of charge.[18] The new contract was signed in August, the Company reserving the right to use Lime Street, Crown Street or Edge Hill Stations as they saw fit. Military horses were carried at 4d. a mile but the Company had not sufficient horse boxes to take any great number at one time.

The Newton Races provided a large volume of extra traffic, although the Board had declined to contribute a prize cup on the grounds that they had no authority to do so. The first meeting the Company had to deal with was that of Wednesday to Friday, 1–3 June 1831, and in readiness for the occasion 26 cotton waggons were fitted up '... in a temporary manner as carriages of the Second Class'. Notices appeared in the press and on wall placards announcing the times of the extra trains, 11 a.m. from Liverpool and Manchester each day, returning half an hour after the last race, but not before 7 p.m. Other trains were retimed in order to be available for the returning racegoers. The 1st Class fare, entitling the passenger to a seat each way, was 5s., and 1200 special tickets for each day were printed for both Liverpool and Manchester, each day of a different colour. Expecting that there might be some trouble the Company asked the Mayor for some extra constables to assist the railway police at Collins Green and the Viaduct, but they were refused. However, the arrangements went fairly smoothly, and on 2 June the B&LR ran a special train to Newton for the event, worked by their *Union* engine; a speed of 35 mph is said to have been reached.

Similar arrangements were made for Liverpool Race Week in July, an extra train for Manchester being provided one hour after the last race, but the Board was taken to task by a Manchester resident who objected to their advertising the fact. In May 1832 Thomas Legh built a branch railway from Haydock Junction to the Newton Race Course, and the Company agreed to raise the 2nd Class fare from 2s. 6d. to 3s., allowing Legh 3d. a passenger. This eliminated much of the confusion of the previous year arising from the traffic being handled at Newton.

The race traffic had increased to such an extent by the summer of 1835, several race weeks having to be carered for, that the Management Committee were asked by the Board to grant extra pay to the clerks, superintendents and porters involved.

The arrangements at Newton Race Course broke down on 16 June 1837 when several L&M trains were detained there all night after the line was blocked by the derailment of a Bolton engine. In the chaos and delay some passengers did not get home until the following morning. The Company considered that it might be expedient another year not to let its trains off the L&M line, but to take up passengers at Collins Green or Warrington Junction; however, in April 1838 Woods arranged with Legh's agent for additional sidings to be laid down at the Racecourse station. By this time the GJR was bringing racegoers from Cheshire to Newton, and the Board asked them to provide one train for the Race Course instead of sending an engine with one or two coaches backwards and forwards throughout the day to the great inconvenience of the L&MR traffic.

A large number of paupers were sent back to Ireland from Manchester every year; Pickford's estimate was 17 to 25 a day and they asked the railway their terms for conveying them to Liverpool. The Company enquired if they were to travel in coaches or vans, the latter presumably if they were to go down to the Docks through the tunnel. On 2 December 1833 it was arranged to carry them in a separate and specially marked 2nd Class carriage at 50s. a trip. In April 1837 the Manchester Churchwardens asked if repatriates could be transported at a cheaper rate by luggage train, but the Board refused to consider treating any class of passengers as livestock.

Another group of unwilling passengers were the prisoners brought by train to Lime Street and taken thence by omnibus to Kirkdale Gaol. On one occasion in May 1839 the police officer from Manchester had put 13 prisoners from the train into the omnibus when Ilbery, the Superintendent at Lime Street, refused to allow the vehicle to deviate from its normal route, and at considerable risk of their escaping, they were transferred to hackney coaches. Ilbery was reprimanded for not using his discretion in interpreting the regulations. With the opening of the lines northwards convicts were transferred from the New Bailey Prison, Manchester, to Lancaster by rail, and on 22 November 1841 the L&MR came to an agreement that they should travel in prison vans placed on flat trucks at 2nd Class fare, the company carrying the vans in each direction free of charge.

In December 1843 the Company considered a suggestion that a siding be provided into the proposed new gaol 'with a view to passing prisoners along the line from the Assize Courts in Lime Street', but it was decided that conveyance by horse van would be more convenient than taking them through the tunnel. The railway offered the use of its 'telegraphic signal' between the Court and the prison.

Having concluded after the Rainhill trials that stationary engines were unnecessary at the inclined planes, the Board considered the alternatives: either to purchase locomotives capable of taking the trains up the gradients unaided or to employ engines of adequate power for the rest of the line, but with assistance where required. The latter course was chosen, the banking engines ordered, engine houses constructed at the foot of each incline, sidings laid and water tanks provided at the top of Whiston bank. *Samson* and *Goliah* were the regular banking engines, *Milo* and *Atlas* the spare ones.

At first the arrangements were not very satisfactory and in August 1831 Stephenson was asked to prepare estimates for fixed engines, engine houses, rope, pulleys etc. at Sutton and Whiston Inclined Planes; it was probably his figure of over £9,000, roughly the cost of nine new banking engines, that led to the abandonment of the plan.

Two years of trial and error elapsed before a set of rules for working the inclined planes was finally formulated.

An order was made in June 1831 that one brakesman attend each train of merchandise drawn by a *Planet* class locomotive and two brakesmen those trains worked by *Samson* and *Goliah*, to peg down the brakes on descending the inclines. At this time the banking engines were regularly employed on normal goods train working, and if no relief engine was available, trains were divided at the foot of the inclines.

In October 1831 it was ruled that at Whiston half

107 *View of the Railway looking towards Manchester, 1831. The four overbridges indicate that it was taken from a short distance up the Whiston Inclined Plane*

of the train was to be shunted into the siding and the other half taken up and put into the siding at the top; the engine was then to cross to the down line and return for the rest of the train. In no circumstances was half of the train to be left on the main line. A month later this rule was revised, it now being considered less dangerous to leave part of the train on the main line and to come back down for it, than to cross to the proper line for the descent, in the sanguine belief that other trains following would know of its presence.

Further instructions were issued in September 1832. Hardly a model of clarity, the directive ran:

'... the Help-up engine is invariably to return down the proper line on the plane. Trains are only to be divided if the help-up engine is not there, or not ready, and the engine may then return on the same line, unless a coach train is following, in which case he must shunt at the bottom in the first instance, and return down the other line.'

In 1832 the L&MR commenced charging other companies a fee of 2s. for each train that required the assistance of a banking engine on the inclined planes, but for a time the charge was waived in the case of passenger trains to encourage the traffic.

Drivers approaching the inclines put on steam to carry the train as far up as possible by its own momentum. After the train had passed the siding the points had to be set and the banking engine usually ran fast up the bank in order to catch up with it; the result was often a more or less violent impact, sometimes resulting in an accident. In September 1834 a siding was placed half-way up the Sutton Incline where the assisting engine could wait instead of '... galloping after the passenger trains as now.'

It was clear that the Company's rules were disregarded on countless occasions, usually without any untoward consequences, but a number of accidents occurred on the inclines. In January 1832 a train of empty Haydock coal waggons was being taken up Whiston Bank by *Black Diamond* when several broke loose and, running back, collided with *Mars*, following with a train. On another occasion one of Hargreaves' enginemen left half his train on the Sutton Incline '... as he would not pay the charge of

2s. for the help-up engine', and was told to use the siding in future.

On 26 May 1842 an extra holiday train from Birmingham came up to the Sutton Incline while the banking engine driver was sitting in the cabin eating his dinner. The fireman took the engine up and hit the last carriage of the passenger train so violently as to damage it and seriously alarm the occupants. This incident cost the driver three days' pay and the fireman was reduced to cleaner. It required some considerable skill to come up gently behind a train and as late as September 1843 a driver was fined for starting his engine too soon and throwing the last carriage of a train from Manchester off the rails at Sutton.

It is told that early one morning a luggage train could not get up the Sutton Incline, whereupon the engineman had a good fire made up, weighted down the safety valves and opened the regulator. He and the fireman then got off and he said to the engine 'Now you follow me when you are ready'; they walked some distance up the incline and after waiting a while their train came slowly up, enabling them to climb back on to the footplate and proceed to Liverpool.[19]

In the winter of 1831 some journeys were taking four hours owing to the engine wheels slipping on the ice-coated rails, particularly on the inclines. It was soon discovered, however, that by pushing two waggons in front of the train they broke the ice off the rails before the engine reached it.

Francis Whishaw[20] rode on the engines and noted the performance of 28 trains on the L&MR during 1839, all but five of them in November; one only was a goods train, eight were GJR passenger trains and 24 of the trips were over only part of the line. Even this small sample shows the great variety of trains to be seen on the line at this period, for no two were alike in composition and none of the passenger trains was made up of carriages of only one class. Most of the trains were between five and eight vehicles in length but the longest was an L&M train drawn by *Arrow* which consisted of two 1st Class and five 2nd Class carriages, a carriage truck and two horse-boxes; the shortest, hauled by the GJR *Oberon*, was of one 1st Class carriage and one mail coach. Five of the trains conveyed at least one road carriage, eight included horse-boxes and several had goods vans attached.

The average speeds recorded by Whishaw ranged from 16.82 mph for *Rokeby* with four carriages to 31.3 mph attained by the GJR engine *Lynx* with five carriages and two goods trucks. A maximum speed of 50 mph was achieved by an engine he omitted to name but *Lynx*, *Torch* (also GJR) and *Rokeby* all reached nearly 48 mph. Generally the GJR trains travelled over the L&MR at slightly higher speeds than its own were permitted to run, but the Company's bye-laws allowed it to control only the starting times of other Company's trains. The one goods train timed ran at an average speed of 17 mph; it consisted of ten partly loaded waggons drawn by *Mastodon*. Several of the trains were banked at Sutton by either *Mammoth* or *Buffalo* and a GJR train from Manchester to Warrington Junction on 3 August, consisting of four first-class carriages and a mail coach, had a Travelling Post Office added at Parkside. It appears from his observations that the average time of stoppages at wayside stations was about one minute.

Although the primary reason for the existence of the L&MR was the cheap carriage of merchandise, the great number of passengers during the first few months coupled with a desperate shortage of locomotives led to a postponement in the starting of a goods service. The first experimental load of merchandise was taken along the railway by *Planet* on 4 December 1830. It consisted of 18 waggons laden with cotton, flour, oatmeal and malt, and with 15 persons travelling on it, the train weighed about 80 tons. The journey, including three five-minute stops, took almost three hours. By this date there were ten engines on the line and in the expectation of more being delivered soon, further experiments were made with a view to starting the regular service in 1831.

It was the Company's wish to have all this traffic handled by carriers, as it was on the canals, and contracts had already been entered into with Harrison of the Grocers Company and with Pickford & Co.[21] Harrison undertook to collect and deliver goods, load and unload the trains, collect the freight charges, accept the risk of bad debts and pay over to the Railway the amount collected, less 2s. a ton on goods into Manchester and 3s. on goods outwards. Pickford's, established in 1646, began their long and close association with the railways on 22 November 1830, when their offer of £2 a trip for one 'contract waggon' was accepted. This waggon had a movable body which was transferred between a horse-drawn dray and a flat railway truck at each end of the line, and was thus the first application of the container principle on the L&MR.

In January 1831 the Company re-affirmed its decision to become a carrier itself, but not exclusively, as it still hoped to attract many more private firms. An advertisement of 3 February announced that the railway would be open to carriers and coach proprietors on payment of tolls from 1 May 1831, and

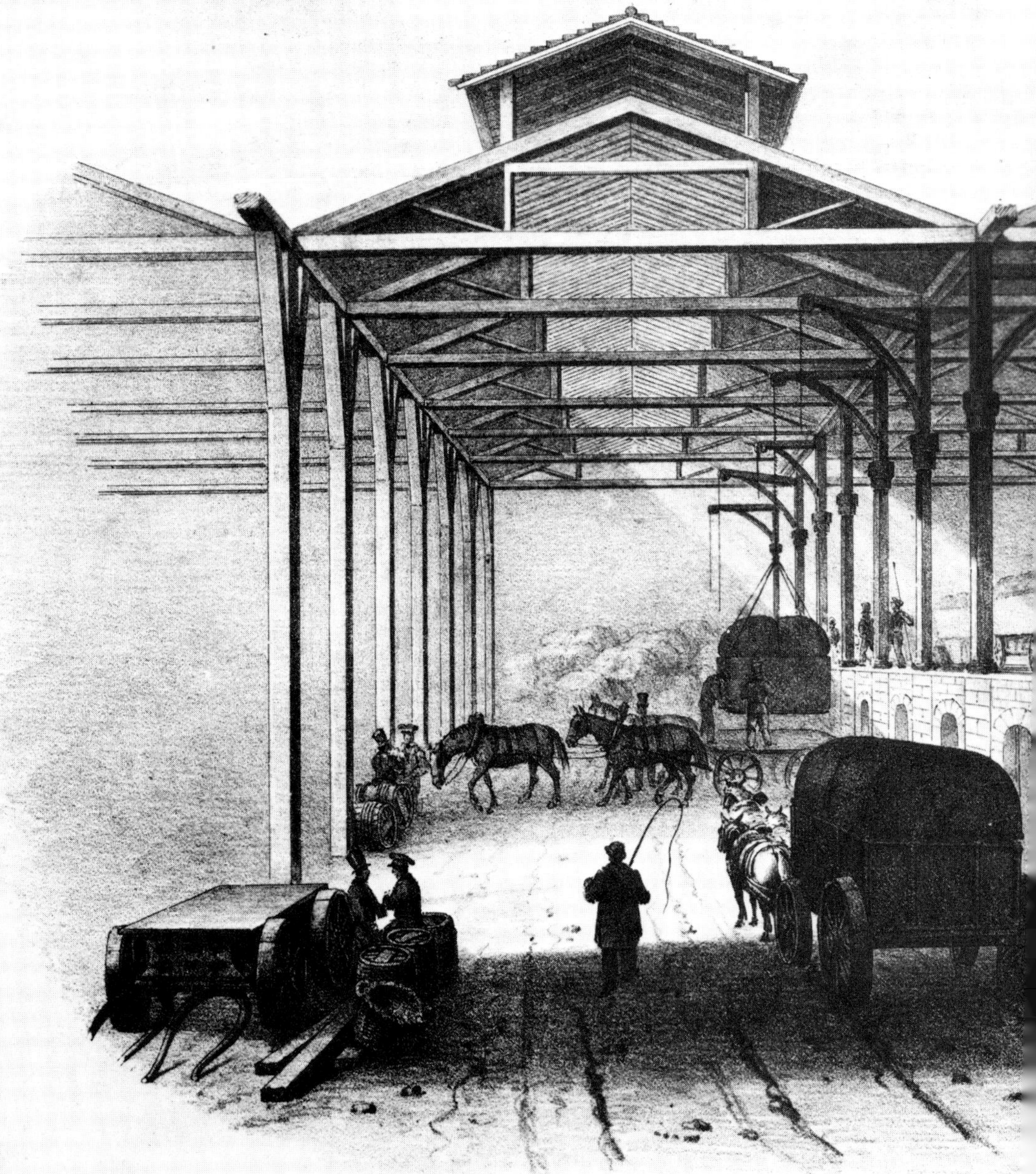

that patterns of approved carriages and waggons could be seen at the Company's yards.

In 1830 the Company purchased one Cheshire acre of land on the north side of the line at Broad Green, about 3½ miles from Liverpool, on which to build a cattle station; this was completed in the summer of 1831 along with the adjoining gate house, and a shed was erected later to protect the sheep carriages. At the Manchester end a wharf for cattle, sheep and pigs was built on the north side of the line adjoining Oldfield Lane; here the waggons stood against a platform upon which the pens were constructed, enabling the animals to be driven straight into the trains, or from the train into the pens. In 1843 a separate pig station was built in Charles Street, Manchester, to handle this rapidly-increasing traffic.

To judge the effect on livestock, four donkeys were taken experimentally on a flat truck in the rear of a coach train in September 1830, and were said to have behaved with more gravity than many of the passengers.[22] The Company started carrying pigs on 12 May 1831 when one truckload of 49 travelled to Manchester; sheep and horned cattle were carried from October. The Board was concerned in May 1832 at the small number of sheep and lambs carried and reduced the rate, but the pig trade was flourishing. By September 1833 over 1500 a week were carried to Manchester—about the same number as went by canal.

Originally a charge was made for each animal but after a while the Company charged £1 per waggon for sheep and 25s. for cattle and pigs, the owner being allowed to load as many as he chose, at his own risk. The double-deck sheep carriages were often used for pigs, 50 being crammed into one vehicle, and their squealing, it was said, could be heard above the noise of the train. In 1841 the Society for the Prevention of Cruelty to Animals protested to the L&MR against the 'wanton cruelty inflicted on pigs conveyed by railway, in the manner of loading them and in the general treatment by the pig drovers who had charge of them.' The drovers brought the animals across from Ireland and an early account refers to them clubbing the pigs on the snout to quieten them.[23]

Within a few months of the commencement of goods traffic a great variety of merchandise was being handled and numerous enquiries were received for special rates or facilities. In August 1831 the Company was asked to carry gunpowder but, because of the fire risk, refused to transport it either by way of normal trade or as army stores. Two months later the

108 *Containers being loaded on to trains*

firm of Leech & Harrison sought terms for the conveyance of boxes of gold, the Company accepting the risk of loss; they were recommended to send it with one of their own clerks by passenger train as ordinary luggage, up to 60lb. being allowed free, with no risk to the Company. For some unexplained reason the charge for carrying oysters was reduced from 14s. to 10s. a ton in January 1832, and in April of that year the railway agreed to haul manure from Manchester to Chat Moss Farm at 1s.6d. a ton, the parties concerned to load and unload it at such times as would not interfere with normal traffic. Special arrangements were made from time to time for other traffic, including salt and copper ore.

The first instance of milk being conveyed by passenger train occurred on 12 March 1832 when the Treasurer reported having received an application to carry three or four cans from Newton to Liverpool morning and evening. The Board agreed to a trial period at a charge of 1s. per five-gallon can, returning the empties free, the milk to be brought on the stations with no trouble or cost to the Company. Apparently the system was firmly established by February 1838, when several farmers sought arrangements to send milk from Newton to Eccles and elsewhere.

At least one stage coach proprietor, Wetherall, made arrangements in August 1831 for his coaches and passengers to be carried between Liverpool and Manchester on the passenger trains, the Company charging £1 for the coach; 5s. was charged for each inside passenger and 3s.6d. for outside passengers. A similar arrangement was made between the Company and the Warrington & Newton Railway in May 1832 for the carriage of the London coach between Liverpool and Warrington, and this service survived until the opening of the GJR in 1837.[24]

A considerable traffic in parcels developed at an early stage in the Company's history. Bretherton the coach proprietor contracted to run a parcel cart between the Dale Street Booking Office and Crown Street Station making 42 trips a week for £3 3s. from March 1832, and when the horse and spring cart of the Manchester contractor was seized for debt in May 1833 the Company purchased it and operated its own collection and delivery service.[25]

On collection of the parcels at either Dale Street or Market Street Offices, they were placed in an inner bag which was then locked in an outer one, and taken to the Liverpool or Manchester stations to be sent by the next passenger train. When a parcel containing £20 disappeared from a locked bag between Manchester and Liverpool on 16 January 1833 the Board ordered all the locks to be changed. This did not prevent a similar mysterious loss of a parcel five months later. On this occasion a parcel was sent to a Liverpool firm, which '... was alleged to have contained, when sent to the office in Manchester, 27 sovereigns and a five-pound note; but when opened it contained only three pence in copper.' The remedy this time was to change the staff, all the clerks and porters from Market Street being sent to Liverpool Road, to be replaced by men from that station; no further losses were recorded. The Company met claims for these incidents as it did when passengers'

109 *Oldfield Lane Cattle Station, near Manchester, 1833*

luggage was lost; in one case of lost or stolen luggage in July 1831 which the owner said contained £136, the Company donated £50.

Occasionally brakesmen were discovered carrying parcels on a private basis for friends, or as a sideline, undercutting the Company's charges. Another profitable activity in the goods department was the sale by the Superintendent of the sweepings from the Corn Room floor; this amounted to about 6s. a week, but when the quantity of corn spilled threatened to become excessive, the Board stopped the practice.

By 1831 an increasing quantity of wines and spirits was being carried and to protect itself against any fraudulent claims for losses, the Company required small samples to be deposited with its agents; these could be claimed within 14 days of the carriage of the main consignment if the Company's charges had been paid. In fact the samples were rarely claimed, and accumulated in the railway warehouses - under lock and key after the seepage of several gallons in the direction of the warehousemen. On average the Company collected about 140 gallons a year, and despite the helpful and apparently disinterested suggestions as to its disposal advanced periodically by the employees, it was all given away to the local hospitals, there to be used for the purpose of rendering insensible those about to undergo operations.

Occasionally in the early days goods sent to Liverpool for shipment were put on to the wrong vessels, involving the Company in claims for compensation. In July 1831 a bale was wrongly sent to Pernambuco resulting in a claim for £94, which the Company paid. The bale was eventually returned and sold to the original owners at $17\frac{1}{2}\%$ discount in February 1832.

All the shunting and 'marshalling of the loads' at sidings by the line was done by locomotives, but at Lime Street the carriages were marshalled into trains by horses in teams of four. The jobbing engines worked the coal, limestone, manure and ballast trains, and assisted wherever they were required.

The directors gave much anxious thought to the matter of fire prevention, both in the warehouses and on the trains. Orders were issued in July 1831 that no lights were to be carried about in the Manchester Warehouses except in glass lanterns and shortly afterwards a fire engine and large cistern of water were installed there, while the gangway between the two buildings was fireproofed; in January 1833 locomotives were prohibited from approaching too close to these buildings. On 18 December 1835 two bags of cotton caught fire in the top room of No 2 Cotton Warehouse, and were thrown out of the window into the timber yard below, without much damage having been done; an enquiry failed to trace the cause of the fire. Generally the precautions taken seem to have been effective as there is no record of any serious fire occurring on the Company's premises.

During the early experiments with goods trains the fire risk to cotton became apparent and double tarpaulins of 'unbleached Russia duck' - a kind of tough canvas - were ordered for all waggons, as a protection against both fire and weather.

There were, however, several cases of goods trains catching fire, the first recorded incident occurring on a train hauled by *North Star* in July 1831, when six bags of Sea Island cotton were destroyed. Near Patricroft on 30 May 1834 a waggon and its load of cotton, silk and woollen goods in the Liverpool train drawn by *Patentee* caught fire from a cinder dropped by the locomotive, the fire on this occasion being extinguished by water from the Worsley Canal. This led to a regulation that the brakesmen must ride on the last waggon giving them a better chance of discovering a fire in time to have it speedily put out. The Company compensated the owners, in this case paying £654 and subsequently recovering about £300 when the damaged materials were sold by auction.

Until this time it had been thought that the fires were caused by sparks from the engine chimneys, particularly when the trains were heavy and the steam full on, and in fact several were started in this way. Grass and furze along the line were set on fire as were several fir trees on the slopes of the Broad Green Embankment; as mentioned, passengers in the open 2nd class carriages often had holes burnt in their clothes before the fitting of roofs to these coaches. The engines were provided with spiral wire cages called bonnets strapped to the centre of the chimneys, and a device referred to as an umbrella was tried, the object being to deflect the sparks downwards; the owners of other engines working over the L&MR were ordered to take the same precautions. It was discovered, however, that the chief danger lay in the dropping of cinders from the locomotives and Brunel testified that the line of the railway glowed red in the night from the quantity that had fallen. Some of these cinders were thrown on to the wheels and if caught between the wooden spokes, were whirled round until, becoming incandescent, they set fire to the wheel or waggon floor. Waggons that had been burned were always the second or third from the engine, whereas sparks from the chimneys formed ' . . . a very large arch and come down farther behind the train'.[26] From a statement by Hardman Earle that ash-boxes had been fitted to all the engines by 1836, it would seem that they had none originally; the new boxes required emptying every 15 or 20 miles.

On 22 July 1835, when *Swiftsure* was descending the Whiston Incline with five waggons of silk, a man by the roadside signalled to the driver that the middle truck was on fire. When the train stopped several hundred yards farther on the driver and fireman managed with great difficulty to detach the last two waggons and pull the rest away; these were totally consumed by the fire, which left the rails red-hot. The Company was not legally liable since the consignment, being of exceptional value, should have been insured, but as they had omitted to post notices to this effect in the Warehouses or York Street Receiving House, they were advised by Counsel not to contest the claims for over £3000 lodged by the silk merchants.

Only two months later several crates of glass sent by Pilkingtons from St Helens to Manchester were lost when the train caught fire at Patricroft, and £88 was paid in compensation.

Despite the precautions taken, fires continued to break out on goods trains, and in 1839 the Management Committee held an enquiry into an incident at Lambs Cottage, Chat Moss, on Saturday afternoon, 9 March. A fire started near the top of a waggon loaded with cotton, the fourth in a train of 20 vehicles, and the driver, Richard Hesketh, quickly stopped and then ran to separate the burning load from the 16 waggons behind. He then drew the four waggons forward out of reach of the remainder and detached the fourth waggon from the other three. Now he, with the fireman, brakesman and a policeman, managed to extinguish fires that had started on the vehicles on either side of it, at no little personal risk to themselves, since the fifth waggon was laden with casks of oil. They then attempted to pull the burning cotton bags from the now isolated waggon and Hesketh told the directors that more could have been saved if they had had long poles with hooks; his suggestion was adopted and from that time all luggage engines carried a number of such poles. The Committee recorded its opinion '. . . that the men had striven hard to save the property in their charge', and awarded them 10s. each and made good the loss of Hesketh's hat and watch.

Both the Royal Exchange and Sun Fire Offices were asked their rates for insuring goods in warehouses and in transit but neither gave acceptable quotations in May 1836. The Company had been insuring silk goods at 1s. per £100 and continued to do so, the Insurance Committee recommending that a fund of £20,000 be built up against fire and other contingencies. Special rates were quoted for occasional consignments; for £2000 worth of silver from Liverpool to Manchester the insurance was $\frac{1}{8}$% and the freight charge 3s.%.

Goods trains were often long and heavy and when only one locomotive was employed there was a great temptation for the driver to overload the safety valve, thereby increasing the boiler pressure. Lawson, the driver of *Sun*, took 20 loaded waggons to Manchester with his safety valves regulated to 60lb. psi instead of 50lb on the instructions of Ralph Hutchison, one of the engineers from R Stephenson & Co., attached to the L&MR in May 1832.

An extraordinary performance was recorded by the then new locomotives, *Samson* and *Goliah*, when one took 52 trucks of cotton and the other 48; amounting to almost 500 tons, this was the entire cargo of a ship which had been discharged direct into the waggons and sent straight to Manchester. Robert Stannard and Forsyth found four broken rails near Eccles after the trains had passed.[27]

As an example of the co-operation of the railway with the traders, a man left Manchester by an early-morning train in June 1836, bought 150 tons of cotton in Liverpool, took it back to Manchester and sold it; returning to Liverpool he bought another 150 tons which was delivered in Manchester, all in 12 hours.[28]

What must have been the longest train to have run over the L&MR to that time arrived at Liverpool from Manchester on Monday morning, 29 January 1838; it comprised 113 waggons of merchandise drawn by five engines, and according to the *Liverpool Mercury*, was over 600 yards long.

The traffic flow was generally towards Manchester, anything up to half the waggons returning empty to Liverpool. Some business had developed from the wayside stations by November 1831 when arrangements were made to attach goods waggons to the light second class passenger trains serving these stations. By February 1833 so many of these trains were being delayed by picking up goods on the road that an engine was sent from each end, after the last train '. . . to clear away all the road goods and coals that may be on the line'. Within a year several of these 'pickup trains' were running every day collecting goods and waggons that had accumulated at the stopping places and junctions, the Company's object being '. . . rather to lay the foundation of a beneficial intercourse in future, than with a view to any immediate profit.'

In the earlier years of the Company's existence, the question was raised in the privacy of the Board Room as to the general policy or expediency of allowing merchandise to be conveyed at all by the railway, since the Company became carriers reluctantly after failing to induce the established firms to undertake the business. Booth was of the opinion that they had no option, for if they neglected to provide a goods service a rival railway company would be established in a very few months. The volume of business brought to the railway by the carriers was negligible; Pickfords, after seeking an abatement of the charge of 35s. per trip for their waggon in 1836, decided in 1837 to run it only three days a week, for which the Company's charge for toll and conveyance was now 50s. By 1844 five firms were involved, the largest being Pickford and Kenworthy. Some of the smaller carriers were quite unscrupulous in their business methods; one of these, Barnby, Faulkner & Co. in June 1844, fraudulently intercepted 10 bags of cotton addressed to the Company, altered the delivery note and took charge of the cotton themselves; (the outcome of the prosecution which followed is not recorded in the Company's Minutes).

The receipts from goods and coal traffic increased from about £53,000 in 1831 to reach a peak of £120,000 in 1838, after which they remained fairly steady at over £100,000 a year; they never exceeded the receipts from passenger traffic. The receipts from 1838 were augmented by the traffic from the GJR and in that year, while the facilities at Wapping were being extended, the local shopkeepers complained to the Company of the loss of trade arising from the congestion in the streets caused by long lines of carts waiting with loads of goods for the railway. As the goods traffic increased, so did the tendency to start in the small hours, and by 1841 the first luggage trains were leaving Manchester at 3 a.m.

Periodically the canals would engage in a price-cutting contest with the L&MR, leading on one occasion to the Company waiving the tolls payable by carriers. In April 1842, however, the Old Quay Navigation, the Bridgewater Trust and the L&MR reached an agreement to fix a common scale of charges.

When the link with the M&LR was made in 1844 the Company became carriers to, and appointed agents in, Oldham, Rochdale, Todmorton, Wakefield, Leeds and Hull. About this time they reclassified the merchandise into three categories, this about three years before the Railway Clearing House was able to institute its general scheme of goods classification. The L&MR, like the GJR, was an early, but not a founder member of the Railway Clearing House.

CHAPTER ELEVEN

Accidents

Inevitably, from the experimental nature of most of the operations on the L&MR in its early days, there were a number of accidents to trains, staff and the general public. The causes were manifold, ranging from the failure of locomotives and rolling stock and the inexperience or sheer incompetence of some of the men, to the negligence or foolhardiness of the public. It is very apparent, however, that many railwaymen met with injury or death through a conscientious determination to carry out duties afterwards recognised to be dangerous. The accounts of these accidents throw much light on the early working of the railway; they illustrate, too, how the Company built up a set of rules and regulations and gradually evolved a rudimentary system of signalling which would eventually do much to eliminate the personal tragedies and suffering which from time to time occurred.

Despite the number of train accidents, very few involved the death of passengers; only one fatal accident occurred in the first two years, although nearly one million passengers had travelled on the line.[1] The figure compared very favourably with the numbers killed and injured on the roads. Some passengers did not realise that they were travelling faster on a train than they had ever moved before; within a few weeks of the opening a passenger lost a limb through jumping off a train travelling at speed. Many passengers paid scant regard to the Company's rules, instructions or advice.

Every accident was investigated by the Board or the Management Committee, who examined witnesses and studied reports from the engineers; they usually discovered negligence or a disregard of instructions to have been the cause, and exacted penalties accordingly.

Theodore Rathbone produced a list of all the accidents that had occurred since before the opening until April 1834 for production to the Secretary of the L&BR, but the Board considered it inexpedient to furnish such a list as, without an explanation of the circumstances in each case, a wrong impression might be created, and it was withheld. In March 1834 a request for a similar list had been received from William Tothill of the GWR Board, and this appears to have been met.

In the foregoing pages many accidents to trains and to individuals have been mentioned. There follows a brief account of others that occurred year by year during the lifetime of the L&MR.

The first mishap after the opening occurred on 7 October at Kenyon when a carriage wheel snapped in two on a train being worked by *North Star*. The carriage was derailed but no-one was hurt; nevertheless some highly exaggerated accounts of the incident appeared in the press.[2]

On 8 December 1830 a collision occurred at the junction for Elton Head Colliery. The 4.30 p.m. from Liverpool drawn by *Meteor*, was preceded by *Rocket* acting as night pilot engine, but the pilot was over a mile ahead of the train instead of the stipulated 400 yds, and in the interval four labourers tried to take a waggon of stones across the points. They threatened the policeman who remonstrated with them, but before they could get the waggon clear of the main line, *Meteor* came up, struck the waggon and was thrown off the road. After an hour *Rocket* came back to find the train, and eventually took it on to Manchester. Warrants were issued against the four men, who had absconded, and Mark Wakefield was ordered to observe the rules when piloting with *Rocket*.

The new locomotive *Goliah* had been at work on the Sutton Incline for only a few days when she was taken down the wrong line by Simon Fenwick and struck a Bolton train, causing some damage. Anthony Harding and John Melling were both admonished by the Board for concealing the facts concerning the incident. About three weeks later, in April 1831, this engine was derailed at the top of the bank by an incorrectly placed switch.

On 1 September 1831 while the 7 a.m. 1st Class train to Manchester was running along the Brosley Embankment the axle of *Etna* gave way and the engine ran down the slope; two carriages were overturned but there were no casualties. An almost identical accident befell the 7 a.m. train to Liverpool on 7 December. As it was approaching Glazebrook Bridge the cranked axle of the *Fury* broke and the driver McCrie immediately shut off steam while the two guards applied their brakes. At about 20 yds beyond the bridge the engine left the rails and plunged down the embankment, dragging the first two carriages after her; these overturned and the passengers had to be got out of the windows. The other two carriages, one of them the mail coach, remained on the top of the slope for some minutes, long enough for the passengers to escape, when the lower ones, sliding farther down, pulled the others after them. Apart from one or two passengers cut by glass, none was seriously injured and they all went on by the next train. The Board asked Sandars to prepare a statement for the Liverpool, Manchester and London papers, and ordered that only engines with the newly-strengthened crank axles should go with coach trains.

The B&LR engine *Liverpool* was involved in two accidents within three days of each other. On Wednesday 22 February 1832 it ran against some 1st Class carriages at Newton Bridge when driven by an engineman named Rogers, who claimed that it was foggy, and although he 'laid down the brakes' he could not stop in time. Mr Dixon, of Mather Dixon & Co., who was on the L&MR train said it was cloudy but not foggy, and two directors said that they saw Rogers drunk the previous Sunday. The following Saturday another driver, Robinson, ran *Liverpool* into a Warrington train at Newton Junction, this time badly damaging the locomotive.

A train crossing Chat Moss in October 1832 was derailed by a switch incorrectly set; the *Mars*, a waggon and a Blue coach were damaged and two women passengers had their legs crushed. Buckley, the switchman, was discharged.

The first train crash in which a passenger lost his life occurred in fog on the morning of 23 November 1832. The 7.15 from Manchester arrived at Rainhill at 9 o'clock having been delayed en route, and was held up for a further ten minutes for the loading of passengers' luggage on to the 1st Class coach. At this moment the passengers in the rear open carriage saw the 8 a.m. fast train from Manchester looming up through the heavy mist and shouted to its driver to stop. Although already warned by the gateman, the train driver could not pull up on the greasy rails, and despite the fact that '... the managers of the stationary train contrived to get it into motion', diminishing slightly the force of impact, a violent collision ensued. The *Fury* smashed the last carriage completely and ripped away the front of the gatekeeper's house. A young soldier going to join his regiment in Ireland, was killed outright and another sustained serious injuries.[3] Strict orders were issued that, in case of fog, gatemen and others must leave the collecting of tickets or stowing away of luggage, and run back 300 yds to stop oncoming trains.

Three passengers were killed outright and a fourth died later from an accident involving two B&LR goods trains and a 2nd Class L&MR train on Friday, 1 February 1833 at about 4 p.m. The Bolton engine *Bee* from Liverpool had stopped on Parr Moss for the machinery to be adjusted and after a while *Ajax* came up with the passenger train for Manchester, stopping a short distance away. The guard, after warning a passenger to keep his seat, went to enquire of the *Bee*'s driver the cause of the stoppage, when a boiler tube on *Ajax* burst, sending clouds of steam across the line; by this time several passengers had alighted, as passengers always did on such occasions, but the engineman, John Wakefield, was too occupied with his locomotive to notice them. Meanwhile the *Liverpool* was coming up on the other line, its driver having seen the *Bee* in the distance but not the *Ajax* behind it, when all was enveloped in the cloud of steam. The passengers standing on the line could neither see the *Liverpool* approaching nor hear her above the roar from escaping steam and water pouring on to the fire; neither could the *Liverpool*'s driver see them, and although by now slackening speed, the first he knew of their presence was the jolt of his engine as it passed over their bodies. The brakesman was thrown off one of the four waggons derailed by the corpses. The inquest on three victims passed almost unnoticed, but that of the fourth, who died in hospital, was reported fully in the Manchester press.[4] The jury returned a verdict of manslaughter against Nathaniel Eckersley, driver of *Liverpool*, and he was imprisoned in Lancaster Castle; the L&MR sent a witness to speak in his favour and at the assizes in March he was acquitted. Following this accident notices were placed in every carriage warning passengers not to leave their seats in similar circumstances.

Another accident occurred in fog on Sutton Incline

in February 1833 when a passenger train from Manchester ran into some waggons left on the line. Despite the Company's strict injunction, no warning of obstruction was given, and the man responsible was fined £5.

On Saturday 2 March a disaster occurred on the Sutton Incline when a goods train drawn by *Manchester* went out of control. Among the witnesses was Ralph Thompson who was half-way down the bank with *Goliah* when he saw *Manchester* at the top, coming on very fast and rapidly gaining upon him. When only about 30 yards away from *Goliah*, *Manchester* jumped the rails '... and was almost broken to pieces'; the engineman M'Carris was terribly injured and died later. Several observers had never seen a goods train run so fast before and one heard something break on the engine immediately before it crashed. Among the claims was one for £42, the value of 15 pigs killed in one of the waggons; the drover was thrown out and escaped serious injury.

Two accidents occurred on Sunday 17 November 1833, both resulting from stoppages for locomotive repairs. The morning 1st Class train from Liverpool, halted for engine repairs at the top of Whiston Incline, was struck by a train following closely behind, its mail coach being badly damaged and several passengers hurt by the force of the impact. The 1st Class train from Manchester had stopped between Newton and Warrington Junction because a cylinder cover had become loose when a W&NR engine came up from Newton propelling its coaches, and with no look-out. Again the mail coach was heavily damaged, and many passengers seriously shaken. The W&NR were informed that the L&MR held them liable for the damage caused by their employees' neglect.

The year 1834 was fairly clear of accidents, although on 11 April a farm cart attempted to cross the Whiston Incline from one field to another when a train coming down at speed was only 40 yds away. Both horses were killed, their driver had his arm and leg broken, the engine overturned and its tender was smashed, but no passengers were hurt. Although it would appear that the cart driver was at fault, the Company gave the farmer £20.

In July the directors were told that a 40-waggon train had got the better of the brakesman in the tunnel and on reaching the Wapping end had left the rails and knocked out one of the iron pillars supporting the warehouse. The two men in charge were each fined a week's wages and an order was issued that trains going down the tunnel were not to exceed 20 waggons.

On 20 February 1835 *Firefly*, the 'picking-up engine' with a luggage train was thrown off the road and down a slope into a hedge on the north side of the line at the foot of the Sutton Incline 'owing to a crossing plate being out'. One of its waggons took the opposite direction and collided with some waggons placed between the engine and carriages of the 8 a.m. from Manchester which was passing at that moment. Luggage was strewn all over the line, but no passenger was hurt. Charles Callan, the engineman of *Firefly*, was held to blame and fined £1.

An occasional engineman, Abel Jones, ran the *Swiftsure* into a stationary luggage train at Parkside on 19 November, crushing a labourer between two waggons; the man died later and Jones lost his turn on the promotion list for entering a regular watering station at 6 mph.

The year ended with *Titan* running into one of Bourne and Robinson's coal trains drawn by their engine *Collier*. The lamp of *Collier*'s train was dirty and dim, but as the L&MR driver had complained of this some days before the Company was able to disclaim liability for the wrecked coal trucks.

The year 1836 was conspicuous for the number of accidents. Traffic on the line was increasing rapidly at this time, particularly the number of trains run by the various collieries and branch lines.

When the drawbar between *York* and her tender broke at the top of the Sutton Incline one day in January, the driver and fireman were thrown to the ground and the brakesman jumped off the train to attend to them. The engine, with tender and train after it, ran down the incline and on to Collins Green, where it stopped without further incident.

During the enginemen's strike of February 1836 there was a curious occurrence, apparently resulting from the inexperience of the relief driver of the Sutton Banking engine. Having assisted a Turner, Evans coal train up the bank, the engine continued to propel it along the Rainhill Level. As the train gathered speed the axle of a waggon in the middle broke, and the consequent strain on the draw chain caused it to break, leaving the engine to proceed with only half its train. The bank engine, still pushing from the rear, broke to pieces several of the waggons which were prevented from moving on by the disabled one. No action was taken against the driver, and Locke, acting as referee, awarded the owners £60 compensation.

On 29 March at Salford Station the 5 p.m. coal train from Liverpool with *Patentee*, driven by Pierce Naylor, ran into the *Leeds* engine which was crossing out of the pig siding where she had left six waggons, and was proceeding with her luggage trucks to

Manchester; *Leeds* and several waggons were badly damaged. John Jones, the policeman who had been absent for a few minutes from his post, was cautioned but forgiven on this occasion in consequence of his good behaviour and long service.

While running near Bury Lane with the 5 p.m. 1st Class coach train from Liverpool on 17 April the front axle of *Patentee* broke, causing the engine to cross the south line and dive headlong down a slope, pulling two carriages after her into a field. Engine and coaches were seriously damaged but the passengers 'escaped without much injury'. After this accident the Board ordered safety mounds to be constructed on all embankments of over ten feet in height.

During this year sections of the line were being relaid with the heavier rails, the work being done without interrupting the traffic. At Parkside the rails were supported by stone blocks standing like pedestals, no ballast having yet been placed round them, when the Sunday morning train on 6 May came off the line. The impact of the wheels against a succession of open stone blocks not only alarmed the passengers but wrecked a number of Blue coaches. On 24 October *Firefly*, taking the 3 p.m. Blue train to Liverpool, was derailed near Parkside Station and ran into the side drain with the tender and two horse carriages; all were damaged although not seriously. Again, new rails being laid there were not properly secured.

In October 1836 *Lightning* ran over a platelayers' lorry left on the line; her ashpan was torn away and jammed under the tender causing a long delay. The Board decided to charge the contractor, Cummings, with the cost of the damage, £45, but some months later released him from liability. That same month the breaking down of one of the Haydock coal waggons while being assisted up the Sutton Incline resulted in *Thunderer* being thrown off the road and its front axle and springs broken.

Joseph Armstrong, engineman of *Ajax*, collided with the 5 p.m. passenger train on 21 November while crossing Chat Moss; he and the driver of *Liver*, Edward Armstrong,[5] were brought before the Management Committee and were spoken to very seriously on the necessity for exercising great care at night.

When the axle of a 1st Class coach broke on the evening of 30 November great alarm was caused to the passengers from the fact that three waggons separated the engine from the carriages, and the guard was unable to make the engineman hear; it took nearly ten minutes to stop the train with the carriage brakes, but no passenger was hurt.

Among other incidents in that year, *Vulcan* with a Blue train ran into some stationary waggons on 13 June and her driver, Hesketh,[6] was discharged for gross carelessness. In July a driver and fireman were dismissed for propelling one train of loaded waggons against a slower train in front of them and later the same month *York* and *Vesta* were in collision on the Whiston Bank. A waggon axle breaking on 12 October near Cross Lane caused '... a piece of brandy and a small cask of wine to be stoved in.' Green thought part of the liquor had been saved, an unusual event where this commodity was concerned; the Company had rarely profited from any salvage of liquor.

The year 1837 soon saw the departure from the Company's service of Henry Holden and his fireman, of the *Eclipse*. These two had driven their luggage train into the rear of a coach train, badly shaking the passengers therein.

Locomotives following too closely behind another engine or train caused several accidents. On 6 March 1837 *Lightning*, driven by engineman Murphy, had assisted a train up the Whiston Bank and had gone on to the top of the Sutton Incline to reverse on to the south line, but before he could complete the shunt, he heard *Milo* and *Orion* almost upon him with the early luggage train. He started his engine forward again, hoping to run ahead, when *Milo* struck his tender and was derailed. Alarmed, Murphy jumped off *Lightning* without shutting off steam, and the engine sped down the Sutton Incline to continue uninterrupted to the Rock Hole beyond Eccles where, the fire and steam nearly spent, a policeman jumped on to the engine and brought her safely into Manchester. All the drivers and firemen concerned were reprimanded after the Board's enquiry.

On 8 April the 7 a.m. from Liverpool ran into some coal trucks left on the line where the passenger trains stopped at Manchester Station. Several passengers were seriously hurt, coaches and trucks damaged and the buffer-plank of *Phoenix* broken.

Pierce Naylor and his fireman were each fined a fortnight's wages in May for running their engine against a shunting waggon, and knocking it into the columns of the omnibus shed at Manchester, bringing two of them down.

The early morning luggage train from Manchester was running near Collins Green at about 6 a.m. on 16 June 1837 with two engines in front and *Cyclops* propelling from the rear, when the leading engine '... dropped between the rails'; the track had been laid the night before, but no ballast had yet been put around the stone blocks. *Cyclops* pushed the train off the line totally destroying five or six waggons and scattering their loads in all directions. Hirst, the engineman, was held responsible, and although '... doing his best to help them on', was aware of the strict instructions regarding the propelling of trains, so was discharged;[7] platelayers were also ordered to ensure that the track was secure before leaving the job at night.

At Broad Green Cattle Station on the evening of 12 September 1837 the *Etna* with the 7 p.m. 1st Class train from Manchester ran into a stationary sheep and merchandise train that had stopped to shunt some sheep waggons. The engineman of the freight train thought he had plenty of time before the 6 p.m. market train from Manchester came up, as this made many stops; he was unaware that it had broken down on Chat Moss and had been passed by the 1st Class train. By the time the approaching train was recognised as the express it was too late to signal it to stop, but its driver, Ellerington, was considered to have been incautious and was reprimanded.

Both lines were obstructed for hours on the afternoon of Saturday 23 September 1837 owing to a mistaken signal at the foot of Whiston Incline. The fireman of *Orion*, with 20 waggons from Liverpool, signalled to the policeman for the banking engine to follow him, but the driver of *Hercules* mistook the constable's signal for one to go before the luggage train, a procedure which was sometimes necessary when the last waggon carried an overhanging load of timber or iron. He put on steam and, emerging from the siding as *Orion* came past, hit her tender; both engines were derailed and lay across the tracks in opposite directions. Passenger trains were stopped on either side of the obstruction and the passengers transferred to other trains, the line eventually being cleared at 8 p.m. As it was a clear case of misunderstanding no penalties followed, but the rule that banking engines must always assist from the rear was strongly reiterated.

The 9 o'clock coach train from Liverpool came near to disaster on 22 November 1837 when one of Turner Evans & Co.'s coal engines attempted to cross the railway at the Haydock Crossing, Warrington Junction, just as the passenger train was passing. The colliery engineman, frightened, had jumped from his locomotive instead of holding on to the brake, and the engine actually caught the steps of the last coach. Correct signals given by the policeman had been ignored and Turner, Evans were instructed to enforce better discipline on the part of their drivers.

At Huyton Quarry Station passengers had to walk along the line from the crossroad to the signal house where the trains stopped. After a man had been killed here by a GJR train in November 1837, a footwalk for passengers was fenced off from the line.

The year 1838 opened with two incidents towards the end of January. William Wood ran his locomotive *Patentee* into the *Phoenix* which was standing quietly on the Whiston Incline, owing to a vague signal from a man left on watch while the policeman went to breakfast. The Board imposed a fine of 5s. and charged Wood with the task of apportioning it between the policeman and his assistant, and of collecting it. In the second case Richard Purdie, engineman of *Vulcan*, and his fireman were dismissed for negligence in running into the back of a Sunday morning 1st Class train on Barton Embankment; two coaches were badly damaged and several passengers seriously cut and bruised.

On a wet Saturday afternoon, 24 March, the *York* with 18 waggons bound for Manchester was going down the Sutton Incline with the brakes of four trucks pinned down. The driver of a train on the opposite line signalled an obstruction ahead as he passed *York*, whereupon her driver T. Hesketh reversed the motion and applied the tender brake. When half-way down he saw a policeman waving his flag so he then sent his fireman to pin down more waggon brakes but to no effect, the rails being too wet. At the foot of the bank was the GJR engine *Sirocco* with two waggons, into which the *York* crashed at 12 mph, demolishing them and five of its own. Amos, the GJR engineman, had reversed his locomotive and could not get her into forward gear again; he said the levers were jammed and he had borrowed a crowbar with which to force them. Hesketh claimed that he could have moved *Sirocco* and was probably justified in his opinion that Amos was incompetent. The Companies each bore their own losses; in the case of the L&MR, several hundred pounds worth of wine, spirits, porter, tea and coffee had been destroyed.

Pierce Naylor, now engineman of *Rapid*, was again before the Board in May 1838 after having run into a coal train crossing on to the main line from a siding at Huyton Quarry. The policeman concerned admitted not having picked up his red flag, while Naylor and his fireman were not keeping a sharp lookout in any case, but were both sitting down when their train passed the Whiston engine shed; all three were cautioned against any further offence.

In the same month *Mercury* and *Orion* were both damaged owing to the former having been stopped to discharge ballast on the Broad Green Embankment. As the line curved at this point the driver of *Orion* did not realise that the ballast train was on the same line and ran into it. Both drivers were reprimanded and told that in future the fireman was to be sent back 400 yds to warn oncoming trains of ballasting operations.

A train crashed into and broke the large spring buffer at Lime Street Station on 17 June having come down the tunnel without pilot or brakesman. The two guards supposed these men were on the train and allowed it to go too far down before applying their brakes, by which time it was too late to stop it.

The policeman at Newton Junction on 22 June opened the gates to allow a Haydock coal train to cross the main lines and then went towards the viaduct to stop any approaching train. The driver of *Star* with the 2 p.m. from Liverpool had passed the Viaduct Foundry when he saw the signal; although all the brakes were applied, *Star* cut straight through the coal train, throwing waggons and coal engine off the line. Many coach panels were scratched or broken but no passengers were hurt, and the driver, of previous good conduct, was reprimanded.

On Saturday, 1 September 1838 the 7 p.m. train from Manchester hauled by *Sun*, arrived at Edge Hill Station at such a speed that both engine and train went into the siding and crashed into three blue boxes, or brake waggons, fortunately standing at the end of the siding. These, although destroyed, absorbed the shock of the collision, preventing serious injury to the passengers. William Holmes the engineman claimed that the reversing gear would not act and the brakes were ineffective owing to the wet weather. The Committee considered that he was guilty of a gross violation of regulations in coming at such a furious speed into the station, and he was discharged.

At eight o'clock on Monday night, 12 November 1838, a long train of 43 loaded waggons was toiling steadily up the Whiston Incline, drawn by two engines in front and assisted by another two behind, when the leading engine, *Patentee*, blew up, with a report heard in Prescot and for miles around. The engine broke away from the train and shot some 400 yds ahead before coming to a halt. The engineman, Charles Warburton and his fireman, Jones, a lad of 17, were found in the dark fields 40 yds from the line, both dead.

At the inquest it was disclosed that Warburton wanted to take only part of the train up the bank, but was persuaded not to divide it by Greenall, the driver of the new locomotive *Lion*. The boiler explosion was caused by the weighting down of the safety valves of *Patentee*, against the Company's strict instructions, and led to an order by the Board that larger valves were to be fitted to all new engines.

Following a collision between a L&MR train and one from the GJR near Huyton Quarry on 26 November, Woods was instructed to find out in what distance a train could be stopped when descending Whiston Incline by reversing the engine but using no carriage brakes. The experiments were held on a dry day in December with an engine, four carriages and a horse box, and were followed next month with a similar series, this time using only one carriage brake. In each case the train was stopped in a reasonable time, and about 300 yds before the spot where the collision took place.

The death of a 13-year-old boy at Rainhill after he ran across the line behind a stationary train into the path of one coming in the other direction led to a new regulation in February 1839 requiring drivers to slacken speed and blow their whistles when approaching a train which had stopped on the opposite line.

On 2 February 1839 the 10.30 a.m. GJR train from Manchester was in collision with a L&MR train of coke and ballast, ten waggons being broken up. The GJR accepted responsibility, the driver of their *Tamerlaine* having failed to keep a proper lookout. The same month a passenger who had left a Liverpool train at Newton Bridge to get a drink at the Legh Arms attempted to mount one of the Blue coaches on the wrong side; the Superintendent Griffiths and a porter, assuming the man to be a stranger attempting to avoid payment of the fare, strove to prevent him from boarding the train, and in the ensuing struggle Griffiths and the man fell. Although the man's legs went under the wheels of the now slowly moving train and he finished his journey in Liverpool Infirmary, he was reported to be 'doing well'.

The practice of slipping the rear waggons from goods trains approaching the Broad Green Cattle Station without stopping the train had developed, apparently with the knowledge of the directors and engineers, but without any regulations either forbidding it or providing safeguards. On the morning of 23 April 1839 two loaded waggons from a Liverpool-bound train '... had been loosed ... near Cave's Gate in the expectation that they would run on to the cattle station, which they did not, by several hundred yards ...', and before a policeman and two platelayers could get them into a siding the 9 o'clock train came up and hit them, causing considerable damage. Another policeman was held partly responsible for failing to signal the passenger train. The driver and fireman of the luggage engine *Eclipse*, the brakesman and both policemen were fined sums ranging from 5s. to 1s., and all were warned of the danger of loosing waggons and leaving them to run nearly half a mile after the train, especially where public roads were to be crossed, as at Broad Green.

After two women trespassers had been killed by a B&LR engine on Whiston Incline in July 1839, small bills were posted along the line cautioning the public against trespass, and all police and gatemen were ordered to '... prohibit and prevent persons walking along the line of way' at the risk of incurring the serious displeasure of the directors.

In August the enginemen of *Goliah* were discharged for attempting to come out of a siding as a GJR coach train was approaching. By some miracle no passengers were injured although '... several coaches were partially damaged by rubbing against the *Goliah* engine and being thrown off the line.'

The Treasurer reported that on the evening of 18 June the 5 o'clock train from Manchester '... was suffered to come down the tunnel at a rapid and dangerous speed into the Lime Street Station; and though the wheels of four or five coaches were locked by the brakes, the train ran violently against the great buffer at the end of the Station forcing all the springs home as well as every buffer spring in the train.' Many passengers were thrown together, some hurt and others alarmed. The brakesmen were held to blame as they allowed this heavy nine-coach train to get out of control on the wet and slippery rails; Flint, who had been with the Company since the opening, was reprimanded and the other reverted to yard porter.

A serious accident involving two luggage trains occurred on the night of 2 July 1840 at the foot of the Whiston Incline. A long train of 32 waggons with two engines in front and none behind had almost reached the summit when the coupling chain between the tender of the second engine and the first waggon broke and the whole train ran back down the hill and on to Huyton Lane Gate. Here it collided with a Bolton train following from Liverpool, the engineman of which, on hearing its approach, reduced speed to about 3 mph and jumped off his engine.

Several waggons were smashed and hundreds of pounds worth of goods, including indigo, raisins and wine, were lost. One of the enginemen, Thomas Leftwich, took what was left of the train on to Manchester, but while returning in the early hours of the following morning with the early goods train he fell from the tender on to the rails and was killed instantly. The other driver, Guest, attended the Directors' enquiry, and having no excuse for not assisting the train from the rear, was discharged. He was not the only one to lose his job that day; the Roby Gateman who '... had got shamefully drunk on wine from the casks which had been stoved in', followed Guest out of the Company's service.

Apart from the Whiston accident, 1840 saw only comparatively minor incidents. On 9 January a collision in fog occurred at Cross Lane when a passenger train struck a luggage train. The next day a GJR train ran into a waggon left on the line at Parkside in darkness at 6 a.m. by the L&MR driver Pilling, with whom the Company parted a few days later. In February *Arrow* collided with a GJR engine in Manchester Station; this, the GJR agreed, was their man's fault.

Carelessness in not replacing points caused several minor accidents. In one case, on 5 April 1841, two horse drivers opened the points near Warehouse Lane Gate, Manchester, to draw out some waggons, and left them open; when the evening train from Liverpool came along it was diverted into the siding except for the last coach which kept to the main line and was dragged off the rails.

The Sunday morning early mail train on 6 March 1842 consisting of one 1st Class carriage, *The Lark* and one 2nd Class, was '... suffered to come down the tunnel without any brake being applied', damaging the large station buffers. There were no passengers and only the railway and Post Office guards were on it; though 'but scarcely hurt', Williams, the railwayman, was sent before the magistrates and subsequently reduced to porter.

On 25 July the Board were concerned to find lurid accounts in some Manchester papers of an accident supposed to have happened at Parkside. They were declared to be completely untrue, no accident having taken place there for many years.

At 10 p.m. on the night of 6 December an L&MR luggage train was divided at the foot of Whiston Bank and one half taken up by *Swallow*. Before the engine could return for the remaining waggons, they were run into by *Vizier*, a GJR engine working an extra train. Thomas Purdie, the L&M driver, admitted that he had broken the rules, but as it was so late he was not expecting any other train from Liverpool, and thought it might be allowed, especially as there was a policeman there. All the GJR driver saw were the two red rear lights of the L&MR train, the lamps at Huyton Quarry having been removed on the orders of the superintendent of platelayers following vandalism the previous April; he ordered that they be kept in the cabin and displayed on the signal post only when required. Five men were involved in the incident, including the superintendent, and all of them were fined one week's wages.

Responsibility for controlling GJR trains descending the Lime Street Tunnel was divided between the train guard and the tunnel brakesman, a L&MR employee. At 5 a.m. on Sunday 2 March 1845 the GJR mail arrived at the top of the tunnel but the brakesman, who had been on duty until late on the Saturday night, was not present. The guard, seeing a man get up at the back of the train, concluded that it was the brakesman and did not realise until the train was nearly at the bottom that the speed was beyond his control. The train rammed the '... large spring buffer at the top of the yard, which was driven home'. Several carriages were damaged and some passengers hurt.

Two separate breaches of rules led to an accident on the Hunts Bank line on 3 March 1845, in which several M&LR waggons were damaged. The 3rd Class 6.30 p.m. train from Liverpool had stalled on the curved incline between Ordsall Lane and the Manchester & Bolton Junction, and a messenger having been sent to the Hunts Bank workshops, the Superintendent, Forsyth, took a locomotive along the wrong line to pull them in. As he approached the junction he came in collision with the M&L waggons which were being propelled from the M&BR. Forsyth was admonished for taking the engine on the wrong line without sending a man ahead '... to ward off danger', but the other company's men were equally at fault for propelling waggons before the engine.

At midnight on 25 March as a GJR luggage train at Newton Junction was crossing from the north line to the Warrington branch a B&LR train from Kenyon Junction bound for Liverpool collided with the last two waggons, which had not cleared the south line; these were laden with pigs, many of which were killed. No warning had been given to the B&L driver as the bell signal from one policeman to the other had not been heard above the rough weather. Nevertheless, the policeman who failed to hear was reprimanded, and the Engineer was instructed to look into the night signalling arrangements at Newton Junction.

At intervals for 15 years the Company's books record accidents to individuals on the railway, usually attributable to their own carelessness or folly. One man was killed by falling from a Blue train in June 1831, and another, a trespasser, was run over in Olive Mount Cutting while balancing himself on one rail. A soldier whose cap fell off jumped over the side of the carriage after it and fell beneath the train, while one of Melling's foundry men, walking home along the railway from Cunliffe's public house, died under the wheels of a luggage engine near Rainhill Gates.

As the two 12 o'clock Blue trains were meeting at Warrington Junction on 22 June 1836, a woman alighted from the Manchester train on the wrong side, contrary to the advice of the guard; while putting up her umbrella, she failed to see the Liverpool train which, about to stop, ran over and killed her. One afternoon at Lime Street two men missed their train; watching their opportunity when the men on duty were at tea, they slipped into the tunnel and started walking through. When about mid-way they were alarmed at hearing a train coming down, and one of them stumbled; he was dragged to one side by the other man, who left him there and went for help. Both survived to be brought before the magistrates charged with trespass.

CHAPTER TWELVE

Rules and Regulations

AT THE FIRST General Meeting after the opening, the Directors were able to assure the shareholders that 'Travelling by the Railway is the safest, as well as the cheapest and most expeditious mode of Public Conveyance ever presented'.

A writer in 1835, commenting on the safety of the railway, observed

'... so great is the momentum acquired by these heavy loads moving with such rapidity, that they easily pass over considerable obstacles. Even in those melancholy accidents where loss of life has been sustained, the bodies of the unfortunate sufferers, though run over by the wheels, have caused little irregularity in the motion, and the passengers in the carriages have not been sensible that any impediment has been encountered on the road'.[1]

A great comfort, no doubt, to the victims, and an encouragement to those contemplating suicide on the railway.

The safe working of the railway was, however, a matter that constantly exercised the minds of the directors and engineers. The Act of Incorporation authorised the Company to make rules, orders and bye-laws for the safe and efficient running of the concern and to publish or exhibit them. At first there seems to have been no distinction made between rules and regulations to be observed by the staff and bye-laws applicable to the general public, although there were few of either. The timetable of February 1831 includes information on luggage, porters' duties, gratuities, punctuality, smoking in carriages and drinking en route, and on 30 May the Board recorded that the 'Rules and Regulations for Working the Railway' had been signed by the magistrates, and that printed copies in large placard form were to be posted up. New bye-laws were added as the occasion arose, the question of Sunday travel being covered by one or more of them, and in February 1839 a revised set was produced and sealed. In June 1841 rules were made for the protection of coach and omnibus passengers, and these, together with the fares to principal destinations, were printed on cards and fixed in all coaches authorised to use the Company's yards.

Staff regulations gradually evolved as a result of experience, all too often dearly bought as in the fatal accidents at Rainhill and Whiston. In October 1837 new rules as to speed at different seasons of the year were printed and added to the existing rules and in March 1839 the rules were in book form, to be carried by all enginemen, guards, policemen, gatemen and overlookers at all times under a penalty of 5s.

Giving evidence before the Select Committee on the Prevention of Accidents upon Railways in 1841, Captain Laws of the M&LR said

'There are certain regulations upon almost all railways that have emanated from the Liverpool & Manchester. Most of them were similar, even in their imperfections, to those that were established upon that line. Having had the precedence in carrying out railway communications, of course it was naturally referred to by new railways coming into operation.'[2]

The signalling and safety of trains was in the hands of the policemen who were stationed at intervals of a mile or less along the line. For years the positive 'all clear' signal was made to drivers by the constable standing erect with arms outstretched. If he stood at ease or was not to be seen, this was to be taken as an indication of some obstruction on the line. Hand-flags of various colours were also used, red to stop a train and blue to indicate to luggage-train drivers that waggons were to be taken on; a black flag was used by platelayers and a green one by policemen as a caution signal.

For passengers wishing to stop a train at a wayside station, the holding up of hat or umbrella was for

216

years a sufficient signal. As train speeds increased, however, it became necessary to give earlier warning to enginemen, and flag-poles with a pulley at the top were erected at all stopping places and junctions, up which flags were run, green to stop a train for passengers, red for danger; at night coloured hand lamps were hoisted on these masts. A flag of any colour waved violently or at night, a lamp moving up and down, was always a signal to stop; a lamp moving from side to side meant caution.

On 17 August 1831 it was ordered that engines going towards Manchester at night show red lights and towards Liverpool 'ordinary yellow lights', with the same at the rear of the train; about a month later the rules concerning signal lamps were printed, probably the first signalling regulations to be put into printed form. By 1833 the last carriage of every train carried a revolving lamp, showing red when the train was in motion but changing instantly to a blue light when it stopped. It probably worked automatically being swung round by a horizontally pivoted weighted lever. At this time it was considered that the engine fire gave sufficient warning ahead of a train's approach. Tender lamps could be turned to show red or white, according to whether the engine was running forward or in reverse.

In order to distinguish GJR engines at a distance, new arrangements were made in November 1838, when it was ordered that the front buffer-planks of their locomotives be painted a bright colour, either red or white, and that they carry two white bullseye lamps throwing the light forward at night; the L&MR engines carried only one such lamp.

At the potentially dangerous Newton Junction a green light visible from the L&MR main lines denoted that the points were set for the Warrington line; a gilt arrow, when pointed towards Warrington, was the corresponding signal by day. The first fixed signals were erected here; these were boards chequered red and white mounted on 12 ft high posts and turning through 90°. When turned to face trains coming from Liverpool, Manchester or Warrington they indicated that another train was just ahead and the driver must proceed with caution; edgewise they denoted 'line clear'. Several lamps illuminated the junctions at night, and four policemen were constantly on duty there.

The Rule Book of March 1839[3] contained 50 paragraphs and, resulting from over eight years' experience, was a pretty comprehensive document. If a train stopped in foggy weather, a gateman, policeman or the fireman was to go back 400 yds to warn any train approaching, and the driver was to make frequent use of his steam whistle. The same precautions were to be taken if a train stopped in the curve of Olive Mount Cutting. Enginemen descending Whiston Incline had their attention drawn to the three flag poles at the bottom, and the need to whistle at Platt's Bridge, the last one on the incline.

Enginemen and firemen were to stand up and keep a good look-out all the time the engine was in motion, and the tools they were to carry on the locomotive were listed – screw-keys, monkey-wrenches, cold chisels, chains and a crowbar among other items. Rule No 12 enjoined drivers to stop if the line was obscured by smoke or steam from another engine with a burst boiler tube, or from any other cause, and not to proceed through the clouds of steam until they were satisfied that their own road was clear. They were also to drive very slowly past any train that had stopped on the opposite line. This rule probably originated in 1833 after the fatal accident on Parr Moss. In evidence at the Inquest Dixon had said that the bursting of a tube was such a common occurrence that enginemen would scarcely think it of sufficient importance to stop. Neither would they stop to render assistance in other cases unless signalled to do so, least of all drivers of trains belonging to another company.[4]

Platelayers were required to report the names of any drivers who disregarded their signals, and luggage engine drivers were to refuse to take out trains if the waggons were not properly sheeted. They were also to ensure that two or three empty waggons were placed between the engine and the rest of the train.

If the banking engine was not ready at an inclined plane, the driver could leave part of his train on the main line and come back for it down the same line if no passenger train was due; otherwise he must shunt it into the siding. If another train came up while waggons were standing on the main line, they were not to be pushed up by that train. Drivers were not to make up lost time by speeding down the inclines, and banking-engine drivers were not to start until the last waggon or carriage in the train they were going to assist had passed across the points – a fairly obvious precaution. Up to three empty waggons at the foot of Whiston Incline could be shunted into the siding by the policeman; more than this number were to be moved by a locomotive.

Enginemen were cautioned against spilling coke on the tracks, engine-turners against the careless turning of engines and tenders on the turntables, and brakesmen on the need to ensure that the large wood-chock was properly replaced near the tunnel mouth at

Edge Hill after a train had gone down to Wapping.

The time-interval system was in operation from the opening of the railway until its amalgamation with the GJR. When it was found that luggage trains frequently started from Edge Hill only a few minutes before coach trains from Lime Street, it was ordered in September 1838 that no luggage or coach train should start at an interval less than 15 minutes from the appointed hour of a coach train starting from Lime Street, and that half-an-hour should be allowed when possible. As the years brought increasing traffic on the line the time interval tended to become shorter. However, in December 1840 Moss suggested that an interval of 45 minutes should be allowed, but in order to achieve it, all coal and goods would have to be moved at night. Although this would not give the traders the service they had previously enjoyed, safety must be the consideration that governed their decisions; he anticipated that the Government would soon compel companies to provide all the locomotive power on their own lines, which would increase safety materially.

110 *Warrington Junction, c. 1848; originally 'Newton Junction', it was renamed Earlestown in the 1850s. The nearer disc signals show 'Line clear'; the station buildings still exist*

A certain amount of latitude was allowed in the application of the time-interval. Coal trains approaching the line near the time a passenger train was due had to wait until the train had half a mile headway, when '... it may come out and make the best of its way'. Another reason why the system was not applied too rigidly was to prevent delay to a 2nd-class train held up with engine trouble, and passed by a 1st-class train; '... if that second class train, after being passed, were obliged to wait 15 minutes, there would be almost an insurrection on the train'.[5] From April 1844 the 8 p.m. GJR London Mail from Manchester, 'a very fast train', was given only five minutes start over the Manchester–Liverpool, a heavy, stopping train.

Some of the earliest rules made by the Board arose from the need to warn all concerned of the rapid approach of trains. In June 1831 orders were given 'That it be the duty of the Firemen of the Locomotive Engines to blow the horns on approaching the Gates at the Public Roads, and that each Fireman be fined 6d. every time he neglects to blow his horn ...'. The guards were also given horns to blow on approaching crossing gates, as were the gatekeepers themselves, who joined in on seeing, or hearing, the approaching train. This old relic of stage-coach practice seems to have been dropped on the introduction of the steam locomotive whistle a few years later.

A number of plans for disengaging the engine from the train in case of accident were examined in the early years, and various experiments were conducted;[6] it is likely that one or other of the contrivances was adopted as in some cases the engine involved in a derailment or other mishap did break away from the train. From the end of 1831 all passenger trains ran with two luggage waggons coupled between the locomotive and the carriages; they were not to be loaded to a height that would obscure the view between the brakesman and the engine.

At the level crossings the gates were, at first, closed across the railway from 10 p.m. until 5 a.m.; any train running between these hours had to stop twice at each set of gates for the fireman to open and then close them. From 1834 the gates were kept shut across the roads and bells were provided for nocturnal travellers to wake the gatemen. Lamps on the gates at night showed whether they were open or closed.

The first suggestion of a communication cord was made in September 1840, when it was put forward as a means whereby the brakesman of a luggage train, riding on the last waggon, could attract the driver's attention by means of a 'check string'.

In the early days the carriage doors on the side adjacent to the opposite line were kept locked but by 1833 there had been so much trouble from passengers impatient to alight at the end of their journey that they were left unlocked. Passengers arriving at Manchester always left the train on the wrong side to avoid having to walk round it. The Board considered a suggestion made by Sinclair of the B&LR that fences be erected between the two lines at stations, of sufficient height to prevent passengers from crossing, but this was not practicable. However, on the opening of the new arrival station at Manchester the passengers alighted on the left, as at Liverpool, and orders were given in April 1838 that the offside doors of all carriages be locked. This remained the Company's practice at least until 1842.

In February 1833 a John Radcliffe of Stockport wrote suggesting that the guard fire a pocket pistol at short intervals in cases of breakdown, but the directors thought it might alarm the passengers while not being heard by oncoming trains.

The subject of night emergency signals arose again in November 1840 when Earle suggested using Blue Lights, fixed at intervals along the line. These were a kind of firework containing a chemical composition which burned with a bright blue flame and were used by the Post Office packets and other vessels. Samples of these and of signal rockets were obtained from the Eastern Counties Railway and from George Green of Liverpool, who gave the Company instructions for making them. Cowper's fog signal, described as a 'small box containing an explosive mixture to be placed on the rail previous to an engine passing' was considered in May 1843 and adopted on the Board of Trade's recommendation in 1844. Until this time the handbells at the gatehouses had been used as signals in foggy weather.

Arrangements were made in 1836 for William Cooke to lay his newly-invented electric telegraph along the L&MR but technical difficulties arose which prevented any trials until 1837 when they were held on the L&BR between Euston and Camden.[7] By 1838 the Company had lost interest and did not even consider offers of Davey's Patent Electric Telegraph

111 *Types of fixed signals, L&MR*

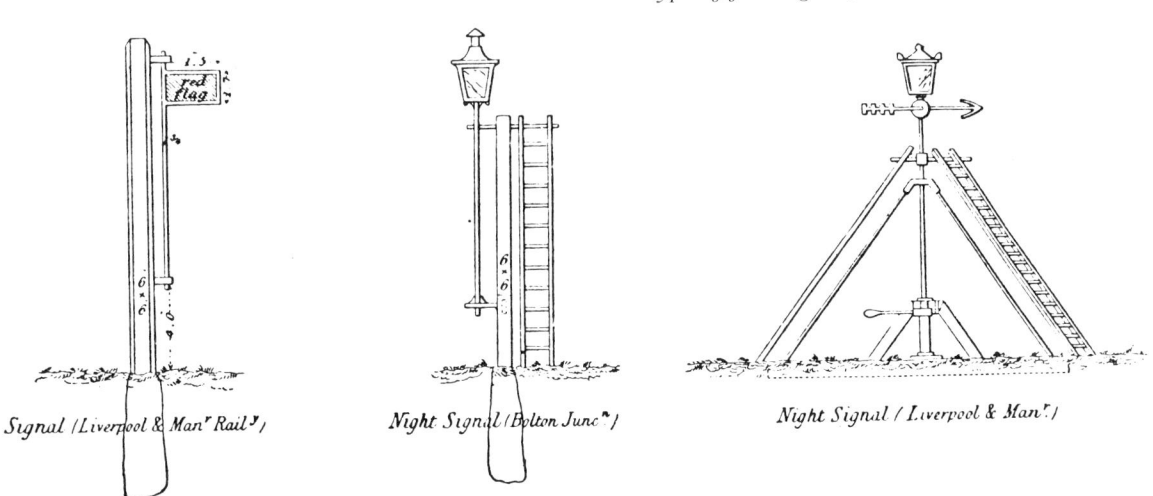

Signal (Liverpool & Man.^r Rail.^y)   *Night Signal (Bolton Junc.ⁿ)*   *Night Signal (Liverpool & Man.^r)*

or Coombes' underground telegraph to be laid along the line in iron tubes. In September 1841 a train was stranded for an hour on Chat Moss owing to the failure of the *Cyclops* engine, and about 30 passengers sent a memorial to the Board urging the adoption of a telegraph for summoning assistance in similar cases. The Directors recorded their opinion that it would be too costly to install for occasional use, overlooking its value in normal signalling; they went so far as to say that with the improved reliability of the locomotive '... the necessity for telegraphs on railways seemed almost superseded.'

In September 1838 the L&BR had sent a list of its signals to the L&MR, suggesting that uniformity was desirable, to which the Board agreed in principle. The matter remained in abeyance for over two years, however, when, at its weekly meeting on 10 November 1840, the L&MR Board resolved to call a conference of Directors of the principal railways in some central town to devise safety measures '... for the reassurance of the public mind'. Although the GJR and GWR disapproved of the plan at first, all the other companies agreed and the L&BR asked the Board to prepare a specimen set of regulations for circulation prior to the meeting.

The General Railway Conference was held in Birmingham on 19 January 1841, and among other things, a uniform system of colours for signalling was agreed upon, viz red indicating danger, green for caution and white for all clear. Before dispersing the conference appointed a provisional committee to watch railway interests; it consisted of the Chairmen of the L&B, GW and South Western Railways, with headquarters at 10 Whitehall, London. The committee went into action almost immediately against the Regulation of Railways Bill of 1841, their principal objection being to the proposal that the Board of Trade be empowered to make rules and regulations for the railways. They secured the appointment of a Select Committee, and as a result the Bill was withdrawn, to be reintroduced and passed in more acceptable form in 1842.[8]

James Loch MP, a director appointed by the Marquis of Stafford, advocated some form of Government control of railways, canals and turnpike trusts by a permanent board back in 1829.[9] His principal object at that time was to ensure that the Government was advised on the best route a railway should take and that opposition from vested interests should not compel a company to accept a compromise since this would prejudice the country's chances of developing a national railway system in the future. Sir Robert Peel, Home Secretary, when approached by Loch on the matter, agreed in principle, but considered that the time was not ripe for such an arrangement, and this first attempt to secure state control failed. In January 1837 Loch urged Parliamentary protection for '... the poorer traveller, who travels upon business, or even he who wishes to move about for pleasure', by the simple expedient of the Legislature making reduced fares for this class of passenger a condition of granting Acts for further powers to railway companies.[10]

In February 1836 the Company added its name to 'The Petition of the Incorporated Railway Companies', urging government action on the many conflicting railway schemes then proposed, and two directors were sent to London to take any action necessary.

The first stirring of interest in railways on the part of the Board of Trade came on 20 September 1836 when the Secretary of the Statistical Department, G. R. Porter, sent a questionnaire to Charles Lawrence and invited his further observations '... on a subject so highly interesting and important'.[11] During the protracted sittings of the Select Committees on Railways of 1839 and 1840, Lawrence, Moss, Rathbone, Earle and Booth all gave evidence; Moss suggested that the Board of Trade issue Engine Drivers' Certificates, with powers of suspension, as in the case of sea captains.[12]

Throughout June 1840 the Board was occupied in considering the implications of the Regulation of Railways Bill, then before Parliament, under which the Board of Trade Railway Department was to be established. While they did not oppose the principle of government supervision the directors objected to some clauses, notably that providing for prosecution in cases of non-compliance with Acts of Parliament. They were informed by their colleagues on the L&BR Board that they considered it a Bill for the suppression of railways, but this did not influence the L&MR who sent two directors to a meeting in London with authority to petition against such clauses as might be injurious '... to the fair and legitimate interests of Railway Companies'. The Bill, one of whose sponsors had been James Loch, was passed on 10 August 1840,[13] and was popularly known as 'Lord Seymour's Act', after its other sponsor. Several amendments had been made to the original Bill, and the Act was generally welcomed. Within a fortnight the Board of Trade informed the Company that it required notification of all new bye-laws and of all accidents involving personal injury. From this time all new lines were subject to inspection before they could be opened for traffic.

Major-General Pasley, the Department's active and most conscientious Inspecting Officer, visited the L&MR in June 1843 during a brief tour of the area. Setting off from the Albion Hotel, Liverpool, on the 20th, to visit the Bolton & Preston Railway, he met Chapman and the directors of the NUR at Euxton. The next day he went to Keswick and Ambleside, and the day after, to Lancaster. On the 23rd he was on the Preston & Wyre Railway and returned to Liverpool where, on the 24th, he met Woods and Dewrance at Edge Hill Locomotive Shops. Here he watched a new method of polishing metal and producing a true plane surface, and the intricacies of the locomotive valves that shut off the steam at $\frac{3}{4}$ stroke were explained to him. He then went to Manchester and back in company with Booth and others before being conducted over the Docks by Hartley.[14]

Despite the rapid developments in signalling of the early 1840s, the L&MR still relied solely upon the policemen with their flags. In September 1842 the police establishment was 59 men; they were under the supervision of the Resident Engineers who were constantly travelling about superintending the operation of the railway. As late as 1841 Booth said of signals that the fewer there were the better, on the grounds that drivers would become so accustomed to seeing them that they would be ignored.[15] When Richard Hall of the ECR sent a description of his patent signals in February 1843, Woods reported that they were ingenious, but suitable for longer and less busy lines than the L&MR.

The year 1845 saw the repeal of the ancient law under which any artefact responsible for causing a death was considered forfeit to the Almighty, in practice to the Crown, but it could be redeemed by the former owner on payment of a deodand assessed by the Court. Railway engines were particularly vulnerable, although the L&MR seems to have been treated leniently by Coroners' juries, the total amount levied on the Company's property for the five years to May 1842 being only £11 0s. 10½d.; this included a deodand of £1 on *Patentee* following the fatal explosion. The amount levied on the M&LR when their locomotive *Irk* blew up at Miles Platting, Manchester, in January 1845 was £500.[16]

Railway vandalism and sabotage are as old as the railways themselves, the first serious incident on the L&MR occurring two weeks before the opening. On 1 September the *Arrow* was taking five loaded waggons along the Roby Embankment when it was momentarily thrown off the track at the points which had been maliciously fastened open in the wrong direction. The contractor George Stevenson, who was on the engine, leapt off, and an instant later the *Arrow*, regaining the track, ran over him, killing him on the spot. The Company immediately offered a reward of 200 guineas for information leading to a conviction; this was the highest amount ever offered, but with the opening imminent the Directors were very sensitive on the question of safety.

One Thomas Pye was fined £5 in July 1831 for placing a stone sleeper on the line at Whiston and a man, I. Birchell, employed at the Rainhill Watering Station was discharged for assaulting a policeman who refused to conceal Pye's action. Later the Board learned that Pye's family were destitute and they returned half of the fine to his wife. Less than a month later a man named Ingham did the same at Sutton, also removing the mile-posts there. He was caught and prosecuted after the Company had offered a £10 reward for his discovery.

The Board was summoned to a special meeting on Wednesday, 3 December 1834 to receive a report on an attempt to wreck the 6 p.m. 1st Class train from Manchester the previous evening. In Kenyon Cutting, approaching Parkside, the *Meteor*, driven by Thomas Milburn, ran into a 'platelayers' small laurie' and was thrown into the side drain with one or two coaches. There was little damage, and no serious injuries, and when the last Blue train from Manchester came up shortly afterwards, the passengers were transferred and proceeded on their way. This second train, when running near the Sandy Mains Embankment, struck an old larch sleeper laid across the rails, passing over it with a severe jolt to engine and carriages – and presumably passengers, although they are not mentioned. As the railway was clear at both spots when the previous train passed, the obstructions must have been placed there in the dark, shortly before these trains were due. The matter was placed in the hands of the Warrington constable Jones for investigation and it was ordered that an iron guard be fastened to the engines in front of the wheels to throw off any obstruction placed on the rails. Four days later, on the following Saturday evening, at the same spot near Parkside, *Mercury* with the 6 p.m. Merchants' Train from Manchester, driven by Ralph Thompson, ran into a stone block placed on the line and smashed it without damage to the engine or train. The Board was convinced it was the work of the same man or gang, and offered £100 reward for their discovery.

A stone thrown from a GJR train hit a gauge glass on the engine of a passing L&MR train causing it to explode, blowing the fireman off the footplate, to lie stunned on the track below. The incident was traced to two boys whose fathers both worked on the L&MR and who were held responsible for their children's behaviour. Brought before the Board in November 1839, they were told that while the Company would not prosecute on this occasion, they could not expect such lenient treatment again, and that they '... would necessarily be marked men'. The boys presumably did not remain unmarked when their fathers carried out the Board's instruction to 'administer proper correction'.

Early in 1840 a £10 reward was offered for information as to who had marked L&MR property with Hargreaves' identifications; in December £50 was offered for the discovery and conviction of the person who placed a sleeper on the line. This was pushed over a quarter of a mile by the engine until it fell harmlessly from the rail. At this time the Board was worried by the increasing number of 'mischievous and wicked attempts to cause accidents to railway trains', and the Postmaster General was asked to use his influence in securing additional legislation to protect the public; it was also suggested that a Royal Proclamation offering rewards for the discovery of the perpetrators might be considered, and the Secretary to the Post Office agreed to bring the matter before the Government.

Incidents, some of a criminal nature, continued despite the Company's vigilance; policemen's cabins were broken into, posts were placed across the line. By 1842 the locomotives were fitted with wheel-guards which usually pushed obstructions off the rails, but the danger remained, and rewards of £50 continued to be offered. In December 1842 a man strongly suspected of interfering with the switches at Manchester was sentenced to a month's imprisonment for trespass.

Widespread strikes and disturbances broke out in Manchester during August 1842 when mobs numbering thousands of millworkers and Chartists rampaged through the town and surrounding district. Green reported to the Board on these riots but as there is no record of the railway having been attacked it was presumably guarded by the troops of the 72nd Highlanders and Bolton Cavalry drafted into the area. The B&LR was immobilised for a time when a mob of 2000 heading for Wigan surrounded the Chequerbent Engine House, removed a plug from the stationary engine and abducted the engineman, compelling him to march with them until he managed to escape.[17]

CHAPTER THIRTEEN

Conclusion

In September 1830 Charles Lawrence was Chairman of the Board, John Moss his Deputy and most of the other directors were those who had guided the Company's affairs during the difficult years now past.

The Board, at its first meeting after the opening, on Monday 20 September, was very preoccupied with the death of Huskisson, and in an attempt to prevent a repetition of such an accident Stephenson was asked to see if the tanks on the tenders could not be made large enough to avoid the necessity for refilling at Parkside. They ordered that each journey should take $2\frac{1}{4}$ hours and that trains should run slowly across public roads, along embankments and near watering places.

In October the shareholders were invited to subscribe to a piece of plate to be presented to General Gascoyne for his zeal in getting the Bill through the Commons, and also to a memorial to Huskisson. A white marble tablet on a black background was set in the cutting wall at the fatal spot in May 1831; it was originally between two buttresses supporting an iron water tank, and is still to be seen, although few traces of the Parkside Station remain.

Early in October 1830 William James wrote to the Board claiming to be the 'original projector of the Railway' and reminding them that he had incurred considerable expense over and above the remuneration he had received. Consideration of his case was postponed for the time being. Apparently nothing was done, for in April 1836 he wrote again claiming some recompense, and the matter was referred to Sandars. A year later James was dead, unrecognised and unrewarded. About 1840 Mrs Elizabeth Mudie, James's sister, sought, by means of a memorial, financial aid on the grounds that the railway system was evolving as a result of those efforts of her brother which had cost him his fortune and left her without provision. A recommendation supporting her case and bearing 14 eminent signatures, including those of J. Walker, R. Stephenson, Locke and Brunel, was appended.[1] Ironically it was her husband who had instituted the proceedings that led to James's imprisonment and bankruptcy. When another proposal was made to the Board Meeting of 12 August 1844 to organise a subscription it was stated that the Company '... had already subscribed £300 to the widow and children of the late William James.'

George Stephenson's active association with the L&MR had practically ceased by 1833 but the successful completion of the undertaking was probably his greatest achievement; none of the railways he subsequently built had works of comparable difficulty. The Lime Street Tunnel incident strained relations between the Company and Stephenson, and having been appointed Chief Engineer to the GJR in 1833, he was replaced by Joseph Locke in 1835, after it became evident that he was incapable of undertaking a work of this magnitude. He lacked the training and experience in civil engineering necessary to produce original plans and estimates, and although his assistants were at first equally inexperienced they learned more quickly, and went off to make their own way in the railway engineering world.

A decade later it was recognised that Stephenson's unique contribution to the establishment of the railway system was not his performance as an executive engineer, but his vision of a nationwide network of lines that would permit travel from any one point to practically any other, coupled with his unswerving faith in the steam locomotive. His connection with the highly successful Liverpool & Manchester Railway gave him enormous prestige and lent authority to his every pronouncement. William James lost his fortune in attempting to promote a railway system and Richard Trevithick, inventor of the locomotive, only narrowly escaped a

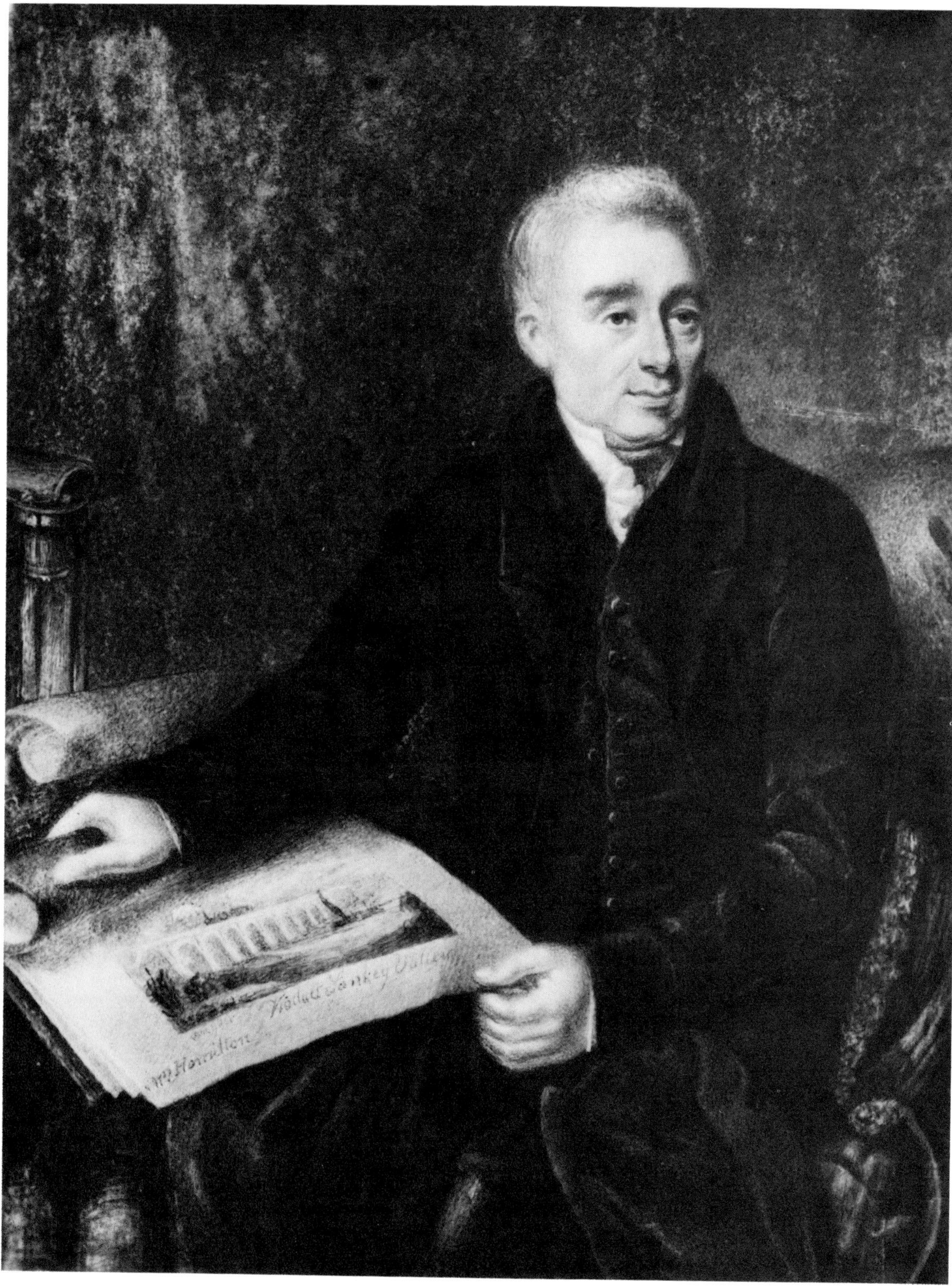

pauper's grave;[2] George Stephenson lived to achieve fame and fortune.

On 26 August 1844 John Moss proposed that a marble statue be erected to George Stephenson, and that Gibson, an eminent sculptor then in Liverpool, be commissioned to execute it; the Board sought the concurrence of the GJR, and in September ordered a prospectus for Stephenson's testimonial to be printed, stipulating that subscriptions should be from railway boards and not individuals; the Board contributed £500.

George Ashby Pritt, the Company's Law Clerk, died in December 1831; when the Chairman referred to the loss of '... their gentle and conciliating ... eminently distinguished friend' at the General Meeting on 5 January 1832, the shareholders voted a gift of £250 to his family. His former partner, William Clay, succeeded him, and the firm now became Clay & Swift. Lawyers in those days were in no hurry for their money, for in August 1840 the Company received a bill for £12,103 covering services rendered over the previous 12 years. The Board protested at the scale of charges and at the delay, and instructed Booth to claim a rebate of £500. Twelve years credit seems to have been normal in the profession; in 1837 Francis Mewburn had rendered his modest account for £11 5s. 6d. for his professional services in 1825 and 1826 during the proceedings on the original Bills. In November 1833 T. M. Sherwood gave up the profession of Parliamentary Agent on being called to the Bar and he was retained as Parliamentary Counsel to the Company.

Foster had received no payment for designing the Moorish Arch, nor for his other services to the Company, and on being offered 100 guineas in September 1834 he said he would prefer the compliment of a piece of plate. Prepared by Robert Jones & Sons, and suitably inscribed, it was presented to him a few months later.

The directors devoted a considerable amount of time to railway business, meeting at least once a week, usually in Liverpool but occasionally at Manchester, when they went by special train and inspected the line. Sometimes they would walk over a section of the line, as on Saturday, 10 December 1836 when they met at Edge Hill at 8 a.m. for such an inspection. Those who served on the Management Committee met every Thursday in addition to the normal Monday Board Meeting, and periodically ad hoc Sub-Committees were formed. The directors were

112 *George Stephenson, from a miniature water-colour, 1836. The drawing he holds is of the Sankey Viaduct*

paid their fee of 1 guinea each Board day but the Management Committee, unpaid until April 1836, then drew 6 guineas a fortnight to be shared among those who had attended; the average yearly total of directors' fees until 1836 amounted to only £300.

Starting with very little knowledge of railways, they mastered the technicalities of the new form of transport quickly. Only a few months before the opening they had seriously discussed the question of whether trains, both passenger and goods, should be drawn or propelled. A great many matters seemingly trivial in themselves, were considered at Board Meetings, since generally no precedent existed and a general policy had to be formulated. Complaints were investigated, such as that of a passenger who, in October 1830, was not allowed to ride on a full train although the other travellers offered to make room for him.

The influential *Edinburgh Review* published an article in October 1832 which was severely critical of the management of the railway; written by Dr D. Lardner, it caused the Board so much concern that within a short time 750 copies of a reply were ready for distribution to the shareholders. The Editor declined to reprint the directors 'answer' in the journal, but he did analyse it in an attempt to justify the original article, one or two of the statements in which were actually uncomfortably near the truth.

The Liverpool & Manchester Railway proved to be a sound investment from its first appearance on the Stock Market until the end of its independent existence. Even during the passage of the Act in April 1826, when the very survival of the enterprise seemed at stake, its shares only hovered around par for a few days, to revive quickly and stand at a premium all through the years of construction, despite the many doubts and uncertainties that assailed the Board so often. Once the railway was opened and earning revenue its shares never fell below £173 (March 1842); in April 1836 they had attained their highest quotation on the London Stock Exchange, £295.

The half-yearly dividend on each £100 share never exceeded £5, but this amount was declared on 16 occasions; neither did it fall below £4, the amount distributed in June 1832. The average annual yield of the shares was £9 10s.

The 10% dividend arrangement agreed to by the Company was observed throughout although, according to George Pritt, William Huskisson would have been willing to see the restriction lifted, but he died before he could make his views public. Sir Robert Peel thought that while the Company operated the limitation it was entitled to some protection against the establishment of rival lines in its territory; others argued that it was a disincentive to economy or the vigorous pursuit of new business. The limitation was circumvented to some extent by the repayment of loans from the proceeds of new shares upon which the dividend could be paid.

Loans were raised for the financing of major works, such as the Lime Street extension. The Exchequer Loan Commissioners, Overend, Gurney & Co. and the Ocean Insurance Co. of Liverpool all lent the Company money at $3\frac{1}{2}\%$ to 4% and for terms of up to seven years. By 1837 the capital of the Company was approaching £1½m.

Before 1838 the Company's accounts were not audited; in February of that year the question was discussed by the Board, who considered that an audit of the voluminous accounts of the carrying department at each end of the line was desirable. Booth suggested that the quarterly accounts and balance sheet prepared at the Lime Street office should be audited by a professional accountant and that one month's accounts of the carrying department be checked. A Mr Prescot carried out the first audit in July 1838 for £36 15s. At this time the goods offices were enlarged '... owing to the accumulation of papers and the extension of business.'

By July 1843 an Audit Committee was set up to check the accounts at Wapping, Manchester and the General Office, Lime Street. This became a Permanent Audit and Finance Committee of three Directors in December 1843; one Director retired every two months. The following year an Audit Office was set up and the accountant Harrison was instructed to put down in writing his method of accounting for the information of the Directors.

Some of the great Quaker families of Lancashire provided the capital for many early railways; the 'Liverpool Party' was a force to be reckoned with at many a shareholders' meeting until the late 1840s. The GJR was financed and controlled from Liverpool and 10,300 shares in the L&BR were held there against 884 in Birmingham itself. They provided the capital for the Eastern Counties and the Midland Counties Railways, not from any particular interest in those districts, but in the expectation of a reasonable return on the investments.

The directors of the L&MR, as bankers and business men themselves, were not anxious to see the canals ruined and all the capital invested in them lost. Largely at the instigation of James Loch in 1829 the Bridgewater Trustees were at first invited, and then urged, to invest in the L&MR to protect their interests, but the perverse Bradshaw spurned the offer. It was even suggested at the time that Parliament should delay projects for new lines that would compete with existing canals, to give the latter an opportunity to convert themselves into railways. The waterway companies, however, showed little desire to co-operate with their new rivals.

In March 1831 Robert Bradshaw's son James resigned his seat on the L&MR Board, a position in which he had never been very happy, and in September 1833 he committed suicide. In early October the elder Bradshaw at last relinquished that sole and absolute control of the Bridgewater Canal that he had exercised for over 30 years. Senile and drink-sodden, he died in 1835. Contrary to expectations, the Bridgewater Canal continued to fourish alongside the railway, and in 1839 it carried twice the tonnage of the L&MR.

The thorny subject of Sunday travel was considered at a Board Meeting a week before the line opened, when it was decided that it should be limited, with an interval between 10 a.m. and 4 p.m. when no trains should run. A Bye-Law, No 11, was framed to cover the arrangement. Some directors thought that the railway should close down completely on Sundays and Adam Hodgson held this view with such conviction that he resigned from the Board on 27 September, to be replaced by Charles Tayleur. On 3 January 1831 the Reverend John Scott of Manchester collected the signatures of 22 Christian Ministers to a resolution 'deprecating Sunday travelling by the railway'. In May the Sunday evening trains were started at 5 p.m., but whether this was to extend the interval or because the evenings were lighter is not clear.

A number of shareholders refused to accept that portion of the dividend accruing from Sunday working, and the Board included in its published accounts a statement of the amount involved, 4s. per share in 1832, 5s. 3d. in 1833. This money remained in a special Sunday Travelling Account.

All through the 1830s the morality of Sunday travel on the railways was discussed in newspaper and pamphlet, Shareholders' Meeting and Board Room. Most railways, following the lead of the L&MR, ran a restricted service, although the stage coaches had no inhibitions on this score. Of nearly 1400 coaches operating to and from London in 1836 over 1000 were licensed to run on Sundays, while in the provinces about one-third of the 1434 coaches ran.[3]

The Warrington & Newton Railway decided, after a special meeting, to run Sunday trains to meet those of the L&MR morning and evening, but in June 1837 the GJR notified the Board of its intention to operate trains all day, since the GPO insisted that mail by their trains should not be delayed. The Board took counsel's opinion and Sir William Follett held that the Company had no power to close their line on Sundays to other railways, although it need not run trains itself. From that time trains ran at all hours over the L&MR, although the Company itself maintained its own restricted service.

The long, severe frost of early 1838 caused great privation and distress in the district and at Moss's suggestion the Sunday Travelling money, which had been accumulating for several years and amounted to £387, was distributed among charities in Liverpool and Manchester; the fund was used in meeting various other appeals which could not be met from the general funds of the Company.

After Robert Gladstone had observed one of the engines being repaired in the workshops on a Sunday in April 1832, it was ordered that no repairs or other work on the line be done on Sundays except in cases of urgent necessity, and then a report was to be submitted to the Board. The Company in November 1831 made it possible for enginemen and firemen to spend Sunday evening at home first by arranging for all trains to stop at Newton, and for the men to change over; when it was found that long delays sometimes occurred while one train waited for the other, it was agreed that the trains could stop wherever they met for the change to be made. Even this arrangement led to disputes when one driver refused to change engines and the Company reminded them that it could be varied only by mutual consent.

The Board made contributions to several charities, but it had to be selective in distributing the Company's money. Fines exacted for various offences were donated to local organisations, on one occasion to the 'Ladies' Charity at Bescot', and in May 1831 the Company gave £100 to the Manchester Infirmary where many employees had been treated during the construction years. However, it declined to devote any of the Company's funds to the relief of sufferers from 'the great fire in Hamburgh' of 1842.[4] The appeal of the vicar and churchwardens for a subscription to the St Helens Church Schools, Manchester, was considered in relation to the number of children of the Company's employees who attended.

In May 1843 the directors refused an invitation to contribute £33 to the cost of repairing the Huyton Church tower, considering that it paid enough already in legal parish rate assessments. The increasing burden of parish rates had long been a sore point with the Board, who in January 1837 raised the matter with the Poor Law Commissioners to no effect. In January 1843 the Chairman met W. E. Gladstone, newly appointed President of the Board of Trade, and referred to the question of the excessive rates to which railways were subjected, but was told that it was a matter for the Home Office and that the Board of Trade had no intention of bringing the subject before Parliament.

The Board received numerous requests for free passes but issued them very sparingly. The wives of policemen and gatekeepers were allowed one each week to go to market from October 1831, although they soon found ways of making about five visits a fortnight. Unauthorised travel brought a fine of 10s. in addition to payment of the fare. A surgeon of Prescot was refused a pass, but free passage was granted to some refugees to return to their storm-

113 *Ivory director's ticket*

114 *Free pass issued to chief officers of associated railways*

wrecked homes, at the request of the Humane Society. In April 1833 it was resolved that former directors be allowed to keep their ivory directors' tickets entitling them to free access to the trains, stations and works and the next year one agent or engineer from each branch railway was given a free pass over the L&MR. Apart from the one free, transferable ticket given to each shareholder to ride on the opening day, they received no concessions.

The Deputy Constable of Manchester applied in January 1834 for free passage for his officers '... when in pursuit of thieves or other offenders against the public peace.' The request was refused, the Directors considering there were no grounds for giving free travel to one class of public officers more than another. When a similar application was received from the Liverpool Police and Watch Committee in May 1836, it was granted, with the curious proviso that if the chase were successful, the normal 2nd Class fare was payable; the arrangement now also applied to Manchester.

Passes to walk along the railway were occasionally granted; Thomas Barlow was given one for himself and his family to attend places of worship in November 1839, all being '... well acquainted with the working of the railway'. However, two clergymen who applied at about the same time were reluctantly refused, as was the Vicar of Eccles some eighteen months later.

Numerous claims were made against the Company, for a variety of reasons, and usually compensation was awarded although in many cases the railway was obviously not at fault. Colts, heifers and other animals strayed on to the line or fell into cuttings and were killed; usually the property of 'a very poor man', payments of £10 or £12 were made, and compensation was even paid to persons injured when horses took fright near the line.

In November 1836 the Company gave £10 to the owner of a horse and milk-cart into which one of the engines had crashed near Monton Lane, although it was clearly the lack of skill on the part of the boy driver of the cart that had caused the accident. When a passenger train on Whiston Incline ran into a farm cart, destroying it, and killing two cart horses and the driver, £15 was paid to the farmer and £10 to the carter's widow, as a charitable gesture in each case.

The directors knew many of the employees and characters on the line and stations. 'Old Richard' the Lime Street Booking Office doorkeeper had to go in April 1841, having become too familiar with a suspicious and objectional element that loitered around the door, and Alice, who used to sell oranges at Crown Street Station was not allowed to transfer her activities to Lime Street. The Directors declined to compensate her from Company funds, but they subscribed privately to a gift of £10 in September 1836.

Whenever possible information or assistance was given to other railway companies, individuals and engineering firms. In June 1833 the Dublin & Kingstown Railway was allowed to send their chief clerk over to see how the railway kept its books, and locomotive performance figures were supplied to them a few weeks later. In April the D&KR was provided with a copy of the L&MR Bye Laws, Rules and Regulations, and in August a Mr Phillips wrote requesting the friendly co-operation of the Company in the formation of the projected Hull & Selby Railway. In April 1833 the Board received two volumes of reports from the Baltimore & Ohio RR and agreed to exchange reports regularly with that corporation, and in March 1834 the Government of the Netherlands was supplied with such reports as the Company could spare. In December 1834 an unusual request for copies of reports came from the shorthand writer of the House of Commons who stated that the '... evidence in the case of the Western Rail-Way had been burnt at the late fire ...', including several L&M reports that had been quoted.[5]

Particulars of salaries, accounting methods, fares and their collection, operating, management and countless other matters were supplied to about 15 separate British companies and to several abroad. Practical help was also given where possible, as when a few dozen brass tubes were hastily despatched to Ireland to keep the D&KR locomotives working. Trials and experiments of every description were permitted to take place on the line. When the Greenwich Railway proposed to extend their line across Greenwich Park, the Governor of The Royal Observatory was given leave to make experiments to determine the vibration caused by loaded waggons and passenger trains travelling at speed down the Wapping Tunnel. Captain H. M. Denham R.N., Marine Surveyor, Liverpool who carried out the tests in July 1835, later reported to the Board that the greatest distance vibration was perceptible on a surface of mercury was 314 yds.

The Board declined a request from the Leeds & Selby Company for the loan or hire of a locomotive for the opening of that line on 22 September 1834, but offered to sell them *Saturn* for £600. Alternatively, if they could hire the *Collier* from Bourne & Robinson, as Edward Bury had suggested, the L&MR '... would lead Messrs Bournes' coals while their engine was engaged.'

In March 1832 Booth was sent to London to give evidence on the London and Birmingham Bill then before Parliament, and in May a similar request from the Edinburgh and Glasgow Railway was met. Occasionally the Company had no option but to render assistance, particularly where Parliament was concerned; in March 1836 Dixon was summoned to London by Speaker's Warrant to give evidence on the London & Brighton Railway Bill. Representatives of the Company gave evidence before the numerous Select Committees of Parliament from 1839 onwards, their views and opinions commanding great respect.

Professor Barlow[6] was allowed to make experiments on the deflection of rails on behalf of the L&BR in September 1835 and, with several of their directors, to inspect the railway and examine different kinds of rails and chairs; an engine and carriage was appropriated to their use and every facility afforded. In February 1836 he was furnished with details of locomotive speeds and power.

In May 1836 Melly Prevost & Co. arranged for '... two young German Engineers to ride on the Locomotive Engines to learn the management of them', for which they offered to pay any fee to the enginemen which was considered proper. A Board Minute of 12 December 1836 mentions that Brunel and Gibbs of the GWR were '... visiting the Railway and Workshops this day'. By March 1837 the directors had evidently forgiven Dr Lardner for his earlier unkind remarks about them, for he was permitted to inspect the engines and form estimates of their performance.

When the author of the first comprehensive book on British railways, Francis Whishaw,[7] sought and received permission to ride on the engines for a few days to make observations in November 1839, it was made clear that if he rode in the carriages he would have to pay.

The British Association for the Advancement of Science was given facilities for 'strangers' attending its meeting in Liverpool in August 1837 to visit the station and works, and the Association was allowed to inspect the railway line and to take tracings of any plans and sections for geological studies in March 1842.

The Railway Society of London was given copies of Acts, maps, reports and other material relating to the Company in July 1839, but the Board declined being a party to the establishment of a central railway office in London for general information on fares, train times, etc. Neither would it become involved in a protest to the Queen, organised in February 1838 by the mill owners and ratepayers of Manchester, against the Incorporation of the Borough.

Distinguished foreign visitors were taken on conducted tours over the railway, usually in special trains. HRH the Duke of Orleans, whose principal object in visiting Manchester in May 1833 was to see the railway, was shown over the Works on the 23rd by the Mayor of Liverpool and several directors; so impressed was he by the experience, not least that of running across Chat Moss at 30 mph, that he left £40 '... for the benefit of the men at the discretion of the directors.'

M Thiers, the French Minister, and his party visited Wapping Station on 12 September 1833, were taken up the tunnel and then travelled to the Sutton Inclined Plane, visiting the St Helens & Runcorn Gap Railway on the way back to Liverpool. On Saturday, 21 July 1838 another illustrious Frenchman, Marshal Soult, Duke of Dalmatia, with his entourage, was taken by special train from Manchester to Liverpool; the following evening the GJR took the party on to Wolverhampton. The King of the Netherlands visited the L&MR in March 1834, and in February 1835 the Turkish Ambassador and suite travelled from Manchester in a special train, stopping to view the Sankey Viaduct and other works.

Foreign observers were most impressed with the L&MR, writing glowing accounts on their return of wonders the like of which could not be seen elsewhere. But they were alarmed at the cost which, although easily borne by wealthy England, would be a serious impediment to the introduction of railways in their own countries. A German Engineer, Joseph Ritter von Baader, who had spent nine years in Britain, described the L&MR at some length, suggested improvements, and advocated an undulating railway as a much cheaper proposition.[8] Years earlier the Prussian engineers C. von Oeynhausen and H. von Dechen had seen the L&MR in the early stages of construction and included a very favourable description of the project in their minutely detailed report on the English railways.[9] Among a party of French engineers was M Navier who, when told any fact concerning the L&MR, would make some hasty calculations and declare 'The thing is impossible, it does not fit at all with the theory!' One of their compatriots observed that they did not leave the English greatly impressed with their ability.[10] By contrast, the Comte de Pambour, after spending several weeks investigating the L&MR and other railways, produced a learned treatise on the subject.[11]

The first of a long line of American engineers to study English railways was Smeaton's student Benjamin Henry Latrobe who published his report in 1808 on his return to the USA. One of his pupils, William Strickland, was in England in 1825, when he spent some time in Liverpool and Manchester after the failure of the first L&MR Bill, and with his assistant Samuel Kneass he produced a detailed illustrated report on railways, canals, docks, etc.[12]

Horatio Allen, armed with Strickland's book and commissioned by the Delaware & Hudson RR to purchase locomotives and rails in England, landed at Liverpool on 15 February 1828. His letters of introduction to the influential William Brown soon led to meetings with Jesse Hartley and George Stephenson, with both of whom he was greatly impressed, and he was shown over the docks, the railway construction works, the S&DR and numerous iron works. His diaries and reports contain a wealth of information that proved invaluable to the early American railroads.[13] Between 1825 and 1828 Moncure Robinson was studying engineering in England and became well acquainted with Stephenson before returning to construct railroads in Pennsylvania.

From November 1828 to May 1829 the engineers Jonathan Knight, William McNeill and George Whistler[14] were gathering information on behalf of the Baltimore & Ohio Railroad, and on their return they put into practice the principles they had observed on the L&MR; it was said that this was evident on the first 12 miles of the B&ORR with its stout masonry bridges and substantial track laid on diagonally-set granite blocks, but for reasons of economy the rest of the line was laid to a less exacting standard. The English standard gauge was adopted and the fish-bellied rails were imported from this country.[15] E. L. Miller,[16] who had come over expressly for the purpose, witnessed the Rainhill trials.

In November 1830 Robert L. Stevens from the Camden & Amboy Railroad unsuccessfully applied to the Board for an 'Order of Admission' to enable him to wander freely over the L&MR and its installations, but arrangements were made for a director to conduct him. He was present at the trials of *Planet* on 4 December, and ordered a similar locomotive, the *John Bull*, for his own railroad. A L&MR engine driver, N. Cummings, went to America with this locomotive, as did William Robertson, who was recommended by the Directors

115 *The Sankey Viaduct, 1847. Mellowed with the passing years, the structure had now blended into the landscape*

and sent with another Stephenson-built engine; he stayed on with the South Carolina Railroad.

Many American engineers returned after their initial visits to observe the progress of the British railways; Miller was given a pass to walk along the L&MR in June 1831, Robinson came back in 1836, Allen spent another three years in Britain and on the continent from 1834 until 1837 and Kneass returned in 1840. The year 1840 saw the first visit to England of the President of the B&ORR, Louis McLane, for the purpose of raising a loan with Baring Bros.[17]

During the years to 1840 a vast literature on railways was published in the United States, much of it reprinted from English sources. Practically everything ever written about the L&MR was reproduced, along with much original material and translations of continental works on the Company. Many of the prominent Liverpool merchants had close business ties with their associates in the USA and a great deal of information was exchanged through this medium.

From its inception until 1835 the L&MR had encouraged the widest possible publicity in all its activities; the construction of the line, locomotive trials from Rainhill onwards and, after the opening, details of receipts and expenditure were available to shareholders and press alike. In the words of the Chairman addressing the General Meeting on 21 January 1835:

'The Liverpool and Manchester Railway being the first great undertaking of the kind, the Directors on the Opening of the Line, were aware that according to the measure of its success, would be the probability of similar Enterprises, founded on this first experiment; every step, therefore, in their proceedings, whether with reference to extent of traffic, mechanical improvements or financial results, was interesting, as well to the Public as to the Proprietors; and under that conviction the Directors published, Half-yearly, those minute details of the concern, which have found their way to every portion of the Globe. During four years the Directors have pursued the plan of unreserved publicity; their difficulties and their mistakes, but notwithstanding these – their success in the great features of their undertaking, have been made familiar to the Public. The subject is now understood in all its parts, and so well satisfied are the Public and the Legislature with the general result that the construction of Railways in Great Lines from North to South of the Kingdom, has become a distinguishing mark of the present age. The object of publicity has thus been gained. It has been determined by the Country and the Government that Railways shall proceed; and the extent to which they will hereafter be carried will depend on the success, not of the Liverpool and Manchester Line, but of those great works which are now in progress.'

All the information so liberally provided by the Company was available to its rivals, the canals and lines planned in opposition, but neither these nor any railway, completed or in progress, revealed any but the barest details of its position. The Board considered that the time had now arrived when it should consult the Company's own interests as a mercantile concern and not disclose its financial situation in such detail; henceforward the half-yearly statements were in a simpler form, showing only gross receipts, expenses and profit.

The pioneering days of the L&MR were coming to an end in the late 1830s; with the opening of several new railways, many of them on a much larger scale, Booth hoped that '... with a liberal understanding and communication between different Companies, the separate experience of each ... may be made of essential service to all.' One valuable advantage the new railways would enjoy was that of having other lines to provide a standard against which to compare their own, a benefit denied the directors of the L&MR. New lines would be constructed more cheaply, but to compensate in some measure for its costly mistakes, the directors and officers of the L&MR gained experience of incalculable value.

The Company had, in Henry Booth, a most conscientious and efficient Secretary and Treasurer. He unquestionably knew more about the Company's affairs since its early days than anyone else connected with it, and until a chief clerk was appointed in July 1833, he dealt with most of the office work. It was now '... the intention of the Board that the Treasurer, as general Superintendent of the various departments of the concern should have power to decide and act on all points arising out of the ordinary operations of the Road and touching the general business of the Company.' Further arrangements were made to relieve him of minor duties and in January 1834 his annual salary was increased from £750 to £1000; in 1838 a further increase brought it to £1500. By 1841 he was referred to as the Treasurer and General Manager of the L&MR, and in 1846 was described as '... one of the earliest improvers of railway administration and the originator of the present mode of conducting railway business.'[18]

He was very conscious of the railway's imperfections, referring in December 1836 to the permanent way, the inadequate drainage system, the

116 *Chat Moss, 1845; within a few years of the coming of the railway, large areas of the moss were brought under cultivation*

need for powerful engines and stronger rolling stock; the previous year had been one of transition, passing from the imperfect and defective to improvements resulting from experience. 'New railways', he observed, 'will have a great advantage ... in everything which constitutes the working of a Railway. They will start at a point which we have not yet reached, or only in solitary instances.'

Booth's advice to the Railway Commissioners for Ireland[19] is that of a professional railway manager with imagination and foresight. He asked:

'Are the railways in Ireland to be considered in the light of mercantile speculations, not to be undertaken except with the prospect of a remunerating profit? – or must we regard them as great and beneficial works ... to be sustained by the hand of Government, where private means are insufficient?'

After a century-and-a-half considerations of a similar nature affect the survival of some railways in Britain itself.

His misgivings on the wisdom of the GWR, about to start construction on the Broad Gauge proved correct in almost every particular, but, like Peter Sinclair of the B&LR, who was '. . . not wedded to the peculiar gauge of the Liverpool & Manchester Railway', he thought 5ft or 5ft 3in. a better width. His suggestion of 5ft 3in. as the standard for Ireland was adopted. He held the view that the main lines between important towns afforded the best scope for the peculiar advantages of railways and that smaller places should be served by branch lines, rather than that the main line should deviate to accommodate them.

This was the time of the first railway mania, when

supplements to the *London Gazette* were necessary to carry all the announcements of new lines projected. Many of these were in competition with existing railways, sometimes taking a better route where opposition had compelled the original company to deviate from the best plan. Others would have traversed country that could not possibly support a line built to acceptable standards, and as Booth observed, '... no line can be a good one where no Railway is required.'

During the hearing of evidence on the L&BR Bill it was stated that the most determined opponents of the L&MR now welcomed the railway, including Lord Sefton and the Liverpool merchant Hardman Earle, now a Director. The line, running through the garden of his palatial house, far from being a nuisance, was regarded as an object of interest; rents of property along the line had doubled, and advertisements recommended a site because of its proximity to the railway. One man actually complained, after opposing the Bill, that the line avoided his land.

Having little in common with the existing colliery lines, the L&MR laid the foundations of the modern railways that were soon to spread across Britain and the world. At home, the railway lent impetus to the Industrial Revolution, providing a more certain and infinitely faster means of transport for the goods pouring from the factories than the roads and canals could ever achieve, while its facilities for cheap passenger travel on a vast scale led to changes in the pattern of social life in Victorian days more radical than anything since the dawn of history. Abroad, whole continents were opened up for settlement, and industries were established where none had previously existed. Men in their tens of thousands found employment for years, not only on lofty viaduct or in gloomy tunnel, but along those endless miles of cutting and embankment hardly noticed by the traveller of today. These mighty feats of civil engineering alone are an enduring monument to the courage and energy of the Victorian railway builders.

The steam locomotive, mainstay of the railways for 130 years, was in its infancy at the time of the Rainhill Trials, when, with considerable courage, the directors of the L&MR decided to adopt it, with all its uncertainties and imperfections. Those archaic engines of 1829 were the precursors of what was to become, if not the most efficient, certainly the most impressive machine ever devised by man. No subsequent development in the world of mass transport has ever had the impact of the railway, where mechanical traction first set man free from his dependence on the horse.

Writing of the Liverpool & Manchester Railway in 1837, one of its directors[20] said:

'That great enterprise, in leading the way in Railway communication, has had to try experiments for all those which have succeeded it; and if it should, in its turn, have to receive instruction from its younger brethren, they must never forget how many lessons have been taught them at its expense.'

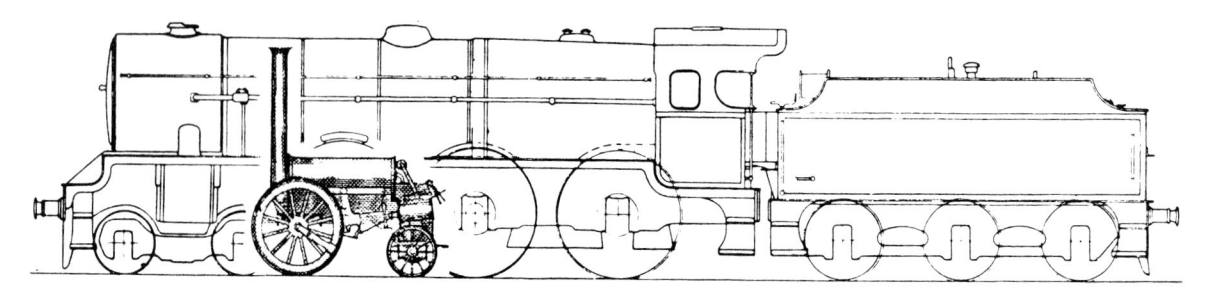

117 Comet, *Liverpool & Manchester Railway, 1830 and* Royal Scot, *London, Midland & Scottish Railway, 1927*

Main Events and Developments affecting the Liverpool & Manchester Line after 1845

1846 Formation of the L&NWR. Capital £6,250,000; route mileage 330

1847 Widening of the Broad Green Embankment to take 4 tracks. Trent Valley line, Stafford–Rugby, opened; north-south services avoid Birmingham. Changes introduced only gradually on the L&M line; L&NWR Rule Book still refers to flags, boards and arrows at Newton Junction. George McCorquodale of Liverpool had joined William Blacklock of Manchester in the contract for the railway companies' printing and stationery, and in 1847 they took over the Legh Arms Hotel, on the north side of the line at Newton; later they acquired the adjacent Conservative Hall. Regrettably, McCorquodale's early records were lost in a fire on 16 February 1865

1849 (1 August) Opening of the line Edge Hill–Waterloo Dock via the Victoria Tunnel (1 mile 947 yds) Edge Hill–Byrom Street and the Waterloo Tunnel (850 yds) Byrom Street–Waterloo Goods Yards, with a short break between the two tunnels. (1 August) Opening of the Manchester South Junction & Altrincham Railway, Ordsall Lane–London Road Station L&NWR (Manchester & Birmingham Railway)

1850 (2 February) Patricroft–Clifton line opened. Widening of the St Helens Railway and the Intersection Bridge to double track

1853 (1 March) The Viaduct Foundry, Newton, leased from Jones & Potts, purchased 1860 (founded in 1833 by Jones, Turner & Evans). Edge Hill to concentrate on locomotives, waggon work transferred to 'Newton Waggon Works'. L&NWR built a township nearby for its employees and named it Earlestown after Sir Hardman Earle, under whose guidance the Company bought and developed the works. Increased from eight to 36 acres; 2000 employed in 1901

1864 (15 February) Edge Hill–Garston line opened. (1 August) Warrington (Winwick Junction)–Golborne line opened, taking north-south traffic off the L&M line, but because of the convenience of exchanging mails between north-south and east-west services at Newton Junction, it was several years before the GPO would allow mail trains to use the direct route. (1 September) Eccles–Tyldsley–Wigan line opened

1865 Work started on extensions to Lime Street Station

1866 Edge Hill–Canada Dock line opened

1869 Runcorn Bridge opened (1 February, goods; 1 April, passengers); journey London–Liverpool shortened by nine miles

1870 Olive Mount Cutting widened and line quadrupled. Locomotives replace rope haulage in Lime Street Tunnel. Tunnel ventilating shaft built; fan 30ft in diameter, 7ft 6in. wide, and running at 45 rpm, cleared smoke in 8 minutes

1871 (1 March) Lime Street Station Hotel opened. (1 November) Huyton–St Helens line opened

1873 Edge Hill Passenger Station remodelled over the previous two years; overall roof removed, passenger subway built in the old winding machinery tunnel

1875 Edge Hill Station, goods depot, sidings, locomotive sheds and other installations now cover about 40 acres and traffic described as of 'gigantic dimensions'

118 *Lime Street Station during reconstruction, 1865; cutting back the tunnel entrance*

119 *Olive Mount Cutting looking east, July 1883, showing widening and quadrupling of line of 1870*

120 Lime Street Station Hotel; photograph taken 28 July 1899

1880 (1 January) Alexandra Dock branch opened. Further widening of part of Olive Mount Cutting. Enlargement of Lime Street Station on south side. L&NWR capital £91 m., mileage 1716. (15 September) Jubilee of L&MR; great disappointment in Liverpool and Manchester at decision 'for certain reasons' by L&NWR to hold no public celebrations, but some of the oldest engine drivers were entertained by the directors at Crewe to mark the event

1881 Lime Street Tunnel opened out. Edge Hill 'gridiron' in operation at the marshalling yards

1883 (11 June) Broad Green–Edge Lane line opened

1884 (13 June) Manchester Exchange Station opened. Platform 3 Exchange joined Platform 11 Victoria to make the longest covered platform in the world, 2194ft

1885 Lime Street Tunnel/cutting widened

1895 (16 February) The Victoria Tunnel rope broke and locomotive working was introduced. (12 June) Riverside Station, Liverpool, opened; reached via Victoria and Waterloo Tunnels but owned by the Mersey Docks and Harbour Board. (4 November) Weaste–Manchester Ship Canal branch opened

1896 (11 May) Rope working of Wapping Tunnel discontinued

1900 Edge Hill marshalling yards now contain over 60 miles of track; had cost over £2 m. to date

121 *Old engine drivers at Crewe, L&NWR, June 1880. Those who served on the L&MR are, back row, standing, 3rd from left, William Manners (1842), and extreme right, Thomas Stockton (1838); seated on the steps in the centre row, 1st from left, is Thomas Valentine (1833), and 2nd from left is John Murphy (1828). Sitting on the wall, extreme left, is Sir Richard Moon, Chairman L&NWR, and in front of him is G. Whale, Assistant Mechanical Engineer. Sitting on the wall on the extreme right is F. W. Webb, Chief Mechanical Engineer; in front of him is A. L. Mumford, also Assistant Mechanical Engineer*

122 Edge Hill marshalling yard, 1895

1903 (14 June) Edward Woods died. He had stayed on with the L&NWR until 1852 to complete the engineering works in hand and then became a consulting engineer in London; elected President of the Institution of Civil Engineers 1886, he was the last surviving officer of the L&MR, and was 89 years old at the time of his death

1905 The staff of Lime Street Station this year totalled 532; at Edge Hill Locomotive Sheds 160 engines were maintained

1923 L&NWR becomes part of London, Midland & Scottish Railway

1930 (15 September) Centenary of L&MR; ceremonies and exhibitions arranged by the LMS and by the civic authorities of Liverpool and Manchester

1940 (20 December) Heavy air raid on Liverpool; Lime Street Station damaged and Canada Dock Goods Station destroyed. (23 December) Manchester Victoria Station bombed and seriously damaged

1941 (1–7 May) Concentrated air attacks on Liverpool causing very heavy damage to railway installations

1947 Railway nationalisation; L&MR line part of London Midland Region, British Railways

1961 Electrification of Liverpool–Crewe line on the 25,000V A.C. system

1965 Park Lane Goods Depot (Wapping) closed

1969 (5 May) Manchester Exchange Station closed

1971 Liverpool Riverside Station closed

1979 Stations now open on the former L&MR are Lime Street, Edge Hill, Broad Green, Roby, Huyton, Rainhill, St Helens Junction, Earlestown, Newton-le-Willows, Patricroft, Eccles, Manchester Victoria

APPENDIX A

1 *List of prominent guests*

The Opening Ceremony, 15 September 1830

List of guests invited to the opening ceremony, 15 September 1830, compiled from various sources including Charles Lawrence's official list and newspaper accounts of those present.

The Duke of Wellington
The Earl and Countess of Wilton
The Earl and Countess of Glengall
The Earl of Brecknock
The Earl of Lauderdale
The Earl of Winton
The Earl of Cassilis
The Marquis and Marchioness of Salisbury
The Marquis of Stafford
Lord and Lady Dacre
Lord and Lady Delamere
Lord Granville
Lord Hill
Lord Wharncliffe
Lord Burghersh
Lord Stanley
Lord Monson
Lord Clive
Lord Grosvenor
Lord Molyneaux
Lord Balcarres
Lord Harrowby
Lord Skelmersdale
Lord Fitzroy
Lord Talbot
Lord Stainforth
Lord Bayning
Lord Mandeville
Lord Leveson Gower
Lord F. L. Gower
Lord F. Somerset
Lord Brougham
Viscount and Lady Belgrave
Viscount Sandon
Viscount Melbourne*
Viscount Combermere
Viscount Ingestre
Viscount Grey*
The Hon. R. Wilbraham

The Hon. S. Wortley
The Hon. E. G. Stanley MP*
The Hon. G. Anson
The Hon. H. Cholmondley
The Hon.—Shore
The Hon.—Neville
The Rt Hon. Sir Robert Peel MP*
The Rt Hon. William Huskisson MP
The Rt Hon. Charles Arbuthnot MP
The Rt Hon. John Calcraft MP
Sir Samuel Scott
Sir Philip Egerton
Sir J. R. Graham MP
Sir H. Mainwaring
Sir Thomas Mainwaring
Sir John Wrottesley MP
Sir Jeffrey Wyatville
Sir G. Smith
Sir George Murray
Sir T. Freemantle
Sir P. Grey Egerton
Sir John Helton
Sir Francis Macdonald
Sir Thomas Stanley
Sir Charles Lithester
Vice-Admiral Lord Colville
Vice-Admiral Hon. C. E. Fleming
Rear Admiral White
General Gascoyne MP
Colonel Cawthorne MP
Colonel Egerton
Colonel Fuller
Colonel Jordan
Colonel Boyd
Colonel Shaw
Colonel Cust MP
Colonel Power
Colonel M'Gregor
Major Kearney

241

Captain Moorsom RN
Captain Cririe RN
Captain Irving
The Bishop of Lichfield and Coventry
Prince Esterhazy (Austrian Ambassador)
The Comte de Demidoff
Count Potocki (Russian Ambassador)
Count Bathiani
Mr Ogden (US Consul)
Mr Henry Brougham MP
Mr Penryn MP
Mr Daniel Sykes MP
Mr John Benett MP
Mr Richard Jenkins MP
Mr Edward Strutt MP
Mr Thomas Legh MP
Mr T. Greene MP
Mr E. J. Littleton MP
Mr Wilbraham Egerton MP
Mr John Doherty MP
Mr John Wood MP
Mr William Holmes MP
Mr Wilson Patten MP
Mr Edward Rogers MP
Mr William Whitmore MP
Mr William Yates Peel MP
Mr A. H. Houldsworth MP
Mr Charles Babbage

Mr W. Cartwright
Mr T. Trafford
Mr H. H. Joy
Mr George Rennie
Mr H. Greville
Mr W. Hulton
Mr W. Gerrard
Mr T. K. Hale
Mr J. Trench
Mr Wainewright
Mr Blackburn
Alderman Thompson MP
Dr Brandreth
Dr Southey
Peter Hesketh Esq (High Sheriff of the County)
Sir George Drinkwater (Mayor of Liverpool)
Boroughreeves of Manchester and Salford
High Bailiff of Birmingham
The Hon. Mrs Stanley
The Hon. Miss Stanley
The Hon. Miss Wilbraham
The Hon. Mrs Penryn
The Hon. Miss Long
Mrs Arbuthnot

Grey, Peel, Melbourne and Derby (Hon. E. G. Stanley) were future Prime Ministers

APPENDIX A

2 Order of trains

Engine	Directed by	Driver	Flagman	Brakesmen	Director in charge of train
Northumbrian	George Stephenson	Robert Creed	Mark Thompson (Lilac)	Jas Scott J. Melling Jnr	Mr Moss
Phoenix	Robert Stephenson Jnr	John Wakefield	Jas Thompson (Green)	James Wood Hugh Greenshields	Mr Earle
North Star	Robert Stephenson Snr	Thomas George	W. E. Gillespie (Yellow)	Thomas Harding Thomas Heaton	Mr Harrison
Rocket	Joseph Locke	Mark Wakefield*	— (Light Blue)	John Wheatley John Gray	Mr A. Hodgson
Dart	Thomas L. Gooch	**	Samuel Bennet (Purple)	Jos Copeland John Cummings	Mr Sandars
Comet	William Allcard	John Robson	Josh Richardson (Deep Red)	Jas Cummings John Melling Snr	Mr Bourne
Arrow	F. Swanwick	**	John Birkinshaw (Pink)	Gordon M'Leod William Day	Mr Currie
Meteor	Anthony Harding	**	William Gray (Brown)	John Harding Thos. Ilbery	Mr D. Hodgson

*Kirwan refers to driver White of the *Rocket*
**The drivers were Robert Hope, John Dunn and Robert Weatherburn, but who drove which engine is not recorded.

APPENDIX B

Locomotives of the Liverpool & Manchester Railway

The Locomotive Registers of the L&MR do not appear to have survived, and this table is based on information derived from the following principal sources:

The Board and Management Committee Minutes
Lists of locomotives as at 1 March 1836 and 18 January 1837, prepared for the Chairman, Charles Lawrence
Report dated 16 December 1842 from Edward Woods to Charles Lawrence
Accountant's list of L&NW (Northern Division) locomotives to November 1854, signed by Francis Trevithick, Locomotive Superintendent, 13 March 1855

Locomotives taken over by the L&NWR in 1846 were renumbered, as shown in brackets under 'Remarks'. An asterisk (*) denotes that the same name had been borne by an earlier engine. Engines withdrawn from service were usually laid aside to be broken up later.

The following abbreviations are used for makers' names:

RS & Co.	Robert Stephenson & Co.
FMJ	Fenton, Murray & Jackson
GBG	Galloway, Bowman & Glasgow
SR & Co.	Sharp, Roberts & Co.
MD & Co.	Mather, Dixon & Co.
TK & L	Todd, Kitson & Laird

No	Name	Maker	Date	Type	Remarks
1	*Rocket*	RS & Co.	1829	0-2-2	Sold 1836 to J. Thompson for £300
2	*Arrow*	RS & Co.	1830	0-2-2	Withdrawn 1837; sold 1840 for £50
3	*Meteor*	RS & Co.	1830	0-2-2	Withdrawn by 1836; sold 1837 for £240
4	*Dart*	RS & Co.	1830	0-2-2	Broken up 1833
5	*Comet*	RS & Co.	1830	0-2-2	Sold 1832 to W. McKenzie for £250
6	*Phoenix*	RS & Co.	1830	0-2-2	Broken up 1833
7	*Northumbrian*	RS & Co.	1830	0-2-2	Offered to L&BR for £450 1836; refused. Broken up (?)
8	*North Star*	RS & Co.	1830	0-2-2	Sold 1833 to W. McKenzie for £275
9	*Planet*	RS & Co.	1830	2-2-0	Withdrawn c. 1840
10	*Majestic*	RS & Co.	1830	0-2-2	Withdrawn by 1833
11	*Mercury*	RS & Co.	1830	2-2-0	Withdrawn c. 1840
12	*Mars*	RS & Co.	1830	2-2-0	Sold 1839 to Tayleur for £358
13	*Samson*	RS & Co.	1831	0-4-0	Withdrawn by 1836
14	*Jupiter*	RS & Co.	1831	2-2-0	Withdrawn c. 1840
15	*Goliah*	RS & Co.	1831	0-4-0	Sold 1835 to S. Ellis for £100
16	*Saturn*	RS & Co.	1831	2-2-0	Beyond repair 1834; broken up
17	*Sun*	RS & Co.	1831	2-2-0	Sold 1835 to Pritchard for £200
18	*Venus*	RS & Co.	1831	2-2-0	Withdrawn by 1836
19	*Vulcan*	FMJ	1831	2-2-0	Sold 1841 to T. Pearson for £399
20	*Etna*	RS & Co.	1831	2-2-0	Sold 1835 to Guest, Lewis & Co. for £250
21	*Fury*	FMJ	1831	2-2-0	Broken up c. 1842
22	*Victory*	RS & Co.	1831	2-2-0	Broken up c. 1842
23	*Atlas*	RS & Co.	1831	0-4-0	Withdrawn c. 1840
24	*Vesta*	RS & Co.	1831	2-2-0	Withdrawn 1836; probably sold
25	*Milo*	RS & Co.	1832	0-4-0	Beyond repair 1834; broken up
26	*Liver*	Bury	1832	2-2-0	Sold 1837 to Mullins & McMahon for £700

APPENDIX C

No	Name	Maker	Date	Type	Remarks
27	*Pluto*	RS & Co.	1832	2-2-0	Rebuilt 1842; withdrawn 1848 (127)
28	*Caledonian*	GBG	1832	0-4-0	Sold 1837 to L&BR for £400
29	*Ajax*	RS & Co.	1832	2-2-0	Broken up c. 1841
30	*Leeds*	FMJ	1833	2-2-0	Sold 1840 to Chester & Birkenhead Railway for £414
31	*Firefly*	RS & Co.	1833	2-2-0	Broken up c. 1840
32	*Experiment*	SR & Co.	1833	2-2-0	Sold 1836 to GJR for £500
33	*Patentee*	RS & Co.	1834	2-2-2	Broken up c. 1841
34	*Titan*	Tayleur	1834	0-4-0	Ballast engine 1842; broken up c. 1844
35	*Orion*	Tayleur	1834	0-4-0	Broken up c. 1840
36	*Swiftsure*	Forrester	1835	2-2-0	Broken up c. 1843
37	*Rapid*	Tayleur	1835	2-2-2	Broken up c. 1843
38	*Speedwell*	Tayleur	1835	2-2-2	Broken up c. 1843
39	*Hercules*	MD & Co.	1835	0-4-0	Broken up c. 1842
40	*Eclipse*	Tayleur	1835	0-4-2	Broken up c. 1842
41	*Star*	Tayleur	1836	2-2-2	Ballast engine 1842; withdrawn 1848 (124)
42	*York*	Tayleur	1836	0-4-2	Heavy repairs 1841; withdrawn 1844
43	*Vesuvius*	Haigh Fdy.	1836	2-2-2	Heavy repairs 1841; withdrawn 1848 (125)
44	*Thunderer*	MD & Co.	1836	0-4-2	Broken up c. 1842
45	*Lightning*	Haigh Fdy.	1836	2-2-2	Rebuilt 1841; withdrawn 1849 (114)
46	*Cyclops*	Haigh Fdy.	1836	2-2-2	Broken up 1843
47	*Milo**	Tayleur	1836	2-2-2	Broken up 1841
48	*Dart**	MD & Co.	1836	2-2-2	Broken up c. 1843
49	*Phoenix**	Tayleur	1836	2-2-2	Broken up c. 1842
50	*Majestic**	Tayleur	1836	2-2-2	Broken up c. 1841
51	*Etna**	Tayleur	1837	2-2-2	Broken up c. 1841
52	*Arrow**	MD & Co.	1837	2-2-2	Heavy repairs 1841; withdrawn 1845
53	*Sun**	Hawthorn	1837	2-2-2	Broken up c. 1842
54	*Meteor**	MD & Co.	1837	2-2-2	Heavy repairs 1842; withdrawn 1849 (115)
55	*Comet**	MD & Co.	1837	2-2-2	Heavy repairs 1842; withdrawn 1845
56	*Vesta**	Hawthorn	1837	2-2-2	Broken up c. 1841
57	*Lion*	TK & L	1838	0-4-2	Rebuilt 1841; withdrawn 1857 (116) and sold to Mersey Docks & Harbour Board 1859 for £400. Now preserved
58	*Tiger*	TK & L	1838	0-4-2	Rebuilt 1841; withdrawn 1850 and broken up (117)
59	*Rokeby*	Rothwell	1838	2-2-2	Heavy repairs 1840; withdrawn 1848 (123)
60	*Roderic*	Rothwell	1838	2-2-2	Rebuilt 1841; broken up 1847 (118)
61	*Mammoth*	Banks	1838	0-4-2	Broken up 1843
62	*Leopard*	TK & L	1838	2-2-2	Heavy repairs 1842; withdrawn 1845
63	*Mastodon*	Banks	1838	0-4-2	Rebuilt 1842; broken up 1849 (119)
64	*Panther*	TK & L	1839	2-2-2	Heavy repairs 1841; withdrawn c. 1844
65	*Elephant*	TK & L	1839	0-4-2	Rebuilt 1841; broken up 1848 (113)
66	*Samson**	Hick	1839	0-4-2	Rebuilt 1841; broken up 1848 (120)
67	*Buffalo*	TK & L	1839	0-4-2	Rebuilt 1841; converted to tank engine for shunting at Holyhead 1859, sold 1862 (121)
68	*Goliah**	Hick	1839	0-4-2	Rebuilt 1841; broken up after boiler exploded, Wigan, 1847 (122)
69	*Swallow*	L&MR (Edge Hill)	1841	2-2-2	The first new locomotive built by L&MR; turned out of Edge Hill Works 8 September 1841. Sold 1850 to St Helens Railway (128)
70	*Martin*	L&MR	1841	2-2-2	Broken up 1849 (129)
71	*Heron*	L&MR	1841	2-2-2	Broken up 1852 (130)

No	Name	Maker	Date	Type	Remarks
72	*Kingfisher*	L&MR	1841	2-2-2	Broken up 1851 (131)
73	*Pelican*	L&MR	1841	2-2-2	Broken up 1852 (132)
74	*Ostrich*	L&MR	1842	2-2-2	Withdrawn 1854; on sale 1855 (133)
75	*Owl*	L&MR	1842	2-4-0	Withdrawn 1854; on sale 1855 (134)
76	*Bat*	L&MR	1842	2-4-0	Sold 1852 Swansea Vale Railway (?) (135)
77	*Stork*	L&MR	1842	2-2-2	Broken up 1852 (136)
78	*Crane*	L&MR	1842	2-2-2	Sold 1854 (137)
79	*Swan*	L&MR	1842	2-2-2	Broken up 1853 (138)
80	*Cygnet*	L&MR	1842	2-2-2	Broken up 1852 (139)
81	*Atlas**	L&MR	1842	2-4-0?	This was a new luggage engine, completed on 1 November 1842, presumably of the standard pattern. Possibly intended for banking duties, hence the name. Sold 1852 St Helens Railway (140)
82	*Pheasant*	L&MR	1842	2-2-2	Broken up 1849 (141)
83	*Partridge*	L&MR	1843	2-2-2	Withdrawn 1854; on sale 1855 (126)
84	*Bittern*	L&MR	1843	2-4-0	Withdrawn 1853; sold to St Helens Railway (142)
85	*Lapwing*	L&MR	1843	2-4-0	Withdrawn 1853 and sold (143)
86	*Raven*	L&MR	1843	2-4-0	Withdrawn 1854; on sale 1855 (144)
87	*Crow*	L&MR	1844	2-4-0	Withdrawn 1853; sold 1854 (145)
88	*Redwing*	L&MR	1844	2-2-2	Withdrawn 1854; broken up (146)
89	*Woodlark*	L&MR	1844	2-2-2	Sold 1852 to St Helens Railway (147)
90	*Penguin*	L&MR	1845	2-4-0	Withdrawn 1853; on sale 1855 (148)
91	*Petrel*	L&MR	1844	2-4-0	Withdrawn 1856; sold to a Mr Stone, but returned, May 1856 (149)
92	*Linnet*	L&MR	1845	2-2-2	Withdrawn 1853 and sold (150)
93	*Goldfinch*	L&MR	1845	2-2-2	Withdrawn 1853; broken up (151)
94	*Bullfinch*	L&MR	1845	2-2-2	Withdrawn 1855 (152)
95**	*Chaffinch*	L&MR	1845	2-2-2	Withdrawn 1853; sold 1854 (153)
	Starling	GJR (Edge Hill)	1845	2-4-0	Withdrawn 1854; on sale 1855 (154)
	Owzell	GJR	1845	2-4-0	Withdrawn 1854; on sale 1855 (155)
	Redstart	GJR	1846	2-4-0	Withdrawn 1856 (156)
	Redbreast	GJR	1846	2-4-0	Withdrawn 1851; broken up (157)
	Condor	GJR	1846	2-2-2	Withdrawn 1853; broken up (158)
	Adjutant	GJR	1846	2-4-0	Withdrawn 1857 (159)
	Flamingo	GJR	1846	2-4-0	Withdrawn 1853; on sale 1855 (160)
	Cuckoo	GJR	1846	2-4-0	Withdrawn 1856 (161)
	Albatross	GJR	1846	2-4-0	Withdrawn 1856 (162)
	Osprey	GJR	1846	2-4-0	Withdrawn 1856 (163)

** No. 95, *Chaffinch*, was the last locomotive turned out at Edge Hill (June 1845) before the amalgamation with the GJR. A further ten 'Bird' class engines were built at the Works by the GJR between then and the formation of the L&NWR in July 1846 in the order given above, but it is not known whether they were numbered in the L&MR series.

The type (wheel arrangement) is that of the engines as originally built.

An engine, *Victoria*, (69), listed by Whishaw, is not mentioned in the L&MR records, nor in Woods' complete list of locomotives as at 16 December 1842.

REFERENCES AND NOTES

Abbreviations
BL – British Library (British Museum)   RO – Record Office   PRO – Public Record Office   ICE – Institution of Civil Engineers   SLS – Stephenson Locomotive Society   U of L – University of London

Railway Archives
Much of the information upon which this work is based has been derived from the Minute Books of the Board of Directors, the Finance Committee and the Management Committee of the Liverpool & Manchester Railway. References to these sources have been omitted from the following list as they are too numerous, but it will usually be apparent from the text where this material has been consulted.

Chapter 1: The Formation of the Company (pp. 11–32)

1. *Hansard*, 1st Series, Vol. 3, col. 522, 15 February 1805
2. VIGNOLES, C. B., Presidential address, Institution of Civil Engineers, *Proceedings*, Vol. 29, 1869–70
3. House of Commons: *Proceedings of the Committee . . . on the Liverpool and Manchester Railroad Bill: Minutes of Evidence*, 1825
4. So named from its terminus at the Old Quay, Manchester
5. James was described as a man of great energy, visiting his establishments in various parts of the country and travelling post haste, day and night; a talented conversationalist with a fund of ready wit and anecdote, and a rapid and stylish writer. 'Though corpulent, his manners were elegant and easy . . .'. *Biographical Notice of William James, Projector of the Railway System in England*, 1840. BL
6. William James to the Earl of Hardwicke: *Report on an Engine Rail Road from Bishop Stortford to Clayhithe Sluice . . .* Hardwicke papers, BL Add Mss 35690
7. VEITCH, G. S., *The Struggle for the Liverpool & Manchester Railway*, 1930, pp. 24–5. Charles Hadfield, biographer of William Jessop, expresses doubt about that engineer's involvement in the project
8. It was of these projects that the old Duke of Bridgewater had remarked 'We shall do well enough if we can keep clear of these damned tramroads'
9. The Rathbones imported the first consignment of American cotton
10. He was employed by Rastrick in 1830, surveying in the Birmingham area. U of L Mss Dept, Rastrick Collection, Ledger. There is an article on Paul Padley by P. R. REYNOLDS in Railway & Canal Historical Society *Journal*, Vol. 23, No. 1, March 1977
11. FALK, B., *The Bridgewater Millions*, 1942, and RICHARDS, E., *The Leviathan of Wealth*, 1973
12. Liverpool RO 385 JAM 1/6/1, 385 JAM 1/3/1, 385 JAM 1/6/2
13. E.M.S.P., [Paine], *The two James's and the two Stephensons*, 1861. Whether the plans were in fact lithographed is doubtful
14. Liverpool RO 385 JAM 1/6/4
15. Letter, W. James to G. Stephenson, 15 October 1822; Liverpool RO 385 JAM 4/2
16. Letter, Lord Derby to W. James, 13 November 1822; Liverpool RO 385 JAM 1/1
17. Records of the King's Bench; King's Bench Prison Commitment Books; PRO Pris 4
18. A rough estimate based on such information as could be gathered from James, who had originally suggested £100,000 for the construction of the line
19. A paper in Sandars' own handwriting dated '1824 5 mo. 24' lists the following as original shareholders: Wm. Ewart, J. Moss, C. Tayleur, Jas. Cropper, W. Rotherham, W. Maxwell, Adam Hodgson, Wm. Jones, S. Blain, Jos. Sandars, Sir J. Tobin, W. Rathbone, W. & F. Maxwell, Isaac Hodgson, Jos. Mill, Jno. Garnett, R. Dawson, Jno. Gladstone, Sandbach, Dr Trail. On the back is added 'Original shareholders in the Liverpool and Manchester Railway, the remainder in Manchester, total 300 shares: John Kennedy, Peter Ewart, Hugh Birley, David Holt, Harbottle, Lees, Garnett'. The *Daily Courier*, 15 September 1880.
20. John Dixon and Thomas Storey
21. Letter and account, Elijah Galloway Jnr to Committee of the L&MR 7 May 1825: Liverpool RO 385 LIV 5/6
22. Letter, G. Stephenson to Sandars 12 December 1824: Liverpool RO 385 STE 14
23. SANDARS, J., *A Letter on the Subject of the Projected Rail Road between Liverpool and Manchester* etc., 29 October 1824
24. N.D. Prepared some time after 5 October 1824. Blank pages interleaved with 24 printed pages.
25. Francis Mewburn was the first railway solicitor, having been associated with the S&DR from 1814. MEWBURN, F. *The Larchfield Diary*, 1876

26 In the event the Birmingham & Liverpool Railway Bill failed
27 The instruments had been lent to Stephenson by Jesse Hartley; letter, Stephenson to Sandars 12 December 1824. Liverpool RO 385 STE 14
28 Liverpool RO 385 LIV 5/3
29 William Holmes, Treasurer of the Ordnance and Conservative whip
30 Liverpool RO; William Cubitt to Sandars 27 February 1825 385 LIV 3/4; 10 March 1825 385 LIV 3/5; Cubitt to Booth 15 May 1825 385 LIV 1/5/1; 19 May 1825 385 LIV 1/5/2
31 House of Commons: *Proceedings of the Committee ... on the Liverpool and Manchester Railroad Bill*, 1825
32 George Leather of Leeds, who had been Resident Engineer during construction of the Surrey Iron Railway, over 20 years earlier
33 *The Creevy Papers*, Vol 2, Maxwell, Sir H., ed., 1903–5
34 In those days committees on Private Bills were open to every MP who chose to attend, even if only for the purpose of voting. VIGNOLES, C. B., Presidential address, ICE *Proceedings*, Vol. 29, 1869–70
35 BASNETT, LOIS, 'The History of the Bolton & Leigh Railway based on the Hulton Papers (1824–1828)', Lancashire & Cheshire Antiquarian Society *Transactions*, Vol. LXII, 1953
36 MATHER, F. C., *After the Canal Duke*, 1970
37 Under the terms of the Will of the Duke of Bridgewater (who died in 1803) the Canal passed first to his nephew, the 2nd Marquis of Stafford, during his lifetime, and was then to go to his second son, Lord Francis Egerton Gower. While enjoying the profits from the Canal, neither had any control over it; this remained with the Superintendent, Robert Haldane Bradshaw. The Marquis of Stafford received a total income of nearly £2¼m from the Canal; on his death as the 1st Duke of Sutherland in 1833, his L&MR shares were inherited by his eldest son, the 2nd Duke
38 POLLINS, H., 'Finances of the Liverpool & Manchester Railway' *Economic History Review*, Vol. 5, 1952. Manchester had neither Member of Parliament nor mayor at the time of the Act, and had no influence in Parliament. Nearby Newton, with about 60 voters, returned two members. The limitation of holdings to 10 shares was lifted after the Marquis of Stafford's investment
39 House of Lords: *Minutes of Evidence* taken before the Lords Committee on the L&MR Bill, 1826
40 7 G4 c xlix, 5 May 1826
41 Mewburn, op cit
42 7 & 8 G4 c xxi, 12 April 1827

Chapter 2: The Construction of the Railway (pp. 33–62)

1 Several directors registered their 'astonishment and disgust' at the Company's failure to appoint the Rennie brothers; *Gentleman's Magazine*, October 1830. Lord Stafford's nominees to the Board, Capt. James Bradshaw, James Sothern and James Loch do not appear to have been entirely convinced of George Stephenson's ability to undertake the task ahead, and Loch urged his fellow directors to appoint a more scientific and experienced engineer to supervise him
2 PICTON, J. A., *Memorials of Liverpool*, 2 Vols., 1875. 'He was the first mason of his day. I remember him, a strange violent, swearing man ... He built the Grosvenor Bridge at Chester, the largest stone arch in the world.' MICHAEL ROBBINS, 'From R. B. Dockray's Diary' (entry of 27 August 1860): *Journal of Transport History*, Vol. 7, No 2, November 1965
3 Thomas Gooch (1808–1882), obit; ICE *Proceedings*, Vol. 72, 1883
4 Horatio Allen (1802–1890), sent to England in 1828 as contracting agent of the Delaware & Hudson RR to study railways and purchase locomotives. He was in England from February until at least July 1828, and his diary for part of this period was reproduced in the Railway & Locomotive Historical Society (USA) *Bulletin* No 89, 1953. Three letters written by him during this period to John B. Jervis, Chief Engineer to the D&H Canal & RR, are in the Society's *Bulletin* No 61, 1943
5 *Great Western Railway Magazine*, Vol. 3, No 25, November 1890
6 John Foster was Liverpool Docks Engineer; 1809, Secretary and Surveyor, 1813, General Surveyor Princes Dock
7 In May 1843 the Company gave Vignoles a sealed certificate to the effect that he had been principal resident engineer for the original survey, had partly laid out the line and had assisted the Company in other ways; he was then about to be appointed Engineer to the King of Wurtemburgh
8 Liverpool and Manchester Rail-Way: *Specification for Excavating the Tunnel at Liverpool*, Liverpool, 25 August 1826. U of L Mss Dept
9 BOOTH, H., *An account of the Liverpool and Manchester Railway etc*, 1830
10 WALKER, JAMES S., *An Accurate Description of the Liverpool and Manchester Railway*, 1831
11 Ibid. and *Description of the Tunnel of the Liverpool and Manchester Railway* reprinted from the *Albion*, 20 July 1829
12 John Gillespie had assisted George Stephenson's elder brother Robert in the construction of the Nantlle Railway.
13 3 m. bricks were made on Newton Common by contract in 1827
14 The Cheshire acre contains 10,240 sq. yds compared with the statute acre of 4840 sq. yds, and was used for mining leases in Lancashire until recently. ANDERSON, D., *The Orrell Coalfield 1740–1850*, Moorland Publishing Co., 1975

15 HOLT, J., *General View of the Agriculture of the County of Lancaster*, 1795
16 BAILEY, W. H., 'A New Chapter in the History of the Manchester and Liverpool Railway', Manchester Association of Engineers *Transactions*, 1889. Stannard's son Robert was also a railway engineer: *The Engineer*, Vol. 72, 2 October 1891
17 Letter from George Rennie: *The Engineer*, Vol. 8, 11 November 1859
18 John Wilson who, with William Jessop, carried out harbour works at Troon
19 Bailey, op. cit.
20 On 1 January 1830 the first passengers crossed Chat Moss in a carriage drawn by *Rocket*. In July 1829 George Stephenson is said to have crossed Chat Moss in a vehicle propelled by sails
21 ASHBURY, T., 'The Early History of the Liverpool and Manchester Railway'; a paper read before the Manchester Association of Engineers, Employers, Foremen and Draughtsmen, 28 February 1880, reprinted in his *Miscellaneous Papers*, 1904. (Leypayers = Ratepayers)
22 10 G4 c xxxv, 14 May 1829. This Act gave the Company powers to raise a further £127,500 by the issue of new shares.
23 9 G4 c vii, 26 March 1828
24 Telford's reports: ICE, Telford Papers T/LM 13
25 Walker, James S., op. cit.
26 Hekekyan Bey, Joseph, an Armenian in the Egyptian service. Born 1807, educated at Stonyhurst, trained in engineering under Francis Giles 1818–30. *Hekekyan Papers*, BL Add Mss 37448
27 Rastrick's Notebook, 13 January 1829; U of L Mss Dept
28 At the opening of the B&LR, 1 August 1828
29 The *Albion*, 20 July 1829
30 The Stockport Junction Railway was a sensitive issue, since it would have been detrimental to the Bridgewater Canal, and therefore to the Marquis of Stafford's interests. As the new company would, in effect, have extended the L&MR beyond Manchester, contrary to an agreement with Stafford, the Company had no option but to obstruct it
31 SMITH, J. F., *Frederick Swanwick; a Sketch*, 1888. Durham County RO, Salvin Papers
32 Capt. James Chapman on leaving the L&MR became Secretary and Manager of the Wigan Branch Railway, and subsequently Secretary of the NUR. He had been at sea with William IV and wore his naval uniform when he met Queen Adelaide at Preston during her journey to Scotland. *Manchester Guardian*, 16 October 1880
33 Probably related to Robert Benson Dockray (1811–71), Resident Engineer, L&BR 1835; *Journal of Transport History* Vol. 7, No 1, May 1965
34 Letter John Dixon to John Moss, 29 June 1835; PRO: RAIL 1008 95
35 By the late 1840s most railways had discontinued the use of stone sleepers. Some of those taken up from the Lancaster & Preston line were used to form the lower part of the spire of St Walburge's RC Church, Preston, built 1850–54. HEWITSON, A., *History of Preston*, 1883
36 Letter, Dixon to Moss – note 34 above

Chapter 3: The Rainhill Locomotive Trials (pp. 63–75)

1 WARREN, J. G. H., *A Century of Locomotive Building by Robert Stephenson & Co., 1823–1923*, 1923. The report is printed in full, pp. 166–170
2 One of the four engines ordered by Horatio Allen
3 Rastrick Notebooks, U of L, Mss Dept
4 STEPHENSON, R. and LOCKE, J., *Observations on the Comparative Merits of Locomotive and Fixed Engines as applied to Railways*, 1830. The 32-page pamphlet also includes an account of the subsequent Rainhill trials and other experiments
5 So spelt in the Board Minutes. Possibly Hahn, of Hahn & Elliott, contractors, B&ORR
6 Letters (5) Robert Stephenson to Henry Booth, 3, 21, 26, 31 August, 5 September 1829. The originals were displayed on the L&NWR stand at the Franco-British Exhibition, London, 1908, and were subsequently destroyed in a fire. They had, however, been reprinted in English and French and issued at the Exhibition as a pamphlet, of which the Science Museum has a copy
7 *The Quarterly Review*, March 1825
8 *The Engineer*, Vol. 58, 17 October 1884
9 Letter John Dixon to his brother James, dated 'Patricroft, 16 October 1829'. Science Museum, 1923-557
10 WOOD, N., *Treatise on Railroads*, 3rd ed., 1838, p. 330
11 Millfield Yard was part of the Crown Street site
12 A modified version was used in Lombardy and the USA, where the expense of a steam locomotive was not justified
13 Born Sussex County, NJ, 1796; of a family of horse-breeding experts. Railway & Locomotive Historical Society (USA) *Bulletin* No 70, 1947
14 William Gowland, one of Hackworth's most trusted drivers on the S&DR. He was the first driver of *Royal George* and after the Rainhill Trials, went with *Sans Pareil* to the B&LR, making his home in Bolton. YOUNG, R., *Timothy Hackworth and the Locomotive*, 1923
15 *The Engineer*, Vol. 4, 17 July 1857
16 Probably the engineer Mr (later Sir) Charles Fox, who rode on *Novelty* at Rainhill
17 The *Albion*, 12 October 1829. All this for £97 16s. 7d.
18 Rastrick's bill for the Rainhill and Winan's waggon trials was £199
19 Letter, C. J. Thompson to C. F. Dendy Marshall, 11 March 1929, in Science Museum Marshall Collection. The writer was the grandson of the purchaser of *Rocket*

20 *The Rocket* had been entered for the competition by Booth and the Stephensons, as joint designers, and as such, the prize was shared by them. Booth, however, had no financial involvement in the construction of the engine, nor in its sale to the L&MR, but George Stephenson had, since he was a partner in R. Stephenson & Co.
21 Hardman Earle, the former opponent of the Railway, joined the Board of Directors on 28 December 1829 on the resignation of William Rathbone

Chapter 4: The Opening of the Railway (pp. 76–90)

1 Letter, G. Stephenson to Michael Longridge, 23 August 1829; Liverpool RO 385 STE 13
2 HEKEKYAN BEY, JOSEPH, *Diary*, BL Add Mss 37448
3 HARE, A. J. C., *Memorials of a Quiet Life*, 2 Vols, 1884, quoting letter dated 19 December 1829 from Catherine Stanley, wife of the Rector of Alderley to Maria Hare; Vol. 1, pp. 281–2. William Scoresby (1789–1857) of Liverpool was an early Arctic explorer. Lords Harrowby and Sandon were father and son; the latter became President of the Board of Trade, 1878–80
4 Account in Minutes after a special Board Meeting following the trials
5 ARMSTRONG, M., *Fanny Kemble*, 1938
6 Letter signed 'Derby' dated 'Knowsley 12 August 1830' quoted in full in the *Daily Courier*, 15 September 1880
7 'Edmondson & Sons, cabinet makers and upholders' [sic]. The firm supplied Board Room furniture etc. to the L&MR. Thomas Edmondson, inventor of the railway ticket system, was originally an apprentice cabinet maker and upholsterer, and presumably of the same family
8 *Blackwood's Edinburgh Magazine*, Vol. 28, November 1830; 'Opening of the Liverpool and Manchester Railroad', article dated 20 September 1830 by A. RAILER [pseud.?]. Other contemporary accounts are to be found in The *Albion*, 20 September, The *Liverpool Mercury*, 17 September and The *Manchester Guardian*, 18 September 1830
9 The tampion had been left in the muzzle of the cannon, and on the firing of the blank round it flew out, injuring four men, one of whom lost an eye
10 Mrs M. M. Sherwood, authoress of *The Fairchild Family*, *Henry and his Bearer*, etc. The extracts from her diary were quoted by her granddaughter in a letter to *The Times*, 15 September 1930
11 About a month after the accident a letter from Dr Thomas Wetherill of Liverpool appeared in the *Lancet* asserting that the surgical treatment provided was 'unscientific, inefficient and imbecile', and that an army or navy surgeon would have amputated, and saved Huskisson's life. In 1913 S. Squire Sprigge, basing his judgement on Dr J. P. Brandreth's letter to Mrs Gaskell after the accident, held the view that, considering the victim's state of health, he would probably have died even with modern operative facilities
12 Letter, Lady Frances Sandon to J. E. Denison, 15 September 1830; Nottingham University Library Os C 77
13 SLUGG, J. T., *Reminiscences of Manchester Fifty Years ago*, 1881
14 *Blackwood's Edinburgh Magazine*, op. cit.
15 Sherwood, op. cit.

Chapter 5: Travelling on the Railway (pp. 91–94)

1 Johnson, Dr James, MD, quoted in *Newcastle Weekly Chronicle*, 9 April 1881
2 DENDY MARSHALL, C. F., *Centenary History of the Liverpool and Manchester Railway*, 1930, quoting from the diary of Col. Pownoll Phipps and PHIPPS, P. W., *The Life of Colonel Pownoll Phipps KC, HEICS*, 1894. (Printed for private circulation)
3 ROBINSON, HENRY CRABBE, *Diary, Reminiscences etc*, 1869, Vol. 3, pp. 26–8
4 Diary of William Wilshere (1804–67) dated 'Liverpool, 18 July 1833'. He was MP for Yarmouth 1837–47. Hertfordshire RO, Wilshere collection, No 60155
5 MOORE, THOMAS, *Memoirs, Journal and Correspondence of Thomas Moore*, ed. Lord John Russell, 1853
6 *An Extract from Miss Kennedy's Diary*; The Lilac Tree Press, Wallasey, 1963 (an edition of 6 copies only). From her diary of a journey from Carlsruhe to England; Liverpool RO
7 *Liverpool a few years since*, by an 'Old Stager', 1869, pp. 173–4
8 *Manchester City News*, 30 September 1865
9 *Notes & Queries*, 4th Series, Vol. 2, p. 101; letter signed 'L.C.R.'
10 *Bradshaw's Journal* (Manchester), Vol. 4, 1843
11 *England in the nineteenth century – Lancashire*, 1842
12 DE TOCQUEVILLE, COUNT CLÉREL, *Journeys to England and Ireland in 1835*, ed. J. P. Mayer, 1958
13 *Liverpool Mercury*, 28 April 1842
14 'Tourist'; *The Railway Companion*, 1833 and *Descriptive Catalogue of the Padorama [sic] of the Manchester & Liverpool Rail-Road . . . . now exhibiting at Baker Street*, 1834. The 1835 edition gives the area as 15,000 sq. ft

Chapter 6: Relations with other Railways (pp. 95–107)

1 Leeds & Liverpool Canal Act; 59 G3 c cv. 1819 B&LR Act; 6 G4 c xviii, 31 March 1825, the session in which the first L&MR Bill failed
2 Robert Daglish (1779–1865), when manager of the Haigh Foundry, Wigan, built the first locomotive to work in Lancashire; known locally as *The Yorkshire Horse*, it was one of three built to Blenkinsop's

designs, and remained in service at the Orrell and Winstanley collieries from 1813 until 1852. ICE *Proceedings*, Vol. 26, 1866–7 and Anderson op. cit.
3 Hugh Steel appears to have committed suicide soon after Stephenson's report; writing from Liverpool to Robert Stephenson in Bogota on 25 February 1827, Joseph Locke refers to '. . . the melancholy death of poor Hugh'. Letter in the collections of the Institution of Mechanical Engineers
4 10 G4 c xxxvi 1829
5 *Utilis* was one of the 8-wheeled engines, probably of the 2-4-2 wheel arrangement and the first of this type; the other may have been *Castle*. SLS *Journal*, Vol. 29, 1953, p. 40
6 11 G4 & 1 W4 c lxi, 29 May 1830
7 6 & 7 W4 c cxi, 4 July 1836
8 11 G4 & 1 W4 c lvi, 29 May 1830
9 1 W4 c lvi, 22 April 1831
10 4 & 5 W4 c xxv, 22 May 1834
11 7 W4 & 1 Vict. c cxxi, 15 July 1837
12 10 G4 c xxxvii, 14 May 1829
13 3 & 4 W4 c xxxiv, 6 May 1833
14 James Bourne was also a director of the L&MR
15 Reports on the North Line by Vignoles and Locke; U of L GL I: 835
16 1 & 2 W4 c lx, 23 August 1831
17 At the end of 1844 there were 2235 miles of railway in operation and 855 miles under construction, involving 104 separate companies. In November 1844 248 Bills were deposited with the Board of Trade for the attention of Parliament in the new year, of which 121 were passed in 1845, authorising a further 2700 miles of railway
18 8 & 9 Vict. c cxcviii, 8 August 1845

Chapter 7: Stations
(pp. 108–134)
1 The *Albion*, 20 July 1829
2 The winding gear was also designed by Grantham, and was said by Fairbairn to have been superior to his own for the earlier tunnels; ICE *Proceedings*, Vol. 2, 1842
3 700 rope sheaves were cast at Crown Street Works in October 1834
4 An exception to the rule was made to enable stone to be brought to Lime Street for the building of the new Assize Court and St George's Hall
5 2 W4 c xlvi, 23 May 1832
6 The full extent of the errors was revealed on the opening up of the tunnel in 1881
7 Other old properties on the station site were sold by the Company for £256, including the Medical Library, a machine house and 'Gorst's old house and shop'
8 Those used for the Crystal Palace, about 2 years later, were only 4ft × 10in.
9 6 & 7 W4 c cxi, 4 July 1836
10 2 Vict. c xli, 14 June 1839
11 5 & 6 Vict. c cviii, 30 July 1842
12 The contractor for the iron bridges was Rigby of Hawarden
13 Pasley's Report; PRO MT6/2/33
14 The *Manchester Guardian*, 19 August 1843
15 Rope block and tackle as originally used on ships
16 *Specification of the work to be done and particulars of the materials which will be required in the construction and erection of a Shed and Offices . . . at Wapping*, Liverpool, 31 March 1838. Clwyd County RO 135/3
17 The Company paid £5 per sq. yd for the 550 sq. yds of land fronting King's Dock, compared with one shilling per sq. yd for farm land
18 *Cornish's Strangers' Guide to Liverpool and Manchester*, 1838

Chapter 8: The First Railwaymen
(pp. 135–150)
1 E. Rigg, shareholder in the L&MR and several other companies
2 Edward Woods (1814–1903); ICE *Proceedings*, Vol. 87, 1886–7, (Presidential address); Vol. 153, 1903 (obituary)
3 On 1 October 1838 Booth wrote to Buddicom on behalf of the directors thanking him for his services to the Company; Clwyd RO, 135/4
4 *The Engineer*, Vol. 51, 15 March 1881; biographical note on A. Fyfe
5 The Chevalier von Gerstner, born Prague 1793, engaged on construction of line St Petersburg–Tsarskoe Selo, emigrated to USA 1838, died Philadelphia 1840
6 The title 'Stationmaster' was not in general use at that time
7 Two enginemen retired in 1880, John Murphy after 52 years' service and Thomas Valentine after 47 years. A platelayer, Thomas Mercer, worked on the line from 1826 until 1887, retiring at the age of 84 while Robert Death, originally of the Crown Street Depot, retired at 80 after 60 years' service
8 de Tocqueville, op. cit.
9 Two of the Company's earliest drivers, Mark Wakefield and Simon Fenwick, had left to join the London & Greenwich Railway by 1837; Fenwick became Locomotive Manager on the Greenwich line. Barned Rice went to France in 1837 and William McCrie applied for leave to join him
10 Strikes were still a novelty in 1836. In the half-yearly Report the word is printed in italics and in the Board Minutes it is referred to as a 'turnout'. A miners' strike in Durham in 1831 was called a 'stick'
11 Enginemen's wages did not change over a period of 70 years; the average weekly wages of the 21,000 engine drivers in 1904 was £1 19s. 0d. McKillop, N., *The Lighted Flame*, (ASLEF), 1950
12 Two engineers from the Horseley Iron Co., the *Star's*

builders, were on the footplate, one of whom was injured. The engine broke away from the train, which was undamaged, and was taken on by another locomotive about 30 minutes later, but *Caledonian* was badly damaged and her tender smashed. The gatekeeper, who had failed to restore the points after the passage of a coal train, was committed to Lancaster Castle on a charge of manslaughter

13 House of Commons: *First Report from the Select Committee on Railways*, 1839

14 LECOUNT, LIEUT. PETER, *Practical Treatise on Railways, explaining their Construction and Management*, 1839

15 Thomas Young was the man who, as a labourer, had been rewarded for his suggestion on blasting techniques

16 3 & 4 Vict. c 97, 10 August 1840. In 1839 the Company expressed the opinion that magistrates should have more power to punish offenders, adding 'In the case of drunkenness, the fine is no compensation for the mischief they might occasion'; *First Report from the Select Committee on Railways*, 1839

17 A man named Appleton, who lost a leg when a boy before the railway was opened, was given £2 in 1842 as he could not find employment

Chapter 9: Locomotives and Rolling Stock (pp. 151–185)

1 VIGNOLES, O. J., *Life of Charles Blacker Vignoles*, 1889, p. 149

2 KIRWAN, J., *A Descriptive and Historical Account of the Liverpool and Manchester Railway*, 1831

3 Two official lists of locomotives, formerly the property of Charles Lawrence, are in the U of L Mss Dept. Ms 584 (xiii) gives numbers and names to 1 March 1836, with a few added later up to *Etna* (51); Ms 584 (xvii) gives numbers, names and cylinder dimensions to 18 January 1837 with additions up to *Tiger* (58), and shows 17 engines withdrawn from service

4 In July 1831 a new engine arrived at Liverpool, and the Board named it *Victory*, only to discover that it was not theirs, but was for shipment to America

5 *Liverpool Mercury*, 4 March and 8 April 1831

6 Kirwan, op. cit

7 *Liverpool Mercury*, 25 February 1831

8 Letter, Hardman Earle to the Rev. Dr Lardner, 16 July 1832, reprinted in *Answer of the Directors to an article in the Edinburgh Review for October 1832*, L&MR 5 November 1832. In a letter to Dixon on 23 May 1832 Earle suggested converting *Phoenix* to 'Planet' class: BAKER, E.; *Catalogue of Early Railway Books*, 1893, p. 98, item 324b

9 CHALONER, W. H., *John Galloway (1804–1894), Engineer of Manchester and his 'Reminiscences'*, 1955, reprinted from the Transactions of the Lancashire and Cheshire Antiquarian Society, Vol. 64, 1954

10 The *Edinburgh Review*, October 1832 and April 1833; *Answer of the Directors* etc., op. cit.

11 HUNGERFORD, E., *The Story of the Baltimore & Ohio Rail Road*, 1928, Vol. 1

12 REED, C. W., 'The Iron "Lion", Locomotive, Pump engine, Film Star'; SLS *Journal*, Vol. 33, 1957, p. 312. The locomotive was used in the film *The Titfield Thunderbolt*, 1952

13 *Specification and Heads of Contract for the Supply of Locomotive Power for the Liverpool and Manchester Railway Company*, June 1837; Clwyd RO, 135/2

14 L&MR: *Treasurer's Report on Comparative Disbursements*, 16 September 1839; U of L, GL Ii 839

15 Report, Edward Woods to Charles Lawrence, 16 December 1842; U of L Ms 584 (xix)

16 L&MR: Staff Register & Wages Book, 1842

17 Letter, Robert Stannard, in *The Engineer*, Vol. 58, 17 October 1884. For a concise account of the *Rocket* based on recent research, see REED, BRIAN, *Loco Profile No 7; The Rocket*, 1970

18 See p. 173

19 Quoted in article 'Improvements in Inland Transport – Railroads'; *Edinburgh Review*, October 1834

20 Brunel was in Manchester on 17 January 1831 and his device was tested at Edge Hill on 31 January. Charles Babbage had previously suggested a similar contrivance for '. . . loosing carriages from the engine in case of accident'; George Stephenson considered it useless. Lord Skelmersdale also had a plan for preventing accidents, no details of which have survived

21 John Reynolds of Pontrhydyrren constructed a rotary engine in 1835, described as similar to the Earl of Dundonald's, and capable of revolving at 60 rpm at a pressure of 50 psi; it was expected that its trials on the L&MR would be in June. The *Public Ledger*, 2 April 1835, quoting The *Cambrian*

22 Scottish RO, GD 233/2/34/20. Specification of rotary engine, GD 233/2/34/1

23 COPELAND, JOHN, *Roads and their Traffic 1750–1850*, 1968, and DAVISON, C. St. C. B., *Steam Road Vehicles*, HMSO (Science Museum), 1953

24 Curtis's brake was adopted by the Greenwich Railway in 1836

25 The Junior Engineering Society: Paper read by David Joy, Vice President on 'The Introduction of Expansive Working in Locomotives by John Gray's Expansive Motion'. *The Engineer*, Vol. 69, 14 February 1890

26 AHRONS, E. L., *The British Steam Railway Locomotive 1825–1925*, p. 32

27 Worsley coke in May 1831 cost £1 3s. 4d. a ton

28 Also referred to as *Prince George of Cambridge* and *Prince George of Denmark*; CLARK, D. K., *Railway Machinery*, 1855

29 Ahrons, op. cit., p. 132; *Condor* was taken into service in March 1846

30 Newcomen Society: *Transactions*, Vol. 27, 1949–51,

p. 165. The principle was anticipated six years earlier in *Railroad Travelling in 1850*, an imaginary account of a future journey on the L&MR: 'The steam trumpet (a substitute for the old guard's horn) has sounded the signal, and the *Comet* will start with the North Mail in a few minutes.' The *Kaleidoscope*, Vol. 10, 3 November 1829

31 In January 1839 Dr Albert was paid £25 for the use of his oleameter for testing the adulteration of oil

32 Abel Turton, Stationmaster Parkside & Lowton (Preston Junc.), remembered the opening of the L&MR, and claimed that he had suggested to Henry Booth the screw coupling to bring the buffers together; NEELE, J. P., *Railway Reminiscences*, 1904

33 DEWHURST, P. C., 'A Mystery Engine – Hargreaves Victoria', SLS *Journal*, Vol. 29, 1953, p. 40, and *Liverpool Mercury*, 2 February 1838

34 Probably *Salamander*. Crook & Dean supplied one other engine to the B&LR, *Veteran*. The *Locomotive*, March 1955, p. 47

35 At Newton Junction on 26 April 1842, two of Turner & Evans' coal trains, drawn by their engines *Magnet* and *Black Diamond*, ran into each other, blocking the main line; the L&MR trains were diverted over the GJR junctions until the line was clear

36 The toll for a locomotive between Liverpool or Manchester and Newton Junction, not employed in working a train, was £1, including the tender if attached and conveyed at the same time

37 Presumably John Smith, contractor to the St Helens Railway in 1839

38 *Asa* was the property of Pearson & Co. of Ince, near Wigan, coal-owners. She was in an accident with a stage-coach at Euxton on 7 September 1841, while running tender first with empty coal trucks. HART, HAROLD, 'Stage-coach and train in Conflict'; Railway & Canal Historical Society, *Journal*, Vol. 24, No. 2, July 1978

39 *The Engineer*, Vol. 58, 26 September 1884, p. 244. Letter from I.W.B. [Boulton]

40 Drab – dull, light brown colour; OED

41 The following have been traced from various sources: *Velocipede, Lord Derby, London, Fly, King William, Queen Adelaide, Duke of Wellington, Sir Robert Peel, Earl of Wilton, William Huskisson, Marquis of Stafford, Sovereign, Clarence, The Lark, Greyhound, Traveller, Harlequin, Victory, Delight, The Times, The Globe, Experience, Treasurer, Despatch, Conservative, Reformer*

42 Walker, op. cit.

43 House of Commons: *Report of the Select Committee on the Prevention of Accidents*, 1841

44 *The Builder*, 13 January 1844, p. 21

45 EARLE, THOMAS, *A Treatise on Railroads*, Philadelphia, 1830 and HEBERT, LUKE, *Engineers' and Mechanics' Encyclopaedia*, 1836

46 FAREY, J., *General View of the Agriculture and Minerals of Derbyshire*, 1811

Chapter 10: Operating the Railway (pp. 186–207)

1 Civil engineers and engine builders; responsible for several railways, including the Edinburgh & Dalkeith and Monkland & Kirkintilloch. Letter, Horatio Allen to Directors of the Charleston & Hamburg RR, quoted in CARTER, C. F., *When Railroads were New*, NY, 1926

2 *Notes & Queries*, 7th Series, Vol. 6, 7 July 1888 and Dixon, *Manchester Courier*, 9 February 1833

3 Copy of letter L&MR to L&BR dated 23 May 1836 on *Liverpool & Manchester Railway Passenger Arrangements*, PRO: RAIL 384/259/3

4 House of Commons: *First Report from the Select Committee on Railways*, 1839

5 Dale Street coach office was closed on the opening of Lime Street Station

6 *Manchester Mercury*, 25 September 1830

7 LEE, CHARLES E., *The Centenary of Bradshaw*, 1940. There is evidence that the first local timetables were issued by Bradshaw in the autumn of 1838, but the L&MR Board Minute suggests that the idea was a novel one in 1839

8 Slugg, op. cit. and *Notes & Queries*, 7th Series, Vol. 6, 4 August 1888. The song, by T. H. Bayly, 1827, was still being reprinted many years later

9 FAY, C. R., *Huskisson and his Age*, 1951 p. 30

10 THORBURN, G., *Men and Manners in Britain*, 1834

11 *The Albion*, 13 September 1830

12 COGHLAN, FRANCIS, *The Iron Road Book and Railway Companion from London to Birmingham, Manchester and Liverpool*, 1838

13 *The Britannia: Jones's Manchester, Liverpool and South British Advertiser*, Manchester, August 1834–December 1838

14 Possibly Wellwood Maxwell and Samuel Blain, two of the original shareholders

15 The election following the dissolution on the death of George IV, when Lord Grey replaced Wellington as Prime Minister

16 The rate was increased in 1832 to include Passenger Duty

17 An assistant sorter at the GPO, John Barrett age 24, was convicted of stealing letters containing approximately £3000, and was publicly hanged at Newgate on 13 February 1832; *The Times*, 14 February 1832

18 The rates included Passenger Duty. The GWR carried only 1 cwt of officers' luggage free

19 *The Engineer*, Vol. 58, 24 October 1884, p. 320 (I. W. Boulton)

20 WHISHAW, FRANCIS, *The Railways of Great Britain and Ireland, Practically Described and Illustrated*, 1840

21 Pickfords operated a carrying network covering the area bounded by London, Bristol, Shrewsbury, Liverpool, Bradford, Leeds, York, Nottingham and Leicester

22 *Manchester Mercury*, 25 September 1830

23 PIKE, RICHARD, *Railway Adventures and Anecdotes*, 1888
24 The carriage of coaches and private vehicles came under the Parcels Department
25 Parcels were accompanied by a waybill, delivered to the addressee by van and signed for in a delivery book
26 House of Lords: *Report of the Select Committee on Danger by Fire from Locomotives*, 1836
27 *The Engineer*, Vol. 62, 19 November 1886, p. 407
28 *Liverpool Mercury*, 10 June 1836

Chapter 11: Accidents
(pp. 208–215)

1 *Edinburgh Review*, October 1832
2 *Gore's Advertiser*, 14 October 1830
3 *The Times*, 26 November 1832
4 *Manchester Courier*, 9 February 1833
5 Apparently they were not related; there is no mention of an Edward Armstrong in the family tree on p. 24 of HOLCROFT, H., *The Armstrongs of the Great Western*, 1953
6 There were several drivers of this name. T. Hesketh was driver of *York* in March 1838 and R. Hesketh was the driver of the train which caught fire on 9 March 1839
7 He soon found employment on the GWR as their first engineman: *GWR Magazine*, op. cit.

Chapter 12: Rules and Regulations
(pp. 216–222)

1 STEVENSON, DAVID, *Observations on the Liverpool & Manchester Railway*, 1835
2 House of Commons: *Report of the Select Committee on the Prevention of Accidents*, 1841
3 Rule Books: PRO: RAIL 1134 221 and 222. Each engineman was furnished with printed instructions at least as early as February 1833. As no copies of these early rules have been traced it is probable that they were collected and destroyed on the issue of revised editions
4 *Manchester Courier*, 9 February 1833
5 *Select Committee on the Prevention of Accidents*, 1841
6 See p. 172 and note 20, p. 252
7 By this time Charles Wheatstone was in partnership with Cooke
8 5 & 6 Vict. c 55, 30 July 1842
9 Mather op. cit. and Fay op. cit., p. 27
10 Letter, James Loch to Lord Viscount Morpeth, January 1837; *Irish Railway Commission; Second Report of the Railway Commissioners*, 1838, Appendix A, p. 78
11 U of L Mss Dept; Ms 584 (xvi)
12 *Manchester Guardian*, 18 September 1880
13 3 & 4 Vict. c 97, 10 August 1840
14 The Pasley Papers, *Diary*, BL, Add Mss 41995
15 *Select Committee on the Prevention of Accidents*, 1841
16 *Manchester Guardian*, 16 October 1880. The Act took effect from September 1846
17 *Manchester Guardian*, 10 and 13 August 1842

Chapter 13: Conclusion
(pp. 223–234)

1 The memorial was originally forwarded to the L&MR Board by Robert Stephenson. On 12 October 1838 Sandars explained to Stephenson that he had held it over until a favourable opportunity arose, and a grant of £300 was paid to Mrs James through Barclay, Bevan & Co. on 19 January 1839. Liverpool RO 358 JAM 2/1/1, 2/2/1 and 2/2/2. The importunate Mrs Mudie appealed to the directors of other railway companies; those of the L&BR and GWR each gave her £5
2 His funeral on 26 April 1833 was paid for, and attended by, his fellow employees of John Hall's engineering works, Dartford, Kent. No stone marks his grave in Dartford Churchyard, but in 1888 he was honoured by a memorial window in Westminster Abbey
3 STURGE, J., *Remarks on the Regulation of Railway Travelling on Sundays, addressed to the Directors and Proprietors of the London & Birmingham Railway by a Railway Director*, 1836
4 Thomas Worsdell, younger brother of Nathaniel, was in Hamburg in 1842 during the great fire, and with other English engineers, blew up buildings to prevent the fire spreading. It is likely that the appeal came from him
5 The fire which destroyed the old Houses of Parliament on 16 October 1834. The papers lost were those relating to the first, unsuccessful, GWR Bill
6 Peter Barlow, mathematics master at Woolwich and later, railway engineer
7 Whishaw, op. cit.
8 BAADER, JOSEPH RITTER VON (1763–1835), 'Announcing a new form of Railway Construction, etc'; *Polytechnisches Journal*, Stuttgart, Vol. 41, 1831, pp. 1–16
9 C. VON OEYNHAUSEN and H. VON DECHAN; *Railways in England 1826 & 1827*, trs E. A. Forward, *Extra Publication No 7*, The Newcomen Society, 1971
10 de Tocqueville, op. cit.
11 THE CHEVALIER DE PAMBOUR, *A Practical Treatise on Locomotive Engines*, 1836
12 STRICKLAND, W., *Report on Canals, Railways, Roads and other Subjects, etc.*, 1826. He had been sent to England by the Pennsylvania Society for the Promotion of Internal Improvements
13 He imported the first locomotive, *Stourbridge Lion*, into America in August 1829. President of the New York & Erie RR, 1843; consulting engineer for the Brooklyn Suspension Bridge, 1870
14 George Washington Whistler (1800–49) was the father of the artist James McNeill Whistler; he became an engine-builder at Lowell, Mass. Major-General William Gibbes Macneill (1801–53) was a member of the ICE (London) from 1851. With Jonathan Knight (1787–1858) they met, among

other engineers, George and Robert Stephenson, Telford, Hartley, Walker, Palmer and Locke during their visit in 1828. ICE *Proceedings*, Vol. 13, 1854 and *Dictionary of American Biography*

15 English-made rails cost $54 per ton and were subject to import duty; US-made rails cost $90 per ton

16 E. L. Miller of Charleston, merchant and Director of the Charleston & Augusta RR, visited the L&MR in 1828, returning to America in October. He attended the Rainhill Trials in 1829, and in February 1830 exhibited a model locomotive he had brought from England. Railway & Locomotive Historical Society (USA) *Bulletins* No 53, 1940 and No 13, 1927

17 HEYDINGER, EARL J., 'The English Influence on American Railroads', Railway & Locomotive Historical Society (USA) *Bulletin*, No 91, 1954. British investment in US railroads in 1914 was $3,090,000,000

18 *Post Office Railway Directory*, 1848. He received a testimonial from the GJ and L&M Railway Companies in 1846

19 Irish Railway Commission, op. cit., p. 76

20 ibid., p. 79

INDEX

Page references in **bold** refer to illustrations

Accidents,
  Barton Embankment, 1838, 212
  Broad Green, 1831, 145
  Broad Green, 1836 (*Vulcan*), 211
  Broad Green, 1837, 212
  Broad Green, 1838, 212
  Broad Green, 1839, 213
  Brosley Embankment, 1831, 169, 209
  Bury Lane, 1836, 211
  Chat Moss, 1832, 209
  Chat Moss, 1836, 211
  Chat Moss, 1839, 213
  Collins Green, 1837, 211
  Cross Lane, 1836, 211
  Cross Lane, 1840, 214
  Edge Hill, 1837, 176
  Edge Hill, 1838, 213
  Elton Head Colliery, 1830, 208
  Glazebrook Bridge, 1831, 209
  Hunts Bank line, 1845, 215
  Huyton Lane, 1840, 214
  Huyton Quarry, 1838 (May), 212
  Huyton Quarry, 1838 (November), 213
  Kenyon, 1830, 208
  Kenyon Cutting, 1834, 221
  Kenyon Junction, 1837, 103
  Lime Street Station, 1838, 213
  Lime Street Station, 1839, 214
  Lime Street Station, 1841, 146
  Lime Street Station, 1842, 214
  Lime Street Station, 1845, 215
  Manchester, 1831, 145
  Manchester, 1837, 211
  Newton, 1833, 210
  Newton Bridge, 1832, 209
  Newton Junction, 1832, 209
  Newton Junction, 1836, 104
  Newton Junction, 1837, 212
  Newton Junction, 1838, 213
  Newton Junction, 1845, 215
  Olive Mount Cutting 1832, 145
  Parkside 1832, 101
  Parkside 1835, 210
  Parkside 1836, (May), 211
  Parkside 1836, (October), 211
  Parr Moss, 1833, 209, 217
  Rainhill, 1832, 162, 194, 209
  Rainhill, 1836, 210
  St Helens Junction, 1835, 141, 161
  Salford, 1836, 210
  Sutton Inclined Plane, 1831 (March), 208
  Sutton Inclined Plane, 1831 (April), 145, 209
  Sutton Inclined Plane, 1833 (February), 209
  Sutton Inclined Plane, 1833 (March), 159, 210
  Sutton Inclined Plane, 1835, 210
  Sutton Inclined Plane, 1836 (January), 210
  Sutton Inclined Plane, 1836 (October), 211
  Sutton Inclined Plane, 1837, 211
  Sutton Inclined Plane, 1838, 212
  Sutton Inclined Plane, 1841, 100
  Sutton Inclined Plane, 1842, 201
  Sutton Inclined Plane, 1843, 201
  Wapping Tunnel, 1834, 210
  Whiston Inclined Plane, 1832, 200
  Whiston Inclined Plane, 1833, 210
  Whiston Inclined Plane, 1834, 210
  Whiston Inclined Plane, 1835 (*Collier* and *Titan*), 210
  Whiston Inclined Plane, 1836, 211
  Whiston Inclined Plane, 1837, 212
  Whiston Inclined Plane, 1838, (January), 212
  Whiston Inclined Plane, 1838 (November), 213
  Whiston Inclined Plane, 1842, 214
  Wigan, 1836, 102
  Wigan, 1838, 102
  October 1836 (*Lightning*), 211
  February 1837 (*Eclipse*), 211
  5 August 1839 (*Goliah*), 214
  see also Employees; Huskisson, William; Vandalism
Act of Incorporation, 30, 31, 225
Acts, further powers,
  deviations, 49
  extension to Manchester, 49
  Leeds Junction line, 125
  Lime Street Station, 116, 118
Adam, William George, KC, 21, 25, 28, 29
Adelphi Hotel, 79, 90
Agreements of service, enginemen, 140, 142
Air raids, 239
Albion Hotel, 221
Albion, The, 79, 85, 194
Alderson, Edward, 25, 29
Ale allowance, 145
Alexandra Dock Branch, 237
Allan, Alexander, 103
Allcard, William, 35, 44, 97, 118, 119, 135, 171, 178, 180
Allcock, (contractor), 44
Allen, Horatio, 37, 230, 232
Amalgamation, L&MR and GJR, 105, 106, 107
Amalgamations, 101, 102
Anderson & James, 65
Anderson, Sir James, 174
Animals in passenger trains, 193
Ankerbold & Lings Railway, 184
Annuity fund, 149
Anthracite coal, 175
Anti-Monopoly Association, 196
Apprenticeship, 168
Armstrong, Edward, 211
Armstrong, Joseph, 142, 211
Army guard railway, 89, 222

Arrow signals, 217
Ashbury, John, 158
Astley Station, 131
Auditing of accounts, 226
Award of premiums, Rainhill Trials, 75
Awty, —, (surveyor), 21

Baader, Joseph R von, 230
Babbitt, Isaac, 174
Badges, 148, 149
Badnall, Richard, 171, 173
Baird, (contractor), 45
Baker Street Bazaar, 94
Ballast waggons, 37, 185
Ballasting, 59, 60, 171
Baltimore & Ohio Railroad, 64, 69, 161, 229, 231, 232
Banking engines, 140, 142, 163, 165, 199, 200, 210, 217
Banks, Thomas & Co., 115, 165
Baring Brothers, 232
Barlow, Professor Peter, 229
Barlow, Thomas, 228
Barnby, Faulkner & Co., 207
Barton Embankment, 49
Barton Moss Station, 128, 131
Baxendale, Joseph, 142
Bedlington Ironworks, 37, 59, 67
Belgrave, Lord, 77
Bellhouse, David, 131
Benefit club, 149
Benson, Robert, 65
Bergin, T. F., 174, 182
Bigland, Amos, 195
Bill, Parliamentary, 1st, 19, 22, 24, 26
  2nd, 29
Birkinshaw, John, 59
Birley, Hugh, 15, 23
Birley, Maj. Joseph, 15
Birmingham, 102, 103
Blackburn, Thomas, 144
Blackburne, John, MP, 33
Blackett, Thomas, 19, 23, 25
Blacklock, John, 45, 47
Blacklock, William, 235
Blackpool Hole, Chat Moss, 47
Blain, Samuel, 15
Blasting, 56
Blue lights, 219
Blue trains, 97, 102, 186
Board meetings, 225
Board of Trade, 61, 148, 197, 219, 220, 227
Board room, 120
Boiler explosions, 115
Boiler houses, 108
Bolton, 95, 97, 106, 186, 197
Bolton & Bury Canal, 125
Bolton & Leigh Railway, 16, 17, 27, 56, 57, 58, 64, 95-98, 107, 133, 151, 152, 157, 169, 179, 198, 199, 209, 215, 222
Bolton & Preston Railway, 102, 221

257

INDEX

Book of Reference, 21, 22
Booking clerks, 130, 139, 143
Booking offices, 186
Booking of omnibus passengers, 190
Booking of passengers, 188
Booking to intermediate stations, 188
Booth, Henry, 18, 19, **20**, 21, 24, 29, 33, 39, 47, 56, 63, 65, 75, 125, 130, 157, 165, 166, 171, 173, 178, 207, 220, 221, 229, 232, 234
Bootle, 106
Boroughreeve, Manchester, 88
Borron, —, (magistrate, landowner), 22, 47
Botany Bay Woods, 48
Bourne & Robinson, 104, 157, 180, 185, 210, 229
Bourne, James, 104
Bradley, John, & Co., 37, 59
Bradshaw, George, 191
Bradshaw, James, 226
Bradshaw, Robert Haldane, 15, 23, 28, 226
Braidley, Benjamin, 195
Braithwaite & Ericsson, 66, 72, 73, 74, 75, 151, 155
Brake, chain, 181
Brake trials, 213
Brakes, carriage, 102, **178**, **179**
Brakes, waggon, 97
Brakesmen, 199
Bramah, Fox & Co., 133
Brampton Colliery Railway, 171
Brandreth, T. S., 47, 69, 183
Bretherton, Peter, 186, 189, 204
Brickfield Station, 103, 108, 136, 168
Brickworks, 44
Bridgen, J., 191
Bridges, 42, 52, 54
Bridgwater Canal, 11, 15, 49, **55**, 207, 226
Bridgewater Canal Bridge, 55
Britannia, The, 195
British Association, 229
Broad gauge, 106, 234
Broad Green, 43, 52, 128
Broad Green Cattle Station, 147, 203
Broad Green Embankment, 41, 52, 56, 235
Broad Green Station, 128
Broad Oak Collieries, 100
Brockbank, J., 50
Brook, Captain, 139
Brosley Embankment, 45
Brougham, Lord, 196
Brougham, William, 29
Brown, Samuel, 65
Brown, William, (later Sir), merchant and banker, 125, 230
Brown, William (waggon builder), 183
Brunel, Isambard K., 172, 196, 205, 223, 229
Brunswick Dock, 133
Brunton & Shields Railway, 63, 64
Brunton, William, 23
Brussells, Railway, 187
Buchanan, R. 186
Buddicom, William, 103, 136, 164, 166
Buffer stops, 182
Buffers, 91, 174, 182, 184
Bugler, Manchester Station, 191
Burgess, Samuel, 139
Burglary at Crown Street Station, 144
Burnett, Matthew, 37
Burstall, Timothy, 65, 68, 75, 151
Bury & Rossendale Railway, 107
Bury, Curtis & Kennedy, 180
Bury, Edward, 56, 96, 111, 142, 157, 162, 166, 177, 179, 180

Bury, G. F., 23
Bury Lane Station, 130
Bury Lane Tavern, 194, 195
Butler, Joseph, 184
Butterley Ironworks, 37
Bye laws, 216, 220, 226, 229
Bywaters, (inventor), 172

Cadbury, R. T., 125
'Caledonia Railway', 106
Caledonian Foundry, 157
Callan, Charles, 140, 141, 210
Callan, Peter, 141
Camden & Amboy Railroad, 231
Canada Dock Line, 235, 239
Canals, 12, 13, 203, 207, 220, 226
Candelet, Peter, 49
Canterbury & Whitstable Railway, 29, 35, 56
Capital, 15, 18, 21, 29, 103, 226
Carriage buffers, 182
  cleaning, 182
  couplings, 102
  Department, 138, 182
  doors, locking of, 219
  'Duke's', 180, 195
  footboards, 182
  Inspector, 186
  lighting, 115, 182
  roofs, 182
  sheds, 95, 115, 124, 127, 182
  Works, 119, 168, 181, 182
Carriages, 101, 180–183
  B&LR, 95, 97
  colours of, 181
  for opening day, 77
  hire of, 100, 182
  M&LR, 183
  naming and numbering of, 92, 181, 185
  road, *see* Private carriages
  2nd Class, 93, 182
  see also Coaches
Carriers, 31, 95, 184, 191, 201, 207
Cassell, John Henry, 62
Cattle traffic, 134, 203
Census returns, 193
Centenary of L&MR, 239
Chairs, permanent way, 59
Chance's glass, 127
Chanter, John, 175, 177, 180
Chapman, Capt. James, RN, 58, 100, 101, 221
Charities, contributions to, 227
Charles Street, Manchester, 103, 106, 133
Charles Street Pig Station, 203
Chartists, 222
Chat Moss, 16, 26, 28, 30, 33, 37, 45–49, **48**, 52, 58, 61, 98, 139, 220, **233**
Chat Moss Farm, 204
Chat Moss Tavern, 130, 158, 195
Check rails, 58
Chequerbent, 95, 97, 184, 222
Chester, 186
Childwall, 83, 89
Cholera, 193
Chorley, 101, 102
Chorley, J. R., 103
Christie, Alexander, & Co., 151
Chubb locks, 144
Clay & Swift, 225
Clay, William Castell, 22, 225
Cleather, Captain, 103

Clerks, 143
Clifton Branch, 107, 235
Clocks, station, 130, 191
Clough, James, 19
Coaches, 'Blue', 182
  Fly, 197
  'Glass', 181
  Gondola (M&LR), 183
  Lark, 214
  London, 181
  Lord Derby, 197
  mail, 181
  Queen Adelaide, 181
  Royal William, 181
  Tourist, (M&LR), 183
  Wellington, 197
  'Yellow', 180, 186
  1st Class, 180, **181**
Coal depots, 108, 115, 116, 131, 133
  locomotive, 174
  -owners' trains, 96
  staithes, 96
  traffic, 185, 207
Coke, 165, 169, 175, 217
Colliery branch lines, 95, 99
Collins Green, 44, 52, 199
Comber, Andrew, 138, 143, 185
Communication cord, 219
Compensation, 141, 147, 210, 228
Complaints, passengers', 193, 225
Comrie, Alexander, 26, 106
Conference of Railway Directors, 220
Conservative Association, 195
Construction, slow progress of, 57
Container system, 184, 185, 201, **202–3**
Contractors, 35–7, 51, 55
Convicts, conveyance of, 199
Cooke, William, 219
Copeland, James, 37, 40, 44
Coppull Colliery, 152
Corn Law Dinner, 196
Cottages for staff, 58, 128, 139, 142
Cotton, 11, 131
Coughlan, Francis, 195
Couplings, chain, 91, 182
  disengaging, 172, 219
  rope, 179
  screw, 178, 179, **179**, 182
Cow-catcher, 174
Cowlishaw, Joseph, 13
Cowper, E. A., 219
Cranes, 133
Crawshay, William, 65, 151
Creed, Robert, 140
Creevy, Thomas, 24, 26
Crewe Locomotive Works, GJR, 103, 166, 237
Cromford & High Peak Railway, 47, 105
Crook & Dean, 179
Cropper, James, 15, **17**, 58, 63, 65, 75, 135, 136, 138, 145, 150, 161
Cropper, John, 147
Crosbie Street, Liverpool, 133
Cross Lane Station, 128
Crown Street Station, 85, 115, 116, **118**, 133, 143, 168, 191, 193, 204
  Tunnel, 41, 92, 110
  Yard, 61, 62
Croydon, Merstham & Godstone Railway, 12
Cubitt, William, 23, 24, 25, 26
Cummings, John, 61, 62, 211
Cummings, N., 231
Cunningham, John, 119

INDEX

Curtis, William, 174
Cuttings, construction of, 52

Daglish, Robert, 95, 100, 151
Daglish, Robert Jnr., 100
Dale Street Coach Office, 186, 189, 190, 204
Daniels, William, 142
Daubhill Inclined Plane, 97
Davidson, William, 146
Dean, Peter, 147
Dechen, H. von, 230
Delaware & Hudson Railroad, 230
Denham, Capt. H.M., RN, 229
Dent, John, 61
Deodands, 221
Derby, Lord, 16, 23, 24, 29, 30, 77, 94, 104
Detonators, 219
Dewrance, John, 138, 166, 177, 180, 221
Director's fees, 33, 225
Discipline, staff, 141–4, 147
Disturbances at stations, 189, 193
Disyntrechon, 94
Dividends, 23, 31, 225, 226
Dixon, John, 35, 47, 49, 57, 61, 62, 68, 74, 75, 104, 118, 119, 135, **136**, 139, 140, 157, 161, 168, 229
Dockray, David, 58, 172
Dodds, Isaac, 161
Donally, Catherine, 139
Dove, Lionel, 144
Dowlais, Ironworks, 178
Dr Parke's Cutting, 59
Drainage, 48, 52, 58
Drais, Baron, 172
Drunkenness, 144, 145
Dublin & Kingstown Railway, 62, 157, 161, 163, 182, 228, 229
Ducie Street Bridge, 125
'Duke's Train', 197
Dundonald, 10th Earl of, 171, 173, 174
Dunn, John, 140, 144
Dyson & Jones, 21

Earle, (Sir) Hardman, 30, 56, 75, 100, **106**, 156, 157, 173, 176, 193, 205, 220, 234, 235
Earle, Richard, 29
Earle, Mrs, 29
Earlestown, 235
Eastern Counties Railway, 148, 219, 221, 226
Eaton, Thomas, 44
Eccles, 28, 58, 88, 98
Eccles cakes, 93, 194, 195
Eccles Cutting, 49
Eckersley, Nathaniel, 209
Edge Hill, 28, 29, 39, **40, 41**, 41, 79, 83, 85, **85**, 108–15, 173, 235, 239
  GJR engine sheds at, 166
  Locomotive Works, 166, 168, 221
  Marshalling Yard, 237, **239**
  New Station, 111, **111**, 115, **116–7**, 235
Edge Lane, 237
Edinburgh & Glasgow Railway, 229
Edinburgh Review, 225
Edmondson, R. & Son, 37, 77
Edmondson, Thomas, 189
Egerton, Lord Francis, 145, 193
Elections, Parliamentary, 197
Electric telegraph, 219, 220
Electrification, 239
Ellerington, William, 212
Ellesmere, Lord, 90
Ellis, Lister, 18, 21, 24, 25, 47
Elton Head Colliery, 104, 180, 185

Embankments, construction of, 52
Embezzlement, 146
Employees, death of, 50, 115, 141, 145, 147, 148, 151, 210, 213, 214
  imprisonment of, 141, 146, 209
  injuries to, 42, 43, 50, 147, 208
Engine cleaners, 139
  drivers, 98, 103, 138, 139–41, 194, 237, **238**
Engineers' banquet, 90
Ericsson, John (*see also* Braithwaite & Ericsson), 151, 173
Euston Station, 120, 189, 198
Euxton Junction, 102, 221
Evans (coal-owner), 101
Evans, Edward, 172
Everton, 16, 17
Ewart, Peter, 15
Ewart, William, 15, 16
Exchange Station, Manchester, 237, 239
Exchequer Loan Commissioners, 32, 50, 118, 226
Excursions, 180, 195–7
Experiments on railway, 173

Fairbairn, William & Co., 109, 123, 157
Fares, 97, 101, 186–7, 191
Farey, John, 157
Faulkner, James, 145
Fawcett, Preston & Co., 151
Fay, Charles, 181
Fencing of railway, 58
Fenton, Murray & Co., 156, 169
Fenwick, Simon, 140, 144, 208
Fiddler's Ferry, 103
Field, Joshua, 51
Fifty-ninth Regiment, 89
Findlay, George, 50, 54
Fines, 141, 142, 144, 145, 148, 190, 210, 211, 212, 221, 227
Fire insurance, 206
  on trains, 205, 206
  precautions, 205
Firemen, 139, 140, 141, 148
Flagpole signals, 104, 217
Fletcher, David, 145
Fletcher, Edward, 66
Flow Moss Station, 130
Fog signals, 219
Follett, Sir William, 227
Ford Colliery, 23
Foreign observers, 197, 229–32
Formby, William, 147
Forrester, George, & Co., 157, 162
Forsyth, Thomas, 135, 206, 215
Foster & Griffin, 162
Foster, John, 37, 108, 119, 123, 225
Foster, Rastrick & Co., 37
Fourth (King's Own) Regiment, 79, 85
Fox, Henderson & Co., 127
Fox's points, 61
Frauds, 135, 146, 189
Free passes, 103, 227, **228**
Fyfe, Alexander, 44, 50, 136, 158, 166, 178

Gadsby, John, 191
Gale, – (engineer), 151
Galloway, Bowman & Co., 157, 162, 169
Galloway, Elijah, Jnr, 19, 23, 25, 27
Galloway, John, 158
Garnett, William, 15
Garston, 100, 235
Gas companies, 41, 119, 151
  lighting, 41, 101, 127, 134

Gascoyne, General, 24, 27, 33, 223
Gaskell, Holbrook, 102
Gatekeepers, 128, 138
Gauge, 50, 59, 128, 231, 234
General Post Office, 101, 166, 191, 197, 198, 227
George, Thomas, 140
German engineers, 229
Gerstner, The Chevalier von, 136, 161
Gibbs, G. H., 229
Gibson, John, 225
Giles, Francis, 26, 47, 76
Gillespie, John, 42
Gladstone, John, 15, 16, 19
Gladstone, Robert, 15, 28, 29, 73
Gladstone, William Ewart, 227
Glasgow & Greenock Railway, 103
Glasgow, Paisley & Greenock Railway, 136
Glazebrook, Bridge, 55
Golborne, 235
Gold, carriage of, 204
Gooch, Thomas, 35, 51, 57, 124, 135
Goods traffic, 201–7
  train, first, 154
  vehicles, 183–5
Gordon, Alexander, 172
Gordon, D., 65
Gore's Advertiser, 157
Gorst, John, 181
Gorton's Buildings, Manchester, 128
Government control of railways, 220
Gowland, William, 72, **72**
Grainger, T., 186
Grand Junction Railway, 60, 62, 102, 103, 105, 107, 119, 128, 133, 135, 136, 138, 139, 165, 182, 197, 198, 199, 207, 215, 220, 226
Grandstands at opening, 79, 86
Grantham, John, 111
Gratuities, 144, 145, 193, 216
Gray, John, 136, 166, 174, 175
Gray, Thomas, 13
Gray, William, 136, 166
'Gray's Yard', 141, 168
Great Britain, S.S., 196
Great Exhibition, 1851, 171
Great Nelson Street, Liverpool, 119, 120 123
Great Western Railway, 106, 142, 220, 229, 234
Green, George, 219
Green, James, 147
Green, Joseph, 138
Green, William, 127
Greenall, Joseph, 141, 213
Greenshields, Hugh, 15
Greville, Charles, 93
Grocers Company, 201
Guard rails, 58
Guards, 139, 143, 148, **149**
Gunpowder, 40, 56, 203
Gurney, Goldsworthy, 65, 151, 172

Hackworth, Timothy, 64, 67, 75, 152
Hague, John, 133
Hahr, O. W., 65
Haig & Franklin, 124
Haigh Foundry, 164
Hall, Percival, 144
Hall, Richard, 221
Hall, Samuel, 174, 177
Hamburg, fire at, 227
Hamilton, George, 15, 16, 17
Hancock, Walter, 173
Harbottle, Thomas, 15

Harding, Anthony, 35, 135, 140, 144, 145, 157, 208
Harding, John, 35, 135
Harding, Thomas, 35, 37, 41
Harford, Davies & Co., 60
Hargreaves, John, 95, 96, 98, 101, 102, 157, 179, 184
Hargreaves, John, Sen., 95, 101
Harrison, George, 25, 26, 29
Harrison, Richard, 29, 64
Harrowby, Lord, 76
Harsleben, Charles, 173
Hartley, Jesse, 17, 19, 34, **34**, 35, 37, 42, 44, 45, 50, 54, 58, 59, 73, 106, 125, 183, 221, 230
Hatherton, Lord, (*see also* Littleton, E. J.) 192
Hawthorn, R & W, 164
Haydock coal trains, 98, 200, 211, 213
Haydock Colliery, 102, 104, 159, 169, 180
Haydock, Henry, 37, 118
Haydock Junction, 199
Hekekyan, Joseph, 76
Hesketh, Richard, 206
Hesketh, T., 212
Hetton Colliery Railway, 18, 23, 25
Hewitt, John, 141
Hick, Benjamin, 164
Hick, John, 152
Higginson, – (contractor), 49
Hill, John, 189
Hill, Thomas, 65, 185
Hirst, J., 46, 212
Hirst, – (Sen.), 46, 49
Hodgson, Adam, 76, 226
Hodgson, David, 106, 145, 168, 173
Holden, Henry, 211
Holme, James, 119
Holme, Samuel, 119
Holmes, William, 213
Holmes, William, MP, 24, 26, 29
Holt, David, 17
Hope, James, 102
Hope, Robert, 140, 144
Hornby, James, 76, 105, 133
Horns, warning by, 218
Horse boxes, 101, 184, 192
 traction, 30, 97
Horseley Iron Co., 161, 180
Hosking, William, FSA, 174
Hotham Street, Liverpool, 120, 123
Houldsworth, A. H., MP, 172
Houldsworth, H, 182
Hours of work, 140, 141, 142, 143
Houses for staff, 139
Huish, Capt. Mark, 103, 104, 106
Hull, 100, 128, 207
Hull & Selby Railway, 128, 136, 229
Hulton Park Colliery, 159, 184
Hulton, William, 95, 96, 131, 144
Humane Society, 228
Hunts Bank Extension, 58, 100, 125, 131, 183
Hunts Bank Station, (*see also* Victoria Station) 125, 127, **129**
Huskisson, William, MP, 24, **25**, 27, 28, 29, 33, 45, 76, 86–8, 90, 223, 225
Hutchinson, – (contractor), 45
Hutchinson, William, 65
Hutchison, Ralph, 206
Huyton, 28
Huyton Church, 227
Huyton Cutting, 43

Huyton Quarry, 104, 173, 212, 214
Huyton-St Helens Line, 235

Ice on rails, 201
Ilbery, Thomas, 138, 143, 195, 199
Imperial mail box, 197
Inclined planes, 34, 43, 60, 64, 99, 140, 199, 200
Inspection's directors', 225
Inspector of coaches, 116, 138
Institution of Civil Engineers, 239
Intersection Bridge, **98–9**, 99, 235
Ireland, 49, 199, 203, 234
Irlam-o' th'-Heights, 106
Iron roofs, 123, 127
Iron Wonders, 74
Ironmonger Lane, Liverpool, 133
Irwell Bridge, 49, 50, **50**, 105, 123
Irwell Bridge, Hunts Bank line, 125, **128**
Irwell, River, 28
Italian Opera Company, 195

James, William, 12, 13, **13**, 15, 16, 17, 18, 19, 46, 223
James, W. H., 174
Jay, John, 120
Jessop, Josias, 30, 33, 34, 47
Jessop, William, 13, 35, 62
Jevons & Sons, 37
Jiggers, 133
Johnson, Dr James, 91
Joint Stock companies, 24
Jones, Abel, 210
Jones, John, 211
Jones, Richard, 181
Jones, Robert & Sons, 225
Jones, Turner & Evans, 235
Jordan, Colonel, 198
Journey times, 190
Joy, Henry Hall, 29
Jubilee of L&MR, 237

Kemble, Fanny, 77
Kendrick's Cross, 54, 71, 142, 194
Kennedy, James, 144
Kennedy, John, 15, 71
Kennedy, Miss, 92
Kenworthy & Co, 207
Kenyon & Leigh Junction Railway, 42, 95, 107, 219
Kenyon Cutting, 45, 53, 221
Kenyon Junction, 95, 97
Kenyon Junction Station, 130
Killingworth Railway, 18, 23, 59, 139
Kilmarnock & Troon Railway, 30, 47
Kilshaw, John, 119
King of the Netherlands, 230
Kings Dock, 133
Kirkdale Gaol, 141, 199
Kirtley, Matthew, 102
Kirtley, William, 102
Kneass, Samuel, 230, 232
Knight, Jonathan, 231
Knowsley Moss, 25
Knox, James, 144
Kyan, John Howard, 61
Kyle, John, 144

Labourers on construction, 55, 138
Lacy & Allen, 181, 189, 190
Lamb's Cottage Station, 128, 130, 206
Lamps, signal, 217
Lancashire & Yorkshire Railway, 100, 181

Lancaster, 106, 199
Lancaster & Preston Junction Railway, 102, 146
Lardner, Dr Dionysius, 161, 225, 229
Latrobe, Benjamin, 230
Lawrence, Charles, 19, 21, 24, 28, 29, 33, 83, 90, 105, 125, 172, 220, 223
Laws, Capt., 216
Leather, George, 26
Lecount, Lieut Peter, 143
Leeds, 100, 127, 207
Leeds & Liverpool Canal, 12, 29, 95
Leeds & Selby Railway, 144, 229
Leeds Junction Line, 133, 189
Leftwich, Thomas, 214
Legh Arms Hotel, 194, **196**, 213, 235
Legh, Thomas, MP, 104, 169, 180, 194, 199
Leicester & Swannington Railway, 163
Leigh, 12
Leigh, John Shaw, 24
Leipsig & Dresden Railway, 180
Leslie, Professor, 65
Level crossing gates, 219
Leypayers, 49
Lime Street Extension, 111, 187, 226
Lime Street Station, 58, 106, 116, 119–23, **120**, **121**, **122–3**, **124–5**, **126**, 138, 143, 182, 192, 228, 235, **236**, 237, 239
Lime Street Station Hotel, 235, **237**
Lime Street Tunnel, 58, 60, 102, 111, 115, 118–9, 135, 193, 223, 235, 237
Lingard, Thomas, 30
Littleton, E. J. (later Lord Hatherton), 86, **88**
Liverpool, 11
Liverpool & Birmingham Railway, 19, 23, 57
Liverpool Assizes, 196
Liverpool Charity Festival, 195, 196
Liverpool Common Council, 19, 24, 29, 116, 119
Liverpool Docks, 16, 28, 34, 42, 133, 196
Liverpool Gas Company, 41
Liverpool Mercury, 11, 15, 64, 104, 206
'Liverpool Party', 226
Liverpool Road Station, Manchester, 50, **51**, 103, 123–4, **126**, **127**, 191, 219
Liverpool Royal Institution, 44
Liverpool shipping, 11
Lloyds of London, 197
Loading gauge, 133
Loch, James, 28, 47, 59, 105, 182, 187, 220, 226
Locke, Joseph, 35, **35**, 37, 50, 57, 62, 64, 88, 106, 118, 120, 135, 166, 174, 210, 223
Locomotive, adhesion (coupling) wheel, 175, **176–7**
 ashboxes, 205
 brakes, 178
 buffer-planks, 217
 building by L&MR, 163, 165, 166
 Committee, 165
 compressed air, 151
 contest suggested, 64
 crank axles, 169, 177
 cylinders, vertical, 159
 Department, 138, 166, 168
 feed-water heaters, 177, **176–7**
 fireboxes, 153, 157, 174, 175, 176, 177
 fittings, ornamental, 171
 headlamps, 217
 power by contract, 165
 repairs, 157, 162, 168
 safety valves, 178, 206

INDEX

sheds, 95, 108, 127, 166
smokeboxes, 152, 171
the, 13, 18, 23, 26, 63, 234
trials, 151, 154, 155, 157, 158, 159, 161, 168, 172, 179, 180
tubes, bursting of, 217
valve gear, 164, 174, 175
wheel guards, 221
wheels, 161, 164, 169. 177
   retractable, 163
whistle, 178
workshops, 115, 166, 168
Locomotives, 'Bird' Class, 138, 166, **167**
   cleaning of, 169
   hiring of, 96, 102, 152, 159, 169
   horse-operated, 70
   inventions relating to, 172–9
   manually operated, 70, 173
   naming and numbering of, 151, 153
   on construction, 56
   painting of, 66, 67, 68
   'Planet' type, 102, 161, 163, **163**
   pooling of, 165
   report on, 166
   short working life of, 162, 172
   sparks from, 205
   standardization, 163, 166
   tenders for the supply of, 157
   tools carried on, 217
Locomotives, individual. (*L&MR engines are denoted by the inclusion of their number*)
Agenoria, 64
Ajax (29) 161, 209, 211
Alpha, 165
Arrow (2), 77, 141, 151, 153, 169, 221
Arrow (52), 164, 175, 201
Asa, 180
Atlas (23), 157, 163, 169, 199
Atlas, 163
Bee, 157, 209
Black Diamond, 164, 200
Buffalo (67), 145, 165, 201
Caledonian (28), 141, 159, 161, **161**
Clarence, 180
Collier, 180, 210, 229
Comet (5), 145, 151, 153, 162, 168, **234**
Comet (55), 164
Condor, 177
Cycloped, 69, **70**, 72, 183
Cyclops (46), 102, 148, 164, 175, 211, 220
Dart (4), 77, 151, 153, 168, 172
Dart (48), 164
Dreadnought, 56
Eclipse (40), 164, 177, 211, 213
Elephant (65), 165
Etna (20), 140, 155, 162, 169, 209
Etna (51), 164, 212
Everton, 164
Experiment (32), 157, **160**, 162
Firefly (31), 161, 169, 173, 175, 177, 210, 211
Fury (21), 156, 162, 169, 176, 209
Goliah (15), 144, 145, 155, **155**, 159, 162, 199, 206, 208, 210
Goliah (68), 165, 214
Hercules (39), 163, 69, 212
Heron (71), 166
Hibernia, 157
Hornet, 168
Irk, 221
John Bull, 231
Jupiter (14), 155, 169
Kingfisher (72), 166

Lancashire Witch, 56, **57**, 58, 72, 95, 140, 151, 152, 175
Leeds (30), 156, 210, 211
Leopard (62), 165
Lightning (45), 164, 175, 211
Lion (57), 164, **165**, 213
Liver (26), 157, 162, 176, 211
Liverpool, 56, 157, 179, 209
'Liverpool Coke Engine' see *Twin Sisters*
'Liverpool Travelling Engine' see *Lancashire Witch*
Lynx, 175, 201
Majestic (10), 144, 145, 153, 169
Majestic (50), 164
Mammoth (61), 165, 201
Manchester, 158, 159, **160**, 210
Marquis of Douro, 146
Mars (12), 141, 155, 156, 162, 169, 200, 209
Martin (70), 166
Mastodon (63), 165, 201
Mercury (11), 140, 147, 153, 155, 169, **170**, 212, 221
Meteor (3), 151, **152**, 153, 155, 169, 208, 221
Meteor (54), 164
Milo (25), 156, 157, 162, 199
Milo (47), 164, 211
Newcastle, 180
Newton, 102
No 1 (L&BR), 144
North Star (8), 77, 88, 140, 152, 153, 155, 169, 186, 205, 208
Northumbrian (7), 85, 88, 140, 152, **152**, 153, **153** 177, 186
Novelty, 66, **67**, 72, 73, 74, 75, 151, 156
Oberon, 201
Orion (35), 163, 169, 178, 211, 212
Ostrich (74), **167**
Owl (75), 167
Panther (64), 165
Patentee (33), 147, 161, **162**, 176, 178, 205, 210 211, 212, 213, 221
Pelican (73), 166
Perseverance, 68, **69**, 75
Phoenix (6), 77, 85, 88, 115, 140, 145, 152, 153, 168
Phoenix (49), 164, 211, 212
Planet (9), 140, 154, **154**, 156, 157, **158–9**, 169, 197, 201
Pluto (27), 161, 162, 173, 175
Prince George, 177, 180
Queen Adelaide, 155
Rapid (37), 163, 175, 212
Rocket (1), 56, 65, **66**, 68, 72, 73, 75, 77, 86, 88, 105, 138, 140, 151, 153, 162, 169, 171, **171**, 173, 208
Roderic (60), 165, 175
Rokeby (59), 165, 175, 201
Royal George, 63, 67, 68
Royal Scot, **234**
Samson (13), 155, 159, 199 206
Samson (66), 165
Sans Pareil, 67, 68, **68**, 72, 73, 74, 75, 95, 97, 151, 152, 169
Saturn (16), 155, 162, 229
Shrigley, 104, 180
Sirocco, 212
Soho, 180
Speedwell (38), 163
Star (41), 164, 176, 177, 213
Star, 141, 161
Stork (77), 168, 175
Stourbridge Lion, 64

Sun (17), 140, 155, 206
Sun (53), 164, 213
Swallow (69), 166, 214
Swiftsure (36), 163, 175, 176, 206, 210
Tamerlaine, 213
Thunderer (44), 147, 163, 169, 211
Tiger (58), 164
Titan (34), 163, 169
Torch, 201
Twin Sisters (L&MR), 56, **57**, 65, 72, 76, 140, 151, 169
Union, 95, 199
Utilis, 179
Venus (18), 61, 155, 162, 180
Vesta (24), 155, 157, 172, 175, 211
Vesta (56), 164
Vesta, 180
Vesuvius (43), 164
Victory (22), 145, 155, 162, 172
Vizier, 214
Vulcan (19), 102, 144, 156, 169, 211, 212
Vulcan, 102
Warrington, 102
Wildfire (L&MR; see also *Meteor* (3)) 151
William IV, 155, 156, **156**
York (42), 147, 164, 211, 212
London, 103
London & Birmingham Railway, 61, 103, 107, 128, 135, 148, 161, 165, 180, 189, 208, 219, 220, 226, 229, 234
London & Brighton Railway, 229
London & Greenwich Railway, 229
London & North Western Railway, 95, 100, 107, 115, 139, 235, 237, 239
London, Chatham & Dover Railway, 102
London Gazette, 234
London Guarantee Society, 146
London, Midland & Scottish Railway, 152, 239
London Tavern, 79
London time, 198
London Underground Railway, 106
Longridge, Michael, 18, 34, 59, 67
'Lord Seymour's Act', 220
Losh, William, 13, 59
Lost property, 193, 205
Lowther, Lord, 27
Lubricants, 178
Luggage, 143, 193
Lynn, William, 79

Macclesfield Canal, 105
Macdonald, Sir Archibald, 28
Machinery, locomotive works, 166, 168
Mackenzie, – (contractor), 118
Mail bag apparatus, 198
Mail coaches, 181, 186
   trains, 103, 197, 235
Management Committee, 225
Manchester, 11
Manchester & Birmingham Railway, 103, 107, 125, 235
Manchester & Bolton Railway, 125
Manchester & Leeds Railway, 95, 100, 106, 107, 124, 127, 128, 135, 183, 207, 215, 216
Manchester & Salford Waterworks, 177
Manchester & Sheffield Railway, 105
Manchester, Bolton & Bury Canal Navigation and Railway, 106, 107, 125
Manchester Courier, 158
Manchester, extension to, 49
Manchester Guardian, 15, 194
Manchester Infirmary, 227
Manchester (Oldham Road) Station, 124

Manchester riots, 15, 222
Manchester Ship Canal Branch, 237
Manchester, South Junction & Altrincham Railway, 235
Manchester Station, *see* Liverpool Road Station, Manchester
Manners, William, **238**
Manslaughter charges, employees on, 103, 145, 209
Manton, John, 174
Manure, carriage of, 204
Market Street Coach Office, Manchester, 189, 190, 204
Markland, William, 98
Marle Cutting, 41, 56
Marsh, Jonathan, 141
Martin, Albinus, 29
Massey, George, 141
Mather, Dixon & Co., 37, 111, 136, 163, 164, 166
McCarris, (engineman), 210
McCormack, – (booking clerk), 144
McCorquodale, George, 235
McCrie, Robert, 144, 190
McCrie, William, 140, 145, 209
McGrath's Farm, 128
McIvie, Daniel, 147
McLane, Louis, 232
McLeod, – (contractor), 43, 44
McNeill, William, 231
Mechanics' Institute, 15, 196
Medals, commemorative, 78, **78**, 79, 103
Melling, John, 136, **137**, 151, 163, 166, 175, 208
Melling, Thomas, 136
'Melling's Shed', 108
Melly, Prevost & Co., 177, 180, 229
Merchandise, classification of, 207
Mersey & Irwell Navigation, 12, 23
Mersey Docks & Harbour Board, 237
Messenger rope, **114**
Mewburn, Francis, 21, 22, 225
M'George, Miss, 17
Middleton Railway, 64
Midland Counties Railway, 128, 150, 177, 226
Midland Railway, 102
Milburn, Thomas, 221
Mileposts, 58, 193
Milk traffic, 204
Miller, E. L., 231
Millfield Yard and Works, 69, 70, 116, 136, 138, 168
Mills, James, 50, 53
Miners, 39
Mitchell, Henry, 144
Molyneux, Lady, 193
Monro, James, 119
Monthly Repository of Theology and General Literature, 24
Moore, Thomas, 92
Moorish Arch, Edge Hill, 108, **109**, **110**, 225
Morgan, W., 65
Moss, John, 15, **16**, 18, 19, 24, 28, 29, 57, 59, 63, 65, 75, 103, 105, 194, 218, 220, 223, 225
Moss, Henry, 73
Mudie, Mrs Elizabeth, 223
Mudie, Peter, 17
Murphy, John, 144, 211, **238**
Murray, Matthew, 175

Nantlle Railway, 57
Naphtha lamps, 134

Nasmyth, Gaskell & Co., 134, 165
Nasmyth, James & Co., 50, 104
Navier, C. L. M. H., 230
Naylor, Pierce, 210, 211, 212
Neville, James, 65
New Bailey Prison, 125, 199
Newcastle & Carlisle Railway, 21, 35, 59
Newspapers, 195
Newton, 28, 37, 194, **196**
Newton Bridge Station, 131, 143
Newton, Conservative Hall, **196**, 235
Newton Embankment, 45
Newton Junction, 104, 142, 215, 217, **218**, 235
Newton Race Course, 147, 198, 199
Newton Station, **46**, 130
Newton Viaduct, 44, 45, **46**
Nicholson, Thomas, 55
Night emergency signals, 219
Nimmo, Alexander, 47
Norman's Lane Gate, 142
Normanton, 100
North Eastern Railway, 66
'North Line', 105
North Midland Railway, 100, 127, 128, 150
North Union Junction (Parkside), 101
North Union Railway, 60, 101, 102, 105, 107, 146, 152, 198, 221

Observers shown over railway, 229, 230, 231
Ocean Insurance Company, 226
Oeynhausen, C. von, 230
Officers, 135–8
Offices, 119, 143
Ogle, Nathaniel, 172
Oil, 178
Oil lamps, 134
Old Botanical Gardens, Liverpool, 118
Oldfield Lane Cattle Wharf, 203, **204**
Oldham, 207
Old Quay Company, 12, 49, 207
Old Quay, Manchester, 106
Olive Mount cutting, 28, 35, 41, 42, **42**, 43, **43**, 52, 56, 60, 76, 91, 128, **149**, 217, 235, **236**, 237
Oliver, Thomas, 23
Omnibuses, 92, 93, 189
Opening Day,
 accident to William Huskisson, 86 7, 90
 attempts to wreck trains, 90
 bands at, 79, 85, 88
 guarding of railway, 79, 85, 89
 hostile crowds at, 89
 instructions to guests, **84**
 menu for banquet, **80**
 orders for enginemen, **81**
 preparations for, 76–9
 special carriages for, 77, 79
 visitors at, 83
Ordsall Lane, 49, 105, 158, 180, 215
Ordsall Lane engine sheds, 168
Ordsall Lane Station, 131, **132**
Orleans, HRH the Duke of, 229
Outram, Benjamin, 13
Outside passengers, 187
Overend, Gurney & Co., 29, 226
Owen William, 187
Oysters, carriage of, 204

Padley, Paul, 15, 16, 17, 19, 21
Palmer, G. H., 172
Palmer, H. R. 26
Palmerston, Lord, 86
Pambour, Comte de, 230

Parcels traffic, 204
Parish rates, 227
Park Lane Station (Wapping Depot), 133, 239
Parkin, Thomas, 62
Parkinson, – (contractor), 45
Parkinson, W., 151
Parkside, 58, 86, **87**, 100, 101, **101**, 103, 143, 177, 223
Parliament, 22
Parliament, Houses of, fire, 29, 229
Parliamentary Standing Orders, 16, 21, 24, 29
Parr Moss, 28, 44, 52, 58
Pasley, Maj. Gen., 125, 183, 221
Passenger diaries, 193
 duty, (tax), 187, 198
 traffic, 186
Passengers, death of, 215
 negligence of, 208
 stranded, 193
Patricroft, 58, 104, **105**, 193
Patricroft Station, 130, 131, 134, 191
Pauling & Henfrey, 125
Paupers, 199
Pease, Joseph, 34
Peel, Sir Robert, 88, 220, 225
Peel, Williams & Peel, 166, 180
Penrith, 106
Perkins, Jacob, 172, 174
Permanent way, 59–62
 maintenance, 61, 62
Perquisites, 205
Peterloo riots, 15
Petition, Railway Companies', to Parliament, 220
Phipps, Col. P., 91
Phipps, G. H., 65
Pickering, – (contractor), 44
Pickering, Peter, 174
Pickford & Co., 67, 138, 185, 199, 201, 207
'Picking-up' trains, 128, 206
Pig traffic, 134, 203
Pile-drivers, 44
Pilferage on railway, 146, 147, 204
Pilkington & Co., 206
Pilot engines, 90 171, 208
Pistol as alarm signal, 219
Plans, deposited, 21, 22
 William James's **14**, 16
 of L&MR, **36**, **96–7**
Platelayers, 56, 62, 138, 148, 211, 217
Platforms, 116, 119, 123, 127, 128, 130
Platt's Bridge, 217
Pleasures of the Rail Road, The, 92
Pneumatic signal, 114, **114**
Points and crossings, 61, 79, 142, 161, 210
Police, Railway, 89, 139, 142, 148, 216, 221
Police Gazette, 131
Police, local, 228
Police sergeants, 145
Pollock, John, 161
Population figures, 1821, 11
Porter, G. R., 220
Porters, 139, 143, 148, 193
Postmaster General, 197, 222
Pownall, John, 138, 182
Practical Treatise on Rail-roads, A., 26
Preston, 101, 102, 103
Preston & Wigan Railway, 101
Preston & Wyre Railway, 102, 221
Price, Bulkeley, 88
Price, James, 62
Price, Peter, 151

Princes Dock, 116
Prison vans, 199
Pritt & Clay, 15
Pritt, George Ashley, 15, 225
Private carriages conveyed by train, 91, 93, 183, 191, 192
Propelling of trains, 151, 211, 215, 225
Prospectus, 21, 29
Provisional Committee, 13, 15
Public Reasons against Railways, 24
Publicity encouraged, 232
Pumping engines, 169, 177
Purdie, Thomas, 214
Purdy, Richard, 212
Pye, Thomas, 221

Quakers, 195, 226
Quarterly Review, 26, 65
Queen Victoria, 150, 229
Queens Dock, 133

Race week traffic, 198
Radcliffe, John, 219
Radley, James, 79
Railway Clearing House, 207
Railway guarded by troops, 89, 222
Railway guides, 195
Railway Mania, 107, 234
Railway Society, 229
Rails, 37, 59, 229
  broken, 60, 61, 62, 206
  cast-iron, 59
  fish bellied, 59, 231
  parallel, 60
Rainford, 100, 106, 107
Rainhill Bottle Company, 104
Rainhill Bridge, 54, **54**, 76
Rainhill Ironworks, 104, 138, 151
Rainhill Level, 43
Rainhill Station, 128, 130, 152
Rainhill Trials, 54, 63, **71**, 151, 169, 231, 234
  award of premium, 75
  Engineers' Dinner, 73
  grandstand, 71
  judges, 71, 75
  preparations for, 70, 71
  regulations, 71
Ramsay, John, 198
Rastrick, John Urpeth, 23, 25, 33, 34, 64, 71, 73, 74, 183
Rathbone, Theodore, 105, 208, 220
Rathbone, William, 15
Rawlins, E., 172
Reading room, Edge Hill, 139
Records, staff, 62, 139, 142
Refreshment rooms, 120, 127
Refreshments served at lineside, 93, 194–5
Regulation of Railways Acts, 104, 145, 191, 220
Relaying of line, 60, 61, 211
Rennie, George, 27, 29, **30**, 33, 43, 47, 53, 54, 59
Rennie, (Sir) John, 26, 27, **27**, 33, 43, 53, 54, 59
Reports on locomotives, 63, 64, 75, 166
  on L&MR, Telford's 53–4
Rewards to staff, 139, 141, 142, 146, 150, 189, 206
Reynolds, J., 172
Rice, Barned, 140
Rice, Thomas Spring, 27
Richardson, Thomas, 29
Richmond, Duke of, 197

Rigg, E., 135
Ritchie, Charles, 138, 166
Riverside Station, Liverpool, 237, 239
Road bed, 59
Road money, 146, 188
Roads, 12
Roadside stations, 128–31
Robertson, William, 231
Robinson, Edward, 139
Robinson, George, 119
Robinson, Moncure, 230, 232
Robinson, H. Crabbe, 92
Roby Embankment *see* Broad Green Embankment
Rochdale, 207
Rochdale Canal, 106, 124
Rope haulage, 63, 97, 100, 110–14
Rope winding machinery, **112–3**
Roscoe, William, 46, 47
Rotary engines, 172, 173, 174
  Lord Dundonald's 173, **173**, 174
Rotherham, William, 65, 105
Rothwell, & Co., 164
Rowley, E., 174
Royal Hotel, Liverpool, 189
Royal Observatory, 229
Rule books, 216, 217
Rules and regulations, 79, 142, 180, 184, 199, 200, 208, 213, 216, 220, 229
Runcorn, 12
Runcorn Bridge, 235
Russell's Patent Steam Carriage, 173

Safety measures, 216
Safety mounds, 211
St George's Hall, 120
St Helens, 26
St Helens Canal & Railway *see* SH&RGR
St Helens & Runcorn Gap Railway, 86, 95, 98–100, 151, 161, 169, 180, 182, 230, 235
St Helens Junction, 128, 130
St John's Church, Liverpool, 191
Salaries, 135–8, 143, 144, 166, 232
Salford, 28, 49, 106, 125
Salisbury, Marquis of, 83, 89, 90
Salvin, Edward, 57
Sandars, Joseph, 13, 15, 17, 18, 21, 24, 25, 29, 47, 65, 75, 105
Sandon, Lady Frances, 88
Sandon, Lord, 76
Sands, Thomas, 106
Sandy Mains Embankment *see* Newton Embankment, 45
Sankey Brook, 44
Sankey Navigation, 44, 100
Sankey Viaduct, 44, **44**, 45, **45**, 52, 58, 76, 86, 195, **230–1**
Satirist, The, 195
Saunders, Charles A., 142
Schools, 227
Science Museum, 151, 152, 171
Scoresby, William, 76
Scott, George, 136, 166
Scott, James, 35, 42, 61, 103, 124, 138
Scott, Rev. John, 226
Seating diagrams, 188
Seaward, John & Co., 173
Sefton, Lord, 23, 24, 234
Seguin, Marc, 65
Select Committees, Parliamentary, 216, 220, 229
Servants, passengers', 193
Share certificate, **31**
Shareholders, 228

Shares, 23, 225, 226
Sharp, Roberts & Co., 157, 173, 177, 180
Sheffield & Manchester Railway, 57
Sheffield, Ashton-under-Lyne & Manchester Railway, 125
Sherwood, Thomas Moulden, 21, 22, 29, 225
Shildon Works, S&DR, 67
Shunting, 205, 217
Shutt End Railway, 64
Sidings, 133
Signals, 208, 214, 215, 216–20, **219**, 221
Silver watches awarded, 139
Simmons, – (contractor), 45
Simpson, – (clerk), 138
Sinclair, Peter, 219, 234
Slater, James, 174
Slave trade, 12
Sleepers, 37, 59
Slipping waggons from trains, 213
Smith, James, 145
Smith, John, 100
Smoke, factory, 49
  restriction on railway, 114
Smoking, 159, 216
Society for the Prevention of Cruelty to Animals, 203
Society of Friends, 13, 195
Soldiers, conveyance of, 198
Soult, Marshal, 230
South Carolina Railroad, 232
South Western Railway, 220
Southern, W. & H., 124
Southport, 100, 107, 186, 190
Spankie, Robert, 25, 26, 29
Special constables, 71, 89
Special trains, 195, 198
Speed of trains, 168–9
Spoil banks, 41, 45, 52
Staff, appointment of, 139
  promotion of, 139
Stafford, Marquis of, 28, 33, 220
Staffordshire Mercury, 173
Stage coach Bill, 187
Stage coaches, 93, 186, 189, 190, 193, 194, 204, 226
Stanley, Lord, 24, 33
Stannard, Robert, 46, 47, 49
Stannard, Robert, Jun., 66, 206
Star Inn, Manchester, 189
Statham, William, 76
Station name boards, 130
Stationmaster, 127
Stations, intermediate, 128–31, 201, 206
Steam engines, stationary, 43, 63, 75, 109, 111, 133, 199, 222
Steam road coaches, 151, 172, 173
Steel, Hugh, 19, 25, 27, 95
Stephens, Adrian, 178
Stephenson, George, *frontispiece* 12, 18, 21, 23, 25, 26, 27, 33, 34, 35, 43, 44, 45, 50, 56, 58, 64, 65, 70, 75, 83, 85, 95, 99, 105, 118, 124, 135, 161, 168, 172, 183, 223, **224**, 230
Stephenson, George & Son, 34
Stephenson, Robert, 15, 16, 18, 64, 68, 75, 135, 161, 185, 223
Stephenson, Robert & Co., 18, 34, 67, 75, 108, 151–2, 154, 156, 157, 161, 177, 184, 206
Stephenson, Robert, Sen., 37, 95
Stevens, Robert L., 231
Stevenson, George, 42, 221
Stevenson, John, 37, 42

Stockport, 105
Stockport Junction Railway, 57, 105
Stockton & Darlington Railway, 13, 18, 21, 25, 29, 30, 35, 50, 53, 59, 61, 63, 64, 67, 135, 169, 230
Stockton, Thomas, **238**
Stopping of trains, unauthorised, 193
Straker, – (engineer), 21
Stratford & Avon Canal, 12
Stratford & Moreton Railroad, 34
Strickland, William, 230
Strike of enginemen, 140
   porters, 143
Strikes, Manchester, 222
Stubbs, George, 103
Studholm, T., 59
Subscription contract, 22, 24, 29
Summers, William, 173
Sunday train service, 186
   travelling, 102, 216, 226–7
   work on railway, 140, 173, 227
Sundial, Liverpool Road Station, 191, **192**
Superintendents, 138, 144, 148
Sureties, 146
Surgeons, 150
Surveys, 23, 28
Sutton Inclined Plane, 61, 73, 89, 99, 145, 173, 193
Swanwick, Frederick, 57, 116, 135
Switches *see* Points and crossings
Sylvester, Charles, 23
Synopsis of Proceedings, 21

Tarpaulin sheets, 143, 183, 205, 217
Tayleur & Co., *see also* Vulcan Foundry, 161, 163, 164, 165, 177, 180
Tayleur, Charles, 15, 17, 226
Taylor, Philip, 23
Telford, Thomas, 26, 33, 37, 49, 50–3
Tenders, locomotive, 66, 68, **178**, 223
Textile trade, 11
Thiers, M., 230
Third Class, 191
Thompson, Benjamin, 63
Thompson, James, (engineman), 148
Thompson, James, (purchaser of *Rocket*), 171
Thompson, John, 139
Thompson, Ralph, 141, 210, 221
Thornton, Joseph, 41, 42
Through booking of passengers, 127, 186
Tickets, 187–9, **189**
   annual, 187
   collection of, 188, 189
   day return, 187
   directors', **227**, 228
   for Opening Day, 79, **82**, **83**
   in advance, 187
   race traffic, 198
   season, 187–8
Timber traffic, 131
   yards, 133
Time-interval system, 218
Times, The, 15, 24
Timetables, 191
Tite, William, FRS, 120
Tobin, Sir John, 15, 19
Todd, Kitson & Laird, 164
Todmorton, 207
Tolls, 96, 207
Toosey, J. B., 193
Tothill, William, 208

Tracks, distance between, 60
Traffic, volume of, 91
Trafford, Sir Thomas J. de, 145
Traill, Dr T. S., 15, 73
Train service, 186, 190
Trains, composition of, 201
   1st and 2nd Class, 186
   length of, 190, 206
   motion of, 92
   speeds of, 201, 223
Tramroads, temporary, 44, 46, 47
Travellers' impressions of railway, 91
Travelling Post Office, 197, 201
Trent Valley Line, 235
Trespassing on railway, 50, 214, 215, 222
Trevithick, Francis, 103
Trevithick, Richard, 12, 68, 223
Trial trips, 77, 103
Tunnel signals, 114, 116
Turkish Ambassador, 230
Turner, Evans & Co, 104, 180, 210, 212
Turner, Richard, 120
Turnpike trusts, 220
Turnplates, 116, 119, 133, 184
Turntables, 133, 217
Twist, James, 145
Tyldsley Line, 235

Uniforms, 79, 130, 142, 148
USA, railway literature in, 232
   railways, 55, 64
   visitors from, 37, 230–2

Valentine, Thomas, **238**
Vallance, John, 65
Vandalism, 61, 90, 214, 221
Vernon, Thomas & Co., 113, 177
Versailles Railway, 180
Victoria Station, *see also* Hunts Bank Station, 58, 127, **130**, **131**, 187, 237, 239
Victoria Tunnel, 115, 235, 237
Vignoles, Charles Blacker, 27, **27**, 29, 33, 37–8, 43, 47, 72, 73, 99, 100, 106, 151, 156, 169
Vignoles, Hutton, 152
Viney, General James, 172
Vulcan Foundry, *see also* Tayleur & Co 15, 162

Wage, guaranteed minimum, 141
Wages, 49, 55, 62, 139, 140, 142, 143, 168
   paid during sickness, 147, 149
Waggon axles, 184
   couplings, 184
   Department, 136
   wheels, 184
   Works, 184
Waggons, anti-friction, 183, **183**
   coal, 97, 184, **185**
   contract, 201
   flat, 183
   for livestock, 183, 184, **184**
   luggage, 193
   numbering of, 185
   timber, 183
Waiting rooms, 116, 127, 130
Wakefield, 207
Wakefield, John, 140, 209
Wakefield, Mark, 72, 140, 208
Walker, James, 23, 64, 106, 124, 223
Walker, James S., 40

Walking passes, 228
Wapping Goods Depot, 96, **132**, 133, 143, 207, 239
Wapping Tunnel, 28, 37–41, **38**, 52, 56, 76, 90, 110, 118, 197, 218, 237
War Office, 198
Warburton, Charles, 213
Ward, John, 172
Warehouses, Manchester, 50, 79, 131, 205
Warrington, 100, 102, 103, 186
Warrington & Newton Railway, 95, 102, 104, 105, 204, 210, 226
Warrington Junction *see also* Newton Junction, 61, **218**
Water cranes, 177
   for locomotives, 177
Water Street Bridge, 49, 50, **51**
Water Street, Manchester, 50, 133
Waterloo Dock Branch, 107, 235
Waterloo Hotel, 72, 79, 93
Waterloo Tunnel, 235, 237
Wavertree Lane, 52, 58, 62, 79, 111, 142, 166
Waybills, 187, 188, 191
Wayside stations, 128–31, 201, 216
Weatherburn, Henry, 141
Weatherburn, Martin, 145
Weatherburn, Robert, 115
Weighing machines, 133
Wellington, Duke of, 77, 83–5, 88, 89, 90
Wellington Harmonic Band, 85
Wellington Rooms, Liverpool, (Adelphi Hotel), 79, 90
West Coast Route, 106
West Cumberland & Morecambe Bay Railway, 106
Whishaw, Francis, 201, 229
Whistle, steam, 115, 178
Whistler, George Washington, 231
Whiston Colliery, 173
Whiston Inclined Plane, 103, 145, 147, 169, 183, 199, **200**, 217
Whitby & Pickering Railway, 135
White, James, 62
Whitsun Week excursions, 196
Widnes, 99
Wigan, 12
Wigan Branch Railway, 60, 86, 95, 100–1, 105, 130, 140
Willey, – (contractor), 47
Williams, – (booking clerk), 143
Willis's Collieries, 104
Wilson, James, 172
Wilson, John, 47
Wilton, Earl of, 30
Winans, Ross, 69, 72, 183
Wines and spirits, 205, 211, 212, 214
Witty, – (engineer), 173
Wood, Nicholas, 23, 26, 71, 73, 74, 75
Wood, William, 147, 212
Woods, Edward, 62, 115, 120, 125, 136, 148, 165, 166, 221, 239
Workshops, 37
Worsdell, Nathaniel, 138, 180, 182, 198
Worsdell, Thomas Clarke, 66, 138, 179, 180, 182
Wrigg, Kersall, 172, 174
Wright, Robert, 65

York & North Midland Railway, 100, 128
York, Archbishop of, 28
Young, Thomas, 56, 145